COMPARATIVE POLITICS

Political Institutions

COMPARATIVE POLITICS

Comparative Politics is a series for students and teachers of political science that deals with contemporary issues in comparative government and politics. As Comparative European Politics it has produced a series of high-quality books since its foundation in 1990, but now takes on a new form and a new title for the millennium—Comparative Politics. As the process of globalization proceeds, and as Europe becomes ever more enmeshed in world trends and events, so it is necessary to broaden the scope of the series.

The General Editors are Max Kaase, Vice President and Dean of Humanities and Social Sciences, International University, Bremen, and Kenneth Newton, Professor of Comparative Politics, University of Southampton. The series is published in association with the European Consortium for Political Research.

RECENT TITLES IN THE SERIES

Mixed-Member Electoral Systems: The Best of Both Worlds
Edited by Matthew Shugart and Martin P. Wattenberg

Parties without Partisans: Political Change in Advanced Industrial Democracies
Edited by Russell J. Dalton and Martin P. Wattenberg

Coalition Governments in Western Europe
Edited by Wolfgang C. Müller and Kaare Strøm

Divided Government in Comparative Perspective
Edited by Robert Elgie

Political Parties: Old Concepts and New Challenges
Edited by Richard Gunther, José Ramón Montero, and Juan J. Linz

Parliamentary Representatives in Europe 1848–2000: Legislative Recuitment and Careers in Eleven European Countries
Edited by Heinrich Best and Maurizio Cutta

Political Parties in the New Europe: Political and Analytical Challenges
Edited by Kurt Richard Luther and Ferdinand Müller-Rommel

Political Institutions

Democracy and Social Choice

JOSEP M. COLOMER

OXFORD
UNIVERSITY PRESS

This book has been printed digitally and produced in a standard specification
in order to ensure its continuing availability

OXFORD
UNIVERSITY PRESS

Great Clarendon Street, Oxford OX2 6DP

Oxford University Press is a department of the University of Oxford.
It furthers the University's objective of excellence in research, scholarship,
and education by publishing worldwide in

Oxford New York

Auckland Cape Town Dar es Salaam Hong Kong Karachi
Kuala Lumpur Madrid Melbourne Mexico City Nairobi
New Delhi Shanghai Taipei Toronto
With offices in
Argentina Austria Brazil Chile Czech Republic France Greece
Guatemala Hungary Italy Japan South Korea Poland Portugal
Singapore Switzerland Thailand Turkey Ukraine Vietnam

Oxford is a registered trade mark of Oxford University Press
in the UK and in certain other countries

Published in the United States
by Oxford University Press Inc., New York

ISBN 0-19-924184-8

Preface

The more complex the political institutions, the more stable and socially efficient the outcomes will be. This book develops an extensive analysis of this relationship. The discussion is theoretical, historical, and comparative. Concepts, questions, and insights are based on social choice theory, while an empirical focus is cast on about forty countries and a few international organizations from late medieval times to the present.

Political institutions are conceived here as the formal rules of the game, especially with respect to the following issues: who can vote, how votes are counted, and what is voted for. Complexity signifies that multiple winners exist, as in plural electorates created by broad voting rights, in multiparty systems based upon proportional representation, and in frameworks of division of powers between the executive and the legislative or between the central government and noncentral units. The efficiency of outcomes is evaluated for their social utility, which is to say, the aggregation of individuals' utility which is obtained with the satisfaction of their preferences.

This is a book that emphasizes the advantages of median voter's cabinets and presidents, divided government, and federalism. It differs from certain arguments developed in other pluralistic traditions in giving the emphasis to the role of institutional rules and decision procedures in the production of different degrees of citizens' political satisfaction, rather than to the predispositions created by social, economic, or cultural structures. Political pluralism is not either praised here for the sake of itself or only as a means for limiting power, as in certain constructions aimed at preserving individual freedom above all. Pluralistic democratic institutions are judged to be better than alternative formulas for their higher capacity of producing socially satisfactory results.

J.M.C.

Acknowledgements

This book was mostly written during my stays at New York University, Georgetown University, and the Institute of Political Studies of Paris during the years 1995–9. I am particularly grateful to my sponsors in the three institutions, Steven Brams, Eusebio Mujal-León, and Jean Léca, respectively. Partial drafts were presented to the graduate students in the mentioned institutions, as well as at the Graduate Conference of Swiss Universities held in Cully, Switzerland, the Latin American Faculty of Social Sciences (FLACSO), and the Center of Research for Development (CIDAC), in Mexico, the University Sanmartín in Buenos Aires and the University Siglo 21 in Córdoba (Argentina), the University of Costa Rica, the University Rafael Landívar in Guatemala, and the University of Panamá.

Among those who provided unavailable data, created occasions of exchanges or made useful comments, I should mention Antonio Agosta, Manuel Alcántara, Alberto Alesina, Gerard Alexander, Klaus Armingeon, John Bailey, Michel Balinski, Samuel Barnes, Michelle Beyeler, Carles Boix, Ana-Sofía Cardenal, Marcelo Cavarozzi, Grace-Ivana Deheza, Alberto Díaz-Cayeros, Patrick Dunleavy, Lars Feld, Peter Fishburn, Bernard Grofman, José-Luis de Haro, Erick Hess, Evelyn Huber, Robert Lieber, Arend Lijphart, Juan Linz, Iain McLean, Beatriz Magaloni, Helen Margetts, Nicholas Miller, Gianfranco Pasquino, Stanley Payne, Rubén-Darío Rodríguez-Patiño, Donald Saari, Ignacio Sánchez-Cuenca, Giulia de Sanctis, Manfred Schmidt, Matthew Shugart, Ligia Tavera, Arturo Valenzuela, and Stephen Wayne. Thanks to Georgetown University, I could rely upon two research assistants, Francesca Vassallo and Eric Langenbacher, and the editing services of Sarah Campbell.

I also enjoyed working with the series co-editor, Ken Newton, and Oxford University Press editor Dominic Byatt. Financial help was provided by the Boards of Scientific and Technological Research of the Government of Spain (CICYT, PR95-249) and of the Government of Catalonia (CIRIT, 1995BEAI400127).

Contents

List of Figures   viii
List of Tables   ix

1. Politics and Social Choice   1
   1.1. The Theory of Social Choice   2
   1.2. The Plan of the Book   12

2. Who Can Vote   14
   2.1. Simple Electorates   15
   2.2. Complex Electorates   29

3. How Votes Are Counted   66
   3.1. Single-winner Rules   70
   3.2. Multiple-winner Rules   116

4. What Is Voted For   137
   4.1. Unified Government   142
   4.2. Divided Government   156

5. Choosing Socially Efficient Institutions   203

References   216
Index   241

List of Figures

1.1. The single-dimensional electorate 7
1.2. Joint and separate elections 8
1.3. Complex electorate with different voting rules 10
2.1. Two strategies of voting rights 47
3.1. Decisions with unanimity rule 72
3.2. Unanimity and majority resolutions in the United Nations 82
3.3. Median winners by proportional representation (PR) and
　　 plurality rule 125
4.1. Strategic divided vote 158
5.1. Types of democratic regime and democratization waves 211

List of Tables

2.1.	Size of the electorate: The 'Anglo' model	44
2.2.	Size of the electorate: The 'Latin' model	45
2.3.	Size of the electorate: The 'Nordic' model	46
3.1.	Frequency of median voter's winners (1945–2000)	69
3.2.	Winning losers with majority rule	86
3.3.	Bipolarized, nonmonotonic Spanish elections (1931–6)	89
3.4.	French presidential elections with no median-winner (1965–95)	96
3.5.	Winning losers with plurality rule	101
3.6.	The United States presidential election (1960)	105
3.7.	Latin-American Presidents (1945–2000)	107
3.8.	Peruvian presidential elections (1962–3)	109
3.9.	Brazilian presidential elections (1945–60)	111
3.10.	Chilean presidential elections (1958–70)	114
3.11.	Votes, seats, and ministries in the French Fourth Republic (1945–58)	129
3.12.	Votes, seats, and ministries in the Italian First Republic (1945–92)	133
3.13.	Votes, seats, and ministries in the Dutch parliamentary Monarchy (1946–98)	137
3.14.	Votes, seats, and ministries in the German Federal Republic (1949–98)	139
4.1.	Re-election of Presidents and Assemblies in North and South America	148
4.2.	Preferences for a divided government	161
4.3.	Nonconcurrent elections and horizontally divided government in North and South America (1945–95)	162
4.4.	Nonconcurrent elections and vertically divided government (1945–95)	163
4.5.	Horizontally divided government (1945–2000)	166
4.6.	Social utility in unitary and decentralized governments	183
4.7.	Preference orders regarding unity, federation, and secession	183
4.8.	National and cantonal majorities	190
5.1.	Political institutions and successful democratization (1874–2000)	209
5.2.	Political institutions and successful democratization, per country (1874–2000)	213
5.3.	Democracies in 2000	215

1

Politics and Social Choice

What is the best regime and the best way of life for most citizens and most human beings?

The political community that is based on those in the middle is best. The best legislators come from the middle citizens. . . .

The better mixed the polity is, the more lasting it is.

Aristotle, *The Politics* (c. 325–324 BC)

The stake of politics is the provision of public goods by leaders. By definition, public goods cannot be provided by private actors unless they are submitted to the appropriate institutional constraints, which implies the embodiment of some political structure. Political leaders may also provide private goods, but this does not distinguish them from other social actors.

Politics always involves exchanges between leaders and citizens to their mutual benefit. The essential exchange is between leaders providing public goods and citizens giving leaders their support or their votes. While public goods can satisfy some citizen groups' common interests, citizens' support to leaders is transformed into opportunities for staying in power, obtaining private goods, acquiring fame, or developing a professional political career.

Some rivalry or competition between different institutional providers of public goods may exist in situations of civil war or in transitory situations of regime change. But public goods are market failures and can be provided effectively only by a monopoly, thus requiring a clear delimitation of every provider's domain. The role of the institutions is to establish the domains of public activity and the rules to select leaders. (For a formal discussion, see Colomer 1995b.)

This basic scheme can be valid for all types of political regimes, whether democratic or not. Some authoritarian regimes may find social support on the basis of delivering certain public goods, whether they be social peace and order, national pride and foreign expansion, or some positive economic performance. However, the smaller the number of people participating in the appointment of leaders and in the decision making, the higher the likelihood that only private good interests or small groups' public interests will be satisfied with policy decisions. Nondemocratic or self-appointed rulers will tend to satisfy the common interests of themselves and their supporters, while resisting the demands of other groups by restrictive mechanisms or repressive means. Conversely, the greater the number of individuals participating in electing leaders and decision making, the greater the opportunities for large groups to develop their demands and be satisfied by policy outcomes.

Ideally, democracy could be defined as the rule of the many in their common interests. Yet public goods can be the subject of democratic competition because all of them involve some redistributive dimension. Certain public goods can be considered to be universal, satisfying very large common interests because they can benefit all citizens in ways they can hardly anticipate. This category may include goods such as defense, security, justice, a constitutional provision for balanced budgets, or environmental protection. Universal public goods may be provided through consensual policies, even in relatively restrictive regimes. Yet even these goods can be provided by policies producing different amounts of citizens' satisfaction and social utility. This is the case, for example, with defense based on either the draft or a professional army. A budget surplus can produce some universal benefits, including low inflation, but it benefits citizens differently depending on whether it is spent in defense, social security, or in any other field. Taxpayers' money can be used to fund either a state-controlled school system or religious schools, although both can satisfy a universal right to go to school. Public works involve choices on location, externalities, and so forth.

Different institutional formulas perform with different degrees of social efficiency in the provision of public goods. In other words, social choices corresponding to different institutional procedures of decision making satisfy different groups of citizens' demands and produce different levels of social utility. Specifically, democratic regimes organized in simple institutional frameworks foster the concentration of power and alternation of successive absolute winners and absolute losers. They favor political satisfaction of relatively small groups, as well as policy instability. In contrast, pluralistic institutions produce multiple winners, inducing multi-party cooperation and agreements. They favor stable, moderate, and consensual policies that can satisfy large groups' interests on a great number of issues.

1.1. THE THEORY OF SOCIAL CHOICE

Social choice theory has developed a research program that touches the core of the study of politics. The founding theorems demolished a naive confidence in the capability of political institutions to guarantee efficient outcomes satisfying citizens' preferences. No decision rule can guarantee outcomes fulfilling some apparently simple requirements of fairness, but all of them are vulnerable to manipulation by voters and leaders and may produce socially inefficient results, according to the 'impossibility theorems' established by Kenneth Arrow (1951, 1963), Duncan Black (1948*a*, *b*, 1958), Allan Gibbard (1973), and Mark Satterwhaite (1975), among others.

Three basic routes from this starting point can be distinguished. First, some of the normative conditions initially established to declare a social choice acceptable have been discussed and relaxed. The corresponding proposals focus on the following conditions: (i) monotonicity, or the requirement of a consistent relation between citizens' preferences and the social choice; (ii) independence of the social choice from individual preferences regarding irrelevant alternatives that cannot win the voting contest; and (iii) a new interpretation of the condition initially called 'no-dictatorship' in order to make the existence of a (nonautomatically) decisive actor acceptable (e.g., Sen 1970; Barberà 1977; Dowding 1997, respectively, for the three conditions mentioned). These contributions usually help the student to mistrust his or her own ethical intuition and to follow reasonable discussions of normative criteria. Yet they also show that any choice of conditions of fairness requires renouncing some possible criterion of value, or at least accepting a trade-off between several of them, which finally depends on subjective judgement.

Second, certain conditions regarding citizens' preferences have been identified in order to guarantee efficient and stable social choices with certain voting procedures. This line of research relaxes the founding theorems' assumption that no restrictions should be imposed on individuals' preferences (or 'universal domain'). The alternative conditions, such as 'single-peakedness' of individual preference curves (Black 1958), 'values restriction' (Sen 1966), and 'extremes restriction' (Sen and Pattanaik 1969), suggest the advantages of relatively homogeneous societies in producing stable and consistent collective decisions. Yet, as will be discussed in the following pages, the restriction of relevant preferences may result from the decision process itself, ultimately depending on the institutional rules of the game.

The third line of research promoted by social choice theory—and the one most closely connected to this book—attempts to evaluate the relative performance of different institutional rules in satisfying citizens' preferences and producing socially efficient outcomes. The 'impossibility' theorems tell us that it is impossible to guarantee stable and efficient social choices with any rule. But the point is not only that it is 'possible' to obtain stable and socially efficient choices with some rules, but also that certain rules produce inefficient choices more frequently than others. In a world of uncertainty, the likelihood of social efficiency may be a useful guide to institutional evaluation and design.

The Study of Political Institutions

The basic perspective adopted in this book is that political institutions shape actors' strategies, and that the latter produce collective outcomes. Institutions provide information, opportunities, incentives, and constraints for both citizens and leaders choosing certain strategies, and it is only through the intermediation of actors' strategic decisions that collective outcomes can be explained.

Debts must be acknowledged, in particular, to certain conceptual contributions dealing with the choice of institutions, the incentives they supply for different strategies, their effects on the outcomes, and the advantages of pluralistic institutions, respectively.

First, Douglass North's theory of 'equilibrium institutions' remarks that the choice and the survival of institutions depend on their performance in providing public goods and reducing transaction costs, as well as on the path by which they are chosen, including the role of small events and luck in gaining adherence. Once institutions exist, they set parameters for further action. But they can also reinforce themselves and make their replacement difficult through the effects of the incentives embodied in their structure. Even certain institutions producing inefficient outcomes can survive as a consequence of actors' learning by use, their adaption to institutional regularities, and the costs of their replacement (North and Thomas 1973; North 1990*a, b*).

The varied panorama of democratic institutional formulas that will parade before the eyes of the reader of this book may be, perhaps, the most persuasive empirical evidence of the variety of equilibrium institutions. Yet, risk-adverse rulers submitted to the challenge of alternative potential winners may choose to change the rules of the game in order to minimize their losses. Also, permanent losers under the existing institutions may try to replace them with other devices favoring wider distribution of power. On this basis, some historical patterns in favor of choosing pluralistic institutions will be identified.

Second, William Riker's seminal exploration of 'heresthetics' has led political students to resuming the classical and too-long forgotten concern with the art of making decisions under given institutional rules. According to this approach, political strategy may consist of such activities as setting the agenda with a particular selection of issues, giving prominence to certain evaluative dimensions of the available alternatives in the public debate, or voting insincerely in order to obtain a more satisfactory collective result (Riker 1983, 1986, 1993, 1996*b*). The corresponding question explored in this book is how different institutional formulas may favor different strategies and how permissive each of them may be for manipulative actions.

Third, Kenneth Shepsle's concept of 'institutionally-induced equilibrium' allows us to understand that actors' strategies and interactions in a pluralistic social setting may produce stable, albeit sometimes undesired or inefficient, social choices thanks to the role of institutions. Stability results from the costs inflicted on certain strategies and from the aggregative mechanisms enforced by institutional rules (Shepsle 1979, 1986, 1989). Accordingly, the analyses presented in the following pages should help us to evaluate different institutional alternatives for their different degrees of constriction on actors' strategies and their effectiveness in producing stable choices.

Fourth, Nicholas Miller's comparison of pluralist theory with social choice theory helps us understand the advantages of pluralism in producing both widespread political satisfaction of citizens' preferences and political stability. In contrast to a concept of stability implying permanent winners and permanent losers, pluralism based on certain strategies, such as exchanges of votes on different issues, multiparty coalitions, and interinstitutional cooperation, gives many different actors the expectation of becoming eventual winners or of sharing power, in this way fostering their acceptance of institutional arrangements (Miller 1983).

The relative performance of some institutional rules has been studied by a number of social choice theorists. Innovative formal analyses of voting procedures have focused on majority rule (May 1952; Plott 1967; McKelvey 1976, 1979; Schofield 1978), unanimity rule (Buchanan and Tullock 1962; Rae 1975), specific procedures (Brams and Fishburn 1983), or systematic comparisons of different rules (Fishburn 1973; Niemi and Riker 1976; Riker 1980, 1982; Nurmi 1987; Merrill 1988; Cox 1997). Institutions with division of powers have been less studied in this approach, but they include some seminal work on federalism (Pennock 1959; Weingast 1995), legislatures (Weingast 1979; Shepsle and Weingast 1981; Laver and Shepsle 1996), bicameralism (Riker 1992a, b; Tsebelis and Money 1997), and multiple elections (Brams, Kilgour, and Zwicker 1998).

This book draws on all these and other contributions. It adds a few formal contributions, it attempts establishing a direct connection between social choice theory and the tradition of empirical study of institutions in political science, it proceeds to some crucial empirical tests of the models, and it develops extensive applied analyses.

Social Utility

The fundamental judgement value used in the following analyses is the greatest satisfaction of the greatest number of individuals, also called 'the principle of social utility'. This classic utilitarian principle, as formulated by Jeremy Bentham (1789), was the basis for what was called 'old' welfare economics. Some eroding criticism developed (which led to the 'new' welfare economics), especially with regard to different individuals' capability of experiencing utility and the consequent impossibility of establishing interpersonal comparisons of well-being.

However, the egalitarian assumption underlying the measurement of social utility as an aggregation of individual utilities can be more solidly grounded as regards democratic decisions. Equal suffrage rights and fair decision rules imply the principle that all individual preferences, whatever the individual subjective capacity of experiencing happiness, ought to have the same value in collective decision making. The classical Benthamite proposition that 'every one counts for one and no one for more than one', however controversial it may be for the elaboration of an economic welfare function, does correspond exactly to the principles of equal individual voting embodied in democratic constitutions.

From this perspective, democracy, which is based upon the choice of rulers by the greatest number of citizens, appears to be highly desirable because it creates better and more regular opportunities than nondemocratic formulas for the satisfaction of citizens' preferences. For analogous reasons, as will be discussed later, pluralistic democracies organized in complex institutional frameworks can perform better in this respect than more simple democratic regimes. (For sources and discussion of utilitarianism, see Rosen 1983; Goodin 1995; Colomer 1987, 1991.)

In social choice theory models, political disutility or dissatisfaction is equated to the 'distance' between voters' preferences and the social choice. This can be expressed as follows:

$$U(W) = \sum \delta_i \, |i - W|,$$

which means that disutility or negative utility U equals the sum $\sum$ of the distances δ between each voter i and the winner W.

The social optimum corresponds to the outcome minimizing the sum of individual distances, which maximizes social utility. Specifically, on a single linear dimension, the sum of distances is minimized by the alternative (candidate, party, or policy) which is preferred by the median voter, that is, the voter whose preference is located in an intermediate position with less than half of voters on both sides. In other words, social utility is maximized when the social choice coincides with the median voter's preference (Davis, Hinich, and Ordeshook 1970; Huber and Powell 1994; Hinich and Munger 1997). In this book, institutional rules favoring the social choice of the median voter's preference will be considered to be relatively socially efficient.

An alternative assumption will also be examined regarding schemes of division of powers, such as separate elections for different offices and

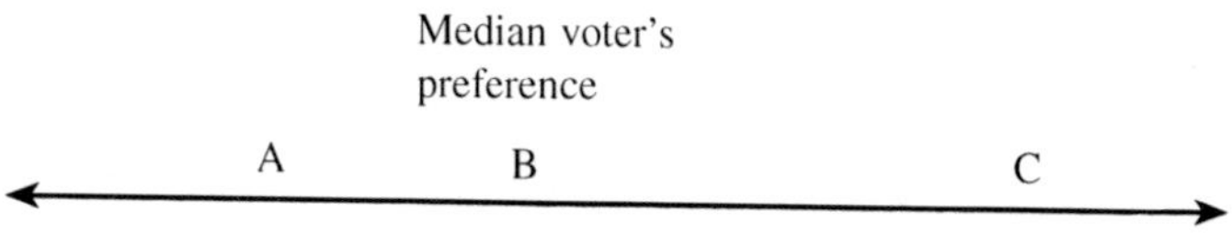

Median voter's
preference

A   B   C

FIG. 1.1. The single-dimensional electorate (N = three voters: A, B, C)

federalism. If significant groups of voters have a different intensity of preferences on various issues and they can vote on them separately, they can find considerable satisfaction in institutional schemes producing different winners on different issues. Under this assumption, social utility can be maximized if different issue domains are allocated to different institutions according to the distribution of intensity of preferences among voters. Also, interinstitutional cooperation can lead to compromise, intermediate decisions supported by broad, consensual majorities producing wide political satisfaction.

A Model of Social Choice

A simple geometrical analysis can illustrate the effects of different institutional frameworks on the stability and collective utility of the social choice. Let us start with the most simple case of an electorate composed of three voters with differentiated preferences (or three voters' groups with the same preferences and a similar number of members).

Initially, we make the simple assumption that voters' preferences can be located on a single issue-dimension, such as A, B, and C on the horizontal axis in Fig. 1.1. Let us assume, for instance, that the distance between voter A and voter B is half the distance between voter B and voter C, as suggested in the figure. If B, which is the median voters' preference wins, the total distance from the voters' preferences to the winner or voters' disutility can be measured as the distance from A to B, say it is 1 unit, plus the distance from B to B, which is zero, plus the distance from C to B, 2 units, so the sum of distances from voters' preferences to the winner, or total disutility, equals 3 units:

$$- U(B) = (|A - B| + |B - B| + |B - C|) = (1 + 0 + 2) = 3.$$

In contrast, if the winner were A, the sum of distances from the voters' preferences to the winner or total disutility would be 4 units; if the winner were C, the total disutility would be 5 units, as the reader can easily check. This shows that the median voter's alternative (B in the example) minimizes the sum of distances and maximizes social utility.

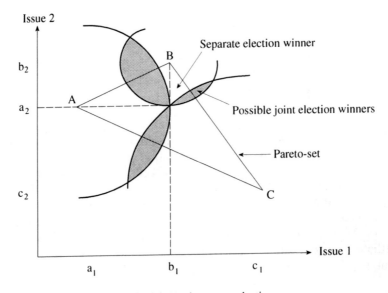

FIG. 1.2. Joint and separate elections

Note: Bold lines circumscribe the 'win-set' in a joint election on two issues
(N = three voters: A, B, C)

Let us turn now to the two-dimensional case. Three voters, A, B, and C, hold different preferences on issue 1 (a_1, b_1, and c_1) and on issue 2 (a_2, b_2, and c_2), as presented in Fig. 1.2. First, we discuss the effects of separate and joint elections. Let us assume that there are two separate elections for different offices dealing with different issues or sets of issues, such as those corresponding to the two dimensions in Fig. 1.2. They can correspond, for example, to separate elections for a president focusing, say, on foreign and defense policy issues and for the Assembly focusing on economic and social policy issues, or to separate elections for two chambers in Parliament, or to other analogous institutional arrangements. Let us assume that, on each separate election, the intermediate alternative close to the median voter is advantaged and wins. In Fig. 1.2, b_1 wins in the election on issue 1 and a_2 wins in the election on issue 2. The social choice is represented by the intersection point of the winning positions on each issue, $b_1 - a_2$.

As can be seen, the social choice of separate elections on different issues under the above assumptions is a somewhat centrist point located inside the minimal set containing all voters' preferences, or the Pareto-set (the triangle A B C in the figure). This point is relatively close to the social optimum, which is the point minimizing the sum of distances from citizens' preferences and thus maximizing social utility. Precisely, in a two-dimensional space such as that in Fig. 1.2, the social optimum point is located at the intersection of the straight lines from each voter's preference to the median of the opposite side in the triangle.

Now, let us assume, alternatively, that the social choice on all the issues is made in a single election, as would correspond to a simple institutional framework, such as a unitary, unicameral parliamentary regime. The institutional setting forces the voters to choose, not between alternatives on separate issues, but between 'packages' of alternatives on all the issues at the same time.

The set of possible winners, or 'win-set', in such a joint election is unpredictable and depends on the status quo. Let us adopt the hypothesis that the status quo is the social choice previously produced by two separate elections, the point $b_1 - a_2$ in Fig. 1.2. The set of possible winners in a single, two-dimensional election from this point is represented by the multipetal shaded area in the figure. This is formed by circular indifference curves around the voters' preferences and crossing the status quo. It is assumed that every voter prefers the alternatives that are closer to the voter's preference and in particular prefers those inside the indifference curve to those outside. Accordingly, the set of possible majority winners in a joint election is formed by all the points at which a majority of voters (any majority of two voters out of three in the example shown in Fig. 1.2) is more satisfied than they would be in the status quo—that is, the win-set is formed by the intersections of pairs of indifference curves.

As can be seen, the set of possible winners in a joint election is relatively large, which makes the prediction of results difficult. The set includes many points located at a relatively long distance from the social optimum point. A number of possible winners are located outside the Pareto-set and even beyond the rank of voters' preferences (for example, the set includes some points located beyond the extreme preference, b_2, on issue 2). The possibility that many different alternatives can win may generate instability in the outcome of a series of successive elections, since any winning point can be further beaten by some other point in the corresponding win-set.

This analysis allows us to state that a joint election on a multidimensional set of issues, as a model for the typical single election in simple regimes, can be more uncertain, produce lower social utility, and be more unstable over time than separate elections on different issues, such as elections for different offices in regimes with division of powers.

The comparative judgement of separate and joint elections might be somewhat different if we replaced the assumption that the median voter's position wins in each separate election with the assumption that extreme alternatives can win (perhaps as a consequence of multiparty competition

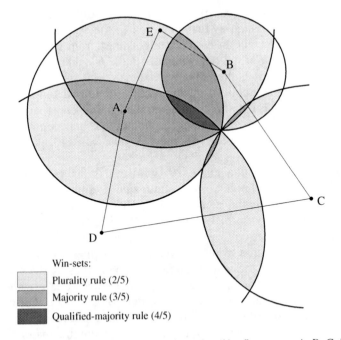

FIG. 1.3. Complex electorate with different voting rules (*N* = five voters: A, B, C, D, E)

with plurality rule). Still, the social choice of separate elections would always be within the rank of voters' preferences and likely inside the Pareto-set. The social choice of separate elections could be less socially efficient than some possible winners in a joint election only if extreme positions corresponding to opposite groups of extreme voters won on the different issues. But, even in this case, the set of possible winners in a joint election would include other points outside the Pareto-set and possibly some beyond the ranks of voters' preferences.

Now, we introduce two new variables in the model. First, let us assume a more complex electorate, composed of five voters with more dispersed preferences than the three previous voters. In other words, the electorate of three voters, A, B, and C, is enlarged with two new voters, D and E, whose preferences are located beyond the rank of the incumbent voters' preferences, as shown in Fig. 1.3. The addition of D and E may correspond to the enforcement of voter rights for new groups, as in a typical process of gradual democratization.

The set of possible winners in a joint election depends on the voting rule. We compare the effects of three rules with different inclusive thresholds: plurality, majority, and qualified-majority. The largest plurality is operationalized as 2/5 (or 40 per cent, not very different from the proportion of votes obtained by the typical winner in certain parliamentary elections by plurality rule in the real world).

The set of possible winners in a joint election with plurality rule for five voters is much larger than the set of winners previously identified for the electorate of three voters, as can be seen in Fig. 1.3. It includes many points located at very long distances from the social optimum point, outside the Pareto-set, and beyond the ranks of voters' preferences. This can produce high unpredictability and instability of the social choice, as well as low social utility.

The set of possible winners with majority rule (or 3/5) is shown in Fig. 1.3. As can be seen, it is smaller than the set of possible winners with plurality rule. This means that the more inclusive the decision rule, the more stable and socially efficient the social choice can be expected to be.

Comparing this result with the set of possible majority winners in the previous electorate of three voters in Fig. 1.2, the electorate of five voters can be considered to be able to produce relatively efficient results. This is not only related to the fact that a higher proportion of voters in a community can increase the sum total of individual utilities. In addition, the new set of majority winners with five voters is located mostly inside the Pareto-set, relatively closer to the social optimum point. This allows us to state that the effects of instability and possible low social utility that come with a complex electorate with highly dispersed voters' preferences may be compensated with the opposite effects produced by inclusive decision rules.

This finding is confirmed with the analysis of a qualified-majority rule, 4/5 in Fig. 1.3. The corresponding set of possible winners is the very small area in black, which is completely inside the Pareto-set and at a rather centrist location. It can certainly produce more stable social choices and higher social utility than the less inclusive rules previously analyzed.

Three institutional variables producing different degrees of stability and different amounts of utility of the social choice have been identified. In the order in which they will be analyzed in the following chapters, they are:

(i)   the different degrees of dispersion of voters' preferences, corresponding to simple and complex electorates;
(ii) the inclusiveness of voting rules and decision procedures; and
(iii) the different number of issue dimensions in single and separate elections, corresponding to schemes of unity and division of powers.

This book argues that pluralistic democratic regimes based upon complex electorates, inclusive voting rules, and division of powers are likely to produce socially efficient results.

Politics and Social Choice

1.2. THE PLAN OF THE BOOK

The findings of the model just presented guide the research program developed in the following pages. The second chapter deals with the historical construction of simple and complex electorates through the development of different strategies in the allocation of voting rights to different groups. Arguments of both suffragists and restrictionists are revised from the perspective of the expected dispersion of voters' preferences that they were ready to promote or to accept. Three basic patterns developed in different sets of countries are distinguished for the social inclusiveness and the political stability that they were able to produce. The basic assumption is that the higher the proportion of citizens with rights to participate in a stably institutionalized political process, the higher the social utility that can be obtained

The third chapter contrasts single-winner voting rules based upon requirements of either unanimity, majority, or plurality, with multiwinner rules based upon proportional representation and multiparty coalitions. The various voting and decision rules are evaluated and compared for their inclusiveness, the relation between the outcomes that they tend to favor and the citizens' preferences, and the corresponding social utility. The different rules are submitted to a broad empirical test regarding the production of socially efficient winners corresponding to the median voter's preference.

The fourth chapter analyzes and compares different schemes of unity and division of powers which promote collective decisions on different amounts of issues at the same time. Parliamentarism, semi-presidentialism, and presidentialism, as well as unitary states and federalism, are compared by applying the categories of unified and divided government to all of them. Different formulas supply different incentives for multiparty and interinstitutional cooperation, in this way creating different opportunities for citizens' preferences to be revealed and satisfied. The emergence of multiple winners in schemes of division of powers is considered to be able to produce broadly diffused social utility.

The fifth chapter concludes with a comparison between the institutional formulas that can be considered to be the most socially efficient ones in the light of the previous analyses, including proportional representation, horizontal division of powers, and federalism, and the institutional alternatives that are mainly chosen in strategic processes of democratization and institutional reform. Self-interested but not all-powerful actors in processes of institutional change tend to choose pluralistic institutions that are considered relatively efficient in the theoretical perspective developed in this book.

The main points of the analysis, including the production of socially efficient electoral results and the frequency of divided government, are tested with data on votes, Assemblies, Cabinets, and Presidents corresponding to the outcomes of 506 national elections and 1,765 regional elections in forty democratic countries in Western and Central Europe, North and South America, and Asia, during the period 1945–2000. The countries are selected for having more than one million inhabitants, high levels of political freedom and at least two consecutive democratic elections by 2000, and available data. The countries selected include more than 90 per cent of the world population living in democracy at the end of the 20th century. The comparative analysis is complemented with a large number of brief case studies of institutional performance and change, including a few excursions several centuries ago (using sources in eight languages). The long-term historical review presented in the final chapter is supported with data on 123 major institutional changes in 85 countries during a 127-year period.

2

Who Can Vote

The laws which establish the rights of suffrage are fundamental to democratic government.

Montesquieu, *De l'Esprit des Lois* (1748)

A political community can be defined as a set of individuals who recognize some basic common interest among themselves and make enforceable collective decisions. Simple communities with concentrated preferences can make decisions relatively easily. When the bulk of the population is sufficiently homogeneous in socioeconomic and cultural terms, as usually happens in small communities, an electorate based upon broad voting rights can identify an acceptable alternative and produce a relatively stable and satisfactory social choice even without sophisticated institutional mechanisms. As will be examined below, small communities with homogeneous interests may adopt virtual universal suffrage and make decisions by unanimity or other highly inclusive voting rules.

In contrast, complex electorates formed by the enfranchisement of differentiated groups in relatively heterogeneous societies can make the achievement of enforceable collective decisions difficult and result in low degrees of stability and utility of social choice. This is usually the case in modern societies in the process of building large, initially heterogeneous nation-states, and undergoing democratization. The more dispersed the preferences of voters' groups on the issues submitted to voting, the more complex the electorate and the more difficult it is to reach agreements.

In modern historical developments, the consequences of giving voting rights to different groups in complex societies have varied enormously. The enfranchisement of certain groups has not produced much political innovation because most of their members have developed similar preferences to those already existing within the incumbent electorate and eventually replicate its voting patterns. This absence of innovation can result from some economic or personal dependence of the newly enfranchised voters upon the incumbents' preferences, or from restrictive political institutions.

Certain new voters' groups, in contrast, have been able to create new political parties, to develop eventually successful strategies to innovate the political agenda, to form a new political majority, or to challenge the

entire political system. This tendency toward innovation can result from more differentiated voters' preferences and from permissive political institutions.

The allocation of voting rights tends to be guided by both collective pressures 'from below' (previously excluded groups) and strategic calculations 'from above' (incumbent leaders). In modern times, landholders, merchants, artisans, workers, servants, women, members of ethnic minorities, young people, and immigrants have been enfranchised in different countries at various historical moments, usually paralleling major rearrangements in the electoral rules, the party system, and other institutional elements.

In certain cases, universal suffrage has been introduced suddenly and without modifying previously existing institutional rules, usually producing high political instability. In other cases, different minority groups of voters have been enfranchised at successive stages in a long lasting process. This strategy can prevent the sudden emergence of a new alternative majority and induce each new small group to enter into a previously existing party. Finally, in some cases, universal suffrage has been accompanied by institutional innovations, such as proportional representation and division of powers, thus producing multiple electoral winners. In this sort of new institutional framework, the social choice is transferred to post-electoral stages in which pluralistic, inclusive agreements can be attained.

This chapter is divided into two sections. The first section presents a certain amount of evidence of small, homogeneous communities in medieval and early modern times which were able to make consensual, enforceable social choices by voting with relatively broad voting rights. The second section approaches the problems of social choice in complex electorates. Different historical arguments in favor of or against the enlargement of the existing electorates are revised and discussed from the perspective sketched here. Different strategies in the allocation of voting rights are identified and associated with different enfranchisement paces, electoral rules, and party systems in a dozen countries during the 19th and 20th centuries.

2.1. SIMPLE ELECTORATES

In medieval and early modern times there were not only numerous feudal enclaves and a few extensive imperial and monarchical structures, but an array of local units where many collective decisions were made by the vote of a large electorate. Typically, these were rather simple communities with relatively harmonious interests, shared values, and a homogeneous

culture in which the identification of a common choice was not a very
difficult achievement. The units in question were small territories, either
villages, communes, municipalities, provinces, counties, towns, boroughs,
colonies, or other communities of minor size. Their collective processes
of decision making dealt with a few local, relatively simple issues. This
was so even when they elected local representatives to larger-scale bodies,
such as the medieval parliaments, due to the absence of large-scale
('national') parties.

Homogeneous preferences developed among the population, reflecting
either social simplicity, especially in rural environments, or the predominance of a middle class of farmers, artisans, or traders in more complex
settings. The homogeneity of the community or the strong appeal of some
socially central position allowed these communities to make enforceable
collective decisions with relative ease, producing stable, widely satisfactory social choices.

Certain institutional features of simple political communities making
consensual decisions were very similar to those that can be found nowadays in meetings of condominium owners—which is another case of
small, simple communities with clearly identifiable common interests.
They include the following:

- Voting rights were given to the heads of households, independently
  on the number of family members, in the assumption that all of them
  had homogeneous preferences; usually only men voted, but the rules
  were rather vague or informal, often allowing young people or
  certain women to participate.
- Decision rules were highly inclusive; unanimity or quasi-unanimity
  rules were used in town meetings and people's assemblies that
  worked by acclamation.
- Several randomizing mechanisms, including turns and lots, were
  used for rotation of officers in charge of implementing the assembly's
  decisions, which was considered a burden rather than a privilege.

The election of representatives induced more innovation in favor of
rules permitting a varied representation of different social categories or
preference groups. Modern formulas of proportional representation were
unknown at the time, but, in communities relatively more complex than
the typical rural villages, interesting instances, such as multimember
districts and the frequent call of elections, were conceived with the aim of
preventing the exclusive rule of some particular group.

Small, somewhat homogeneous units dealing with local issues could
maintain open, large participation in collective decision making by resisting pressures from large-scale Emperors, Popes, monarchs, and colonial

powers. Yet, when the traditional local communities experienced growing internal complexity and more differentiated groups emerged, their own traditional criteria in favor of broad suffrage rights and unanimous agreements became a source of conflict and instability. External trade, wider communications, and the increasing prominence of larger-scale public goods leading to the formation of modern nation-states induced major institutional rearrangements. These included the redefinition of the qualifications for voting, even including the disenfranchisement of certain voting groups, as well as more explicit regulations of elections. (For a related historical perspective, see Manin 1995.)

Cases: Communes, Parliaments, and Colonies

According to legend, the German tribal groups of the early Middle Ages held primary assemblies of warriors in which they approved resolutions offered by the king by clashing spears against shield or disapproved them by silence. The survey presented in the following pages focuses on simple electorates of three modern types of political units. First, we will approach decision making procedures in independent small communes, including the Swiss rural villages and cantons that have existed since the late Middle Ages and certain famous medieval Italian towns. The medieval commune in Central Europe was initially a private association of households organized to provide some basic public goods. They assumed the administration of justice, military defense, maintenance of a food supply, and other basic services. To the extent that the counts and the bishops were unable to perform these tasks effectively, the communes gradually replaced their authority. Eventually, they, in fact, ignored the sovereignty of the German Emperor or the Roman Pope.

Second, elections in local units within certain large kingdoms will be reviewed. They include town assemblies, provincial estates, and the Estates-General in pre-revolutionary Bourbon France, as well as counties and boroughs in parliamentary elections in Hanoverian England. Initially, the members of medieval assemblies summoned by the kings were not elected by popular constituencies, but selected from among those who were thought to be representatives of the mood and interests of diverse social categories in large territories. However, popularly elected representatives of communes or other local units also sent delegates to medieval parliaments. Modern parliamentary elections were established largely upon this precedent.

Third, some notorious colonial institutions will be discussed. They include the British dominions in North America before the formation of the United States, as well as certain Spanish colonies in North and South America in the process of attaining independence. Although based on different models, in both cases the enforcement of relatively restrictive regulations of elections in the metropolis permitted more permissive practices in the colonies located at the other side of the Atlantic. Participatory elections were in fact crucial events in triggering independence. Only when small independent units formed larger nation-states, were certain initially vague criteria of enfranchisement replaced with more specific requirements.

Evidence of the cases of simple electorates here discussed has emerged or has been recently re-elaborated among historians. But, apparently, different country cases have not been put together, or at least they have not been compared, from the perspective adopted here.

The Swiss Communes and Cantons

During the Middle Ages, German communes were recognized as the maximum legal and political authority over their rural population. They made decisions at people's assemblies with a fixed membership of the masters of households who were at least 14 or 16 years old. Married women and children were allowed passive membership and attended the meetings, but usually they did not vote, under the presumption that every house and family held homogeneous interests. Based on the commonality of private goods, the commune's membership was determined in the same way attendance to owners' meetings in modern urban condominiums is decided: only residents in the commune, and not aliens or temporary tenants without a stake in the common property, were admitted.

The assembly was called to the sound of bells, typically on Sunday morning, and gathered in a circle in a green meadow. It opened with a silent prayer. Anyone could present a proposal to the assembly. Voting was by show of hands and decisions were made by majority. The homogeneity and transparency of the community created strong incentives for attending the meetings and also for transforming a majority into unanimity. After voting, an oath of membership and obedience to the commune was taken. Other rules could be applied for other purposes: proportional partition of resources and burdens held in common, or rotation of access to public goods. Lots were used to appoint officers in charge of implementing the assembly's decisions. Cooperative action expanded among neighboring communes. Yet the homogeneity of every unit remained very high, including language, religion, and other cultural traits. Communes in which conflict became too persistent were partitioned in order to preserve the homogeneity of each decision unit.

From 1291, the little forest cantons of Uri, Schwyz, and Unterwalden began to break away from the Counts of Habsburg in Austria. Eventually, they formed a league which expanded to eight cantons in the mid 14th century, and thirteen cantons between the 16th and 18th centuries. For centuries, this Swiss confederation was little more than a loose alliance aimed at preserving local autonomy with respect to the Empire, without containing any central authority. The cantonal assembly became the form of government of most of the German cantons. Somewhat more ceremonial than the village assembly, the canton meeting could include a parade of the little army of the canton, with the magistrates arriving on horseback amidst banners and horn-blowing. The procedures were slightly less permissive than in the communes. Here, membership was limited to men over the age of 18 or 20 years and proposals had to be previously channeled through the elected council. The assembly voted on cantonal laws and motions, taxes, and admission of new members, and elected canton officials with judicial, police, and other executive functions, as well as the federal deputies. An oath of allegiance to the Constitution was taken from all attendants, including women and children. Fines for nonattendance existed in some cantons.

Continuing into the early 20th century, the size of the cantons' electorate was small, each with a membership between 3,000 and 12,000 men. Their homogeneity is still very high nowadays. Most of the twenty-two cantons created in Switzerland in 1848 have differed more from each other than they do from neighboring countries. Also, the cities developed electoral formulas to appoint a Council and the mayor very early (starting with Freiburg in 1248). Merchants and artisans predominated in these urban settings, especially since the 16th and 17th centuries. Popular assemblies have remained more powerful in rural cantons with small, homogeneous populations. In the late 20th century, the Helvetic Confederation was still mainly an instrument for preserving local popular self-government (Lloyd 1907; Head 1995).

Italian Communes

Throughout the 12th century, the North Italian towns, led by their consuls, became autonomous from the Emperor and the Church authorities. Genoa, Pavia, Pisa, Siena, and many other communes organized themselves around the Assembly of all the citizens, or 'harangue' (*arengo*). They approved the appointment of the Consulate by acclamation, a procedure close to unanimity, or by indirect election. In the second half of the 13th century, the participation of the people expanded. In towns like Genoa and Bologna, regular participants in people's Assemblies numbered between 7,000 and 8,000, which was equivalent to the majority of adult men, or about 15 per cent of the total population (author's calculation with data from Waley 1988: 33ff; Hyde 1973: 115).

In the case of Venice, the election of the doge (duke) by the entire population dates from 697. For almost five hundred years, powerful doges were elected by the Assembly, or harangue, formed by 'a great inclusion of the upper, the middle, the lower, and many other Venetians' (majores, mediocres, minores et magna Ventorum englobatio; Wiel 1895). Since 1172, the people's general Assembly indirectly elected the Great Council (usually attended by about 1,000 to 1,500 men, 30 or more years old), which became the supreme authority, and the Senate.

As the doge's powers were restricted, he ceased to be popularly elected and began to be appointed by the Great Council. In order to do so, the latter adopted an increasingly complicated procedure with up to nine stages of approval ballots and lots which was conceived with the aim of making insincere voting and manipulative strategies unviable. From the 13th to the 15th century, the people's Assembly had to ratify the election of the doge by the Council. Other elected offices, from the 13th century until 1789, included magistrates, procurators, advocates, and a High Chancellor. 'The Republic was founded on the politics of compromise, conciliation, and consensus . . . the patrician Republic gave Venice 500 years of domestic peace and stability' (Finlay 1980, in Lines 1986).

In Florence, republican forms of government, including the election of rulers, existed for more than two hundred years from the late 13th century. During the first republican period, which extended from 1291 to 1433, the people's Assembly was formed by residents over the age of twenty-five who paid some minimum local taxes. This produced Assemblies of more than 6,000 voters, which was equivalent to about 15 per cent of the total number of inhabitants in a city with many youth and immigrants, and certainly included a majority of its adult men (author's calculation with data from Najemy 1982; Brucker 1977: 252, 1983: 133).

The government of Florence was organized around the standard-bearer of justice (*Gonfaloniere*) and the other eight members of the Lordship (*Signoria*). They were elected by a complex system of approval voting and very frequent lots. The *Signoria* was supported by twelve elected advisors or 'good men', sixteen *gonfaloniers* representing the quarters of the city, as well as many other elected offices for which most voters were eligible for short terms (six months or a year). The Council of the People (300 members) and the Council of the Commune (200 members) were selected by a mixed procedure of people's election and appointment by the *Signoria*. As in Venice, albeit with different formulas, an extremely complex procedure of elections was conceived to prevent the fraudulent manipulation of the electoral process and to avert the commune's domination by a few of the city's powerful families. Rulers and officeholders were frequently replaced, and this instituted a certain feeling of apparent instability. Yet a more basic stability was secured by the 'large degree of agreement within the guild community on certain issues, particularly in the economic sphere' (Brucker 1983: 66, 70, 388ff.).

The rule of the Medici, established in 1433, introduced some restrictions and frequent interruptions in the regular schedule of elections. Yet, although some families were disenfranchised, 'new people' were included in the electorate, which, parallel to the growth of the population, reached about 8,000 voters in the late 15th century, again about 15 per cent of total population (according to data in Rubinstein 1966: 214–15). The new republic established in 1494 was based upon the popular election of the traditional offices and of a new Great Council inspired by the Venice model, formed in this case by about 3,000 members. After some decay of the Council's powers, a new period of Medici rule again replaced regular elections with direct approval by people's Assembly. The last Florentine republic re-established the election of the rulers, including the Great Council, from 1527 to 1530 (Brucker 1977, 1983; Guidi 1992).

The end of the republican regimes in the Italian communes has been attributed to frequent violence, disorder, and instability provoked by political factionalism, family feuds, and class conflicts. Even Dante famously scorned, in the *Divina Commedia*, the bitter factional disputes, the personal animosities, and the impulse to destroy one's enemies possessed by his Florentine neighbors. In fact, Dante had been a member of the Council of the Commune on several occasions (Zenatti 1984: 341–3). Interestingly, his worrisome complaints included some regret for the inclusion in the electorate of 'new people' (*gente nuova*) who generated 'pride and excess' and were able to challenge the traditional ruling group (Dante 1265–1321: Canto xvi, 73–5).

However, according to modern historians, pluralistic negotiations and agreements developed under the incentives provided by a complex institutional structure. 'The relatively peaceful fusion of old and new elements in Florentine society had been the normal pattern throughout the city's history' (Brucker 1962: 392). 'Florentinism' even became a common expression in Italian and other modern Latin languages, synonymous for sophisticated political maneuvering and coalition building.

Strictly speaking, there is no instance of a single Renaissance Italian city in which violence and civil disorder made for a direct exit into authoritarian rule. As has been remarked by some historians, certain cities, like Siena, Lucca, and Florence, which occasionally experienced intense civil conflict, were able to retain their republican governments after many other cities had fallen to aristocratic rule. In contrast, others, such as Genoa, Bologna, and Pavia, with lower levels of visible conflict, went back and forth between aristocratic and republican governments more frequently. Furthermore, as shown by the cases of Bergamo or Bologna, the incoming aristocratic rule did not secure order and peace (Martines 1979: 79–80).

However, in certain cities using less sophisticated decision making procedures than those enforced in Venice and Florence, a feeling of political dissatisfaction was relatively widespread. In particular, the predominance of artisans' guilds in making political decisions induced negative reactions from other groups. The hypothesis, which will be developed further in this book, points out the negative effects of simple institutions and rules in complex electorates. Specifically, the virtual unanimity rule so commonly used in people's Assemblies making decisions by acclamation does not always produce quick, agreeable decisions in an increasingly complex electorate, such as those of some urban settings of Renaissance Italy, in contrast to the efficiency of unanimity rule in more simple, rural environments. As suggested by one of the most authoritative historians on the period: 'A major source of political frustration [in certain Italian communes] was the government's inability to deal squarely with controversial issues—the result of a belief that unity was essential, and of an etiquette that frowned upon the exposure of irreconcilable viewpoints' (Brucker 1962; 393).

French Municipalities and the Third Estate

Local autonomy was a Roman tradition in some Southern European towns, but it was also created by the privileges given to certain communes by their lords. Perhaps under some influence from the Italian communes, with which they maintained regular trade, many French municipalities were governed by people's assemblies from the late 13th century. Especially in the Southern region of Languedoc, and more famously in towns like Montpelier and Nimes, among others, the 'General Assembly of Inhabitants' was attended by all heads of households (including widows) if they were natives or long-standing residents. Attendance was commonly regarded as an obligation rather than a right. The Assemblies elected proctors or syndics, as well as the collective consulate usually called the 'town body' (*corps de ville*), over whose legislation they exerted control. Municipal offices were held for short terms of about two years. Some restrictions regarding re-election and office accumulation by members of the same family promoted openness and circulation of the appointees (Babeau 1882; Petit-Dutaillis 1947).

In addition, provincial Estates were created and elected in many French provinces by the middle of the 15th century, although they only met by the King's command. During the 16th and 17th centuries, local and provincial Estates retained or even expanded their powers. Taxes, loans, and expenses were submitted to a vote, frequently by secret ballot. Suffrage was expanded and there was an increase in popular participation. The increasingly centralized control of the country by the Crown gradually curbed the autonomy of town and province offices, in particular by way of introducing advantaged 'official candidacies' in the elections (Babeau 1894; Bisson 1964; Temple 1973; Major 1980).

Similarly, the Estates-General, which evolved in the direction of becoming a modern parliament, were eventually limited to being the King's consultative body. Initially, they had taxation powers and their agreement was required for settling the kingdom's religious conflicts and other major crises. The Estates-General met regularly, albeit in rudimentary form throughout the 14th century (in 1302, 1308, 1314, and in frequent meetings between 1344 and 1358), more formally once in the 15th century (1484), and again with some regularity during the 16th and 17th centuries (1560, 1576–7, 1588–9, 1614–15), only to be forgotten for 175 years until they were called again in 1789.

Initially, voting rights to elect the national deputies of the Third Estate were given to all heads of family or household (depending on the town, and somewhat more flexibly in rural settings). 'In this framework, women's vote was regular for the women who were heads of family; widows and daughters living in a different house had also the right of voting' (Cadart 1952: 46–7). Beginning in the 15th century, the franchise was extended to the inhabitants of small towns and country districts. While in some urban towns the election of national deputies was usually confined to municipal officers, representatives of the guilds, and other notable citizens, in the country districts 'the system approximated closely to one of adult male suffrage' (Bridge 1921: 56). 'It has been customary to regard the delegates of the Estates-General of France as being chosen by what amounted to universal manhood suffrage in rural areas' (Howard 1930: 132, but see comments by Major 1951: 44).

For the election of representatives of the Third Estate to the Estates-General in 1789, the number of electoral districts was increased and the number of seats was enlarged in proportion to the population of each district. Suffrage rights were given to all men aged over 25, French or naturalized, domiciled locally, and on the local tax roll (as well as to the women members of the clergy) (*Regulations for the Convocation of the Estates General*, 24 January 1789, in Baker 1987: 180–4). According to recent interpretations, 'this was not far removed from manhood suffrage' (Jones 1988: 63); 'the elections [for the Estates-General] of 1789 were the most democratic spectacle ever seen in the history of Europe, and nothing comparable occurred again until far into the next century' (Doyle 1989: 97).

From the 15th century, most national deputies of France had been elected indirectly by local councils or provincial Estates. Each of the three orders elected representatives at separate primary assemblies, the Third Estate having many more representatives than the other two. But the representatives of the three estates in towns or provinces formed a single electoral Assembly and elected together the deputies of the Estates-General by individual voting. National deputies were thus elected in multimember districts by majority rule. Every seat was filled separately by voting on several rounds, if necessary, until a candidate obtained a majority support (in 1789 a majority was required only in two rounds, the third round deciding by plurality). Although seemingly vulnerable to strategic voting, this procedure could have induced exchanges of votes at the different rounds, permitting a roughly proportional representation of different categories of interests. Yet, not many voting rounds were usually required because large majorities could be formed on the basis of widely shared objectives, compromises, and agreements. The joint election of deputies by the representatives of the three estates was supported by their common elaboration of a single 'book of grievances' (*cahier de doléances*) in every district. Even in 1789, the elections were remarkably harmonious; the 'cahiers' displayed a wide measure of agreement about how France should develop in the immediate future, replacing authoritarian monarchy with constitutional, representative government, individual rights, and economic modernization (Doyle 1980).

The English Parliament
According to certain historical sources, there was a wide electoral franchise in medieval England. Town meetings and shire (county) courts were called periodically to settle disputes, proceed with judicial matters, and choose tax collectors. Towns and boroughs elected delegates to represent their interests in the county courts. When the king summoned what was to be known as the

modern Parliament in 1295, it included two knights from each of 37 rural shires or counties and two burgesses from each of 115 cities and urban boroughs.

Until the 14th century in the rural counties, 'every inhabitant and commoner in each county had a voice in the election of knights whether he were freeholder or not, or had a freehold only of one penny, sixpence or twelvepence by the year' (Bishop 1893: 71). 'Previous to the 15th century it is probable that any free man residing in the county might vote for the knight of the shire. Sheriffs were elected by universal manhood suffrage and the entire male population was assessed for the knight's wages as representative, so that we may assume that Parliamentary elections doubtless followed the same principle.' Similarly for the urban districts, 'it is probable that boroughs elections were held on the basis of universal manhood suffrage, every freeman of the town taking part in the choice of a burgess . . . In some boroughs, probably, the great mass of the inhabitants took part in the election' (Seymour and Frary 1918, vol. 1: 66).

Only from the 15th century was the franchise somewhat limited to holders of 'free land or tenement to the value of forty shillings by the year, at the least, above all charges'. The very Act establishing this regulation explained that previous elections 'had been crowded by many persons of low estate, and much confusion' had resulted. The new electorate was formed by peasant farmers of some wealth or townsmen of the middle classes for whom it was relatively easier to identify common interests and produce enforceable collective decisions (Seymour and Frary 1918, vol. 1: 69).

Beginning in 1688, the House of Commons decided the franchise in various boroughs. While several formulas of residence and contribution to municipal charges resulted in virtual universal manhood suffrage at the local level, in most boroughs 'freeman' became a more restrictive category excluding serfs, villains, and other unprivileged. The proportion of enfranchised population at the national level in 17th- and 18th-century England was lower than in some of the other European cases previously mentioned. But the limits to franchise were vague and uncertain, and the participation was still notable in many local constituencies. The system was based on multimember districts with loose national parties and many independent local candidates, which permitted some varied representation of different preference groups.

A number of historical studies have presented a picture of the elections in Britain before the electoral reforms of the 19th century in which widespread political participation was the rule rather than the exception. A high number of contested elections and an electorate capable of much action developed between 1689 and 1715 and again between 1734 and 1832. Many general elections provoked debates over national issues in a wide range of constituencies. 'The electorate was a numerically impressive and, for most of this period, steadily increasing entity. It comprised a vast, if somewhat nebulous, electoral pool of fairly wealthy, propertied individuals. Its members participated with commendable frequency in elections whenever the possibilities of such participation were open to them.' The election campaigns were open events, public spectacles, inclusive and popular. Control of elections by local elites became difficult and most elections were open to innovative candidates and uncertain results (O'Gorman 1982: 389ff.).

The active electorate was partly curbed by certain restrictive institutions, most prominently the control of the Parliament by the Cabinet, single-party Cabinets, and the restriction of the political agenda to a few issues on which a homogeneous group could promote some dominant interest. As will be seen in the following section, a series of electoral reforms during the 19th century established more and better defined constituencies across the country, but also more rigid bounds over the groups of citizens entitled to participate in the electoral process than had existed in some of the previous periods (Plumb 1967, 1969; O'Gorman 1982, 1989; Phillips 1982, 1992; Taylor 1997).

Anglo-American Colonies

Elections by virtual universal suffrage in the British colonies in North America date from the election of the House of Burgesses in Virginia in 1619, followed closely by the Assembly of Maryland and the annual choice of governor in Plymouth. In the early part of the history of each colony, the qualifications required of electors were neither numerous nor well-defined, allowing in many cases all inhabitants to vote. Later, suffrage restrictions previously introduced in Britain were extended to the colonies, especially in the form of land-property requirements. In fact, this was not an extemporaneous condition. As with the other European cases already mentioned, the assumption that all family members shared some common basic interest, allowing them to be fairly represented by the head of household, was strongly grounded on the familiy property. In addition, the absence of feudal lords, a much greater availability of land, and the wide diffusion of real and personal property in the North American colonies rendered the British requirements for voting much less restrictive.

Until the independence of the colonies in 1776, large consensus was found in most communities. Unanimity was considered a highly valued goal and conflict over public issues was something to be avoided. In the very earliest times, the right to vote in a colony was claimed in very much the same way as the current right to vote of stockholders in a modern corporation. The early colonies were business corporations in agriculture, hence the real property qualification was considered the appropriate requirement to entitle the holder to a vote. The assumption was that suffrage was the way to identify the common good of the community and only those who clearly had an interest in the colony should be permitted to participate in its governance (Porter 1969; Dinkin 1977).

The requirements for voting rights were loosely defined and differed in every colony. They were adapted to different circumstances in order to make feasible the identification of common interests among the voters and the stability of the social choice. The rules were flexible and were frequently modified, using either land property, wealth, or moral qualifications as indices of the individual's capability to make reasonable choices on collective matters.

More specifically, those who had not been residents a sufficient length of time were excluded from voting. But the length of time required varied from six months to one or two years, depending on the colony, and did not exist in Virginia, New Hampshire, and New York. The standard minimum age requirement was 21 years old (20 in Plymouth, 18 in Rhode Island). Yet 'minors did sometimes vote' (Bishop 1893: 65); 'boys and other [legally] unqualified persons voted' in the Carolinas (Seymour and Frary 1918, vol. 1: 223); 'boys' and 'youth' 18 and 19 years old participated in certain elections in North Carolina, Pennsylvania, New Hampshire, and Massachusetts. All women could vote in New Jersey (Dinkin, 1977: 30–1). Other voting criteria included the character of the man's employment and his moral qualifications. Land-property was measured in acres in the South, but in New England, where land was more expensive, much smaller portions were validated for its monetary value.

On the one hand, criminals were disenfranchised and, in several Northern colonies, the absence of correctness in moral behavior could lead to the suppression of a freeman's rights and even to his total disenfranchisement, in some cases making resource of the testimony of his neighbors. In Massachusetts and New York, electors were required to be members of some church; Roman Catholics in general, and Jews and Quakers in some cases, could not vote. On the other hand, in the Southern colonies, where the majority of the black, red (or native), and mulatto population resided, they voted until rather late (1716 in South Carolina, 1734 in North Carolina, 1723 in Virginia, 1761 in Georgia). In the North, no state ever eliminated nonwhites from the ballot, including Indians in parts of New England.

A number of historians have found the franchise to have been extremely widespread despite the qualifications imposed upon prospective electors. 'Fairly uniformly the electorate seems to have varied, on a freehold basis exclusively, from about 50 to 75 per cent [of the male adult population]. Some communities exceeded, some fell below this range, but probably not as many as came within its limits' (Williamson 1960: 38). 'In some colonies like Virginia the degree of eligibility may have run as high as 80 per cent, in others, such as New York, it was closer to 50 or 60 per cent.' In general, enfranchisement was larger in rural districts. According to some sources of the 1770s, qualifications were rarely scrutinized: 'anything with the appearance of a man' was allowed to vote. Actually, only 'one-fifth to one-half of the adult males' were unable to exercise the right to vote (Dinkin 1977: 41–9). Accordingly, and quite similarly to other continental European cases previously discussed, between 10 and 20 per cent of the total population seem to have had voting rights in the British colonies in North America before their independence.

In colonial times, the annual election day was a gala event, conceived as an occasion for the colonists to come together and socialize. Procedures included oral voting, show of hands, polls, a booth with a poll-book with the names of the candidates over and against which were set down the votes, or corn and bean ballots to approve or reject the candidates for certain offices. Written ballots have been used in some places since the early 17th century, and some forms of the modern perforated ballot with the names of all the candidates were used from the late 17th century.

The elections of local representatives were instrumental in the process towards independence. Yet, between 1776 and the approval of the Constitution of the United States in 1789, a tendency towards higher uniformity developed across the states. Wishing to preserve harmony in a larger, more varied society, most patriot leaders thought that political participation should be preserved for those who had a 'common interest with, and an attachment to the community', those with a 'stake in society', for they alone could make competent, reasonable judgements.

Interestingly, a new strategy of simultaneous enfranchisement and disenfranchisement of different electors' groups, which would be steadily developed throughout the 19th century, can be identified as early as in the independence years. On the one hand, property requirements were reduced and became similar in all thirteen states, religious requirements were substantially moderated so as to make almost all Christians eligible, and several states allowed blacks to possess the franchise for the first time. Yet, on the other hand, formal requirements of 21 years of age, male gender, citizenship, and residence were established in all states, and eight states altered their own constitutions in order to exclude blacks, slaves, and most Indians from voting. All in all, the electorate of the 13 states 'probably expanded from 50–80 per cent [of the male adult population] in the late provincial period to about 60–90 per cent by the close of the revolutionary period' (Dinkin 1982), which is to say about 15–25 per cent of the total population.

Iberian-American Colonies

Universal men's suffrage at the local level was introduced into the Spanish colonies in North and South America more abruptly than in the British colonies. Following the Napoleonic invasion of Spain in 1808, an improvised people's resistance was coordinated by means of elected local *juntas*, which initially adopted the rules of the surviving medieval Assemblies (*Cortes*) and local councils. In 1809, representatives of the Central Junta of Spain were indirectly elected with restricted suffrage by municipal and parish councils using a mix of choices and lots.

The election of new 'Cortes' in 1810 and 1812 was based on a combination of old rules and the new suffrage of family heads. The 1812 Constitution approved in Cádiz introduced virtual male universal suffrage for indirect elections, as was used for the elections of municipal councils and provincial deputies in 1812–14. Paralleling the enlargement of the electorate, the proportion of representatives from the Spanish colonies in the Americas and the Philippines was augmented. In 1812, all men aged over 25, and natives of the province, whatever their status, could vote. Exclusions were devised for some groups on the basis of the presumption that they did not share some basic common interest with the rest of the community. Among those excluded were the members of the military orders, state debtors, servants, and those lacking employment, a trade, or any other 'honest livelihood'. Native Indians in the colonies, however, were allowed to vote (Chavarri 1988; Demélas-Bohy and Guerra 1996).

This initial electoral mobilization, which was soon interrupted in Spain with the re-establishment of the traditional monarchy, was a major episode in the Spanish colonies' process of gaining independence. More than one hundred American cities were involved in the first Spanish elections and electoral politics mobilized large groups in the immediate aftermath. The fall of Spanish domination fostered territorial fragmentation and localism. Electoral expectations were concentrated at the first electoral level, including rural towns, small cities, and provincial states (Botana 1995). This push explains the 'early existence [in 1820] of a relatively wide suffrage in the Spanish world . . . With a few exceptions, in most Latin American countries the idea of an extended suffrage gained ground during the first half of the 19th century to an extent which has few parallels in the Western World' (Posada-Carbó 1996: 6).

Particularly interesting developments include those in New Spain (today's Mexico) in 1812–20. For the election of representatives to both the Spanish *Cortes* and local and provincial councils, electoral districts were defined as corresponding to the traditional parishes, which were socially somewhat homogeneous units. In many places the Indian Republics were transformed into town councils. The Indians were thus given access to the election and the holding of all the offices, while maintaining the homogeneity of every electoral unit. In this way, voting practices enjoyed large consensus within the communities. In 1814, voting rights were given to all adult men 18 years old or younger if married, including not only all Indians but also 'patriotic foreigners' (Annino 1995, 1996).

Similarly, the province of Buenos Aires, as well as other provinces in Rio de la Plata (today's Argentina), organized elections with flexible rules in 1811. More formally, universal suffrage for direct elections of representatives was established for all men more than 20 years old in 1821. Foreigners were excluded, but voting rights were given to about 20 per cent of the total population (Chiaramonte 1995; Alonso 1996).

The Crown of Portugal called elections in 1821, according to the rules provided by the Spanish Constitution of 1812. In Brazil, 'the elections mobilized the interest of the majority of the male adult population of the towns. There were no restrictions of race or literacy'. Economic requisites were low and could be fulfilled by all 'except beggars and vagabunds [sic]', and slaves. Elections were lively, popular events with relatively wide participation. 'Approximately, a half of free men 24 years old or more were in the census and, in some provinces, the number rose to 85 per cent' (Graham 1995).

Political mobilization was curbed and voting rights were substantially reduced in the second half of the 19th century in most of the new states in Iberian America as well as in Spain and Portugal. Relatively small, homogeneous communities were, thus, able to make important collective decisions on the basis of elections with broad voting rights. But the sudden creation of new large states with wide franchise produced greater political instability.

2.2. COMPLEX ELECTORATES

The complexity of large electorates in modern polities derives from new demands of public goods and new policy issues that are submitted to binding collective decisions by voting. The more the number of issues in the political agenda and the dispersion of the corresponding voters' preferences increase, the more uncertain the social choice becomes. Stable and satisfactory outcomes can be obtained only with the introduction of new institutional devices.

The introduction of new voters into the electorate can be considered to be either innocuous, hazardous, or threatening, from the point of view of the incumbent voters and rulers, depending on the number of new voters, their political information, the 'location' of their preferences, and the degree of homogeneity of their interests, as well as on the fragmentation of the incumbents. Specifically, dependent people with preferences similar to the incumbent voters, like children, youth, women, and servants, can be considered innocuous or susceptible to being manipulated in order to enlarge the support of incumbents' preferences and even to counteract the potential threat derived from the enfranchisement of other groups of voters. In contrast, other politically unorganized and uninformed new voters, especially those in rural areas, can produce less predictable social choices because of persuasion by intrepid political entrepreneurs. Finally, colonized peoples, dominated ethnic groups, or compact working classes, if allowed to vote, are often expected to threaten the survival of existing states, property rights, and moral standards and to reverse the previous political equilibrium.

Incumbent rulers, especially if they have a high degree of internal cohesion and face weak opposition movements, tend to prefer reduced electorates and restrictive electoral systems producing total winners and total losers, as was the case with most incumbent Conservatives and Liberals in the 19th century. Emergent minorities, in contrast, tend to pressure for the enlargement of the electorate and, at the same time, for proportional representation or other pluralistic institutional formulas, as the Socialists did in many countries in the late 19th century.

However, if the incumbent rulers are submitted to a sufficiently credible challenge, they may prefer to lead the enlargement of the electorate in

conjunction with the introduction of pluralistic institutions which guarantee them some power-sharing, as certain Conservatives did in the late 19th
century and early 20th century. Conversely, the challenging opposition
may bet for universal suffrage, but also for maintaining simple institutional formulas, including, in particular, single-member electoral districts,
in the expectation of becoming absolute winners under the existing framework.

This section has two parts. First, arguments for and against the enlargement of the electorate are reviewed. Second, different strategies of voting
rights are identified on the basis of different combinations of enfranchisement of new voters' groups and institutional arrangements.

Arguments on Suffrage

Arguments for and against the extension of suffrage rights became more
controversial and sophisticated in modern times, as new, large political
units encompassed potentially complex electorates, than those of the
earlier, local-type discussed in the previous section. The development of
communications and travel, bigger markets, larger-scale economies, division of labor, and other factors supporting the creation of modern nation-
states, make political communities more complex and the allocation of
voting rights more intricate.

Traditional doctrines of permanent, natural rights have been widely
used in favor of the enlargement of the electorate. On this view, equal
voting rights are defended on the assumption that all human beings are
created equal. Yet this assumption may suggest a substantial degree of
harmony and homogeneous interests among the potential members of a
political community, which is relatively hard to find in modern societies.
A logical evolution of the natural rights argument has led some of its
believers to emphasize certain supposedly common social and cultural
characteristics of human nature, actually making the requirements for the
corresponding voting rights more restrictive. At the same time, collective
natural rights have been argued in order to maintain traditional estates'
'organic' representation or the privileges of incumbent voters.

Partly as a result of these theoretical weaknesses among early promoters of broad-based suffrage, alternative arguments more clearly based on
the expected consequences of enlarging the existing electorates have
tended to replace the natural rights argument, especially on the side of
those against creating new voting rights. In fact, hardly any social group
has been indisputably recognized to bear natural voting rights and most
have been excluded, or at least proposed to be excluded, at some moment
or place for a variety of reasons.

Children, aliens, the mentally ill, criminals, and the homeless are almost always barred from voting, on the assumption that they are unable to make reasonable choices on collective matters or that they do not share sufficiently significant common interests with the other members of the community. Analogously, women were traditionally considered to be insufficiently involved in public affairs to participate in political elections; many youth and children are still considered too immature to make political choices; the elderly have been seen as particularly vulnerable to manipulation due to their dependence on state pensions; Indians, blacks, and Jews have been considered extraneous to the interests of incumbent dominant voters; and industrial workers have been widely viewed as a threatening majority which should be prevented becoming an electoral force.

Conversely, but also on the basis of expected political consequences, landowners, monarchists, and Catholics were threatened with deprivation or effectively deprived of voting rights by modern liberal movements because of their allegiance to the old regime. Attempts to exclude peasants from voting were based on their servile obedience to the owners. Artisans, shopkeepers, and other 'bourgeois' people were attacked for their social dominance in some industrialized settings with a growing proletariat.

In all these different arguments, the crucial social choice variable is the dispersion of voters' preferences, that is, the number of new potential voters and the 'location' of their preferences relative to the number and preferences of the incumbent voters. When the enfranchisable group is presumed to have very similar or interlaced preferences as the incumbent voters, no significant change in the social choice can be predicted from its enfranchisement. When new voters' preferences are uncertain and one suspects that they will make hesitant, shifting choices, the room for manipulation of the social choice is great and the outcome appears to be unpredictable and unstable. When new voters have compact, differentiated preferences and can form an alternative majority, they may produce a new social choice which can be considered very damaging for the incumbent voters or, from the opposite viewpoint but coincidental analysis, very satisfactory for the newly enfranchised. The arguments that correspond to these analyses are reviewed below. (For a comparable threefold typology of rhetorical arguments regarding civic liberties, universal suffrage, and social policy, see Hirschman 1991.)

Innocuousness

Certain authors have held that 'dependent' people, as they are led by those who are active in politics and share the same interests, are not likely to develop differentiated political preferences. Children, youth, women, servants, serfs, and slaves have been considered to have the same stake in the society as those already enfranchised.

The idea of virtual representation emerged in rather homogeneous societies during the Middle Ages. At that time it was believed that, like the father of a traditional household could vote on behalf of his wife and children, paternalistic rulers could act on behalf of those under their care. When adapted to modern times, this argument was based upon the presumption that nonvoters did not bear a potential distortion of the social choice, but were unnecessary participants in a process in which they would vote like the members of the incumbent winning group.

The concept of virtual representation without voting was used as an argument against the enfranchisement of the colonists, in particular in the British colonies in North America. During the controversy that led to the war for American independence, certain British politicians asserted that the House of Commons did in fact represent the colonists, even if they did not elect their own representatives to the House, because they shared the same interests as those voting in Britain.

As a consistent reply to these statements, the independence of the colonies was supported by the argument that the Americans had become 'a different people', that is, that they had ceased to have preferences similar to and amalgamated with those of the Britons and had developed differentiated interests and new issues, which were not sufficiently dealt with in the House of Commons. However, this did not prevent the independent American communities from using similar arguments in order to keep certain people disenfranchised or to add other groups to those already banned from voting, including women and children, under the presumption that they did not have different interests from those of the enfranchised male adults.

The English liberal James Mill drew from this discussion the implication that certain dependent groups in the society were not worth being given new voting rights. Mill supported significant enlargements of the electorate in Britain in the early 19th century, but he stopped short of including 'superfluous' voters. In a series of articles published between 1820 and 1829, just before the first British electoral reform in 1832, Mill emphasized the leading role of the 'middle class' in promoting stability and prosperity for the whole society, in the same way the 'median voter' has been considered able to produce high social utility in modern social choice theory. Specifically, Mill hoped to curb the role of the minority aristocracy in order to promote liberal reforms. He also counted on the fact that a vast majority of people feeling an immediate and daily dependence (through jobs, income, protection, housing, and health) upon the members of the middle class 'would be sure to be guided by their advise and example'.

Accordingly, James Mill was in favor of a broad men's suffrage including 'certain classes, professions, or fraternities' that had become central in modern society but had been excluded from voting during the previous period. Yet, he thought that any other portion of the community beyond these groups, 'if erected into the choosing body, would remain the same'. The logical inference for Mill was to recommend a virtual men's suffrage, while noting that 'all those individuals whose interests are indisputably included in those of other individuals, may be struck off [the electorate] without inconvenience'. These included, in particular, all children and youth whose interests are involved in those of their parents. James Mill expected that, since the great majority of old men had children, whose interests they regarded as an essential part of their own, even without voting the interests of the young would not be sacrificed to those of the old. Likewise, he considered that voting rights could be fairly denied to women since 'the interest of almost [sic] all of whom is involved either in that of their fathers or in that of their husbands' (Mill, 1820–9, in Lively and Rees 1978).

Interestingly, this point was eventually recycled by the suffragist movement as the basis for the harmlessness of giving voting rights to women. 'If the opinions and interests of women are identical with those of men of a similar social grade', said the American suffragist Lydia E. Becker, 'there could be no possible harm in giving them the same means of expressing them as are given to men' (Becker 1872).

In further developments, the expectation that women would reveal the same political preferences as their previously enfranchised fathers and husbands led some political leaders to perceive women's suffrage as an opportunity to counteract the innovative influence of other newly enfranchised groups with more differentiated preferences, including workers, immigrants, and blacks. The American suffragist Mary Putnam Jacobi, in particular, developed this 'counter-weight' argument. She praised women's values in favor of 'conservatism, their economy, their horror of waste, their interest in personal character, the very simplicity of their judgement, their preoccupation with direct and living issues, all qualities generated by the special circumstances which have surrounded women, and must continue to surround them', as reasons for giving them the vote. Jacobi expected that 'the influence of the women who are now busily engaged in civilizing the hordes of uncivilized people in our midst, will be utilized, not only to kindle the lagging interest of the men of their own class, but to so guide ignorant women voters, that they could be made to counterbalance, when necessary, the votes of ignorant and interested men' (Jacobi 1894).

With a similar orientation, Catholic and conservative women created the French Union for Women's Suffrage, the first specifically suffragist national organization in France, in 1909. They equated women's emancipation to the defense of the Church, the family, and the fatherland. More specifically, they promoted a formula of 'family suffrage' by which only the head of the family would vote, but with as many votes as there were members of the family, including women, grandparents, and children, in the assumption that all of them shared the same interests (Rosanvallon 1992).

The 'innocuousness' argument became more sophisticated as the suffragist movement proceeded. As the traditional sphere of women in the household was becoming more public through the development of food stores, laundry operators, and public schools, as well as more women entering the labor market, it was argued that their basic interests merged with those of the incumbent male voters in two different ways. First, these changes provoked new family relationships, making men's tasks closer to certain traditional women's household jobs. Second, women began to share similar professional and economic interests with their male counterparts (Kraditor 1965, esp. ch. 3; Harvey 1998).

Hazard

Paralleling the self-confident argument of innocuousness, there is an age-old tradition that points to the risks of permitting the electoral participation of ignorant people who are likely to be deceived in their political choices. As the 'hazard' argument was formulated, for instance, in a mid 18th century French local assembly regarding the election of artisans as deputies, certain people can be considered 'easy to delude, incapable of understanding by themselves what might be in the town's interests, and sometimes unable to write the name of those for whom they were voting' (Temple 1973: 78).

Lack of political understanding has typically been considered to be the result of illiteracy, which may prevent an individual from even recognizing the names of candidates. This argument has taken precedence in countries in which a sudden enlargement of the electorate has been introduced or proposed in an environment of massive illiteracy and the absence of sufficiently well-organized political parties, including those in many 19th-century European states. To the alarmed observer, misinformed voters could be the victims of patrons, would-be dictators, demagogues, fanatics, or extremists of varied colors. Then the social choice would be unpredictable and unstable since shifting majorities could be formed at the initiative of ambitious leaders. Suffrage rights were typically seen in this perspective as a 'slippery slope' leading to the unknown.

This type of warning was issued against the 'innocuousness' argument mentioned earlier, and was developed by Chancellor Otto Fürst von Bismarck when he promoted universal male suffrage in the North German Confederation (and later in the German Empire). He implicitly expected that peasants, who were loyal to the King overall, would also be obedient to their manor lords or employers when voting (Ludwig 1927: 242). Yet, as was pointed out by the lawyer Robert von Mohl, certain potential political entrepreneurs who had been previously marginalized from the political, such as the Catholic clergy in the rural areas and the Socialist or Communist leaders in factories and mines, might take control of new voters and produce a high fractionalization of the elected representatives. 'Universal manhood suffrage, without firmly established and well organized political parties', he warned, 'especially in a federated state like Germany, would bring forth numerous fractions incapable of forming a majority—a parliament built upon quicksand' (Mohl 1860–9, in Anderson and Anderson 1967: 427).

This position could also be found on the left wing of the political spectrum. In situations in which large sections of the population were deprived of voting in political elections, a number of Liberal, Radical, and Socialist leaders were reluctant about significant enlargements of the electorate. They feared that uninformed new voters would be deceived by unscrupulous political entrepreneurs or by their own bosses and patrons. Instead of focusing on voting rights, many political leaders of the left gave priority to promoting public education and compulsory schooling, which was considered to be a tool for building a better society and, more specifically, a necessary condition for shaping more 'conscious', homogeneous constituencies that would support progressive programs.

The British Socialist Robert Owen, for example, did not refrain from referring to 'the ignorance, vulgarity, and most disgusting assumptions of the laboring classes' and, accordingly, considered that a government based upon popular elections 'could be tolerated only as the best known means of leading to an advanced state of society, by a superior education of all classes' (Owen 1828, 1844, in 1993, vol. 1: liii; vol. 2: 121).

When universal male suffrage was introduced in France in 1848, the Socialist Pierre-Joseph Proudhon held that 'universal suffrage given to a people of so neglected an education as ours, far from being the instrument of progress, is only the stumbling-block of liberty' (Proudhon 1923, vol. XVII: t. 1). On the same occasion, the Socialist Louis Blanc asked to adjourn the elections in order to prevent 'the numerical superiority of the ignorant peasantry over the enlightened population of the towns' (Blanc 1848: 297). Likewise, the revolutionary Louis-Auguste Blanqui referred to the oppressed workers as a 'blind flock', due to their control by the Church, and announced that 'the elections, if they are held, will be reactionary' (Bastid 1948).

In Italy, the proposal to abolish literacy tests for allocating voting rights in a largely illiterate population was viewed as running the risk of having the rural masses of the South being politically manipulated by traditional local powerholders. This was particularly risky for national cohesion in such an early period of unification of the Italian state. Meanwhile, in Spain certain 19th-century Liberals rejected universal male suffrage in the fear that new, uneducated voters would be deceived by their patrons, *caudillos*, and local bosses (*caciques*). In the face of that risk, the progressive Sabino Herrero stated: 'It is better to delay universal suffrage rather than falsify it' (Serrano 1993: 215–16).

Regarding women's suffrage in particular, certain Liberal leaders in European countries feared that women would be manipulated by the Church and would submit to reactionary influence. This was a reaction to the conservative 'counter-weight' arguments for women's suffrage previously described. The British Liberal William E. Gladstone held that women's 'personal attendance' at elections would constitute a 'practical evil not only of the gravest, but even of an intolerable character' (Lewis 1987: 67). The Radical French Prime Minister Georges Clemenceau believed that 'if the right to vote were given to women tomorrow, France would all of a sudden jump backwards into the middle ages' (Hause 1984: 16).

According to some Socialist leaders of the early 20th century, women's voting rights should be subordinated to their economic liberation, which implied the abolition of private property. Only by suppressing the existing family relations supported by a capitalist economy, they thought, would gender equality come about as a natural consequence, while, under capitalism, women's vote would be somewhat adrift from the point of view of progressive purposes. The French and Belgian Socialists voted for a long time against women's suffrage, fearing the more conservative preferences of women and their domination by the priests.

As late as 1931, most Spanish left-wing Republicans opposed the introduction of female suffrage into the newly established Second Republic on the grounds that the new voters would be won over by the conservative clergy. The opposition included two outspoken Radical-Socialist and Socialist female politicians (the latter in disagreement with most of her male party companions), Victoria Kent and Margarita Nelken, respectively. Kent, in particular, confined women's voting rights to their achievement of a 'university education and the liberation of their consciousness' (Capel 1992).

Threat

In contrast to the presumptions that nonvoters would be either innocuous or easily manipulated, they can also be seen as threatening by incumbent voters when they share some compact common preference which is opposed to the prevailing rule, especially regarding property or moral standards. A new majority entering the electorate can change the social choice dramatically at the expense of the previous winners. In early modern periods of enlargement of voting rights, this foresight was simultaneously feared by enlightened members of the groups likely to lose in the future and celebrated by leaders of the expected winning groups.

Thomas B. Macaulay, an English moderate Liberal, was one of the advocates of the British limited electoral reform introduced in 1832. On the eve of that bill, he emphasized the risks of giving the vote to workers and women. Macaulay reflected a very widespread fear that a radical reform of the franchise would undermine the security of private property. Like many other members of the incumbent electorate of the time, he suspected that under universal suffrage it would be a numerical majority, a poor majority, who would govern, and this majority, following its immediate interests, would seek to dispossess the rich minority. Accordingly, Macaulay thought that suffrage should be limited. On the one hand, 'every decent farmer and shopkeeper might possess the elective franchise', he said. But, on the other hand, the deprived of property should be excluded, especially 'in countries [like the United Kingdom] in which the great majority live from hand to mouth'.

This was not an absolute, natural law-based position, but rather an argument of expediency and social utility that could be adapted in different forms to different contexts. In particular, the criterion in favor of a stable social choice led Macaulay to accept that—in a society not based on class and with greater opportunities for work, wealth, and decent life, like the United States—'it is not very decidedly even for the immediate advantage of the poor to plunder the rich'. Voting rights for the poor, he concluded, would not be so threatening in such a society and, as such, be acceptable there.

Macaulay likewise rejected women's suffrage because he saw women to be, across the world, 'in a state of personal slavery'. Precisely because they were so oppressed by men, he believed, their voting would not be so innocuous as others (such as James Mill) claimed. Women could develop alternative interests and political wills if they were given the opportunity, thus for the sake of men's self-protection, so stated Macaulay, they should be denied voting rights (Macaulay 1829, in Lively and Rees 1978).

Fears regarding private property were also revealed by leading French moderate Liberals of the time. Praising the role of intermediate voters in producing outcomes with high social utility, Pierre-Paul Royer-Collard held that 'all new interests in the society belong to the middle class'. Yet, when dealing with the electoral laws to be approved during the French constitutional monarchy, he postulated that 'a certain degree of personal wealth' should be required for a person to be given voting rights. Wealth was used here as an index of the individual capacity for making 'free and enlightened judgement'.

In contrast to the typical 'hazard' argument regarding unpredictable and unstable social choices, this personal wealth requirement for being able to make 'reasonable' choices was not advanced with the aim of avoiding ungrounded, shifting choices of misinformed voters that would produce unstable outcomes. This restriction on voting rights was promoted in the acknowledgement of a substantial conflict of interests between the incumbent and the newly eligible voters. Wealth was considered to be the proof of an individual's 'political aptitude' and ability to vote 'rightly'—in other words, in favor of the enlightened interests promoted by the middle class (Royer-Collard in 1817, according to Barante 1863: 103–17).

Along similar lines, and perhaps more explicitly, the French Liberal politician and Romantic novelist, Benjamin Constant, stated that for voting, as with being a 'member of an association, a person needs some degree of enlightenment and a common interest with the other members of the association'. From this perspective, the voters' enlightenment was conceived as a sufficient condition for producing an acceptable social choice if the necessary condition that the voters shared a common interest with the previously winning group was fulfilled. Education was a tool to avoid being manipulated, in a similar way as for those who feared the 'hazard' of unpredictability and instability previously discussed. But in this new approach, avoiding manipulation of the voters meant the ability to identify the voters' interests in accordance with the preferences of the incumbents. While 'hazardous' suffrage implied that ignorant voters might be deceived and vote against their own interests, 'threatening' suffrage implied that voters could vote in their own interests against those of the incumbents. They could be attracted to the dominant viewpoint only by way of enlightenment.

The implications of this approach for excluding certain categories of people from voting rights were straightforward. The excluded should be, first, children, because they are not enlightened. Second, foreigners should be excluded because they do not share common interests with the indigenous population. And third, it excludes all those lacking 'the leisure indispensable for the acquisition of understanding and soundness of judgement', which is to say, 'those to whom destitution retains in a situation of perennial dependence and condemns to work every day [because] they know as much of public affairs as children and do not have more interests than the foreigners in national prosperity' (Constant 1815, ch. 6).

The Spanish Conservative leader, Antonio Cánovas, repeatedly resisted the introduction of universal male suffrage on the basis of similar arguments. From 1868 to 1871, he held that: 'Universal suffrage and property are antithetical and will not live together, because it is not possible, for long . . . Universal suffrage will always be a farce, a deceit to the crowd, brought about by the malevolence and violence of the few, of the privileged by inheritance and capital, under the name of ruling classes, or it will be, if it is enacted in freedom and with full independence and conscience of action, unavoidable and irreducible Communism'. In 1888, facing a new attempt to introduce broad suffrage in Spain, he noted a difference between the hazard of voting by illiterates and the threat of voting by the poor. 'I believe', he said, 'that universal suffrage, if it is sincere, if it gives a real vote in the governance of the country to the crowd, not only the unlearned, which would be almost irrelevant, but to the miserly and beggar mob, it would be the triumph of Communism and the ruin of the principle of property' (Cánovas 1884–90).

Interestingly, the prospect that alternative winners could develop under the opportunities created by broad adult suffrage and reverse the basis of the existing social structures was also confirmed by the opposing side. For most Socialists, the experience of universal suffrage in France in 1848, which led to the direct election of Louis Bonaparte as President of the Republic and eventually to the dissolution of the Assembly by coup and the re-establishment of the Empire, was extremely disappointing. This episode made most of them highly suspicious of such mechanisms of social choice and, as mentioned, led them to put their trust, instead, in the long-term effects of public education or, more generally, in the guidance of educated leaders. In one of its branches, this Socialist approach supported the role of intellectuals leading the ignorant working masses in the formation of workers' political parties, which inspired both the formation of Socialist parties under Karl Kautsky's leadership and the organization of the 'revolutionary vanguard' in Communist parties by Vladimir Lenin.

However, some ambiguity remained, which permitted the development of the alternative opinion in favor of universal suffrage as an opportunity for a new majority to be formed. As early as 1852, Karl Marx had written that, in contrast to what was happening in France, 'universal suffrage [would be] the equivalent of political power for the working class in England, where the proletariat forms the large majority of the population', confirming thus the implicit 'threat' that defenders of private ownership had perceived in workers' votes. Marx speculated that 'the carrying of universal suffrage in England would be a far more socialistic measure than anything which has been honored with that name on the Continent. Its inevitable result, here [in the United Kingdom], would be the political supremacy of the working class' (Marx 1852: 332).

After the introduction of virtual universal men's suffrage in Germany, Marx noted in 1880 that 'the franchise has been transformed from a means of deception, which it was before, into an instrument of emancipation'. Further developing this insight, Friedrich Engels sketched a potentially winning coalition under universal suffrage elections starting with 'the most numerous, most compact mass, the decisive "shock force" of the international proletarian army' that would 'conquer the greater part of the middle strata of society, petty [sic] bourgeois and small peasants, and grow into the decisive power of the land, before which all other powers will have to bow, whether they like it or not' (Engels 1895: 421). This approach was further elaborated by Edward Bernstein in the early 20th century and eventually became the basis for the electoral participation of the Social-Democrats.

Analogously, the expectation that not only workers' but also women's political rights could bring about substantial changes in certain social structures and moral standards was not only feared by certain men, as previously mentioned, but sustained by some outstanding leaders of the feminist movement. In the early days of the movement, Mary Wollstonecraft had outlined this idea. She openly acknowledged that the existing ignorance of women generated their 'folly'. But she argued for women's rights in the expectation of obtaining beneficial social consequences, specifically 'the moral improvement that a revolution in female manners might naturally be expected to produce' in the dominating men's society (Wollstonecraft 1792, ch. 13).

Just as anti-feminists held that social order required a family model that involved the political subordination of women, some radical suffragists hoped that women's political rights would produce significant changes in family relations. Women's political participation would give salience to new issues related to education, social welfare, and children and, as a consequence, public life would be morally elevated. Governments based on women's suffrage would even be 'less likely to go to war, without real necessity', as stated in the American Congressional Union for Woman Suffrage (Kraditor 1965: 63).

These arguments were also developed by some outstanding male supporters of women's voting rights, such as John Stuart Mill, one of the founders of the British women's suffrage movement. On the one hand, Mill shared the worries of other progressive leaders previously mentioned regarding the votes of uneducated people. 'Universal teaching must precede universal enfranchisement', he said. Mill even supported giving different numbers of votes to different individuals on the basis of their respective educations (Mill 1861, ch. 8). Yet, on the other hand, if women were educated and enfranchised in all aspects of life, Mill thought, they would make a substantial contribution to public life on the basis of their distinctive intellectual and moral qualities. With women's political participation, 'all the selfish propensities, the self-worship, the unjust self-preference, which exist among mankind would be permanently rooted out'. Women's influence would be 'nothing but favorable to public virtue' (Mill 1869, ch. 4).

Susan B. Anthony, the foremost agitator for women's suffrage in the United States in the 19th century, argued more specifically that the prevalence of such social plagues as prostitution, sex crimes, and wife murders proved men's incapacity to cope with social problems, that they were caused by women's dependence, and that their cure would be women's economic independence and political equality. 'I am a full and firm believer', she said, 'in the revelation that it is through women that the [human] race is to be redeemed. And it is because of this faith that I ask for her immediate and unconditional emancipation from all political, industrial, social and religious subjection' (Anthony 1875).

Similarly, the leader of the French suffragists, Hubertine Auclert, claimed that women's political liberation would reduce war, immorality, and alcoholism and would create the opportunity for building a 'maternal State' in charge of public health care, and the protection of children, ill people, the unemployed, and the elderly (Auclert 1885, in Hause, 1987).

Voting Rights Strategies

As has been seen, natural rights arguments regarding the enlargement of the electorate were largely replaced with social-utility arguments in the modern intellectual debate. For some of the authors and politicians mentioned, voting rights were openly acknowledged to be a means for the goal of social utility. For others, the argument of social utility was adopted only as a means for persuading reluctant incumbent rulers and voters of the advantages of 'natural' equal suffrage. In the latter approach, the expediency argument was itself an expedient, but in some ways it also induced its bearers to pay attention to the collective consequences of individuals' voting rights.

In some cases, universal suffrage has been established in modern times in parallel with a decrease in the dispersion of preferences among different social groups on certain relevant issues. Certainly, universal suffrage can produce widely satisfactory and stable outcomes, while becoming itself a stable feature in the polity, on the basis of certain voters' characteristics, such as high educational levels, significant opportunities for economic well-being, and low barriers between different ethnic and gender groups. Yet, certain institutional arrangements can attain similar objectives, either by reducing the number of the available alternatives at voting, or by transferring the social choice to a post-electoral, institutional stage of moderating negotiations in a pluralistic framework.

Among the authors and politicians previously discussed, some wanted to exclude those without property from voting in order to preserve the existing social equilibrium. Others pointed to the socially efficient potential role of the 'middle class', but they only conceived this by way of obtaining adhesion from other groups to the middle group's interests through some 'enlightened' or 'sound' judgement. Others, finally, sought to establish the supremacy of the 'working class', but relied upon 'the conquest' of the middle strata of society.

All these strategies were aimed at maintaining or creating a single absolute majority in favor of one group's interests. They had in common the assumption that the act of voting can immediately produce a social choice. But further institutional refinements in the process of decision making, including in particular proportional representation, were able to create a different framework. Even if each member of a group votes according to some differentiated group's interest, further multiparty bargaining and compromising within a pluralistic institutional setting can produce intermediate, moderate, 'middle', 'enlightened', or 'sound' social choices able to distribute social utility widely and evenly. This was a relatively late discovery. Accordingly, different choices of institutions have paralleled different strategies of voting rights in various countries on the basis of the social choices they can be expected to produce.

From the point of view of incumbent voters and leaders, a successful strategy of voting rights allocation should achieve two major aims. First, it should keep within safe limits the instability effects of new, uneducated voters prone to shift their choices with successive elections or, in the words introduced earlier, to limit the 'hazards' of enlarged franchise. Second, it should prevent the formation of an alternative electoral majority able to change existing social structures and moral standards radically, or to neutralize the 'threat' posed by new voters. As suggested before, 'innocuous' voters—those likely to duplicate the voting patterns of the incumbents, as it was widely expected that would be the case, in particular, with women's enfranchisement—can be used by incumbent leaders to enlarge the electoral support of prevailing positions and to neutralize the influence of other newly enfranchised voters with hazardous or threatening preferences.

Two basic institutional elements can be manipulated in order to achieve these aims: (1) legal requirements for access to voting rights; (2) institutional regulations that can shape the party system, particularly the electoral rules.

On the basis of different combinations of these and related elements, three basic strategies of voting rights can be identified in the history of the early processes of democratization. The first, the 'Anglo' model, is based on a gradual allocation of voting rights to different minority groups through a slow, lengthy process of moderate reforms while the available political alternatives are reduced to a two-party system by institutional means. In this way, each small step in the enfranchisement of a new minority group forces its members to enter into collaboration with one of the two existing larger parties, thus giving the incumbents the possibility of maintaining significant control of the political agenda and retaining some winning positions. The result of this process, which refers to the cases of the United Kingdom, the United States, and other ex-British colonies, brings about high stability in the long term, but also some significant institutional restrictions over the development of varied political preferences, as well as relatively low levels of political participation.

The second strategy, the 'Latin' model, involves a sudden jump from a small electorate to universal men's suffrage, typically at the initiative of the political left or new groups, and under single-winner electoral rules. In conditions of mass illiteracy and the absence of well-organized political parties, as was the case at the moment of introducing broad suffrage rights for first time in France, Italy, Spain, as well as in some 'Latin' colonies in the Americas and Africa, this strategy tends to provoke high electoral unpredictability and instability, often leading to conflict and nondemocratic comebacks.

Finally, the third, the 'Nordic' model, which was developed in Germany and in Northern European countries, such as Sweden, Norway, and Finland, makes the sudden enfranchisement of a very large electorate compatible with appreciable degrees of political stability. In order to achieve this, new institutional devices in favor of political pluralism are introduced 'from above' by the incumbent rulers. In particular, proportional representation or similar institutional 'safeguards' promoting multiparty politics are adopted. Governments can then rely upon parliamentary coalitions in which centrist and moderate parties can expect to play a decisive role. In this way, the risk of instability and the threat of turnabouts are limited, and incumbent voters and leaders can expect continued opportunities of being included in government and maintaining a significant influence on the political process. As a consequence of self-reinforcing multiparty strategies, the new pluralistic institutional arrangements tend to last.

Tables 2.1, 2.2, and 2.3 show different stages in the process of enlarging voting rights in several countries. The size of the electorate is given as the percentage of enfranchised voters out of total population. The relative increase (or decrease) at each step (presented in the far right column) shows that the United Kingdom, the United States, as well as the former British colonies, Canada, Australia, and New Zealand, have developed a pattern of successive moderate enlargements, never enlarging the existing electorate by more than a few percentage points of the total population, and in two-digit points for women's suffrage only. The smoothness of this path has been reinforced by additional devices that distort representation in favor of traditional incumbent voters or that discourage electoral participation.

In contrast, both the Latin group formed by France, Italy, and Spain, and the Nordic group formed by Germany, Sweden, Norway, and Finland have

Who Can Vote

TABLE 2.1. *Size of the electorate: The 'Anglo' model*

Country	Voting rights requirements	Electors as % of total population	Percentage points increase
United Kingdom			
1716–1831	Loose rules	3	
1832–1866	Adult (age 21) men, with tax	4	+1
1867–1884	Adult men, with lower tax	8–9	+4
1885–1917	Adult men, with even lower tax	15–19	+6
1918–1927	Adult men, some women	44–49	+25
1928–1970	Adult men and women	65–70	+16
1971–	Men and women (age 18)	72–78	+2
United States			
1776–1788	Loose rules	15	
1789–1878	Adult (age 21) white men, property or tax	16–20	+1
1879–1919	Adult white, non-southern black men	21–24	+1
1919–1963	Plus adult women	49–55	+25
1964–1970	Plus southern blacks	60	+5
1971–	Men and women (age 18)	67–70	+7
Canada			
1891–1917	European adult (age 21) men	25–30	
1918–1959	European adult men and women	50–55	+20
1960–1970	Plus Indians and Innuit	55–60	
1971–	Men and women (age 18)	60–65	
Australia			
1901–1902	Adult (age 21) men, with tax, some women	25	
1902–1967	Adult men and women, except Aboriginals	50–55	+25
1968–1972	Adult men and women	55	
1973–	Men and women (age 18)	60–65	+5
New Zealand			
1851–1875	European adult (age 21) men, property or rent	15	
1876–1892	Adult men	25–30	+10
1893–1964	Adult men and women	48–55	+18
1965–1973	Younger (age 20) men and women	55	
1974–	Men and women (age 18)	60–65	+5

Note: Value ranges regarding total population are due to demographic changes.

Source: Author's own calculations with data from Mackie and Rose (1991) and Mitchell (1992–5).

experienced dramatic increases of the electorate. In all cases, the introduction of male adult suffrage implied that the previous number of voters was multiplied in a single move and that the new voters were a two-digit percentage of the total population. Yet, while in the mentioned Latin-European countries early sudden enlargements of the electorate produced conflictive, short-lived, or fake experiences of virtual universal male suffrage, in their Northern European counterparts a more institutionalized framework allowed pluralistic democracy to last for a number of decades.

Figure 2.1 compares the paths of two extreme cases that experienced

TABLE 2.2. *Size of the electorate: The 'Latin' model*

Country	Voting rights requirements	Electors as % of total population	Percentage points in increase
France			
1791–1795	Adult (age 25) male family heads, with tax	15	
1801–1814	Adult (age 21) men	20	+5
1815–1847	Adult men, with tax	1	–19
1848–1851	Adult men	27	+26
. . . .			
1871–1936	Adult men	20–29	
. . . .			
1945–1972	Adult men and women	63–57	
1973–	Men and women (age 18)	65	+8
Italy			
1861–1881	Adult (age 25) men, with property, tax, literacy	2	
1882–1911	Adult (age 21) men, with tax, literacy	7	+5
1912–1918	Adult (age 21) men with literacy or draft (age 30)	28	+23
1919	Adult men	32	+4
. . . .			
1946–1974	Adult men and women	64–68	
1975–	Men and women (age 18)	78	+10
Spain			
1810,20,36	Adult (age 25) male family heads	28–33	
. . . .			
1834–1867	Adult men, with tax	1–4	
1868–1875	Adult men	25–29	+21
1876–1889	Adult men, with tax	5	–24
1890–1923	Adult men	23–25	+20
. . . .			
1931–1932	Adult men	26	
1933–1936	Adult men and women	53–55	+27
. . . .			
1977–1978	Adult men and women	70	
1979–	Men and women (age 18)	77–80	+7

Note and *Sources*: As for Table 2.1. Dotted lines indicate authoritarian periods.

stable results: the United States with its long, gradual process of enlargement of the electorate, and Sweden with its sudden, dramatic mass enfranchisement.

Cases: Creating Complex Electorates

The three voting rights strategies identified are illustrated here with the corresponding stories in the countries mentioned, including the United Kingdom, the United States, and some other ex-British colonies in the

Who Can Vote

TABLE 2.3. *Size of the electorate: The 'Nordic' model*

Country	Voting rights requirements	Electors as % of total population	Percentage points increase
Germany			
1871–1917	Adult (age 25) men	18–22	
1918–1933	Adult (age 20) men and women	64–68	+44
. . . .			
1946–1971	Adult men and women	67	
1972	Men and women (age 18)	70	+3
Sweden			
1866–1909	Adult (age 25) men, with property or income	6–7	
1910–1920	Adult (age 24) men	20	+13
1921–1940	Adult (age 23) men and women	55–65	+35
1941–1969	Adult (age 21) men and women	68–69	+3
1970–1973	Men and women (age 19)	70	+1
1974–	Men and women (age 18)	72–76	+4
Norway			
1814–1896	Adult (age 25) male family chiefs	5–9	
1897–1906	Adult (age 24) men	20	+11
1907–1912	Adult men and some women	32–34	+12
1913–1918	Adult men and women	46	+12
1919–1945	Adult (age 23) men and women	51–62	+5
1946–1968	Adult (age 21) men and women	68	+6
1969–1977	Adult (age 20) men and women	69	+1
1978–	Men and women (age 18)	73–76	+4
Finland			
1900–1906	Adult (age 25) men, with property or income	9	
1907–1940	Adult (age 24) men and women	48–50	+49
1944–1969	Adult (age 21) men and women	62	+12
1970–1971	Adult (age 20) men and women	67	+5
1972–	Men and women (age 18)	82	+15

Note and *Sources*: As for Table 2.1. Dotted line indicates as authoritarian period.

'Anglo' model; France, Italy, and Spain in the 'Latin' model; and Germany and the Scandinavian countries in the 'Nordic' model.

The 'Anglo' model

The typical Anglo-American strategy for allocating voting rights is a continuing combination of carrot and stick measures. On the one hand, there is a process of successive moderate enlargements of the electorate by gradually relaxing legal requirements for voting. On the other hand, the rulers introduce new legal or political barriers to the enforcement of voting rights, all of this under the framework of highly restrictive electoral and party systems. The process seeks to prevent the sudden formation of a new alternative majority to the incumbent electorate by permitting only

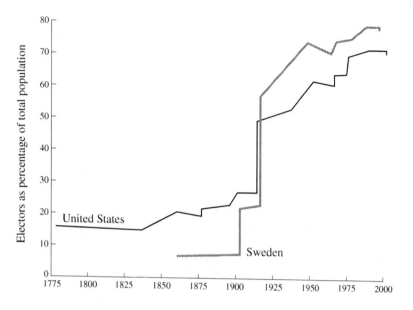

FIG. 2.1. Two strategies of voting rights

a gradual increase in its complexity and by reducing the number of poten-tially winning alternatives to two.

United Kingdom

The introduction of equal universal suffrage rights in the contemporary United Kingdom took more than one hundred years. Until the early 19th century, as has been sketched in the previous section, British elections were based upon the enfranchisement of a relatively low number of local communities (counties and boroughs) governed by local customs and special provisions which created virtual universal male suffrage in a number of places. A series of Electoral Reform Acts enacted in 1832, 1867, and 1885 established increasingly homogen-eous rules across the British territories, gradually resulting in an enlarged franchise, but also introducing some new restrictions on electoral repre-sentation. Later, women's suffrage was approved in a two-stage process: 1918 and 1928. Certain remnants of old distortions, like the plural vote, were not abol-ished until 1948 (Seymour 1915; Seymour and Frary 1918; Conacher 1971; Cox 1987).

We can examine the permissive and restrictive elements of this series of reforms separately. The two basic elements introduced to create a more complex electorate were the following: higher numbers of voters, a more proportional distribution of seats across the territory, and the reduction of corrupt practices.

First, the number of voters was gradually increased in the first three stages mentioned (1832, 1867, and 1885) by successively co-opting new groups of voters. These new groups amounted to only about 1 per cent, 4 per cent, and 6 per cent of the total population, respectively (see Table 2.1). Specifically, in 1832 new legal requirements in counties and boroughs delimited the electorate to men inhabiting houses worth more than some minimum value, as well as to certain categories of copyholders [*sic*], leaseholders, and tenants. Yet, 'if the borough electorate in the years surrounding the 1832 Reform Act was open and popular it became less so in subsequent years [1841–66] as demographic change led to a relative diminution of adult male voters' (Taylor 1997: 70).

To counteract this evolution, a high number of householders in the boroughs were enfranchised in 1867. However, the representatives of the rural boroughs could still outvote the members of industrial districts in the Midlands, the Northwest, and the North. A uniform regulation of household requirements was finally established in 1885, with particularly inclusive results in certain urban counties. Parallel to these new enfranchisements, a number of nonresident borough voters, however previously qualified, were disfranchised.

Second, new distributions of parliamentary seats to the disadvantage of the boroughs and Southern counties and in favor of urban and industrial areas gradually approached a closer correspondence of political representation to the distribution of population. As a result of these reforms, at the end of the 19th century the British electorate amounted to about 15 per cent of the total population. Some demographic changes expanded its numbers to almost 20 per cent during World War I. In 1918, there was a first partial enfranchisement of women who were either 30 years of age, owners of land, or wives of voters, introducing a new quarter of the total population into the electorate. As previously discussed, it was expected that most of the new female voters would vote similarly to 'their fathers and husbands' in the middle and upper classes of the society. Literally, certain Conservative leaders expected the enfranchisement of women to be a counterweight to the votes of working-class men. Universal adult women's suffrage was completed ten years later and an additional portion of about 15 per cent of the total population was added.

Third, the introduction of the secret ballot in 1872, as well as new regulations regarding campaign expenses and corrupt practices in 1883, allowed new voters to express their political preferences more sincerely than before. With the previous practice of viva voce voting, the decision of each elector was often recorded together with his name, thus allowing the opportunity for bribery or intimidation and checking the votes. It was during only the late 1880s that these practices were seriously curbed.

The restrictive elements introduced by successive reforms can be summarized as follows. First, for the first time a system of voters' registration was created in 1832. The requirements for a person to be put on the electoral lists were so complicated that a very large proportion of individuals who were actually qualified did not become voters. Many people were victims of residential or rate-paying requirements, other people's objections, or the numerous bureaucratic complexities involved. The power of official electoral agents identified with the interests of incumbent voters in making the electoral lists did not give way to party activists' pressures and decisions by an impartial tribunal until the very end of the century.

Second, plural vote was gradually replaced with equal vote for every individual. Yet, more than one-tenth of the electorate still held more than one vote on the basis of their property or education qualifications after the 1885 reforms. Between forty and eighty seats in each election were determined by those voters. Some business people and members of university communities held dual votes until 1948.

Third, the electoral system remained based upon plurality rule, which allows overrepresentation to the largest parties and reduces or eliminates the role of any other parties. In addition, there were some significant restrictive reforms. Until 1885, most districts elected two representatives, which, on the basis of loose parties and the correspondingly relevant role of candidates' personal standing, permitted a somewhat varied representation of the electorate. In 1867, the introduction of the limited vote in a few three- and four-member districts promoted multiparty-coalition candidacies, while a number of voters tended to split their votes among candidates of different parties, thus creating some pluralistic representation. However, these practices were curbed in 1885 by the establishment of single-member districts inducing, single-party vote.

Fourth, local candidates and political elites were gradually replaced with national party leadership. A crucial institutional development was the centralization of legislative power in the Cabinet, which induced more cohesive party voting in the House of Commons. As individual members of parliament became less powerful and nationwide party organization and discipline increased, national leaders were able to nominate party candidates in elections, and voters usually adapted to the narrow choice offered by a two-party system. In fact, more cohesive parties in a two-party system diminished the scope of possible choices of candidates by the electorate.

Conservatives and Liberals dominated British political life during the 19th century, while minority Radicals promoted more pluralistic forms of representation unsuccessfully. Eventually, a new potential majority gradually emerged, not as a sudden replacement of any of the two existing dominant parties, but through intermediate stages involving, first, electoral coalitions between the Liberals and labor representatives and, later, the split of the Liberal party (by Lloyd George's faction). When, on the grounds of a larger electorate, the Labour party obtained some success at the polls in the 1920s and Labour leaders forecast a possible party victory under the existing electoral rules, they turned against its former proposals for proportional representation. The existing rules thus allowed a significant change in the two major parties by replacing the Liberals with the

Labourites, and, finally, the institutional system was capable of reinforcing its most restrictive features.

United States

The process of allocating voting rights has been even slower and more restrictive in the United States than in the United Kingdom. Initially, as mentioned in the previous section, some British regulations of voting rights during the colonial era, especially those requiring land ownership, produced a much greater enfranchisement in the British colonies in North America than in Britain because of the colonies' widespread diffusion of land-property. Yet, starting with an electorate as large as more than 15 per cent of the total population prior to independence, a very slow process of gradual enlargements of the electorate developed during the subsequent two hundred years.

The basic stages of the enlargement of the electorate included: the suppression of property or tax requirements for adult men to vote during the 19th century, the enfranchisement of women in 1920, the enfranchisement of African–Americans, first in the North after the Civil War in the 1870s and later in the South in the 1960s, as well as the inclusion of young voters in the 1970s. This series of successive limited enlargements was accompanied by parallel measures aimed at demobilizing voters and reducing the scope of their political choice, especially regarding immigrants at the turn of the 19th and 20th centuries, and at reinforcing the two-party system.

Between independence and the Civil War, a variety of state regulations were passed that can be summarized as follows: fourteen states holding land ownership requirements for voting eventually replaced them with less stringent qualifications. The process of abolishing land requirements started in 1778 (in South Carolina) as was completed in 1856 (in North Carolina). Typically, real estate property requirements gave way to personal property alternatives, taxpaying, and then to no limitations. However, at least five states required tax qualifications for voting until 1870. Residence requirements varied from six months to one or two years, although aliens were permitted to vote in six states. Universal women's vote was suppressed in New Jersey in 1807 while a limited number of voting women with property (including widows in particular) were banned from the polls in Massachusetts, New York, and other states, and from voting in local elections in most of the ex-provinces—all of this against the usual practices of the colonial period. In eight of the former colonies and in eleven Southern states of the Union, as well as in the newly created states, African–Americans were excluded from voting (they could vote in only six states in New England). Also, soldiers, students, the mentally ill, the poor, and criminals were denied access to suffrage in most states.

This process, made up of both permissions and restrictions, was led not only by pressures from the excluded, and cautious calculations by the incumbent voters and leaders, but also by competition among states. One state would abandon, for example, the property test, in order to retain workers that were attracted by new enfranchising rules in another state; certain states in the Midwest tried to attract immigrants from other states by agreeing to let them vote; and a border state between the South and the North would oppose African–Americans' suffrage because of fear that many of them would flee from the highly restrictive laws in their native Southern states (Porter 1969).

African–Americans were legally enfranchised in most states only after the Civil War. However, they remained actually disfranchised in the eleven Southern states. In addition, eighteen states introduced literacy tests between 1890 and 1926, with restrictive effects directed in three cases against African–Americans, in five against Indians, Mexicans, and Asians, and in six against recent European immigrants (especially Irish and Germans) (Riker 1965: 59–60). In a similar vein, seven states increased the length of their residence requirements. These measures were particularly restrictive in a period when about one-fourth of the male adult population was foreign born and about 10 per cent was nonwhite.

A countermeasure that was perhaps even more effective was found with the generalization of voluntary registration of voters. Only three states had adopted this device by the early 1800s. But most Northern states introduced voluntary registration between 1876 and 1912, up to thirty-one states had followed by 1920, and almost all of them instituted it in the following decade. Typically, the states required annual, in-person registration to allow citizens to enter the electoral lists. This barrier was particularly powerful at the turn of the century in preventing uneducated immigrants in the North and blacks in the South from becoming regular voters and has maintained significant effects regarding immigrants in more recent times (Piven and Cloward 1988).

The set of restrictive measures directed against immigrants, blacks, and other people paying relatively high costs for voluntary registration, implemented at the end of the 19th century, are usually referred to as 'the great disfranchisement'. They seem to have been crucial in preventing the formation of a socialist party strongly based with industrial workers, in marked contrast to Britain and most advanced countries of the time.

Women were gradually given (or restored) voting rights in a number of states, beginning with Colorado in 1893, and ending in 1920 with national recognition of their rights. As discussed earlier, some of the suffragists' arguments pointed out the potentially countervailing role of new female voters regarding more unpredictable or threatening groups of disfranchised men. In the North it was expected that women's suffrage might help maintain the political supremacy of incumbent voters because there were more native-born women, likely to replicate their male counterparts' electoral behavior, than recent immigrants, men and women combined. In fact, by introducing formal citizenship requirements, no state permitted aliens to vote since 1928. In the South, similar effects of women's suffrage were expected due to the fact that there were more white women than blacks of both sexes (Kraditor 1968: 18–19, 261–5).

Poll taxes and literacy tests were prohibited in national elections only in 1964, allowing most African–Americans in the eleven Southern states to have access to the polls for the first time. Residence requirements were lowered to 30 days in 1970. And, in parallel to similar decisions in most democracies, 18-year-olds were co-opted to the electorate a year later.

As a consequence of this lengthy process of carrot and stick measures, about 20–25 per cent of the United States' total population was enfranchised between 1870 and 1920, while most immigrants and blacks remained excluded. With the countervailing enfranchisement of women, enfanchisment rose to between 50 and 55 per cent from 1920, and it reached between 60 and 70 per cent only after 1964. Registration procedures, however, have moved only between two-thirds and three-fourths of legally qualified citizens to become registered voters, with the result that only about a half of the total population is actually enlisted in the polls.

Electoral participation has also been discouraged by the institutional restrictions of the electoral system and the limited choice offered by a stable, rigid two-party system. Before the Civil War, third parties obtained an average of 15 per cent of the vote in national elections for the House of Representatives. Even after the emergence of the Republican party as the other major party together with the Democrats in the mid 19th century, third parties maintained regular organizations, won state legislatures, elected governors, and sent delegates to the Presidential electoral college. During the 19th century and into the early 20th century, minor parties had a significant influence on the political agenda by introducing issues, such as the abolition of slavery, income tax, immigration laws, protection of agriculture, prohibition of alcoholic beverages, regulation of working hours, etc.

Yet, in addition to the constraints created by an electoral system in which 'the winner takes all' and by the typical bipolarization produced by presidential elections, further measures against third parties were introduced from 1892. These included restrictions to ballot access, denial of pre-election financial subsidy, denial of media access, and persecution of radical leaders. Local and state party machines pre-empted representative offices against intruders. The national average vote for third parties in House elections went down to 4 per cent in the first half of the 20th century and less than 1 per cent in the second half. Nevertheless, an array of less durable third candidacies, such as those of the Progressives, the State-Rights Democrats, and a number of independent candidates for President, have revealed some broad dissatisfaction with the political supply provided by the two dominant parties (Rosenstone, Behr, and Lazarus 1996; author's own calculations with data in Gillespie 1992).

Voter turnout gradually declined in the first decades of the 20th century (down to 8 per cent of the electorate in the mid term election of Congress in 1942). It increased in the first fifteen years after the World War II, but has suffered a steady decline since 1960 until reaching about 50 per cent in Presidential elections and 30 per cent in mid term Congress elections by the end of the 20th century.

Other former British colonies

Some of the cautionary devices for allocating voting rights previously surveyed have been replicated in other ex-British dominions by developing similar strategies of gradual enfranchisement of the population. In contrast to other colonial rules, British dominion was characterized by promoting significant degrees of political organization and participation among sectors of the native populations before independence. In this sense, in former British colonies the creation of new states was only one step in the process of gradual enfranchisement of new voters which did not provoke such hazardous surprises as it did in other processes of decolonization.

In Canada, a number of different provincial suffrage laws enforced between 1867 and 1920 gave the vote to adult men meeting income or property requirements, with particularly strong restrictions in Quebec, Nova Scotia, and New Brunswick. Women were enfranchised at the national level in 1918, but their electoral participation at the local and provincial levels came later. Indians were banned from voting until 1960, as were Asians in certain provinces. Citizens born in 'enemy' countries were disfranchised during both World Wars.

During the 19th century, there had been virtual men's suffrage in colonial Australia, as well as women's suffrage in two of the country's six colonies, while in only one, Tasmania, were there small property requirements. The formation of the federation in 1901 led to unifying different states' laws around adult men's suffrage, while women were initially enfranchised in four states. However, aliens and the aboriginal inhabitants of Australia, Asia, Africa, and the Pacific Islands were excluded from voting until 1967. Relatively high residence requirements were also imposed.

In New Zealand, the suffrage laws of the six provinces, which were previously limited to adult European men with property or income qualifications, were unified in 1876 in favor of European men's suffrage, whereas the aboriginal Maoris were given four separate parliamentary seats of their own. Women's suffrage was established comparatively very early, in 1893 (Seymour and Frary 1918; Hughes and Graham 1968).

Despite the fact that these countries adopted more inclusive provisions than those in the United Kingdom and United States, in all three cases mentioned—Canada, Australia, and New Zealand—the percentage of voters out of the total population remained below the relatively low level of 50–55 per cent until the 1970s, when the vote for 18-year-olds increased that amount by about five to ten percentage points (see Table 2.1). In all cases, the electoral system was based upon single-member districts and majoritarian voting rules, severely restricting the number of alternatives available to voters.

The 'Latin' Model

The 'Latin' strategy for allocating voting rights is the sudden introduction of universal men's suffrage under restrictive electoral and institutional rules. In 19th- and early 20th-century France, Italy, and Spain, this decision involved the creation of new mass electorates largely formed by illiterates. Political parties were weak, not well organized, or simply nonexistent. Electoral systems typically based upon small districts and plurality or majority rule did not create incentives for the emergence and consolidation of nationwide political parties. Hazardous voting results and new, threatening electoral mobilization provoked fears of instability among the incumbent voters and rulers, moving them to search for or support authoritarian reactions in order to re-establish the old political order.

France

Universal suffrage was not recognized during the French Revolution. The electoral system put in operation after 1789 gave voting rights only to those male heads of the family over the age of 25 who paid taxes equivalent to three day's labor and it explicitly excluded, among other groups, all domestics servants. Voluntary registration was established, one-year residence required, and the new elector had to swear fidelity to the Constitution, the nation, the law, and the king, and to fulfill 'with zeal and courage' the civil and political functions confided to his care. Deputies were indirectly elected and voting was by viva voce. As a result of these provisions, only about one-sixth of the total population became legal electors in 1791, while turnout in Paris fell to 10 per cent of registered voters. The further approval of universal men's suffrage for direct elections to the National Assembly during the First Republic in 1792 was never enforced. The re-establishment of the monarchy in 1814 reduced the electorate to a very small minority of wealthy men (Gueniffey 1993).

Universal men's suffrage was enacted in France for the first time with the Second Republic in 1848. The election of a Constituent Assembly in April of that year was the first mass election in contemporary history and the occasion of a huge mobilization of new voters. At a single shot, the French electorate was expanded from about quarter million to more than eight million people and to ten million one year later for the election of the legislative Assembly, which is to say that it was multiplied by 40 virtually overnight. Turnout was initially 85 per cent. Under the circumstances, universal suffrage was widely considered to be a risky experiment with unknown results. France was at that time a largely rural society with an illiterate majority. Political parties were not previously organized, local issues predominated in the electoral debate, and deputies decided their alignments on constantly changing issues, and there was also a very high mobility in party membership. Hazardous electoral outcomes could be reasonably expected in this environment. In fact, two different political majorities, one in favor of the Republic, the other in favor of the Monarchy, were elected within a year (Huard 1991; Rosanvallon 1992).

In addition, the new Constitution approved in 1851 introduced the direct election of the President of the Republic by universal men's suffrage. Several cautious provisions were brought in, particularly the transfer of the election to the Assembly if no candidate obtained an absolute majority of people's votes at the first round, and the withholding of certain powers from the President including the dissolution of the Assembly.

However, the move was openly acknowledged to be highly risky. Alexis de Tocqueville, its strongest supporter from the center-right, stated in the Assembly that 'for a great number of our fellow citizens, the Republic is nothing but this act [of choosing the President by universal suffrage]' which should be approved despite the fears that the people could choose 'a name hostile to the Republic'. After delivering this influential speech, he deeply 'regretted having spoken on that occasion' (de Tocqueville 1851: 176–80).

Alphonse de Lamartine, a key supporter from the center-left, had previously and extensively discussed the 'grave perils' of universal suffrage. Shortly after the establishment of the Republic, he feared that 'a confusing and unintelligent mass, groping in the dark', would vote at 'hazard' because unlearned people 'deceive themselves or are deceived by others', including demagogues, men of bustle, intriguers and dreamers, 'converting the electoral urn into a genuine lottery'. Yet, once at the Assembly, Lamartine blamed those with 'lack of faith' in the people and held that 'even if the people will choose the one whom my foresight, badly enlightened, perhaps, would regret to be chosen, it doesn't matter: Alea jacta est! God and the people will tell' (Lamartine 1850).

The nonpartisan, politically inexperienced, well-known family member candidate, Prince Louis Napoleon Bonaparte, nephew of the Emperor, won the first direct election of President of France by universal men's suffrage in 1851. He obtained almost 75 per cent of votes with a turnout of more than 75 per cent of the electorate. In addition to his symbolic representation of the past grandeur of France, most observers saw in this election an expression of 'the spirit of opposition', 'protest', and 'general discontent'. The victory of a candidate unanimously opposed by the press and the political clubs was interpreted as being the choice of those 'submerged in ignorance and misery', a 'mobile opinion', 'the politically unorganized people'. As feared by many politicians, the election of Louis Napoleon shortly preceded his illegal dissolution of the Assembly by a *coup d'état* and the re-establishment of the Empire. Universal men's suffrage with some minor new restrictions was officially maintained for further elections to the Assembly, but most governmental candidates secured their victory through the active support of the prefects and public officials in the Emperor's service. Turnout declined to 40 per cent in the 1860s (Tudesq 1965: esp. 79–111).

Universal male suffrage was re-established in France by the Third Republic in 1871. However, some irregularities in registering electors and the maintenance of open ballot reduced the people's participation and political competition for several decades. Electoral rules were constantly shifted for short-term partisan or factional purposes. Somewhat restrictive formulas were alternating, basically plurality rule in multimember districts and majority rule in single-member districts. Low levels of party competition developed and no stable party system was formed for a very long time.

A new significant enlargement of the electorate was enacted by the Fourth Republic at the end of the World War II, with the establishment of universal adult men's and women's suffrage. However, a tradition of political instability and electoral reform-mongering has remained in France throughout the more recent period. From 1789 to the end of the 20th century, there have been ten different political regimes, about fifteen constitutions, and at least sixteen major changes of the electoral law. Since 1945, the succession includes two republics, the replacement of proportional representation (mostly supported by the left) with a mixed system, majority-runoff (supported by the conservative right), proportional representation again, and majority-runoff again (Cole and Campbell 1989).

Italy

The first franchise laws that followed the unification of Italy were very restrictive. Beginning in 1861, only men over the age 25 who were property-holders, able to read and write, and who paid a certain amount of taxes were allowed to vote. After 1882, the voting age was lowered to 21 years with requirements of literacy and some minor tax payments. While the property and tax qualifications were not very much stricter than those required at about the same time in countries such as the United Kingdom and the United States, illiteracy in Italy was so widespread that only about 2 per cent of the total population during the first period mentioned and 7 per cent during the second period were enfranchised. The government also proceeded to further disfranchise of about one-fourth of the electors in 1895 by administrative means.

The electoral rules were based on single-member districts, except for the short period 1882–91, when multimember districts with individual limited voting might have allowed some varied representation. But no robust party system was formed. Elections were controlled by the prefects at the service of the government and based upon local issues and submissive candidates. Official pressures were complemented by bribery, fraud, and trickery, especially in the South. Moderate governments centered around the Liberals were persistently supported by temporary groupings of local or corporate representatives, Radicals, Democrats, and Reformists, through permanent bargaining. Many deputies frequently changed their parliamentary group allegiance, a practice called *transformismo* which prevented the development of strong national parties (Ranzato 1991).

As a result of pressures from the excluded and internally divisive calculations within the ranks of rulers, a massive electoral enfranchisement was suddenly implemented in Italy during the turbulent years around World War I. Initially, the Liberal leader, Giovanni Giolitti, tried to promote a 'limited and cautious' enlargement of the electorate for 'reasons of expediency in the self-interest of the ruling classes'. As he said in his memoirs, Giolitti thought he was acting in favor of social security on the grounds that 'the exclusion of the working mass . . . has always the effect of exposing them to the suggestions of revolutionary parties and subversive ideas', whereas political participation, in contrast, develops in them an interest in the maintenance of the state. Giolitti's government designed a reform to multiply the electorate by two, while relying upon a relatively high degree of abstention among new voters. On this basis, the Liberals expected that the traditional practice of coalition-building through *transformismo* would be extended to new popular representatives and would neutralize innovating pressures. Accordingly, in 1913, voting rights were given to all men over the age of 21 able to read and write, as well as to a small group of men over 30 who had undergone military service (Giolitti 1967, ch. 10).

However, in 1918, immediately after the war, mass electoral enfranchisement was implemented by a new Radical government to include all men over 21 and any ex-soldiers under this age. As a consequence of the two reforms, the electorate jumped from 2.5 million to 11.5 million people, a multiplication of the prewar number of voters by almost five and an addition of 25 per cent of the total population. Both the supporters and foes of universal suffrage coincided in seeing the creation of an electorate so large and new as a challenge to the stability of the previous political order.

As mentioned earlier, the incumbent rulers were poorly organized; they were also divided among themselves, especially because of their differing positions regarding the war, and they proved unable to adapt to and absorb the new voters. Instead, two incompatible and extreme alternatives developed. On the left, the Socialists were led by maximalist leaders in favor of revolution and the establishment of a dictatorship of the proletariat. Just after the war, the Italian Socialist party joined the Communist International led by the Russian Bolsheviks, condemned collaboration with the 'bourgeois state' in any form, and demanded 'all power' for the workers. On the right, and at about the same time, the Pope cancelled the more than forty-year-long prohibition on Catholics participating in Italian political affairs as either voters or candidates, while retaining his rejection of the Italian state. The new Popular party began to mobilize Catholics and large groups of peasants against the establishment.

The results of the first election with universal men's suffrage in 1919 were astonishing in the eyes of most participants and observers. The two new, extreme parties, the revolutionary Socialists and the anti-Italian state Catholics, together gathered more than half popular votes and parliamentary seats. For the Socialists, electoral success was only viewed as a means of expediting the destruction of Parliament and 'the organs of bourgeois domination'. They supported industrial strikes and factory occupation in the North of Italy and engaged in parliamentary sabotage. The Catholics, meanwhile, organized land seizures in the Center and the South and, not being a cohesive party, they were unable to commit themselves to any governmental collaboration (Seton-Watson 1967; Farnetti 1978; Noiret 1994; Clark 1996).

The next election in 1921 produced about the same results with the significant novelty of a group of Fascist deputies being elected. No stable majority government could be formed with such hazardous electoral results produced by a sudden mass enfranchisement. Social conflict, violence, and political bipolarization rapidly increased. A Fascist dictatorship was established for more than twenty years, which eventually led to an open civil war. (For the common characterization of the political conflict in the mid 1940s as a civil war by historians from both the right and the left, see, respectively, Pisano 1965–6 and Pavone 1991.)

Spain

Four major attempts to introduce suddenly universal suffrage in Spain during modern times failed. The first attempt in favor of large-scale men's suffrage was made during the war against Napoleon for elections held between 1810 and 1813. The so-called Constitution of Cádiz, approved in 1812, formally established virtual universal men's suffrage for those aged over 25 and became 'the classical liberal constitution in Latin Europe in the early 19th century' (Carr 1966: 94). About 28 per cent of the total population was enfranchised, the largest proportion of a country's population ever having been given voting rights in the modern world at that time. The same rules were re-established in 1820 and in 1836, but they were suppressed by military *pronunciamentos* induced by authoritarian monarchs.

The second attempt took place in 1869 at the initiative of the Liberals and Republicans previously excluded from legal political activity. A new constitutional monarchy based upon parliamentary elections by universal male suffrage was very soon followed by an even shorter-lived Republic, which was abolished by another *coup d'état*. Liberal political parties were at that time very weak. Traditionalist Catholic monarchists (*Carlists*) on the right and radical anti-clerical republicans (*exaltados*) on the left, promoting incompatible regime alternatives, were able to produce permanent political instability.

A much more durable political regime was established with the restoration of the monarchy by the Conservatives in 1874. Initially, the electorate was limited to about 5 per cent of the total population. The central government was able to control elections by promoting official candidates and organizing fraud through the administration of justice and the prefects. In parallel, a number of local bosses (*caciques*) developed relations of patronage with voters by distributing private benefits (including public employment) in exchange for political support, with the help of bureaucrats, judicial officers, mayors, and provincial governors. These restrictions to political participation and competition induced the development of extra-parliamentary, anti-system political movements, including Anarchism (Romero 1973; Varela 1977; Tusell 1991).

A resumption of the coalition of ostracized Liberals and Republicans for local elections in the mid 1880s appeared as a major challenge and threat to the Conservative rulers, leading them to co-opt the Liberals into the regime by allowing their temporary access to the Cabinet. The Liberals, led by Práxedes-Mateo Sagasta, then tried to incorporate a fraction of the Republicans into their own candidacies by introducing universal men's suffrage, while maintaining a restrictive electoral system mostly based upon single-member districts and plurality rule. In 1890, voting rights were given to all men aged 25 with two-years' residence and other minor restrictions. The new electorate encompassed about one-fourth of the total population, that is, the number of voters was multiplied by five at one shot, almost half of them being illiterate.

Control of elections by the central government weakened, but the role of local networks increased, including new practices of direct purchase of votes. By these means, the incumbent rulers were able to delay the potentially explosive effects of the sudden enfranchisement of a politically uninformed, unorganized electorate under a restrictive electoral and political system. Turnout was only about 50 per cent in the 1890s. However, in 1893, anti-system Republicans won the election in Madrid, in 1901, Republicans and Catalan Regionalists won in Barcelona, and new victories of Republicans in Valencia, as well as Republicans and Socialists in Bilbao, and other cities followed. A new electoral law approved in 1907 by the government of the reformist Conservative Antonio Maura made corrupt practices more difficult and reduced the role of local *caciques*. Turnout rose to 70 per cent in the 1910s, giving Republicans, as well as Regionalists and Socialists, increasing proportions of votes (Ull 1976).

The Liberals, with the support of the Republicans and Socialists, passed a proposal in Parliament for introducing proportional representation in 1919 and again in 1921. On both occasions, the Conservative Government began to prepare the corresponding bill which could have created a more pluralistic, integrative framework (Tusell 1997). But the process failed when the King and military reacted to social unrest with a *coup d'état* and the establishment of a dictatorship in 1923.

The fourth opportunity for universal suffrage was created, in counter-reaction, with the proclamation of the Second Republic in 1931 by a leftist coalition of Republicans and Socialists. Voting rights were extended to women one year later. A majoritarian electoral system promoted increasing political polarization between two blocs supporting incompatible regime alternatives, as will be discussed in the next chapter. In 1936, a new military coup resulted in a civil war which ended with the victory of General Franco's dictatorship. It was only in 1977 that universal suffrage was successfully established in Spain, together with proportional representation in a new parliamentary monarchy (Colomer, 1995a).

The 'Nordic' Model

The 'Nordic' strategy of voting rights coincides with the 'Latin' one in that it implements a sudden massive enfranchisement of voters, in contrast to the gradual, step-by-step model in 'Anglo' countries. Yet, unlike the 'Latin' model, the introduction of universal suffrage in Germany, Sweden, and other Northern European countries, typically at the initiative of the political right, has been parallel with the establishment of pluralistic institutional frameworks which permit a multiparty system to exist. This gave way to large multiparty coalitions and relative moderate Cabinets. Democratic stability was thus achieved on the basis of matching a new complex electorate with pluralistic institutional arrangements.

Germany
At the time of the unification of German territories in the second half of the 19th century, the introduction of universal suffrage by the political left under the French model had failed. Following the short-lived liberal period between 1848 and 1850, Prussia (which embraced about two-thirds of German territories and population) was organized as a three-class corporative system. Landowners and financiers chose a third of the representatives, owners of small businesses and public officials chose another third, and workers selected the remaining third. Voting rights were acknowledged within each group to men aged over 24. Representatives were indirectly chosen by electors chosen in single-member districts by majority rule using public ballot. There was universal suffrage for the election of the local Diets in only a few of the small states of the Empire, including in particular Baden and Würtemberg (in the latter case with proportional representation) (Seymour and Frary 1918, vol. 2).

It was the rightist Chancellor Otto von Bismarck who outbid the Liberals by proposing an immediate introduction of universal men's suffrage for the North German Confederation in 1867, and for the Imperial Parliament (*Bundestag*) in 1871. The Chancellor, who at that time was accused of 'opportunism' for embracing his rivals' program, had sophisticated motives for this unexpected proposal. First, Bismarck had been pressured and enticed to introduce universal suffrage during a series of private meetings with the Socialist leader, Ferdinand Lassalle. The two leaders thought that this could curb the Liberal majority in the incumbent Prussian Parliament by promoting, on the one hand, the peasants' and lower-middle class vote for the Conservatives and, on the other, the workers' vote for the Socialists. Also, with this proposal Bismarck eluded a new challenge by Austria to strengthen the German–Austrian Confederation (to the detriment of Prussian domination) under a nondemocratic regime.

The most significant institutional element to contain the political consequences of the new large electorate was the absence of parliamentary control of the Cabinet. The Chancellor (or chief executive) was not chosen by the lower chamber, but by the federal upper chamber (*Bundesrat*), which was not directly elected but appointed by the component states of the German Empire and by its President, the Emperor. Also, this design was based on Bismarck's prudent calculations. As he said in his memoirs, 'The measuring of the limits within such a struggle [of the conservative Government with Parliament and freedom of the press] must be confined, if the control of the government, which is indispensable to the country, is neither to be checked nor allowed to gain a complete power, is a question of political tact and judgement' (for his motives for introducing universal suffrage, see Bismarck 1899: 65–9).

Majority rule with second-round-runoff was again adopted for the election of Parliament, but this time with direct, equal, and secret elections. Under these rules, locally concentrated minorities were able to support different party candidates for the second round in different regions, thus producing a national multiparty system. The Parliament was organized around four basic parties, but about twelve parties regularly obtained representation. Catholics, workers, and farmers developed innovative political mobilization, with an increase in turnout from 50 per cent in 1871 to 85 per cent in 1907–12. Challenged by these new competitors, the Conservatives and Liberals restructured and changed from parties of notables into active mass parties (Ritter 1990a, b).

After the German defeat in World War I the so-called Weimar Republic was established in 1918. Voting rights were extended to men and women who were 20 years old, together with the introduction of proportional representation, which had previously been supported by the Socialists. The institutional framework of the Empire was adapted to more democratic formulas. The executive branch was made responsible to the lower chamber, but the elected President of the Republic (replacing the previous Emperor) retained significant powers by the appointment of a Chancellor in a 'semi-presidential' relationship. Bipolarization was partly encouraged by the direct election of the President. However, about ten parties obtained representation in Parliament, in such a way that the so-called Weimar coalition, formed by the Christian, Liberal, and Socialist parties, was able to form a majority supporting the regime for most of the period from 1918 to 1930.

Two extreme, anti-system parties, the Communists and the National-Socialists, obtained increasing support until they blocked the formation of centrist coalitions in 1932. However, in the historical perspective sketched here, the rise of the Nazis to government, followed by the suppression of civil liberties, the implementation of racist and war policies, and the establishment of a totalitarian regime, can hardly be attributed to the sudden enlargement of the electorate. In fact, the introduction of universal men's suffrage at the moment of the creation of the German Empire had been followed by more than sixty years of remarkable political stability.

One of the most provoking and controversial interpretations of the electoral success of the Nazis and the suppression of democracy in Germany in the 1930s focuses on the effects of proportional representation, most prominently in the work of Ferdinand A. Hermens (see especially Hermens 1941, ch. 10). Against this link, several points can be made. First, as mentioned, a multiparty system had already existed in Germany for almost fifty years before the introduction of proportional representation. Even if it is true that some of the previously existing political parties were not strongly ideologically oriented, political pluralism and parliamentary coalitions, which developed after 1918, were not an absolute novelty in German politics.

Second, the crucial point in Hermens' argument is that an alternative electoral system based on plurality rule would have prevented the Nazis from obtaining representation when they enjoyed minority popular support and, in this way, it would have made their further growth baseless. However, it can be argued that plurality rule, although it reduces the number of parties, does not always prevent a new, initially small political party from entering into political competition and obtaining representation, as the paradigmatic case of Britain (with the replacement of the Liberals with the Labourites at the turn of the century) clearly shows. New parties are not 'created' by proportional representation, but by political entrepreneurs on the basis of voters' new political preferences engendered from social, economic, and cultural changes. The formation and rise of the National-Socialist party should thus be explained by factors such as certain German ideological traditions, and the party leadership maximalist initiative and organizational effectiveness against the backdrop of Germany's defeat in World War I and its further social disarticulation during the 1920s. Under these inducements, it is highly likely that plurality rule would have worked against centrist parties and increased political bipolarization between the Socialists and Communists on one side and the Nationalists and Nazis on the other, as similar 'majoritarian' electoral systems did in France and Spain, with their own rise of new, extreme parties at about the same time in 1935–6.

In fact, the Nationalists and far right political positions obtained not only a widespread appeal among German voters in the 1920s and early 1930s, but also local strongholds of support in Bavaria as well as in many other regions. It seems reasonable to consider that plurality rule would have made them local winners. Even under proportional representation, the Nazis obtained votes by attracting those who previously supported the Nationalists and other small parties on the right, especially in small cities, partly because they appeared as potential absolute winners at the national level. Plurality rule, which promotes more strategic vote for likely winners than proportional representation, would have reinforced the tendency towards a concentration of votes. If it had any effect, proportional representation might have delayed bipolarization in German politics perhaps for a few months or years. (For a discussion, see Lepsius 1978; Kolb 1988; Nicholls 1991; Feuchtwanger 1993.)

Finally, proportional representation was again adopted with the re-establishment of democracy in West Germany in 1946, despite—or in the memory of—the Weimar experience. The corresponding multiparty system originated a long-lasting practice of coalition governments around the center that consolidated democracy. After the 1966 elections, the Christian-Democrats in government offered the Social-Democrats a change of the electoral system into plurality rule. An independent commission was appointed to this purpose including most remarkably, F. A. Hermens himself, who had returned from the United States a few years earlier. However, the Social-Democrat leadership found the gamble for a two-party system too risky and rejected the proposal, which was also opposed by the smaller Liberal party. (Jesse, 1990). This was a somewhat fortunate decision since the maintenance of a highly proportional representation system was instrumental in making the reunification with the Eastern part of Germany in 1990 feasible by consensual means. It permitted a new enlargement of the elect-orate with differentiated social groups and political preferences, including in particular the ex-Communists as a regular minority party, without major constitutional changes. Political equilibrium remained around moderate Cabinets with center-like policy positions, while the inclusiveness of the system promoted continuous support for democratic stability.

Northern Europe
Sweden, Norway, and Finland experienced processes of sudden introduction of universal suffrage, including, very early on, women's voting rights, together with the enforcement of proportional representation leading to multiparty coalition politics.

In the early 20th century, the Swedish incumbent rulers explicitly exchanged the enlargement of the electorate for a proportional representation electoral system. Previously, Sweden had adopted in 1866 a two-chamber parliament formula supported by very restrictive suffrage rights as an alternative to the traditional four-Estate corporative representation. The new upper chamber was organized on the basis of territorial representation through provincial councils elected by plural vote based on wealth. For the lower chamber, the vote was given to 21-year-old men fulfilling property or income qualifications. Representatives were elected in single-member districts by majority rule. Only between 5 and 8 per cent of the total population was enfranchised in Sweden during the last third of the 19th century. Landowners and farmers dominated political decisions. While the Liberals and the Socialists demanded universal suffrage, the Conservative rulers feared that broadening the franchise would disturb social stability.

However, in the first years of the 20th century, Liberals and Socialists achieved increasing parliamentary representation with the support of the lower-middle class and industrial workers who, because of economic growth, were increasingly able to fulfill the economic requirements for voting. Under plurality or majority rule, this evolution could have produced a total overturn, eventually making the opposition parties absolute winners and the Conservative rulers absolute losers. However, suddenly, and to other actors' and observers' general surprise, the Conservative government led by Arvid Lindman proposed the introduction of universal men's suffrage together with proportional representation in both chambers.

From the incumbent rulers' perspective, a new electoral system permitting multipartism was conceived to be a protective device. The Conservatives would become a minority, but they would not be expelled from the system as might be risked with a majoritarian rule. The incumbent rulers took the initiative of introducing universal suffrage 'with guarantees' rather than witnessing their own defeat. Proportional representation was adopted as an institutional safeguard in place of the traditional safeguards of wealth, property, or income qualifications.

As Lindman reasoned in 1907: 'With universal suffrage and elections in one-man constituencies, the time will not be distant when the interests of farmers here and there in the country are not well represented in elected bodies'. In contrast, with proportional representation, 'the danger of a shift in the direction now indicated is very greatly diminished. Even if farmers are no longer in a majority, agriculture should nevertheless have a chance to enjoy its fair share of representation' (Lewin 1988, ch. 3).

This proposal caused a dramatic reversal of institutional preferences among political parties. Some dissident Liberals joined the Cabinet's proposal, but the Liberal and the Socialist parties' leadership voted against the bill introducing universal suffrage because they refused proportional representation on the basis of their recent optimistic expectations under majority rule. Voting rights for all men over 24 years of age were finally approved in 1909. A few years later, in 1918, a new bill enlarging the electorate to all men and women aged 23 years was also introduced. As a result of these, the Swedish electorate was enlarged in about 50 per cent of the total population, multiplying the number of voters by eight in less than ten years.

The combination of universal suffrage and proportional representation created a very long-lived democratic stability while at the same time confirming to some extent the moderate expectations of the Conservatives. Under the new electoral rules, no single party obtained an absolute majority of seats in Parliament. Until 1930, governments were alternatively led by the Liberals, Socialists, and Conservatives (who returned to power in 1923–4 and again in 1928–30). The emergence of a centrist Agrarian party in the 1920s created a moderating bridge between the two blocs. The Agrarians (nowadays called the Center party) formed coalition Cabinets with the Socialists in the 1930s and the 1950s and with the Liberals and the Conservatives in the 1970s and the 1990s.

A similar, albeit somewhat slower process developed in Norway. A traditional four-Estate corporative representation had been based upon a narrow electorate still encompassing less than 9 per cent of the total population by the 1880s. Indirect elections in multimember districts gave the Norwegian Liberals absolute control of the chamber. Yet the formation of the Labour party in 1887 induced the Liberals to compete more strenuously for popular support. Using the same risk-adverse strategy used by the incumbent Conservative rulers in Sweden, the Norwegian Liberals introduced men's universal suffrage 'from above' in 1897. Women were partly enfranchised in 1907 and given equal electoral rights in 1913.

After the dissolution of the union between Norway and Sweden in 1905, the Norwegian parliament began to be directly elected in single-member districts, with majority rule in the first round and plurality rule in the second round with all previous candidates running again. This formula, while not producing proportional representation, permitted a multiparty system and gave the Liberals the opportunity to remain in power, together with the Conservatives and new Moderates, and to resist the threatening growth of the Labourites. As the electoral decline of the Liberals remained steady, however, they finally introduced proportional representation in 1919.

The results of these institutional reforms positively matched their promoters' basic expectations. No party obtained an absolute majority of seats (leaving room for minority Cabinets relying upon other parties for support). Liberals, Conservatives, and Agrarians alternated as the head of Cabinets against the largest Labour party until the first of a series of Labour governments was formed in 1935. A new reform for a more proportional representation formula (modified Sainte Laguë instead of d'Hondt) in the 1950s resumed the previous alternation of parties allowing once more the non-Socialist parties to share power.

The case of Finland corresponds even better to certain features of the 'Nordic' model previously identified. Since 1863, the Finnish corporative four-Estates had begun to be convened regularly under the control of the Russian Empire. They were elected with a highly restricted franchise, however, elections in multimember districts permitted some political pluralism. The Swedes, who were concentrated in Southern and Western Finland, predominated in the Estate of the nobility and also in the Estate of the burgesses for most of the 19th century. Yet by the end of the century, the Finns predominated in the Estate of burgesses as well as in those of the clergy and farmers, giving them control over parliamentary legislation (since the decision of three out of the four Estates was required). Almost all political groups promoted a modern unicameral parliament in order to fend off Russian domination. When the Swedes' leaders realized that this new institutional framework was going to be adopted, they held out for a system of proportional representation as the only guarantee of the continued representation of minorities in parliament. Since no party then had expectations of achieving an absolute majority of seats by plurality or majority rule, the proposal was accepted.

In 1905, virtually overnight, a unicameral parliament based on universal suffrage of men and—for first time in Europe—also women, was established in Finland, together with an electoral system of proportional representation. About 40 per cent of the total population was introduced into the electorate at one shot, multiplying the existing electorate by more than five. With this highly innovative, pluralistic framework, the Finns were able to confront the continued interference of the Russian Tsarist regime in their local politics, survive the Russian Bolshevik revolution and the following civil war, and achieve independence and a new Constitution in 1919. Since then, multiparty coalition Cabinets have been formed, mostly led by either the Agrarians or Social-Democrats (or both), with the minority Liberals and Swedes (the Swedish People's party) being very frequent partners with both the right and the left (Carstairs 1980, chs 9–11).

3

How Votes Are Counted

The race is over!
But who has won?
Everybody has won, and all must have prizes.
Lewis Carroll, *Alice's Adventures in
Wonderland* (1865)

In relatively simple, homogeneous communities, simple voting and decision rules producing a single, absolute winner are usually chosen. Single-
winner rules, such as unanimity, qualified-majority, simple majority, or
plurality, dominated the history of voting and elections until the 19th
century. They have survived in countries with several-centuries-old political institutions and are still a common institutional choice in small, relatively undifferentiated communities.

In pre-modern times many supporters of these rules considered them as
devices for discovering the truth, be it called God's will or the People's
will. They expected that the social choice obtained with those rules would
be widely accepted and very stable. This expectation is quite reasonable
in the context of simple communities whose members may not have very
disparate preferences on a small number of issues. They can be aggregated
into a single enforceable decision without much effort. However, in large,
complex societies in which a high number of policy issues arise and are
submitted to binding collective decisions, single-winner rules tend to
produce a highly uneven distribution of political satisfaction between
winners and losers, and low social utility. As a consequence of the incentives created for the absolute losers to try to overthrow such unfavorable
decisions, single-winner rules may also induce instability of the social
choice.

Modern utilitarian reasoning aimed at achieving the greatest satisfaction of the greatest number of people inspired the search for alternative
voting rules. They include those producing multiple winners, such as
proportional representation and other institutional devices favoring negotiations and agreements between differentiated groups. Multiple-winner
rules distribute satisfaction more widely among the different groups of a
society, and tend to produce more consensual and stable decisions and
higher social utility than single-winner rules.

Social choice theory can help to make the basic intuition sketched in the previous paragraphs more precise. The questions identified here will also guide formal and empirical analyses of the working of different voting rules in real-world politics.

According to social choice models, for a given electorate the stability and efficiency of the social choice heavily depends on: (i) the number of issue-dimensions which are prominent at voting; and (ii) the number of available alternatives to be voted for (in the form of candidates, parties, policy proposals, bill amendments, etc.).

When voters' preferences can be formed along a single issue-dimension, such as the typical left–right ideological axis, the social optimum coincides with the median voter's preference. The median, that is, the point with no more than a half of voters on both its right and its left, minimizes the sum of distances from the voters' preferences and, therefore, can be considered to maximize social utility.

Efficient outcomes can be achieved by single-winner rules, such as majority or plurality rules, if only two alternatives are available, since the winner can be expected to have the support of the median voter. However, likely losers in a relatively simple issue space can have incentives to introduce new issues and new alternatives in order to alter the outcome in their favor. By the creation of a multidimensional space of issues, new winners and instability of the social choice will appear. The outcome can become unpredictable and move away from the socially efficient median point. The more inclusive the rule (the most inclusive one being unanimity), the more new issues and alternatives are needed to destabilize the winner. The more exclusive the rule, such as simple plurality, the more potentially unstable, arbitrary, and inefficient the winner can be as a consequence of former losers' new strategies. In contrast, multiple-winner rules, such as proportional representation and the subsequent negotiation process, tend to organize multiparty coalitions around the alternative supported by the median voter.

In this chapter we will explore whether and how different voting rules create incentives for actors' strategies to develop new issues, new alternatives, confrontation, or negotiation which can lead to more or less efficient and stable social choices.

In particular, two characteristics of voting rules that have been targeted by social choice theory will be discussed. The so-called 'monotonicity' condition requires that a voting rule does not put at a disadvantage an alternative obtaining more support among the voters. We will examine whether votes and seats maintain 'monotonic' relations under different voting rules, that is, whether both increase or decrease in parallel. Specifically, situations in which one alternative becomes the winner despite having obtained less popular support in votes than some other alternative will be considered clear and blatant cases of nonmonotonicity.

The second condition is known in social choice theory as 'independence of irrelevant alternatives'. Basically, it states that the winning alternative should not depend on how many other alternatives are available at some particular moment of decision making. If one nonwinning alternative ceases to be available, the outcome should be unchanged as long as individual preferences over the remaining alternatives do not change. The lack of fulfillment of this condition for a voting rule makes it vulnerable to such well-known strategies as 'divide and win' and 'merge and win'. In general, minority winners and, more precisely, minority winners located at an extreme position on the issue space, will be considered as lacking this desirable property since they could be beaten by a potential majority if the appropriate alternative existed.

The Efficient Median Voter

The frequency of winners supported by the median voter with different voting rules is analyzed for 451 parliamentary and presidential elections in forty countries for the period 1945–2000 in Table 3.1. We consider 'winners' the party or parties in the Cabinet in parliamentary regimes and the party or parties supporting the President in popular elections in presidential and semi-presidential regimes. Roughly speaking, median voter's Cabinets and median voter's Presidents were produced in slightly more than half (54 per cent) of the elections by plurality rule and almost three-fourths (73 per cent) of the elections by majority rule (or qualified-plurality rule in a few presidentialist countries). In contrast, Cabinets based on proportional representation have the support of the median voter in more than 90 per cent of the cases. Most of the countries in the list that elect representatives with proportional representation and have parliamentary regimes have *always* included the median voter's party in the Cabinet (in 138 elections in ten countries).

This allows us to state that the outcomes of elections producing multiple winners with proportional representation are relatively more socially efficient than those of elections with single-winner rules. Among the latter, the more inclusive the rule, as is majority compared to plurality rule, the more efficient the social choice.

Voters' preferences can be identified on the basis of their voting or by using opinion surveys. Some simplification of issue preferences is needed to make comparisons feasible. In fact, voters and leaders themselves usually proceed to this kind of simplification in order to communicate political messages along a single dimension, such as the typical left–right scale, which usually synthesizes voters' varied preferences, political party platforms, and governmental agendas on many issues. The available evidence shows that most citizens in most democratic countries can place

TABLE 3.1. *Frequency of median voter's winners (1945–2000)*

Plurality rule		Majority rule		Proportional representation	
Parliamentary Cabinet		*Parliamentary Cabinet*		*Parliamentary Cabinet*	
Canada$_{17}$	41	Australia$_{21}$	33	Austria$_{17}$	94
India$_{13}$	69	France 5th$_{11}$	82	Belgium$_{17}$	100
New Zealand$_{15}$	73	Japan$_{13}$	100	Czech Rep.$_3$	67
United Kingdom$_{15}$	0			Denmark$_{21}$	76
		President		Finland$_{15}$	100
President		Argentina$_4$	100	France 4th Rep.$_5$	100
Argentina$_6$	100	Bolivia$_5$	40	Germany$_{14}$	100
Brazil$_4$	25	Brazil$_3$	67	Greece$_{16}$	100
Chile$_5$	20	Bulgaria$_2$	100	Hungary$_3$	67
Colombia$_{10}$	80	Chile$_3$	100	Ireland$_{16}$	100
Ecuador$_5$	0	Colombia$_2$	50	Israel$_{13}$	100
S. Korea$_3$	33	Costa Rica$_{12}$	83	Italy$_{11}$	100
Peru$_4$	75	Ecuador$_6$	67	Netherlands$_{16}$	100
Philippines$_3$	67	France 5th Rep.$_6$	50	Norway$_{13}$	46
United States$_{13}$	77	Peru$_3$	100	Spain$_7$	57
Uruguay$_{10}$	70	Poland$_2$	50	Sweden$_{17}$	82
Venezuela$_{10}$	60	Portugal$_5$	100	Switzerland$_{15}$	100
		Uruguay$_1$	100		
Election average:	54		73		91
Country average:	53		76		88

Note: The numbers are percentages of elections which produced a cabinet or a President supported by the median voter's first preference. Subindices are the number of elections for each country.

For parliamentary regimes, the data refer to the party composition of the longest lasting cabinet within every legislature, if there are more than one.

Source: Author's own calculations. Data for party relative positions in Daalder and Mair (1983); Sani and Sartori (1983); Castles and Mair (1984); the collection in Laver and Schofield (1990, appendix B; Huber and Inglehart (1995); Mainwaring and Scully (1995); Jones (1995), Colomer (1996a); Knutsen (1998); *Europa World Year Book*.

themselves and the parties or candidates on a linear scale which allows us to establish relative global positions of voters and leaders. Since the substantive content of the left–right dimension (or other comparable constructs) varies from country to country and from election to election, it is used here not to imply any essential definition of the left, the center, or the right policy positions, but for its communicative and heuristic value. (For discussions, see Budge, Robertson, and Hearl 1987; Riker 1993; Budge 1993; Klingemann Hofferbert, and Budge 1994.)

The party or candidate chosen by the median voter may not coincide with the median voter's ideal preference. Yet the distance between the two can be expected to be short the higher the number of alternatives available, since the parties and candidates will tend to distribute themselves along the space and fill the intermediate positions. Even if it does not coincide with the median voter's preference, the alternative which is chosen by the median voter can be considered to be the most socially efficient outcome for a given set of alternatives.

Fortunately, we do not need cardinal values for the distances between voters' preferences and political parties or candidates in order to make a qualitative judgement of social efficiency. Even if the outcome does not coincide with the median voter's ideal preference and is therefore not the social optimum, we can consider it to be relatively more socially efficient than any other available alternative if it corresponds to the median voter's actual choice. Social utility is maximized by the median voter's choice within the framework of citizens' available choices or 'revealed' preferences, although it may not be maximized in the ideal world of all imaginable voters' preferences.

The only information needed for our analysis is the relative position of some nonwinning alternatives with reference to the winner. If we are able to observe that, say, a majority of voters has voted for parties or candidates on the same side of the winner, whether on its left or on its right, or on whatever one side of the pertinent dimension, we can be sure that the winner is not the median voters' choice. In that case, the winner can be considered to be relatively socially inefficient, whatever the cardinal positions of the parties or candidates on the scale and the value of the distances from voters' preferences. With this artifact, most political outcomes in the real world (and the corresponding institutions) can be evaluated with standard empirical information. The median voter's party is identified on the basis of party-relative positions with the sources mentioned in Table 3.1. When available, further refinements will also be used.

This chapter is divided into two parts, dealing with single-winner rules and multiple-winner rules, respectively.

3.1. SINGLE-WINNER RULES

The choice of a single-winner rule always implies a trade-off between effectiveness and efficiency, that is, between the rule's capacity for producing outcomes and the social utility of these outcomes. As will be seen more specifically in the following pages, unanimity rule is highly ineffective in producing new outcomes different from the status quo, but when the outcome exists, it is usually relatively efficient in social terms. Majority rule is relatively ineffective in complex societies in which varied preferences can develop among voters. Socially efficient and stable outcomes can be produced by majority rule only under certain restrictive conditions. Finally, plurality rule is very effective in producing an outcome. But this is likely to be socially inefficient, as well as highly unstable since it can be replaced with some other alternative with relatively small innovations.

The trade-off thus works as follows. The more inclusive the rule (such as unanimity), the more consensual and efficient, but the less effective in producing outcomes it will be. The more exclusive the rule (such as simple plurality), the more effective it will be, but more inefficient outcomes will be produced. The above-mentioned voting rules, as well as other intermediate rules, such as qualified-majorities or qualified-pluralities that are also found in a number of real-world political institutions, will be analyzed for their results regarding these important aspects of social choice.

Unanimity

Unanimity rule is usually considered to be a procedure favoring consensual decisions. By definition, a unanimous decision requires the agreement of all and must be considered to be better for all voters than the status quo or the absence of a decision. In this sense, unanimity outcomes are considered to be 'Pareto superior' than any alternative occurrence and they certainly fulfill the monotonicity condition.

However, if voters' preferences can be located along a single dimension, unanimity rule leads to immobility. No decision can be made to alter the status quo because any voter can veto a move away from his preference. Initially advantaged voters (those whose preferences are closer to the status quo) can consolidate their privileges. The outcome will remain stable independently of its distance from the social optimum located on the median of voters' preferences.

With the introduction of new issues or new values of judgement creating a multidimensional space, several unanimous decisions can be made available from the initial status quo. But each one of the possible decisions will give different voters different degrees of satisfaction of their preferences and will produce different amounts of social utility. Since costly negotiations can be needed to achieve a single decision, the cost of making decisions or the control of the agenda may produce biased and socially inefficient outcomes.

Bias and Inefficiency

The biases in social efficiency of the outcomes produced by unanimity rule in a multidimensional space can be illustrated with the help of Fig. 3.1. From the initial status quo point (SQ), unanimity decisions by voters A, B, and C are possible in favor of any alternative located inside the lens-shaped area in the figure. This area is formed by circular indifference curves

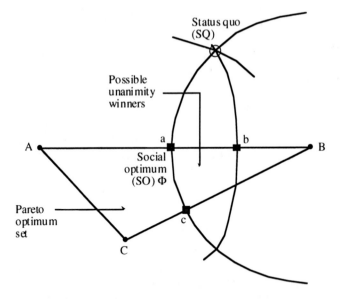

FIG. 3.1. Decisions with unanimity rule

around the voters' preferences A, B, and C that pass through the initial point SQ. All the points in this area are preferred by all voters because they are a shorter distance from the voters' preferences than SQ.

The set of possible decisions by unanimity intersects with the Pareto optimum set, which is the minimal set containing all voters' preferences (the triangle A B C). Any outcome within this intersection (the shaded area) is stable because none of the points in the area can be beaten by unanimity by any other alternative. No new unanimity can be obtained in favor of a move from it because at least one voter would find the new proposal less satisfactory and would veto it.

The set of stable winners by unanimity may or may not include the social optimum point (SO). As can be seen, SO is not included in the set of unanimity winners in Fig. 3.1. Only if the status quo is very distant from the voters' preferences, that is, the initial state is very unsatisfactory for the voters, will the social optimum point be within the set of stable decisions by unanimity. Precisely, the social optimum point can only be reached by a unanimous decision from an initial status quo placed outside an area which is at least three times larger than the Pareto optimum set. If the initial status quo is closer to the voters' preferences or less unsatisfactory (as in Fig. 3.1), only socially nonoptimum decisions can be made. From highly unsatisfactory initial states, dramatic changes leading to highly satisfactory and stable outcomes are feasible; from less unsatisfactory initial states, mediocrity tends to endure (Colomer 1999*a*).

Different voters will prefer different outcomes out of the set of possible unanimity decisions, as shown in Fig. 3.1. Voter A, for example, will prefer the alternative a, while voter B will prefer b, and voter C will prefer c. If voter A is the agenda setter, A can submit the alternative a to voting against the unsatisfactory status quo (SQ). The agenda setter A can expect an agreement on a on the basis of the higher level of satisfaction of all voters' preferences produced by this alternative, the cost for the other voters of negotiating another proposal or replacing the agenda setter, and the pressures of the institutional environment to make an effective, quick decision. In contrast, if voter B is the agenda setter, B will submit the alternative b to voting against the status quo in the expectation of analogous developments in favor of b, etc. A unanimous decision in favor of any of these or the other alternatives located inside the shaded area becomes stable. In this sense, unanimity social choices are dependent on irrelevant alternatives; having different sets of proposals to vote for may produce different winners.

Thus, unanimity rule produces stable social choices. However, the social efficiency of the outcome is highly dependent on the status quo, the distribution of bargaining costs among voters, and the agenda setter's maneuvering. This is significant because on many political issues, including policy choices and other provisions of public goods, the status quo is not typically chosen by voters nor does it necessarily depend on their preferences or on available alternatives. Given the usual existence of several possible outcomes, unanimity social choices are uncertain. The satisfaction they provide is biased in favor of advantaged voters, such as those with the power of making proposals first or those with a greater capacity for paying negotiation costs. Unanimity stable social choices are monotonic and included in the Pareto optimum set, but they may be socially inefficient from the point of view of social utility.

Cases: Medieval Assemblies and International Organizations

Unanimity rule has been enforced in at least two different types of institutions which will be briefly reviewed below. (1) The Christian Church in the Middle Ages and a few medieval parliaments, including in particular the Aragonese and Catalan Corts and the Polish Diet; (2) Most international organizations, with two major examples surveyed here, the United Nations Security Council and the Council of the European Community.

As will be seen, a common pattern can be identified in the evolution of these as well as other political institutions making decisions with unanimity rule. First, some initial socially efficient decisions can be made, in the sense of choosing outcomes that approach the Pareto optimum set of alternatives in which all participants are better off than in the previous status quo. Second, there can be further stagnation and absence of new decisions due to the veto power of every participant, even if the previous outcomes do not correspond to socially optimum solutions. Finally, a change to a nonunanimity rule may be expected in order to regain institutional capability to make efficient social choices.

God's Single Will

Unanimity rule was prevalent in the Christian Church for many centuries, as it was considered to be the only rule that could assure the participants that their decision was right or inspired by God. At the beginning of the Christian era, most bishops were unanimously elected with participation of the Christian faithful ('the people'). The election of a bishop, including the Bishop of Rome whose primacy over the other bishops was only gradually asserted, was conceived as a way to discover God's will. Hence the maxim 'vox populi, vox Dei', or the 'people's voice is God's voice'.

The Church also restated the Roman law principle (embodied in the Justinian code): 'What concerns similarly all ought to be approved by all', by affirming that 'He who governs all should be elected by all'. Popular participation induced unanimous consent and obedience from the faithful and gave the Church solid ground for expanding its influence and attracting a large following in the first few centuries after Jesus (Benson 1968).

However, dissidence over several candidates for bishop or for pope, as well as the frequent ineffectiveness of unanimity rule in producing a winner, became a source of popular tumult, conflicts, and schisms relatively early. Even before Christianity had been officially accepted by the Roman Emperor, at least one simultaneous election of two different popes had taken place (in 250, after eighteen months of failure to elect). In 366 and 418, the election of two popes by different factions of the Church provoked hundreds of deaths and the intervention of Roman troops. These conflicts put the Church for several centuries under the protection and domination of political powers, especially Italian noble families and emperors. The Church obtained the Emperor's effective renunciation of the right to appoint the pope only at the Concordat of Worms in 1122. The present Catholic Church recognizes 159 Popes from 1 to 1122, but at least thirty-one 'anti-popes' were recognized by certain factions. From the mid 9th to the mid 10th century, twenty-two out of twenty-six popes were overthrown (twelve were removed from office, five sent into exile, and five killed) (author's own calculations with data in Levillain 1994.)

The ineffectiveness of unanimity rule eventually moved the Church to adopt alternative rules. First, the laity was excluded from the election of the pope and voting was reserved for the cardinals (by a Papal Bull in 1059). However, unanimity among the cardinals was also difficult to reach. Priority was then given to the vote of the cardinal-bishops, who were entrusted with gaining the assent of the cardinal-priests and the cardinal-deacons, as well as the approval of the other members of the Church. More ambiguously, the identification of the '*sanior et maior pars*' (the 'sounder and greater part') of voters was introduced in order to persuade some dissidents to support a candidate and create apparent unanimity when it did not exist. Moral qualities like seniority, zeal, and the dignity of voters were considered relevant because voting was conceived as a way to discover the truth. But the 'sanior pars' often did not coincide with the 'maior pars'. In elections of bishops, the determination about which was the 'sanior' part in a divided electorate could be submitted to an arbiter, such as the metropolitan bishop or even the pope, but no such arbiter existed for the election of the pope after the suppression of imperial control. Three 12th-century elections by cardinals under unanimity rule ended in the appointment of two rival candidates which, together with their successors, produced eight anti-popes and only nine 'official' popes in less than fifty years.

Unanimity rule was associated with a mystical and theological notion of the Church's unity. Whereas voters' unanimity was believed to be inspired by God, any failure in obtaining such a total consensus was seen as an instigation of the devil. Nevertheless, the frequency of conflicts led to abandoning unanimity rule and to the adoption of two-thirds majority rule by Pope Alexander III (himself previously in competition with an anti-pope) at the Third Lateran Council in 1179. Alexander III's six-month stay in Venice during 1177, during which he reconciled with the Emperor Frederick Barbarossa who had supported the anti-pope, may well have exposed him to the city's sophisticated voting procedure for electing a doge (sketched in the previous chapter) and induced him to adopt a more effective nonunanimity rule for elections of the Church soon thereafter (Baldwin 1968).

The basic aim of the qualified-majority rule of two-thirds was the formation of a consensual, large coalition of cardinals without giving any of them veto power. The outcome could be considered to be rather stable because, in order to overthrow a winning candidate with two-thirds support, the losers would have to persuade at least *a majority* of the winner's original supporters to change their mind. The expected stability of qualified-majority winners allowed the Church to consider this rule also as a right procedure for discovering God's will. In the words of Pope Pius II about his own election in 1458, 'What is done by two thirds of the sacred college [of cardinals], that is surely of the Holy Ghost, which may not be resisted' (Gragg and Gabel 1959: 88). The rule of two-thirds also came into play in elections of bishops and abbots.

In contrast to the previous history of conflicts and schisms, two-thirds rule was efficacious and did produce rather stable outcomes. However, a qualified-majority rule is still somewhat demanding, which can be effective at the expense of rather long delays in decision making. Under the rule of two-thirds, negotiations to form a sufficiently large coalition to elect the pope caused extremely long vacancies in the Holy See during the 13th century (up to thirty-four months).

This led to establishing the practice of locking up cardinals until they reached a decision, which was formally shaped as the *conclave* (from the Latin: with key), first in 1274 and again from 1294. The cardinals are given incentives to make a quick decision by being submitted to external isolation, certain physical and material restraints, scanty information about candidates, and restricted communication among themselves. This certainly makes qualified-majority rule effective in producing outcomes, but it also leads the cardinals to precipitate decisions driven by the desire to leave such an uncomfortable environment. (For a broader and more detailed discussion, see Colomer and McLean 1998.)

From the 17th to the 19th centuries, the leaders of cardinals' factions in the conclave were based on ecclesiastic orders, political allegiances, or geographical origins. They bartered their support for future appointments or doctrinal reforms. Usually, a committee of independents called the 'flying squad' (*squadra volante*) was formed to bargain with the factions (Lector 1894). Beginning with the 20th century, several prominent issue-dimensions to promote candidates were developed, including progressive-conservative, bishop-Curia member, and Italian-foreigner. The endogenous creation of issues and candidates tends to raise the bargaining costs. This leads cardinals in conclave to look for intuitively appealing focal points, shifting to favor those candidates who obtain increasing support and appear as potential winners in the first rounds of voting. The analysis of voting rounds in modern conclaves shows that any front-runner who loses one vote from one round to the next immediately becomes a 'dead horse'. In contrast, candidates who maintain or increase their votes, even from a very low initial support, can attract particular attention, even if they are not highly consensual or have hardly been mentioned as *papabile* a few hours before being crowned (Colomer 1996c).

In sum, the ineffectiveness of the initially adopted unanimity rule was traded off in the Church for the lower consensus of a qualified-majority rule. The latter rule has been relatively more effective. But additional environmental pressures were implemented in order to induce the cardinals to make quick decisions. A number of popes have been elected as a result of these institutional pressures rather than for their proximity to well-informed, sincere preferences of many of the cardinal-voters. Frequent surprises in favor of inefficient candidates gave rise to the popular saying, 'He who enters the conclave a pope, leaves it a cardinal', which has had the status of an 'empirical law' since the 14th century.

Consensual Medieval Parliaments

Medieval kings, emperors, and popes called assemblies of great feudal nobles, ecclesiastical dignitaries, and other notables to ask their counsel or opinion, or simply to highlight new legislative measures, foreign treaties, or dynastic marriages. The Magna Carta conceded by King John of England in 1215 is usually mentioned as the starting point. Representative institutions flourished particularly in the kingdoms and principalities of Latin Europe, including Aragon, Catalonia and Valencia, Leon and Castille, Navarre, Portugal, and Sicily from the 13th century onwards, as well as in France, the German Empire, and the Northern European kingdoms in later periods. While many of these assemblies remained consultative bodies, some of them developed more significant initiatives and decision power and eventually became relevant institutions of government.

The doctrine of unanimous consent emerged from practice. By the late 12th century, not only the Church, as previously discussed, but also some civil powers had adopted virtual unanimity rule by referring to the Roman principle: 'What concerns all ought to be approved by all'. A further evolution, however, moved most of these bodies from 'the primitive unanimity' to alternative criteria, such as the 'sounder and greater part' (already mentioned regarding the Church), qualified-majorities, or simple majority rule (Konopczynski 1930; Marongiu 1968; Wilkinson 1972; Myers 1975).

Two cases corresponding to different periods, the *Cortes* of Aragon from the 13th century and the Polish Diet from the 16th century, are discussed here for their basic similarities: both achieved great control over legislation and both formally adopted unanimity rule for important decisions. Also, in both cases, the requirement of unanimous agreements eroded their capability of decision making and made the parliaments vulnerable to the rule of more effective, less consensual institutions.

The Aragonese and Catalan '*Dissentimiento*'

One of the earliest meetings recorded of a representative assembly in Europe was in 1064, in Barcelona, Catalonia, for the approval by consensus and acclamation of public laws later compiled in the celebrated Customs of the city (*Usatges*). By the middle of the 12th century, the counts of Barcelona also became Kings of Aragon. Beginning in 1162, they summoned regular assembles of representatives of the clergy, the nobles, and the knights, as well as the towns.

The 'General Cortes' developed in parallel to separate meetings of the Cortes of Aragon and the Corts of Catalonia, as well as the Corts of Valencia after its conquest. From the mid-13th century, the Catalan-Aragonese confederation expanded its dominions south into the Iberian Peninsula against the previous Muslim domination, parallel to the expansion of Castile, and became the major power in the Mediterranean. The Aragonese Cortes were the model for the Sicilian and Sardinian parliaments.

The King of Aragon was bound to summon the Cortes once every five years and, after the union with Catalonia, every other year, although the actual calendar of meetings was highly irregular. The business of the Cortes included solving justice disputes (especially 'grievances' or complaints from individuals or towns, concerning the King's officers or other Estates' members), approving legislation, and voting on taxes. For the approval of all the more important laws, the Aragon

Cortes required that each of its four component Estates had to come to a unanimous decision ('*nemine discrepante*'). Every member could veto any decision by his *dissentimiento*. Yet, when total consent was not achieved, the accord was registered as made by '*unanimiter excepto N.N.*', leaving room for further debates and discussions, although they often ended in 'no result'. Eventually, some individual objections were declared to be 'absurd', 'not pertinent', or 'irrational' and the matter was referred to a permanent committee formed by two representatives from each Estate as an arbiter to judge on the soundness of the existing majority will (see the discussion in González Antón 1978).

The Catalan parliament was institutionalized at an assembly in Barcelona in 1283, when a long and formal list of participants was established, including representatives of 'the citizens and men of the towns'. King Peter the Great promulgated a series of legislative decrees to guarantee both the rights of his subjects and just administration, especially in matters of justice and taxation. He committed himself and his descendants to enact any general constitution or statute of Catalonia only with 'the approval and consent' of the prelates, barons, knights, and citizens of the country. The Catalan Corts should have been summoned once a year 'to treat of matters of common utility for the country', but after repetitive delays, triennial convocations were adopted in 1301, although the permanent parliamentary commission, the *Generalitat*, might call Extraordinary Assemblies.

Unanimous agreements were laboriously constructed in the Catalan Corts in several ways, including deliberation; lengthy negotiations within each of the Estates, between solicitors of the different Estates, and between solicitors of the Estates and the King; by attracting voters to the bandwagon in public and ordered voting rounds which started with the higher or 'sanior' parts; and by bribes from the King offering jobs and money to the dissenters.

Yet, given the relative ineffectiveness of unanimity rule in making decisions, the Corts asked the king to interpret the founding constitution as allowing to replace unanimous consent with the opinion of the '*major e de la pus sana part*' in matters of legislation (according to the example of the Castilian Cortes, as well as the Church's practices previously mentioned). Consequently, certain measures were declared valid if they were approved by the nobles' and the citizens' estates with disagreement or abstention of the clerical representatives or by other qualified majorities.

In the Corts of Valencia, unanimity was required for the Estate of nobles. But at least on one occasion, in 1645, unanimity was reached by throwing a recalcitrant member out into the street and then proceeding to a vote.

After the union of the Crowns of Aragon and Castille in the late 15th century, the unanimity-inspired, consensual Cortes were gradually curbed by the Habsburg monarchs of Spain. The Cortes of Aragon abandoned their virtual unanimity rule after 1592, but some of their tasks were transferred to other bodies. The Catalan Corts gathered together in 1626, after twenty-seven years without sessions, but were unable to make a single decision, whether on grievances, legislation, or taxes, thus preparing further constitutional and secessionist conflicts. The Corts held a few more meetings, but were formally suppressed after the victory of the Bourbon dynasty in the Succession War and the corresponding establishment of a 'New Plan', inspired by the French centralized model, in 1716 (Coroleu and Pella 1876; Ferro 1987; Gil 1991).

The Polish *'Liberum Veto'*

The Diet or 'Noble Parliament of Poland' (*Sejm*) worked with unanimity rule from the 16th to the 18th century. The General or Great Diet was formed by the King (elected by the Diet since the late 13th century), the Senate (with up to 150 members), and the Chamber of Deputies (with up to 236 members). Before attending the General Diet the elected deputies gathered together at provincial Diets, where they received compulsory mandates, especially on taxes. According to the procedure formally established by law in 1572, the Diet held ordinary sessions of six weeks every two years. All decisions should be adopted by unanimity (*'nemine contradicente'*), that is, by general agreement of all senators and deputies with every voter enjoying *'liberum veto'*. At each session, all laws were to be approved in a single package. The president of the Chamber, known as the 'marshall', played a prominent role in inducing negotiations and agreements.

During the 16th century, the Polish Diet was able to make unanimous decisions in favor of significant 'modernizing', nationally oriented reforms, such as the expropriation of lords' properties; the creation of new legal institutions, territorial homogenization, and monetary unification; the annexion of Lithuania; affirmation of sovereignty in the face of the German Empire and the Papacy; the declaration of freedom of thought; and the termination of religious wars.

However, from the early 17th century, the ineffectiveness of the Diet began to increase. 'Unended' or 'broken' Diets, that is, biennial sessions where no decision could be made as a result of some member's veto, proliferated. Every deputy or senator could nullify all decisions taken during a session just by using a formula such as 'I declare nullity of the Diet', 'I do not permit', 'I protest', or others. Among the intended remedies to the Diet's decadence, was a suggestion that the debates be prolonged beyond the previously established period of six weeks. But the proposed prolongation had also to be approved by unanimity. From 1669, several vetoes blocked not only proposals to prolong the deliberations but also the ordinary sessions. In 1689, the session ended even before the marshall was appointed. In the words of certain historians, the feeling that 'the sense of public interest was being lost' spread widely. Complaining popular slogans, such as 'Individualism is the master of Poland!', arose. During the 17th century and due to the Diet's decadence, 'the Republic entered into a period of anarchy, paralysis and obscurantism' (Lesnodorski 1959).

Finally, the Diet rules were drastically reformed. In 1764, majority rule was introduced for affairs of minor interest (excluding taxes). In 1791, a new

Constitution established that the Diet could make decisions by majority or by two-thirds qualified-majority on certain issues (such as overthrowing ministers). However, this new period of more efficacious decision making granted by the adoption of new, nonunanimity rules, was short. In 1795, Russia, Prussia and Austria occupied the country and divided Polish state between them (Konopczynski 1930; Davies 1982).

Intergovernmental organizations

Unanimity rule is usually applied in those institutional settings in which the members claim 'sovereignty' and reject any collective decision which is not made with its explicit approval. The councils of two paramount modern international organizations formed by 'sovereign' states are reviewed here, those of the United Nations and the European Community. In both cases, the veto right of every member-state has produced decreasing efficacy in decision making, prompting the replacement of the central or exclusive role of the unanimous council with some alternative institutional scheme.

The Inefficacious United Nations

The relative ineffectiveness of unanimity rule as compared with majority rule can be observed in the two major institutional bodies of the United Nations Organization (UN), the Security Council and the General Assembly, since they work by virtual unanimity and majority rule, respectively. When the UN was created in 1945, the victors of World War II had drawn up a plan to organize a Security Council in which the United States, the Soviet Union, the United Kingdom, France, and China were to be permanently represented. At the first conference of delegates from fifty-one states in San Francisco, these five powers insisted the UN should give them the authority to veto actions of the Security Council. The smaller nations opposed this without success, but they did succeed in adding other UN organs, especially the General Assembly.

The UN Security Council is now formed by the five permanent members mentioned above and ten temporal members elected for two-year terms. Each member has one vote, the five permanent members have veto power, and decisions are made by at least nine votes. The Security Council basically works with the rule of unanimity of its five permanent members (or, in fact, their abstention). It is not difficult for the permanent members to find sufficient support among the temporal members for the proposals they agree upon. The permanent members' power, seen as the probability for them to succeed in approving a common proposal (and ignoring the possibility of abstention), has been calculated to be very close to unanimity, at about 98% (both when the number of temporal members was six and the decision rule was seven votes, and under the above-mentioned rules adopted in 1965 (Brams 1975: 182–91).

The record of annual decisions of the Security Council has remained fairly constant from 1946 to 1990. Its average number of resolutions adopted annually was 89 in the late 1940s and 102 in the late 1980s. During the first forty-five years of the Council, the permanent members of the Council exercised a total of 279 vetoes on sixty-seven different issues (the most conflictive issue being that of the Middle East, with forty-two vetoes). A substantial number of vetoes cast during the Council's early existence were made by the Soviet Union. However, during that same period, a great number of resolutions failed to be adopted because the United States managed to get sufficient support from certain temporal members to defeat the required majority (the so-called 'hidden veto'). The United States also cast a significant number of 'nonhidden' vetoes during the 1980s.

The UN General Assembly includes representatives from every member state (185 in 1999). Each member has one vote and decisions are made by majority. In contrast to the regular performance of the Security Council, the record of the General Assembly during the same period shows a higher degree of efficacy in decision making and a steady increase in the number of resolutions approved each year. The Assembly's record has evolved from an annual average of 117 resolutions adopted in the late 1940s to more than 340 in the 1980s (only nonprocedural but substantive matter resolutions are included in this account). The disparate evolution of the two bodies in their effective decision making is shown in Fig. 3.2 (Marín-Bosch 1987; Patil 1995).

It is of note that the Security Council has a relatively lower degree of efficacy in making decisions despite of its dealing with a high number of issues and the advantage of having much fewer members than the General Assembly. The most important decisions regarding the maintenance of international peace and security have initially been allocated to the Council. But in practice, and due to the inefficacy of its virtual unanimity rule, some questions that have not been resolved in the Council have been added to the General Assembly's agenda. The increasing membership in the UN might have created more difficulties forming majorities among the varied members of the Assembly. But, thanks to the greater efficacy of majority rule, the General Assembly has enlarged the range of its concerns and has steadily increased the number of resolutions adopted.

European Unanimity

When the European Economic Community was founded by the Treaty of Rome in 1957, the Council of Ministers of the initial six member-states—Belgium, France, Germany, Italy, Luxembourg, and the Netherlands—was conceived as its basic institution, although it received initiatives from the European Commission and the Assembly (later transformed into the Parliament). Initially, the six members chose to make decisions in the Council by unanimity, as it would correspond to the 'intergovernmental' or diplomatic model of decision making in international organizations, subject to moving to majority rule on selected subjects in the future. In its first years the European Economic Community, led by the Council's unanimous decision making, was remarkably innovative; it was able to

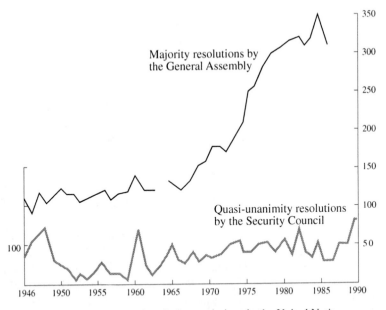

FIG. 3.2. Unanimity and majority resolutions in the United Nations

Note: The left scale shows the number of resolutions approved by the UN Security Council under
the veto right of five members. The right scale shows the number of resolutions approved by the UN
General Assembly under majority rule. (The 1965 General Assembly is not included because it was
a short session)

Source: Marín-Bosh (1987, table 1); Patil (1995).

create an industrial and agricultural common market by lowering customs barriers between its members and to establish common external tariffs favoring trade.

Further development, however, was significantly curbed by the unanimity
procedure. In 1963, the French delegation, presided over at that time by General
Charles de Gaulle, vetoed Britain's first attempt to join the Community, despite
of the fact that negotiations were far advanced. In 1965, when majority rule was
due to be introduced for selected matters, the French government began to
boycott the Council meetings, provoking the so-called 'empty chair crisis'. This
led the members of the Community to agree on the so-called 'Luxembourg
compromise' in 1966, a statement in which the right of veto in the Council was
formally asserted 'when very important interests were at stake'. For two decades
civil servants and ministers of the member-states had to hold lengthy discussions
in the Committe of Permanent Representatives and the Council of Ministers until
unanimous decisions were reached, leading the Community to a long period of
stagnation or 'Eurosclerosis', as it was called at the time. The accession of new
members, including Britain in 1973 (after de Gaulle's demise), was a source of
new vetoes against further integration, especially during the premiership of

Margaret Thatcher in the early 1980s. Denmark also insisted on the national sovereignty of its institutions, while Germany wanted to preserve the autonomy of its national bank.

In the words of some standard presentations: a 'combination of hostility and inertia . . . impeded the sharing of sovereignty, and stunted Community development between 1965 and 1985' (Pinder 1995); 'decision making was becoming virtually impossible under the practice of unanimity . . . The unit-veto system of the European Council would, in the absence of complex package deals, lead to stalemate on an increasing number of issues. For a major advance in policy integration to take place, these package deals would have had to be so complex that the costs of negotiating them would have become prohibitive' (Keohane and Hoffmann 1990).

Only the adoption of new, nonunanimity decision rules escaping from the limits of the 'intergovernmental' model was capable of furthering more effective decision making. New rules embodied in the Single European Act of 1986 included the 'cooperation procedure', by which the Council shared certain legislation powers with the European Parliament, and the adoption of qualified-majority voting with weighted votes in the Council for most of the decisions concerning completion of the single market program. In the view of the then-President of the European Commission, Jacques Delors, 'the old 'inequality-unanimity-immobility' triangle has been replaced by a new 'equality- majority- dynamism' triangle, the key to success' (Delors 1989).

New revisions of the Community Treaties and further major decisions towards a closer union then became possible, including the creation of a new common currency, the euro, and further enlargements. Specifically, the Maastricht Treaty on the European Union (EU) in 1992 introduced the 'co-decision' procedure in which new legislative powers of the European Parliament were linked to qualified majority voting in the Council of the European Union (as the former Council of Ministers is called since 1993). The 1997 Amsterdam Treaty virtually abolished the cooperation procedure and extended the scope of the co-decision procedure in economic policy making. However, unanimity decisions on important matters are still made at summit meetings of the European Council, composed of the member-states' chief executives, and unanimity in the Council of the European Union is required for decisions on the Common Foreign and Security Policy and on Justice and Home Affairs (Nugent 1994; Crombez 1996; Hayes-Renshaw and Wallace 1997).

Majority

The theological idea of the general will of God, which had been forged within the ancient and early medieval Christian Church, was transformed into the idea of the general will of the citizens in 18th-century French political thought. Accordingly, the praise of unanimity rule, initially associated with God's will, was replaced by certain philosophers' by a similar tribute to majority rule.

For Jean-Jacques Rousseau, the general will was considered to be 'always right' and could be discovered by voting by majority rule. However, Rousseau did not elaborate very much on voting procedures to discover the majority, general will of the people. Rather, he relied upon moral incentives leading citizens to adapt to the general will, however discovered, and substitute it for their particular wills. As an alternative procedure, he suggested resorting to a temporal dictator able to establish or re-establish the people's general will (Rousseau 1762: iv, 2, 6).

Inspired by Rousseau's basic principles regarding the people's general will, Marquis de Condorcet promoted a voting procedure by which the winner should be the alternative preferred by a majority against every other alternative. What is known as Condorcet voting procedure or exhaustive pairwise voting (if multiple rounds of voting between pairs of alternatives are implemented) may be difficult to implement because it requires a complete ordering of preferences, and is highly ineffective in producing an outcome. However, Marquis was eager to counterbalance these drawbacks by asserting the rightness of the outcome when it exists. Voting with multiple majority was conceived as a way to discover the 'best' or the 'correct' decision, one through which 'the people as a whole' could express 'a common will' (Condorcet 1792: 71ff.). A relatively more effective but still difficult variant had been devised in the 13th century by the Catalan philosopher Ramon Llull (1283, ch 24, and 1299).

Majority rule, even with one round of voting by categoric ballot, is certainly much more effective in producing innovative decisions than unanimity rule. In contrast to the latter, majority rule does not give any individual veto power to prevent moves away from the status quo to more efficient outcomes.

Yet, we know from social choice theory that even when a majority winner clearly exists, it may not be socially efficient in terms of social utility. Majority rule is also more vulnerable to instability than unanimity rule. Majority losers can attract sufficient voters' support and overthrow the winner by introducing a relatively lower number of new issues and alternatives than those required to do so under unanimity rule. If appropriate institutional devices exist in order to produce a stable winner, this can be arbitrary and unpredictable from the perspective of voters' preferences, since it will be just one among the many potential winners. The less inclusive the rule, for example, simple majority as compared to qualified-majority rules, the smaller the number of new alternatives and issues that are sufficient to produce instability or unpredictability of the social choice.

Specifically, only in the very simple case of social choice between two alternatives located on a single-dimensional space (such as the left–right axis), it is assured that the majority winner will be stable and socially efficient. By definition, the alternative obtaining more than half the votes will obtain the support of the socially efficient median voter. Even if there is no 'convergence' between the two alternatives (e.g., two parties competing in mass elections) and they keep some significant distance from each other's policy or ideological positions and from the median voter's preference, the alternative closer to the median voter's preference can be expected to win. Given the restricted number of alternatives available, the relative closeness of the winner to the median voter's preference can be taken as a measure of the social efficiency of the social choice (Downs 1957; Davis, Hinich, and Ordeshook 1970).

Yet, if new issues are introduced and a multidimensional space is created, then, even with two alternatives, unstable or arbitrary outcomes can be produced. It has been proved that if any pair of alternatives can be offered to voters, any alternative can be beaten by some other alternative in pairwise contests (Plott 1967; McKelvey 1976, 1979; Kramer 1977). Then, in a single election the majority outcome can be unpredictable. Rather than depending on voters' sincere preferences, the winner depends on which issues take salience in the political debate and the electoral campaign and on the specific pair of alternatives (policy proposals, party programs, or candidates) made available at the election.

Relatively efficient social choices can be produced only in a series of elections by majority between two alternatives in which every outcome becomes the initial state for the following round. It seems reasonable, then, to expect that the emerging new alternatives and the corresponding outcomes, instead of increasingly dispersing themselves, will approach a central area of points in the multidimensional space and not lead out again. The dynamic process in successive elections between two alternatives will not be as 'chaotic' as the static model previously mentioned may suggest, although it is still unstable (Ferejohn, McKelvey, and Packel 1984; McKelvey 1986; Milller, Grofman, and Feld 1989). Yet, if more than two alternatives are created, majority rule lacks effectiveness, even in a single dimensional space.

Majority winners may maintain nonmonotonic relations with voters' choices. Specifically, in Assembly elections with multiple districts, the majority loser in popular votes can become the majority winner in seats. A minority alternative in the electorate can obtain a higher number of seats than its popular majority rival if it obtains narrow majorities in a greater number of districts, as can be seen in Table 3.2. Even if the winner in every district corresponds to the choice of the median voter in the district, the multiple-district winner may not correspond to the alternative preferred by the median voter in the electorate. As will be seen in real-

TABLE 3.2. *Winning losers with majority rule*

		Parties:		
		Left		Right
Districts:	A	40		*60*
	B	40		*60*
	C	*80*		20
	Total votes	160	>	140
	Total seats	1	<	2

Note: The table illustrates two-party competition in three single-member districts. The numbers in each district refer to percentages of votes. The winners of a seat in each district are shown in italics. As can be seen, party Left has a majority of votes (160 to 140) but party Right obtains a majority of seats (2 to 1).

world cases, the apportionment of the electorate, that is, the drawing of electoral districts and the territorial allocation of seats, can favor such paradoxical results.

Majority Procedures

Since a majority winner between three or more alternatives may not exist with a single categoric ballot, two major procedures requiring voters to express their ordinal preferences regarding several alternatives are commonly used in mass political elections.

First, majority-preferential voting (also called alternative vote) takes into account not only the first voters' preferences but their second and further ordinal preferences, which can be revealed in a single ballot, in order to make a winner with majority support. Alternative vote is currently used to elect a few Assemblies, including the Federal Lower Chamber in Australia.

Second, the majority-runoff procedure includes a second round of voting in order to choose a winner between the two alternatives which obtained more votes in the first round. Variants of the runoff procedure are used in parliamentary elections in France, as well as in most direct presidential elections in Europe and Latin America.

In contrast to categoric ballot, the above two procedures of majority voting guarantee that a majority winner exists in contests with more than two alternatives. However, neither procedure guarantees a socially efficient outcome, not even in a single-dimensional space. As will be seen in a number of real-world cases, the winner with a majority of votes in a single-dimensional space may not be the alternative favored by the median voter.

The winners by majority-preferential voting or by majority-runoff depend on irrelevant alternatives. Specifically, a socially efficient alternative can be eliminated at the first round of counting votes (with the first procedure) or at the first round of voting (with the second one). Then the final winner could be beaten by majority by the eliminated alternative if the opportunity to choose between the two were given to the voters.

Only the winner with the Condorcet procedure of voting in a single-dimensional space, that is, the alternative winning by majority against every other alternative on its right or its left, would correspond to the median voter's preference and be socially efficient. By definition, the median voter is always necessary to form a consistent majority in a single dimension. Yet, in a multidimensional space, the Condorcet procedure of voting is highly ineffective (on many occasions an alternative able to win by majority over all the others does not exist) and may be inefficient since the winner may not coincide with the social optimum. Given these disadvantages and the difficulty of voting, the Condorcet procedure has never been used in mass political elections.

Cases: Majority Parliamentary and Presidential Elections

Different cases of mass political elections using the majority principle will be discussed here: (1) Parliamentary elections, including those during the Second Republic of Spain in the 1930s, which used a mixed majoritarian electoral system; the House of Representatives of Australia, with major-ity-preferential voting; and the National Assembly of France during the fifth Republic, with majority-runoff not always limited to two candidates; (2) Presidential elections with majority-runoff and a second round of voting between the two most voted for candidates in France, producing certain surprising results.

The electoral outcomes analyzed here will show that practical voting procedures based on majority rule do not fulfill such basic requirements of social choice as monotonicity and the independence of irrelevant alternatives. In many of these cases, the social utility of majority winners can be compared unfavorably to likely results with alternative voting rules.

The Spanish Pre-Civil War

Nonmonotonic electoral results in which the loser in popular votes becomes the winner in seats can help to explain high levels of political bipolarization that, under certain circumstances, may lead to revolution, *coup d'état*, and civil war. This was the case in the Spanish Second Republic, which was established in April 1931 in reaction to the previous involvement of the Monarchy in a military dictatorship.

A few weeks after the Republic was proclaimed, the Provisional Government decreed new electoral rules for parliamentary elections to the Cortes. As was explained by the Prime Minister, Manuel Azaña, in a further discussion in Parliament, a majoritarian electoral system was chosen in order to produce a clear parliamentary majority upon 'the indestructible conviction that Republicans and Socialists were the majority of the country'. To the protest that the minorities would be crushed, Azaña, however, acknowledged that he 'didn't know yet whom we are going to crush, or even who will be the crushers and the crushed' (in Mori 1933, vol. XIII: 345ff.).

The electoral system combined majority and plurality rules. About one-seventh of the deputies were elected in ten urban districts and the rest in fifty rural districts with an unfair apportionment of seats. Every elector was given a limited vote for a lower number of candidates than seats to be filled in the district. In each district, the seats were distributed between the two party or coalition lists with higher numbers of votes, respectively called 'the majority' and 'the minority'. If a list was supported by a majority of voters, it was given the proportion of seats they had been allowed to vote for (about 80 per cent). If no list obtained a majority of votes, the most voted list was given 67 per cent of the seats under the proviso that it had obtained at least 20 per cent of votes (40 per cent since 1933). If no list obtained this minimum support, a second round of voting was held. Thus, the second candidacy in votes, the so-called 'the minority', was given only between about 20 and 33 per cent of seats in the district independently of the amount of votes obtained.

It was presumed that these 'majoritarian' rules would favor the fabrication of an oversized, clear parliamentary majority at every election. But unfair district apportionment of seats combined with uneven distribution of votes for different parties across the territory could make the winner in votes a loser in seats.

The electoral system created strong incentives to form large, heterogeneous coalitions of parties at the first round, in the expectation of obtaining the over-representation promised to the most voted list in every district. The numerous, small parties in the broadly populated political center tended very quickly to join either of the two large coalitions with more extreme parties that were formed on the two sides of the left–right spectrum, thus producing increasing bipolarization. The party leaders' strategies to form electoral coalitions were developed asymmetrically on the left and the right and with no continuity from one election to another. In these conditions, the electoral system produced two winners in seats with a minority of votes: in 1933 in favor of the right and in 1936 in favor of the left. On both occasions the opposition to the winner in seats took the form of an armed rebellion.

In the first election in June 1931, the Republican parties (including Left-Republicans, Radical-Socialists, Radicals, and Liberals), running together with the Socialists, obtained a very large, centrist majority over the Monarchists. The Republicans obtained over-representation and a large majority of seats on their own (even without those of the Socialists). In contrast, the disunited Monarchist groups, including Catholics, Agrarians, and Basque and Catalan regionalists, were under-represented.

In the second election in November 1933, the Republican center split into two factions. In contrast to the so-called Left-Republicans and the Radical-Socialists, center-right Republicans, like the Radicals and the Liberals, were now ready to collaborate with the recovered Monarchists.

The center-right Republicans reached irregularly distributed, sometimes informal, pre-electoral agreements in most districts with a reinforced right which was able to organize a new large party, the CEDA, with the Catholics and the Agrarians. Both the candidacies of the center-right and those of the right obtained fewer votes but were given more seats than the more separated center-left and left parties if the latter are counted together, as shown in the electoral results compiled in Table 3.3. Specifically, while the separated center-left and left partes obtained (22 + 14) 36 per cent of votes, they were given only (13 + 8) 21 per cent of seats. This was because the parties on the right half of the spectrum attained narrow majorities or pluralities in a high number of districts and were rewarded with oversized representation. In contrast, the center-left Republicans and the left Socialists, now running separately, became frequent district 'minorities' and were badly affected by the electoral system favoring the larger candidacies.

After the 1933 election, a rather moderate Cabinet led by the center-right

TABLE 3.3. *Bipolarized, nonmonotonic Spanish elections (1931–6)*

1931			1933			1936		
	Votes	Seats		Votes	Seats		Votes	Seats
Republican–Socialist Conjunction	85	89	Left	22	13	Popular Front	46	60
			Center-left	14	8			
			Center-right	30	37	Center-right	23	15
Right	15	11	Right	34	42	National Front	31	25
	100	100		100	100		100	100

Note: Under majoritarian rules, large coalition candidacies obtain higher proportions of seats than votes, in contrast to separated candidacies. Votes and seats are given in percentages. As in other tables in this book, percentages are rounded by the method of greatest remainders: the integers with the greatest remainders are rounded up until they sum 100, and then the other integers are rounded down (following Balinski and Rachev, 1997).

Left: Socialists (PSOE, USC); Communists (PCE); and minor groups.

Center-left: Left-Republicans (AR/IR, UR); Radical-Socialists (RS), Regionals (ERC, ANV, ORGA).

Center-right: Radicals (PRR); Liberals (PP, PC, ASR, DLR, LD); Regionals (PNV, LC); Independents.

Right: Catholics (AN/CEDA); Agrarians (PA); Monarchists (RE, CT); Fascists (FE).

Source: For 1931, Author's calculations with data from Tusell (1982). For 1933, Irwin (1991: 269). For 1936, Linz and de Miguel (1977: 34); Linz (1978: 147–9) with data from Tusell (1971, 1976). More details in Colomer (2000*b*).

Radical party was formed, thanks to the parliamentary support of the right. The largest party in votes and seats, the Catholic CEDA, did not enter the Cabinet directly. Despite this, and in the belief that the CEDA would eventually obtain more influence, in October 1934 the extreme left of the Socialists and the Anarchists organized an armed rebellion to which they were able to attract some center-left Republicans. The rebellion was fought by the army and resulted in more than 1,500 deaths (on both sides) and about 15,000 prisoners.

The election of February 1936 was a kind of revenge. The center-left Republicans and the left Socialists and Communists united and formed the Popular Front. This was basically an electoral coalition that demanded amnesty for the prisoners of the 1934 rebellion and the re-establishment of previous reforms. Significant disagreement on other issues between moderate reformists and revolutionaries was reflected in the programmatic weakness of the coalition.

The center-right Republicans, and especially the Radical party, were badly affected because of their record in the incumbent Cabinet, which underwent several scandals concerning corruption. Some members of the Radical party joined the Popular Front. A new Center party improvised by the incumbent prime minister was not even able to recruit candidates in half the districts. Therefore, this time it was the center-right that was weaker than the large coalition of the center-left and left parties. In addition, the fear of wasting their votes moved a significant number of citizens to vote strategically either for the Popular Front or for the rightist National Front formed by the Catholics, Agrarians, and Monarchists.

The increasing bipolarization promoted by the incentives supplied by the electoral system did not correspond to the degree of bipolarization that could be found among voters' sincere preferences. Using the preferential vote available on the ballot, the citizens gave more votes to the moderate candidates within each coalition or bloc. The center-left Republicans obtained more support than did the Socialists or the Communists in the same lists, while the Catholics received more votes than the Monarchists. In the knowledge of these voters' preferences, party leaders facilitated these choices by placing the more moderate candidates at the top of the lists. Moderate candidates within each of the two blocs were much closer by aligned to each other than to the extreme candidates of their own bloc. In fact, some of the candidates running on opposite coalitions had been members of the same electoral candidacy (or even the same party) just a few years earlier. The more extreme parties obtained almost no support. The Fascists of Falange, with less than 1 per cent of the vote did not obtain representation. The Communist party obtained only 2 per cent of votes, but it was given some over-representation through the coalition lists of the Popular Front (Jackson 1965: 518–25; Linz 1978).

This time it was the Popular Front that obtained fewer votes but was given more seats than the less unified center-right and right parties, if the latter are counted together, as shown in Table 3.3. Specifically, while the separated center-right and right parties obtained (23 + 31) 54 per cent of votes, they were given only (15 + 25) 40 per cent of seats. Out of 60 districts, the Popular Front was given over-representation by winning in 30 districts (including all the urban constituencies), frequently with narrow majorities, and in three districts by plurality against the disunited majority of the center-right and the right. The right and center-right candidacies won in the remaining twenty-seven districts, including all the five that needed a second round due to their division in the first round, with relatively larger electoral support.

If the center-right and right parties had run in perfect unity in the first round and had obtained the same amount of votes that they had received separately, they would have collected a majority in votes but still fewer seats than the Popular Front, according to district-per-district calculations (Tusell 1976: 111). This indicates that the perverse results were not only the consequence of party leaders' asymmetrical skill in forming electoral coalitions but also a mechanical result of majoritarian electoral rules and unfair apportionment. The uneven distribution of votes for the different political groups in the territory only amplified the distorting effects of the drawing of districts. As a consequence of both the electoral rules and the coalition strategies, relatively minor changes in voters' choices between successive elections produced upheavals in institutional representation.

Following the 1936 election, a rather moderate Cabinet led by center-left Republicans was formed without direct participation of the Socialists or other leftist parties. Yet, a military uprising, initially supported by the Catholics and Agrarians, was consummated less than five months after the election. The division of Spain into two camps supporting the Republic and the rebel military, roughly conformed to the territorial division of votes in the previous election. The two blocs, however, were soon dominated by the initiative of the Communists and the Fascists, respectively. During an almost three-year cruel Civil War, about 300,000 people were killed and a comparable number went into exile. The outburst of a bipolarized conflict at the induction of electoral institutions, rather than from social unrest, greatly surprised many Spaniards. The lack of understanding why civil war had occurred fed a great fear that a similar conflict might reappear in the future. The subsequent military dictatorship lasted for almost forty years.

Australian Winning Losers

Majority-preferential voting or 'alternative vote' has been used in Australia to elect most state parliaments and the House of Representatives since 1918 (it was also used for the election of the Australian Senate between 1919 and 1948). According to some expert analysis, 'the introduction of preferential voting in single-member districts in the last few years of the 19th century [in some state elections] followed recognition of the fact that plurality elections had often given results noticeably inconsistent with the wishes of the voters' (Wright 1984: 129).

These inconsistencies included the production of oversized parliamentary majorities as typically happens with plurality rule. More distorting, plurality rule had produced some visibly nonmonotonic relations between votes and seats. At least in one Australian federal election with plurality rule in 1903, the Protectionist party obtained fewer popular votes than both the Free Trade and the Labour parties, but it was allocated more seats than either of them. In addition to correcting generic inconsistencies, 'some people in the Labour movement believed that preferential voting was introduced specifically to reduce the chances of the election of Labour candidates', whose electoral support was more concentrated in the territory than the Conservatives (Wright 1986: 127–8).

Majority-preferential voting is an eliminatory method. Each voter ranks all candidates in the ballot and if one candidate obtains a majority of first preferences in the district, he or she is elected. If not, the candidate with the lowest total is eliminated from the count. The votes of the eliminated candidate's supporters are transferred to their next preference and a new scrutiny is proceeded with, just as if the excluded candidate did not appear on any ballot. The process is repeated until one candidate attains a majority.

Thus, not all individuals' votes are valued equally. For some voters, only their first preference is accounted; for others (those favoring minority candidates), several preferences are taken into account. The process of transferring votes to the secondary preferences of some voters may lead to the election of a candidate thanks to the second, third, or a lower preference of some voters with minority tastes despite the fact that some other candidate is preferred by a majority of voters.

Although the elimination procedure might favor centrist, relatively socially efficient candidates in every district, uneven multiple districts tend to produce globally nonmonotonic results. Majority losers in votes have become majority winners in seats in a significant number of Australian elections with majority-preferential voting, both at the state and federal level. Specifically, the Labour party obtained more votes but was allocated fewer seats than any other party in three federal elections before the end of World War II (in 1922 and 1925 in favor of the Nationalist party and in 1937 in favor of the United Australia party). In a later period, 1949–98, the winner in votes has become a loser in seats in nine out of twenty-one federal elections, always to the disadvantage of the Laborites and in favor of the Liberal party (in 1949, 1951, 1955, 1958, 1963, 1975, 1977, 1980, and 1998). In three other elections (in 1954, 1961, and 1969), despite the fact that the sum of votes for the Liberal party and for the National (previously called Country) party was lower than the votes for the Labour party, their seats were sufficient to form a parliamentary majority and a coalition Cabinet against the most voted party. All of this is due to the uneven distribution of Labour votes in the territory, which is made relevant by the boundaries of electoral districts and the apportionment of seats. (On apportionment in Australia, see Hughes 1990.)

In the period after World War II, two-thirds of Australian parliamentary Cabinets did not contain the median voter's most preferred party. The median voter's party can be identified on the basis of ordering the political parties along the left–right axis. In this case, just the noncontroversial location of the Communist party on the left of the Labour party and the sum of their votes is sufficient to identify whether the Labour party or any alternative winner contains the median voter. In precisely fourteen out of twenty-one elections, the median voter's most preferred party was not included in the winning Cabinet (in 1954, 1958, 1961, 1963, 1969, 1972, 1974, 1983, 1984, 1990, 1993, and 1998).

In sum, majority-preferential voting in the election of the lower House of Australia has not suppressed the kind of inconsistencies previously experienced with plurality rule (although it might have given satisfaction to those seeking to undermine the representation of the Labour party). In most elections since 1949, majority-preferential voting has fabricated a winner that does not reflect the wishes of the voters monotonically and can be considered to be socially ineffi-cient.

The French Nonmonotonic National Assembly

Majority rule with a second-round-runoff was introduced in France for the elec-tion of the National Assembly by Louis Napoleon after his *coup d'état* in 1851, was enforced most of the time during the Third Republic (1873–1940), and was reintroduced by decree by General Charles de Gaulle after his *coup d'état* in 1958. In the French Fifth Republic, all those candidates who have obtained a certain percentage of votes in the first round of the election can run in the second round. Since the threshold was initially placed at 5 per cent of votes cast, at 10 per cent in 1967, and at 12.5 per cent of registered votes from 1976, the proced-ure may allow more than two candidates to run in the second round and therefore it does not guarantee a majority winner. But, party strategies have favored desist-ing in favor of the largest candidate on the same side of the left–right spectrum, in order to avoid the victory of a more distant rival by plurality, thus creating two-candidate races in most districts. 'Divide and win' is, however, still a strategy that certain party leaders have incentives to try.

With this procedure, de Gaulle aimed at producing Gaullist narrow majorities in many districts, many of them filled at the second round, thanks to the elimina-tion or the withdrawal of Conservative and centrist candidates after the first round. In particular, his aim was to cut off the Communists, who had been the first party in votes in the five elections of the Fourth Republic (with an average of over 25 per cent), to a few districts where they would obtain majority or substantial support at the first round.

Accordingly, 'small rural departments were over-represented. Moreover, urban areas were frequently divided and attached to neighboring rural areas in constituencies in which the rural votes would predominate. This was in part the result of the instruction to the prefects that the boundaries should be drawn in such a way as to weaken the Communist Party (but not to discriminate against any other political force). The Ministry of the Interior checked the draft boundaries and sometimes modified them, for De Gaulle was anxious not to penalize leading non-Communist opponents' (Campbell 1965: 129; Cole and Campbell 1989: 92; similar presentations can be found in Macridis and Brown 1960: 238; Williams 1970: 102–3).

The first Assembly election with majority-runoff in 1958 produced effects overwhelmingly oriented in the expected direction. The Gaullist party (at the time called National Union for the Republic, UNR) obtained 21 per cent of votes but was given 43 per cent of seats. The Communist party, which was second in votes (the first in metropolitan France excluding overseas territories), was given only 2 per cent of seats, becoming the sixth largest group in the Assembly. Similar results occurred in the following four elections from 1962, in which the Communists ran second in votes behind the Gaullists, but became third or fourth in seats, and always behind the less-voted for Socialists.

Extreme candidates like the Communists were disadvantaged because many voters of the moderate left turned to other candidates in the second round. But, all the left parties were globally disadvantaged. In 1958, Communists and Socialists together obtained more than 7 million votes and the Gaullists received 4.2 million. But while the first two were given in total only 54 seats, the latter was given 198 seats. Likewise, in 1962, 1967, and 1973, the two major center-right and right parties, the Gaullists and their Republican allies, were together given a majority of seats despite having obtained fewer votes than the Communists and the Socialists, counted together. This created incentives for the left to unite at the first round. By doing so, the Socialists became the first party in votes in 1978, but they were still relegated to the third place in seats behind the Gaullist Rally for the Republic (RPR) and the center-right Union of French Democracy (UDF).

De Gaulle's strategy had been one of bipolarization in the expectation of drawing support from intermediate voters for his nationalist, populist, anti-Communist alternative at the second round. Eventually, the growing electoral support for the nonextreme Socialist Party (PS), mostly at the expense of the Communists, backfired. In 1981, the RPR and the UDF, running separately, obtained together more votes but fewer seats than the PS, which was given a majority of seats in the Assembly. In 1988, the two center-right and right parties mentioned earlier ran together in the first round; their candidacy was the first in votes, but became the second in seats after the Socialists.

In sum, major distortions and nonmonotonic relations between party votes and seats have occurred in eight out of the ten Assembly majority-runoff elections in the French Fifth Republic (in all but those of 1993 and 1997; the 1986 election was held with proportional representation).

From the point of view of social utility, however, the results of the National Assembly elections have been less inefficient than the previously presented distortions may suggest. In a number of cases, the party which was unfairly rewarded with seats by the electoral system was able to form a majority in the Assembly that included the median voter's preference. The median voter was captured by all the center-right parliamentary coalitions and Cabinets in the 1960s and early 1970s, as well as that of the first Socialist parliamentary majority and Cabinet in 1981.

However, on at least two occasions the winner cannot be considered to be socially efficient. In 1978, the most voted PS and its allies of the left gathered together a majority of votes, thus containing the median voter on the left–right axis, but the RPR and the UDF were together given almost two-thirds of seats and formed a Cabinet. In contrast, in 1988 the most voted united coalition of center-right contained the median voter (due to some significant electoral support for the extreme right), but the Socialist party was able to form a parliamentary Cabinet.

Biased Presidents
The rule of majority-runoff was introduced by General de Gaulle not only for the election of the French National Assembly but also for the direct election of himself and the following Presidents of France. It was ratified by referendum in 1962. Majority-runoff has produced more inefficient results in the French presidential elections than in the Assembly elections discussed earlier.

Relatively moderate or popular candidates, such as Georges Pompidou in 1969 (still under the influence of de Gaulle's period), Valéry Giscard d'Estaing in 1974 (broadly), and François Mitterrand in 1981 (narrowly), won with the support of consistent majorities including the political center. Yet in the other three out of the first six elections, the bipolarization enhanced by the electoral system made nonmedian voter's candidates elected Presidents. De Gaulle in 1965 and Mitterrand in 1988 were not the median voter's candidates by relatively narrow margins, and Jacques Chirac was certainly not in 1995. All of them won as a result of the role of irrelevant candidates at the first round.

The electoral results of the first round of the French presidential elections in 1965, 1988, and 1995 are shown in Table 3.4. The median voter's candidate, that is, the only one who would win by majority against any other candidate (or Condorcet winner), is in brackets, while the winner by majority at the second round is in italics. These socially inefficient elections are now submitted to a summary analysis.

The dimension of 'regime support' became highly salient during the electoral campaign of 1965. This was the first direct election of President after de Gaulle's coup against the Fourth Republic and the end of Algeria's war after he granted the colony its independence. The salience of the regime dimension can be captured by the fact that, in the second round, de Gaulle attracted about one-fourth of leftist voters to his policy of political 'stability' and national 'grandeur', while virtually all pro-French Algeria, extreme right voters, joined the left against de Gaulle. On the regime dimension, the Democratic center candidate (supported by the Christian-Democrats and some Radical groups), Jean Lecanuet, occupied an intermediate, potentially more consensual position. (Data on the salience of dimensions during the electoral campaign are given by the polls and analyses of

TABLE 3.4. *French presidential elections with no median-winner (1965–95)*

	1965		1988		1995	
LEFT			Laguiller	2	Laguiller	5
	Barbu	2	Lajoinie	7	Hue	9
			Juquin	2		
	Mitterrand	32	*Mitterrand*	34	Jospin	23
			Waechler	3	Voynet	3
	Marcilhacy	2				
MEDIAN	[Lecanuet]	16	[Barre]	17	[Balladur]	19
	de Gaulle	44	Chirac	20	*Chirac*	20
					de Villiers	5
RIGHT	Tixier	4	Le Pen	15	Le Pen	16
		100		100		100

Note: Numbers are percentages of votes at the first round. The median voter's candidate is between brackets; the winner at the second round is in italics.

For the relative spatial position of the candidates, see Mendès-France and Laumonier (1967); Pierce (1995, tables 4.2 and 8.1).

Fondation Nationale des Sciences Politiques 1967.)

On the left–right dimension, Lecanuet was placed in the middle, between the Socialists and the Communists on one side and the Gaullists and the extreme right on the other, obtaining the support of the median voter in the first round. The bridging role of Lecanuet on the two issue-dimensions is also shown by the fact that, according to both the available polls and post-electoral analysis, in contrast to the consistency of the other candidates' voters' behavior in the two rounds, Lecanuet's voters split: about 60 per cent chose de Gaulle at the second round and about 40 per cent chose Mitterrand (Mendès-France and Laumonier 1967).

There is some additional, perhaps persuasive evidence in support of the hypothesis that had Lecanuet had the chance to be compared with the other candidates by pairs he would have been the majority winner. An expert's summary of a collection of pre-electoral polls states that 'the opinion sector who is favorable to Lecanuet [Democratic Center] bends mostly for an arrangement with the Gaullists, whereas the opinion sector identifying with Mitterrand against de Gaulle wishes, mostly, a rapprochement with the Democratic Center' rather than with the Communists. This may suggest that, first, some relative ideological closeness between most Lecanuet's and de Gaulle's voters, which could form a majority against the left, and, second, the readiness of most leftist voters to support Lecanuet against de Gaulle had the chance been given. Also, post-electoral polls showed large support for the Centrists' balancing role. An absolute majority of voters thought that if the Gaullist Cabinet had needed the support of Lecanuet's party in the Assembly, this would have allowed the latter to control the Cabinet's action (as wished by the left) without the risk of provoking Cabinet instability (against the fears of the Gaullists) (Rossi-Landi 1967). In future years, Lecanuet was seen as embodying 'the nostalgia of centrism, the refusal of two blocs, of manicheism, of bipolarization. Yet this was to fight against the voting rule, against the presidential thing, against the mood of the time' (Duhamel 1983: 73).

The median voter's candidate for President of France in 1988 was the former Prime Minister (under Giscard), economist Raymond Barre, then the candidate of the center-right coalition UDF (formed by Conservative Republicans, Christian-Democrats, Radicals, and Social-Democrats). On the basis of his previous record in government, his party support, and his policy program, Barre was located between two other major candidates, the incumbent Socialist President Mitterrand on his left and the Gaullist Prime Minister Jacques Chirac on his right.

According to some expert analysis of the election, in order to gain access to the second round, the 'Chirac campaign was fundamentally a first-round campaign directed, in spite of its ostensible targeting of Mitterrand, against Raymond Barre' (Gaffney 1989: 134). The latter's entourage, in response, asserted on every occasion that Barre was the best candidate to face Mitterrand in the second round. Finally, the incumbent Mitterrand and the more populist Chirac (the latter in particular criticizing Barre's free market-oriented economic policy proposals) obtained greater support in the first round. As could be expected from the previous insights, the Socialist candidate Mitterrand won in the second round.

It may be interesting to note that, in the honeymoon of his re-election, President Mitterrand immediately dissolved the Assembly and called a new legislative election, but the Socialist party did not obtain an absolute majority. Despite of Barre's defeat, 'Mitterrand's [further] appeals to the center, [his] calls for *ouverture*, and the results of the legislative elections, placed Barre in a nodal position in French politics' (Gaffney 1989: 137).

At the next presidential election in 1995, the retirement of François Mitterrand after fourteen years in the Elysée and the discrediting of the Socialists after a number of scandals concerning corruption gave the center-right a better opportunity to win the Presidency of France. According to the dominant opinion of the time, whichever serious candidate from the mainstream right could make it to the second round was almost certain to win.

After the victory of the center-right in the nonconcurrent Assembly election of 1993 (in one of the few 'monotonic' elections previously analyzed) and the corresponding Cabinet formation, Prime Minister Edouard Balladur was almost taken for granted as the future President by public opinion polls and most of the media. Balladur, a member of the RPR led by Jacques Chirac, was seen as 'reassuring, unpolemical, managerial, thoughtful and competent' in style, as well as 'circumspect, wise, slightly older, moderate in manner, more centrist in outlook and policy proposals' and more pro-European than Chirac (Gaffney 1997, 102–4). Balladur's 'cohabitation' as Prime Minister with President Mitterrand in 1993–5 is widely considered to have been much more effective, smooth, and cooperative than the previous, rather conflictive 'cohabitation' between Mitterrand and Chirac

(1986–8). Balladur was backed by nearly all the center-right UDF and some prominent members of the Gaullist RPR, including all his ministers from both parties, while Chirac had to rely mostly upon his control of the RPR party machine.

We have a very interesting series of opinion polls which were collected and published before the first round of the 1995 election. They include an unusual and enlightening question about the citizen's future electoral choice in different hypotheses of pairs of candidates surviving to the second round. According to the poll results, Balladur would beat Jospin (at least 55 to 45), Balladur would beat Chirac (at least 54 to 46), and Chirac would also beat Jospin although by lower margins (53 to 47, on the same poll). On all the polls Balladur was the Condorcet-winner, the only candidate who would be preferred by an absolute majority of voters to any alternative. (The series of three IFOP polls including this question was completed and compiled in the weekly magazine *L'Express*, 16 February 1995.)

Yet, after a very active campaign for the first round, Jacques Chirac obtained 21 per cent of votes, scarcely one and a half percentage points more than the perhaps too self-confident Balladur, and went to the second round together with the Socialist candidate. Chirac's first round score was barely more than his own in the elections of 1981 and 1988, and far less than any previous successful presidential candidate in France. In the second round, Chirac beat Jospin by almost exactly the margin forecast in the poll mentioned above (53 to 47). Balladur, the median voter's candidate, 'appeared to many after his defeat as the best President France had just lost, a statesperson deprived of office because he did not know the street-fighting rules of party political clashes' (Gaffney 1997: 111).

Interestingly, on two of the three mentioned occasions the nonmedian elected President was eventually forced to 'cohabitate' with a winning median voter's Prime Minister of different ideological orientation, thus creating the opportunity for intermediate, probably more socially efficient compromises between President and Cabinet. This was the case with Mitterrand and Balladur in 1993–5, and with Chirac and Jospin in 1997–2002. In a later section of this book we will discuss how and to what extent cooperation between different winners in separately elected institutions can 'correct' some of the distortions in social utility produced by single-winner electoral rules such as majority-runoff.

Plurality

Plurality (or relative majority) rule is the most effective voting rule. Even with simple categoric ballot, it always produces a winner (except in the case of ties, which is practically negligible in mass elections).

It seems that relative majority rule emerged as an accepted, although not widely noticed, principle for collective decision making in late medieval Europe merely as an expedient resource in response to the failure of unanimity and absolute majority rules to guarantee an outcome. In England, a 1430 statute introduced the majority principle for direct elections in shires. Those with 'the greatest number' of supporters were to be chosen for the Parliament. The sheriff in charge of electoral assemblies could estimate the people's desires either by listening to the shouts of supporters of different candidates or by counting heads and declaring elected those who had more votes than anybody else. Usually, however, the official did not bother to ensure that a candidate was elected by absolute majority, especially if the electoral assembly was a tumultuous affair. 'The rule of the bare majority was thus established' and members of Parliament continued to be elected by relative, not absolute, majority in a system which came to be known as 'first-past-the-post' (Hart 1992: 5).

Even if there might have been similar processes in other countries, the English rule directly expanded to political elections in British colonies and a few imitators in four continents. From the United States, it also expanded to Latin America for direct elections of presidents. While plurality rule might have produced relatively efficient results in simple late medieval societies, it tends to produce highly inefficient results in complex electorates.

With plurality rule, the alternative with the highest number of votes, whatever that number may be, becomes the absolute winner. Thus, the higher the number of alternatives submitted to election, the higher the likelihood that the winner will have only a minority support and the smaller the winning minority can be. However small the potentially winning minority, the general principle of single-winner rules applies and the 'winner-takes-all'.

Plurality rule is most vulnerable to losers' strategies. By introducing relatively few new issues or creating a few new alternatives, plurality losers can alter the winner, thus producing high instability and unpredictability of the outcome in the long run. Plurality rule is more vulnerable to these strategies than majority and qualified-majority rules.

Stated more precisely, plurality winners are highly 'dependent on irrelevant alternatives'. This means that which alternative becomes the plurality winner depends on whether or not some other alternatives are available and can be voted for. Let us assume, for example, that party Left wins against party Right in a pairwise election. Yet, the same voters with the same preferences and voting with the same procedure may make party Right the winner if the choice is presented as being between parties Left, Center, and Right (and a sufficient number of voters prefer Center to Left). The previous loser can become the winner for the same electorate with the same preferences, despite obtaining the same or perhaps even fewer votes than in the previous voting. The new winner depends on the introduction of a new alternative, Center, which does not win (it is 'irrelevant').

Thus, plurality rule works differently with different numbers of parties or candidates. The strategies aimed at altering the number of contenders, such as 'divide and win' and 'merge and win', are highly encouraged in elections by plurality rule. The difference in results that can be produced by plurality rule with different numbers of available alternatives can be most prominently observed by comparing the cases of the United Kingdom, where a three-party system in votes has existed during most of the 20th century, and the United States, which is much closer to a two-party system. As will be documented below, the proportion of parliamentary elections producing socially inefficient winners is higher in the United Kingdom than in the United States.

The plurality winner can be socially efficient if there are only two candidates (then it is equivalent to majority rule) or if a large centrist party is able to maintain its rivals on the left and the right at sufficiently distant positions so as to win the election (as essentially occurred in India with the Congress party, from the country's independence in the late 1940s until the 1980s). However, plurality rule does not usually produce socially efficient winners close to the median voter's preference with more than two parties, as will be observed in the following empirical analyses.

In plurality elections with multiple districts, inconsistent or 'nonmonotonic' relations between votes and seats include the paradox that the loser in popular votes can become the winner in seats. This distortion can be even more striking with plurality rule than with majority rule, as illustrated in Table 3.5. In an election with three (or more) alternatives, even the alternative obtaining the smallest number of votes can become the largest majority alternative in seats. In the example in Table 3.5, an alternative with less than one-third of votes obtains two-thirds of seats against two other more voted alternatives. With plurality rule, the winner may not correspond to the median voter's preference either at the district level or at multidistrict level with relatively high likelihood.

Plurality Procedures

Alternative procedures to categoric ballot based on plurality rule include rank-order count and approval voting. The 18th-century French academician Jean-Charles de Borda invented the first procedure. Rank-order count, also called Borda procedure, requires the voter to order preferences over all the available alternatives giving zero points to the least preferred one, one point to the second-to-least preferred, two points to the next, and so on. The alternative with the highest sum of points becomes the winner (Borda 1784).

Approval voting with plurality rule allows the voters to vote for those alternatives that they consider acceptable, from a minimum of one to a maximum of all minus one. The alternative with the most votes becomes the winner (as formulated by Steven Brams and Peter Fishburn 1983).

Both procedures tend to produce results that are more consistent with voters' preferences and bring about higher social utility than plurality rule

TABLE 3.5. *Winning losers with plurality rule*

		Parties:		
		Left	Center	Right
Districts	A	35	25	*40*
	B	30	30	*40*
	C	40	*45*	15
	Total votes:	105 >	100 >	95
	Total seats:	0 <	1 <	2

Note: The Table illustrates three-party competition in three single-member districts. The numbers in each district refer to percentages of votes. The winners of a seat in each district are in italics. As can be seen, the order of parties in votes, Left > Center > Right, is exactly the opposite to the order of parties in seats.

with categoric ballot. Yet both rank-order count and approval voting are vulnerable to strategic voting, which made Jean-Charles de Borda warn that his scheme was conceived 'only for honest persons'. Voters with information regarding others' preferences and whose preferred candidates have wide support can concentrate their votes on one or a few candidates and relegate their intermediate preferences to the bottom or make them unacceptable. In conditions of complete information, strategic voting should lead most voters to vote as they do with categoric ballot. Similar favorable conditions for strategic voting would likely be created by mass survey polls (Brams 1982; Merrill and Nagel 1987; Weber 1995).

Neither of the two procedures guarantees a Condorcet winner; in other words, the winner by rank-order count or by approval voting could be beaten by majority by some other defeated alternative. This means, in particular, that the median voter's preference on a single dimension—the alternative producing maximum social utility—may not win with either of these procedures.

A form of approval balloting with qualified-majority rule was used for the election of forty-one popes by the cardinals from 1294 to 1621. The original voting rules written in Latin by cardinal Jacobi Gaytani in the late 13th century were found by the author in a collection of ecclesiastical rules called *Ordinarium Sanctae Romanae Ecclesiae* (Mabillon and Germain 1689, vol. 2: 245ff.; story and analysis in Colomer and McLean 1998).

Nowadays, both rank-order count and approval voting with plurality rule have been used in a few academic and professional organizations (Brams and Nagel 1991). Yet, comparing unfavorably with the easiness of categoric ballot, none of these procedures have been used in mass political elections.

Cases: Plurality Parliamentary and Presidential Elections

Plurality rule with categoric ballot is used for mass elections in two sets of political institutions: (1) Parliamentary elections in parliamentary regimes based on the British model, that is, in the United Kingdom and most former British colonies. (2) Presidential elections in presidential regimes in the United States and in almost every Latin-American democracy until the 1970s. However, frequent distorted results, including some presidential elections in Peru, Brazil, and Chile which are analyzed below, moved most Latin-American countries to adopt the majority-runoff rule for presidential elections in order to avoid some of the drawbacks usually associated with the former formula.

As will be seen, dependence on irrelevant alternatives, nonmonotonic results, and relatively low social utility outcomes can be found with relatively high frequency in elections with plurality rule.

Absolute Minority Winners

Plurality rule is used for parliamentary elections in the United Kingdom and in most former British colonies including the United States of America, Canada, New Zealand (until 1993), and India (Australia moved to majority rule in 1919, as explained above). Under plurality or relative majority rule, a party can be given an absolute majority of seats even if it obtains much less than a majority of votes. In British-style parliamentary regimes (all of the above except for the United States) the single-party Cabinet becomes the absolute winner. The less restrictive the number of parties competing in elections and obtaining the voters' support, the higher the likelihood that the typical popular minority-based, parliamentary majority Cabinet will be socially biased and less socially efficient than any hypothetical alternative organized around the median voter's preference. This is, in fact, the typical occurrence in the United Kingdom, which is replicated with relative frequency in the other countries mentioned. In a certain proportion of cases in which a minority party in popular votes becomes the single-party Cabinet, it could be said that, in contrast to the conventional motto of the electoral system, the loser takes all.

Precisely, Cabinets supported by a minority of voters were formed in the United Kingdom in twenty-four out of thirty-nine elections to the House of Commons in the period 1885–1997, that is, in 62 per cent of the cases (more precisely, in ten out of twenty-four elections before World War II and in fourteen out of fifteen elections afterwards). On two occasions, in paradoxical contrast, a single-party absolute majority of votes was not awarded with a majority of seats (in 1886 and 1900). In six British parliamentary elections, the loser in votes became the winner in seats: in 1892 and twice in 1910 in favor of the Liberals against the most-voted Conservatives; in 1929 and February 1974 in favor of the Labourites against the most-voted Conservatives; and in 1951 in favor of the

Conservatives against the most-voted Labourites. The alternative victories of Conservatives and Labourites since the 1930s provoked high political instability and heavily biased Cabinets supported by socially extreme minorities. None of the British Cabinets formed after the fifteen elections of the period 1945–97 was supported by the median voter.

In New Zealand, Cabinets in minority among the voters were formed in 65 per cent of the cases, that is, in twenty-two out of thirty-nine elections in the period 1890–1993 (until plurality rule was replaced with proportional representation). In four New Zealand elections, the loser in votes became the winner in seats: in 1911 and 1928 in favor of the Reform party against the most voted Liberals, and in 1978 and 1981 in favor of the National party against the most voted Labourites. These distortions produced by the electoral system reduced the social efficiency of New Zealand Cabinets despite the fact that the country had a very simplified, almost pure two-party system that might have produced majority popular support for the winning party: less than three-fourths of Cabinets in the period 1946–93 were supported by the median voter.

Results are not better in India. Cabinets with a minority of voters' support were formed in 69 per cent of the cases in the period 1952–98 (in nine out of thirteen elections). The median voter supported slightly more than two-thirds of Cabinets thanks to the already mentioned central role played by the Congress party.

The frequency of social biases and nonmonotonic results is somewhat less notorious, although still highly remarkable, in North America. In Canada, fifteen out of thirty-three parliamentary Cabinets in the period 1878–1997 (45 per cent) were supported by a minority of popular votes. On three occasions the loser in votes became the winner in seats: in 1896 in favor of the Liberals against the most-voted Conservatives, and in 1957 and 1979 in favor of the Conservatives against the most-voted Liberals. In the period 1945–97, only seven out of seventeen Cabinets were supported by the median voter.

Finally, plurality rule produced a single-party parliamentary majority with a minority of votes in 30 per cent of elections to the United States House of Representatives, that is, in twenty-six out of eighty-seven cases in the period 1828–1998. Nonmonotonic results have been relatively frequent. On ten occasions, the loser in votes became the winner in seats: in 1846 and 1854 in favor of the Whigs, in the first case against the electoral majority of the Democrats and in the latter producing an absolute majority of seats for the Whigs despite having obtained only 12 per cent of popular support and being the fourth party in votes; in 1836 and 1848 in favor of the Democrats against the most-voted Whigs, in the first case again against an electoral majority for the other party; in 1880 and 1888 in favor of the Republicans against the most-voted Democrats; and in 1858, 1914, 1942, and 1952 in favor of the Democrats against the most-voted Republicans (who obtained an absolute majority of votes in 1942).

Minority White House

The President of the United States is not directly elected by the voters but chosen by the Electoral College, a body which is nowadays elected mostly by plurality rule in fifty-one multimember districts (the states plus the District of Columbia). As in multidistrict parliaments of the British model previously analyzed, the US Presidential Electoral College tends to oversize the representation of the most voted candidate and, with relative frequency, to produce an absolute majority of College electors on the basis of a minority of popular votes. Despite the fact that a simplified party system based on two major alternatives has existed for most of the time since the introduction of competitive presidential elections in 1828, 37 per cent of United States presidents since then, that is, sixteen out of forty-three presidents, have been elected with a minority of popular votes. Minority presidents elected in the period 1828–1996 are the following: the Whig Zachary Taylor in 1848; the Republicans Abraham Lincoln in 1860, Rutherforf Hayes in 1876, James Garfield in 1880, Benjamin Harrison in 1888 and Richard Nixon in 1968; and the Democrats James Polk in 1844, James Buchanan in 1856, Grover Cleveland in 1884 and 1892, Woodrow Wilson in 1912 and 1916, Harry Truman in 1948, John Kennedy in 1960, and William Clinton in 1992 and 1996.

At least on two occasions, the winner in popular votes became the loser in the College and thus in the presidential choice. In 1876, the Governor of New York, Democrat Samuel Tilden, received over a half of the popular votes cast (51 per cent), leading the Republican Rutherford Hayes by more than a quarter million votes or three percentage points. But three disputed Southern states in which fraud and intimidation of black voters was widespread, Louisiana, South Carolina, and Florida, as well as Oregon, sent double sets of College elector returns. The contest was held still in the ashes of the Civil War and, faced with new racial issues, 'at the time probably more people dreaded an armed conflict than had anticipated a like outcome to the secession movement of 1860–61' (Haworth 1906: 168). An Electoral Commission established by Congress and made up of a majority of Republicans, recognized Republican Rutherford Hayes' electors from the above-mentioned states. Hayes was elected by the Electoral College by 185 to 184 votes (Michener 1989: 78–91).

In 1888, Benjamin Harrison obtained less than 48 per cent of votes but was elected president by the Electoral College over the most-voted, Grover Cleveland, who received 49 per cent of votes (a difference of 0.8 percentage points). Harrison ascribed his victory to 'Providence'. (Cleveland was elected with a minority popular support before and after that occasion, as recorded above.)

The 1960 election was particularly controversial. While the Republicans concentrated their support for Richard Nixon, the Democratic candidate John Kennedy ran in parallel to a minor states rights' candidate of his own party, Harry Byrd, who promoted hot positions on racial issues and had significant support in some Southern states. Depending on how the votes of the state of Alabama are

TABLE 3.6. *The United States presidential election (1960)*

| | Counting method A | | Counting method B | | Electoral |
	Votes	% votes	Votes	% votes	College
John F. Kennedy	34,220,984	49.48	34,049,976	49.46	303
Richard M. Nixon	34,108,157	49.32	34,108,157	49.55	219
Harry F. Byrd	638,822	0.93	491,527	0.72	15
Others	188,559	0.27	188,559	0.27	—
Total	69,156,522	100.00	68,838,219	100.00	537
					(Majority: 269)

Note: By method A, under which Kennedy is the popular vote winner, the Democratic votes in Alabama are counted twice, both for Kennedy and Byrd. By method B, under which Nixon is the popular vote winner, the Democratic votes in Alabama are divided 5/11 for Kennedy and 6/11 for Byrd, proportionally to the number of electors from the state supporting each candidate in the College.

In the College, Byrd obtained the votes of six unpledged electors from Alabama, the eight from Mississippi, plus one vote by a Republican elector in Oklahoma who defected from Nixon.

Source: Peirce (1968: 101–5). Very close results were previously published in *Congressional Quarterly*, 17 February 1961: 285–8.

counted, the candidate with most votes was either Kennedy, with a plurality of 49.48 per cent of popular votes and an advantage of 0.16 per cent, or Nixon, with a plurality of 49.55 per cent of popular votes and an advantage of 0.09 per cent, as shown in Table 3.6. Without counting Alabama, Nixon won in twenty-six states and Kennedy in twenty-three, but, thanks to having small pluralities in the more populous states, Kennedy was given a majority of electors in the College and was chosen for president.

The Democratic ballot in Alabama included five electors pledged to Kennedy and six unpledged electors who voted for Byrd in the College. Most Democratic voters in the state voted for both pledged and unpledged electors, hence creating a counting problem. If all Democratic votes in Alabama are credited to be for Kennedy, he would have won the national popular vote, but then the electors supporting Byrd would not be credited with any popular votes. Kennedy would have also won if the Democratic votes in Alabama are counted twice, both for Kennedy and for Byrd, but this would make the total number of votes higher than the total number of voters. If, in contrast, the Democratic votes in Alabama are somewhat arbitrarily distributed between Kennedy and Byrd proportionally to the number of electors supporting each candidate, Nixon would have won the national popular vote. Interestingly, the Democratic National Committee used the latter formula in allocating the number of delegate seats each state would have to the following party Convention, implicitly accepting a counting system under which Nixon would have been the popular vote winner. 'In fact, it was impossible to determine exactly what Kennedy's popular vote plurality—if it existed at all—really was' (Peirce 1968: 102).

The result of the election remained uncertain hours after the polls had closed. In the early morning hours of the following day, 9 November 1960, John Kennedy telephoned his father's longtime friend, the Mayor of Chicago, Richard Daley, who told him: 'Mr. President [*sic*], with a little bit of luck, and the help of a few close friends, you're going to carry Illinois'. Later it was discovered that Nixon had won in 93 of the 102 counties of Illinois, but lost at the state level thanks to huge numbers of votes in favor of Kennedy in Cook County (Chicago). Kennedy carried Illinois by a difference of 8,858 votes out of 4,757,409 (less than 0.2 per cent). Speculation of vote fraud was widespread, but electoral recounts bogged down in legal maneuvering on both sides. Even without the twenty-seven electors from Illinois, Kennedy would have had an absolute majority in the College. Yet, with a shift of 4,480 votes in Illinois and 4,491 in Missouri (0.01 per cent of total votes in the United States), Kennedy would not have won the Electoral College (Peirce 1968: 100–10; Reeves 1991: 213–7; on the fraud in Chicago, Kallina 1988; the loser's version in Nixon, 1990: 410–13).

From Plurality- to Majority-Latin-American Presidents

Plurality rule was used to elect the president in virtually every presidential democracy in Latin America until the 1970s. Presidential elections by plurality rule produced biased minority winners leading to political and social turmoil with relatively high frequency. As a consequence, most Latin-American countries moved to more inclusive, alternative rules, mainly majority-runoff, during their processes of redemocratization since the 1970s.

Plurality rule was replaced with majority-runoff or qualified-plurality rule in Ecuador in 1978, El Salvador in 1984, Peru and Guatemala in 1985, Brazil in 1986, Chile in 1989, Colombia in 1991, Argentina in 1973 and again in 1994, the Dominican Republic and Nicaragua in 1995, Uruguay in 1999, and Venezuela in 2000. While Costa Rica retains the rule of 40 per cent since 1936, new variants of rules based on qualified-pluralities were adopted in Argentina, where the Electoral College was replaced with the requirement of either 45 per cent of votes or 40 per cent with 10 percentage points of advantage to the second runner in the first round, and Nicaragua, with the requirement of 45 per cent in the first round. Plurality rule is still used in 2000 in Honduras, Mexico, Panama, and Paraguay. In Bolivia, the second round is transferred to Congress according to rules initially established in 1967. (Majority rule with the second round in Congress was previously used in Mexico in 1864, Cuba in 1901–25 and 1940–6, Costa Rica in 1913–32, and Chile in 1932–70. In Peru a one-third rule with the second round in Congress was enforced between 1933 and 1963, as explained below; Jones 1995*b*, 1997*a*, and the author's direct information. For discussion on the advantages of qualified-plurality rules, Shugart and Carey 1992, appendix A; see also Colomer 1999*b*.)

Table 3.7. Latin-American Presidents (1945–2000)

	Plurality rule		Majority or qualified-plurality rules	
	Majority support	Median voter included		Median voter included
			Costa Rica$_{12}$	83
Argentina$_6$	33	100	Argentina$_4$	100
Brazil$_4$	25	25	Brazil$_3$	67
Chile$_5$	20	20	Chile$_3$	100
Colombia$_{10}$	50	80	Colombia$_2$	50
Ecuador$_5$	0	0	Ecuador$_6$	67
Peru$_4$	25	75	Peru$_3$	100
Uruguay$_{10}$	20	70	Uruguay$_1$	100
Venezuela$_{10}$	40	60		
Election average:	30	59		85
Country average:	27	54		83

Note: Numbers are percentages of elections. Subindices are the number of elections for each country.

Source: Author's own calculations. In order to calculate whether the winner is the median voter's candidate, we need to establish relative candidate's or party's positions regarding the winner, but not necessarily the exact position of the candidates or parties located on the same side of the winner or even less their cardinal positions on the issue space. For this purpose, relative party positions have been found in Nohlen (1993); Mainwaring and Scully (1995); Jones (1995a); Huber and Inglehart (1995).

Results for eighty-eight presidential democratic elections in nine Latin American countries in the period 1945–2000 are shown in Table 3.7. Of these elections, fifty-four were decided by simple plurality rule, while whereas thirty-four were decided by majority or qualified-plurality rules in more recent times. The set of countries analyzed here include all of South America except for Bolivia (where all presidents since 1982 have been elected by Congress) and the nondemocratic Paraguay, plus the stably democratic Costa Rica.

A very small proportion of presidents elected with simple plurality rule obtained a majority of popular votes (16 out of 54, or 30 per cent). In only 59 per cent of elections the winning president obtained the support of the median voter.

Relatively more socially efficient results were produced by plurality elections of presidents in those countries with a simplified, almost two-party system, especially in Argentina. In cases like these, there are usually only two main candidates for president and the winner in a single round tends to collect an absolute majority of votes including that of the median voter. Yet two-party systems in pres-idential regimes may provoke relatively high levels of conflict and institutional paralysis when the President's party does not obtain a majority in the Assembly. Divided government with two parties can become an opportunity for confrontational strategies which can be overcome only by difficult unanimity agreements, as will be discussed in the next chapter. In contrast, multiparty Assemblies are more prone to produce viable, nonunanimous majorities able to develop cooperative strategies and to reach compromises with the president. Plurality elections of president in multiparty systems, however, can produce surprising winners dependent on irrelevant alternatives, as will be illustrated below.

Presidential elections with majority or qualified-plurality rules have produced more efficient results than those with simple plurality rules. With qualified plurality rules, no election needed a second round in Costa Rica and Argentina, while only eight out of eighteen elections with majority-runoff needed a second round in the other six countries. In only five of the eight second rounds the winner was different from the plurality front-runner at the first round. This suggests that majority rule induces wider coalition formation already at the first round than plurality-rule.

Precisely, in 85 per cent of the cases (twenty-nine out of thirty-four elections), the winner by majority was the median voter's candidate, in contrast to the 59 per cent of elections by plurality rule previously found. In almost all countries in which the electoral rule was changed—Argentina, Brazil, Chile, Ecuador, Peru, and Uruguay—the proportion of median voter's presidents elected by majority-runoff is higher than with plurality rule in the previous period. Only in the case of Colombia is the new proportion lower, due to the high results obtained in the noncompetitive presidential elections of the previous period of National Front agreement between the two parties (1958–70).

Three Military Coups in Latin America

A very high number of authoritarian regimes in Latin America have resulted either from military coups against weak, minority presidents elected by plurality rule, as will be illustrated below, or from unlimited re-election of a president (as will be discussed in Chapter 4, section 4.1). Presidents are particularly 'weak' or vulnerable when they are chosen with socially biased and minority support, and especially when the majority of voters would prefer an alternative candidate, that is, when the elected is not a Condorcet winner.

Three cases of presidential elections by plurality rule producing nonmedian winners and ending in military coups against 'weak' presidents are analyzed below: those in Peru in 1962–3, Brazil in 1955–60, and Chile in 1970. In the Peruvian case, the military acted merely as self-appointed arbiters: they called a new election under the same rules, which produced a different outcome; in the Brazilian case, the military were innovative electoral rule-makers; and in Chile, they became direct rulers—although, after a period of harsh dictatorship, they introduced new electoral rules too.

One-third of Peruvians

Two presidential elections in Peru in 1962 and 1963 illustrate some of the hazards produced by plurality rule: different candidates can win from the same electorate with the same preferences as a consequence of the role of irrelevant candidates with no expectations of winning.

The voting rule for the election of President of Peru, as established in the Constitution of 1933 (Art. 138), required one-third of valid votes for the candidate to win. If no candidate obtained such a proportion, the election was to be transferred to Congress, which could choose by majority any of the three most-voted candidates.

Three major candidates ran for President of Peru 10 June 1962. On the left, Víctor-Raúl Haya de la Torre was the first viable candidate presented by the American Revolutionary Popular Action (APRA). This populist party, which had a long record of enmity with the Army and had promoted mass action and resistance against a former dictatorship, had not been allowed by the military to run with their own candidates for president in the previous election. Relatively close to Haya were three other minor leftist candidates, respectively supported by the Communists, the Socialists, and the Social-Progressives.

At the center, the major candidate Fernando Belaúnde Terry led the Popular Action Party (PAP). But a close, minor Christian-Democrat, Héctor Cornejo, ran independently. On the right, General Manuel Odría, who had been dictator in 1948–56, led his own candidacy (UNO). (For a longer-term perspective, see Chang 1985; McClintock 1994.)

The three major candidates in 1962 obtained around one-third of votes each (with the former dictator in last position), as shown in Table 3.8. Yet, due to the fragmentation introduced by the minor candidacies, none of the three achieved the required one-third of votes. APRA's Haya de la Torre lacked 5,676 votes (0.33 per cent of total votes). Yet Haya obtained an advantage of only 0.85 per cent of votes over Belaúnde. Had Haya gathered together the votes of any of the other leftist candidates, he would have obtained more than one-third of total votes. But the same threshold would have been achieved by Belaúnde had he collected the votes of the Christian-Democrats. Thus, irrelevant (nonwinning) candidates crucially interfered in the electoral outcome.

TABLE 3.8. *Peruvian presidential elections (1962–3)*

	1962		1963	
LEFT	Pando	2	Samamé	1
	Haya de la Torre	33	Haya de la Torre	34
	Castillo	1		
	Pérez Eldredge	1		
CENTER	Belaúnde	32	*Belaúnde*	39
	Cornejo	3		
RIGHT	Odría	28	Odría	26
		100		100

Note: Numbers are percentages of votes. The winner is shown in italics.

As established by the Constitution, the election of the President of Peru was transferred to Congress in cases in which no party had an absolute majority of seats. Each of the three major candidates was considered to be a potential majority-builder at some moment during the negotiations. However, on 4 July, the chiefs of Armed Forces vetoed Haya's candidacy. Haya in fact, withdrew. In a party meeting two days later he declared: 'We have to acknowledge what was perceivable the day after the election. The APRA party, in the electoral field, cannot be called "party of national majorities" any longer. We should put this honorable title that we have borne for 30 years in the refrigerator and wait to retrieve it in other elections' (Chirinos 1962, 1984: 107).

A military junta took over and annulled the election five weeks after it had been held. Remarkably, they called a new election for the following year 6 June 1963), with no significant persecution of political parties or leaders nor visible repression of political activity in between. The same three major candidates ran again. Eventually, the minor leftist candidates withdrew, while only one new candidate emerged. More decisively, the centrist Belaúnde attained a formal agreement with the Christian-Democrats to jointly support his candidacy. On 13 January 1963, the two party leaders, Belaúnde and Javier Correa, formalized an electoral and, if winning, governmental coalition which came to be known as 'the pact of Salaverry Avenue' (Ramirez y Berrios 1963).

There was increased voter participation this time. Haya obtained a higher number and percentage of votes than he had in the previous election, more than the required one-third. But so did Belaúnde, thanks to the 3 per cent of votes previously given to the Christian-Democrats (as well as a few more from the right and from new voters). In contrast to the previous election, Belaúnde won by plurality.

The following presidential election in Peru was to be held in June 1969. A few months before, the incumbent President Belaúnde experienced increasing unpopularity, the coalition between his party and the Christian-Democrats was broken as a consequence of disagreements in governmental management, and even the rightist candidacy, UNO, had split in two. Again, the APRA party looked as if it had an opportunity to win the presidential election. But a military coup in October 1968 prevented the election and established a ten year dictatorship. The first APRA presidential candidate who was allowed to take office in the history of Peru was Alan García, who won the 1985 election at the first round after plurality rule had been replaced with majority-runoff rule.

Eccentric Brazilians
Several presidents of Brazil elected during the democratic period, which began in 1945, obtained minority popular support. Extreme minority candidates without support of the median voter, that is, no Condorcet winners, alternated in office until a military coup halted the experience in 1964. (For a longer-term perspective, see Lamounier 1994; Mainwaring 1997.)

TABLE 3.9. *Brazilian presidential elections (1945–60)*

	1945		1950		1955		1960	
LEFT	Finza	10						
					Kubitschek + VP Goulart	36	Lott + VP *Goulart*	33
			Vargas	49				
	Dutra	55			Barros	26	Barros	19
			Machado	21	Tavora	30		
							Quadros	48
RIGHT	Gomes	35	Gomes	30				
					Salgado	8		
		100		100		100		100

Note: Numbers are percentages of votes. The winner is shown in italics.

In October 1945, a coup d'etat dismissed dictator Getúlio Vargas and led to the first competitive election with broad suffrage in Brazil. Marshal Enrico Dutra, with last-minute Vargas endorsement, won an absolute majority of popular votes and a majority of seats in Congress. For further presidential and vice-presidential elections, the 1946 Constitution and the 1950 electoral code (Art. 46) established 'the majority principle', which was interpreted by the Superior Electoral Tribunal in 1951 as not requiring more than a plurality of votes. The President and the Vice-President were elected in separated sections of the ballot.

The party system was organized around three basic poles. On the left, the Brazilian Labor Party (PTB), led by Vargas, mobilized voters in industrial and urban areas. The Communist party (which obtained about 10 per cent of votes in the first election) was banned after 1947, and basically supported the PTB candidates in the further process.

At the center, certain Vargas associates created the Social-Democrat party (PSD), with bases in small towns and rural areas, with the aim of joining and moderating the PTB candidates and forming a stable majority. Two minor parties, the Progressive PSP, especially strong in São Paulo, and the Christian-Democrats, also competed for the centrist electorate. On the right, the conservative National Democratic Union (UDN) competed with some minor parties and candidates with similar orientation.

Getúlio Vargas himself ran for President in 1950 with the support of the PTB, the PSP and the Communists, and won with 48.7 per cent of votes, as shown in Table 3.9. Vargas was close but still short of a majority; he was located on an extreme position that did not allow him to be considered the median voter's candidate. Under attack for scandals concerning corruption and the country's economic disaster, and fearing a new military coup, Vargas resigned and committed suicide in August 1954.

For the election of 1955, the pro-Vargas parties supported Juscelino Kubitschek, from an internally divided PSD, for President, and João Goulart, from the leftist PTB, for Vice-President, both also endorsed by the Communists. Kubitschek won with only 35.6 per cent of votes and was certainly not the median voter's candidate. Kubitschek's strength was eroded by the success of the progressive candidacy of Adhemar de Barros, who attracted substantial numbers of Vargas' former voters, especially in São Paulo. Supporters of Juárez Távora, the candidate of the right and some centrist groups, speculated on the victory of his candidate if the irrelevant, independent rightist candidate Plínio Salgado had not ran (Távora and Salgado together collected three percentage points more than the winner).

Kubitschek's inauguration found significant resistance. In September 1954, one month before the election, Congress had defeated a proposal to send the election to the Chamber of Deputies if no candidate received an absolute majority of popular votes and, after the election, the Conservatives argued again before the Superior Electoral Tribunal that the election should be considered invalid for not having produced a majority winner. Prominent political leaders launched accusations of fraud and intimidation and called to establish an 'emergency regime'. A military chief declared that 'to sanction a victory of the minority' and give it 'the enormous sum of power that is concentrated in the hands of the Executive' would be 'an indisputable democratic falsehood'. The progressive Vice-President Cafè Filho experienced heart problems and was replaced as acting President by the chairman of the Chamber of Deputies, Carlos Luz, who was a PSD member but Kubitschek's foe and suspected of conspiring to keep him from taking office. However, a 'preventive' military coup installed Kubitschek as President.

Five years later, in the 1960 election, the candidate for President supported by the pro-Vargas parties, PTB and PSD, obtained still less support than on previous occasions, again in competition with the irrelevant Barros. The winner was Jãnio Quadros, the candidate of the now united right and center-right, with 48.3 per cent of votes. Quadros was close but still short of a majority; he was located on the opposite extreme position, also without the median voter's support. Moreover, the winning Vice-President was João Goulart, the leftist candidate, thanks to a significant number of split-ticket votes. First, President Quadros appointed a national 'concentration Cabinet', with members from the right and the left. But, surprisingly, he undertook a number of leftist policy initiatives, including approaching the new revolutionary Cuban regime, and attempted ruling without Congress.

In August 1961, Quadros resigned eight months after his inauguration, apparently on miscalculation to provoke a fervor of popular support, which would have allowed him to take exclusive powers. According to constitutional provisions, he was replaced by Vice-President João Goulart, who became the most extreme minority President since 1945. The military leaders accepted the appointment of the new president only by depriving the office of significant powers and imposing a parliamentary regime (one of the rare experiences of parliamentarism in

Latin America in the 20th century). However, Goulart regained full presidential powers at a plebiscite in January 1963. A few months later, he formed a Cabinet with the exclusive support of the PTB-PSD parties. Goulart's request for a state of siege was refused by Congress, but he launched a series of mass demonstrations that were widely interpreted as an attempt to override the established institutional mechanisms. In March 1964, the PSD officially split from the government, which was left exclusively in the hands of the minority PTB. Three weeks later, a military coup disbanded the elected leaders (Skidmore 1967; Dulles 1970; Stepan 1971, 1978).

The military Junta established in Brazil in 1964 experimented with some new rules, not with much success. It curbed Congress powers, while keeping regular legislative, state governorships, and mayoral offices elections. The traditional political parties were replaced with two parties formed from those above and tried to represent both the right and the left. Presidential elections were allocated to Congress, with the requirement of absolute majority in two rounds and only plurality in the third round. The last indirect presidential election was held in 1985, but the opposition demands of *diretas-jà* (direct elections now) was widely associated to effective democratization and legally established in 1986. The following democratic presidential elections used majority-runoff rule.

The Chilean Way to *Coup d'État*

As with other presidents elected by plurality rule, the 1970 Chilean winner, Salvador Allende, was dependent on irrelevant alternatives. The median voter was not included among his supporters. Further confrontational strategies between the extreme, minority winner and a potential alternative majority led to social conflict, *coup d'état*, and military dictatorship. (For an extensive analysis, see Valenzuela 1976, 1978, 1994.)

The Chilean Constitution of 1925, which was continuously enforced from 1932, established that the President should be elected by absolute majority of popular votes. Had no candidate obtained a majority support, the President would be chosen by Congress from between the two candidates with the highest number of votes. In the elections of 1946, 1952, and 1958, Congress always elected the plurality-winning candidate, even if the parties that supported the president in the popular election did not have a parliamentary majority.

Plurality rule was thus not legally established in Chile (in contrast to most other Latin-American countries), but it was stringently enforced by political parties. Usually, the second candidate in votes conceded the election in favor of the plurality winner without waiting for the decision of Congress. In 1964, the Christian-Democratic candidate formally declared, even before the election, that he would not accept the presidency if he were not the candidate with the most popular votes.

There is remarkable evidence that the basic distribution of Chilean voters' preferences, as can be located on left, center, and right positions of the ideolog-

TABLE 3.10. *Chilean presidential elections (1958–70)*

	1958		1964		1970	
LEFT	Allende	29	Allende	39	*Allende*	37
	Zamorano	3				
	Bossy	15	Duran	5		
MEDIAN	Frei	21	*Frei*	56	Tomic	28
RIGHT	*Alessandri*	32			Alessandri	35
		100		100		100

Note: Numbers are percentages of votes. The winner is shown in italics.

ical spectrum, did not change significantly throughout the 1950s and the 1960s (Prothro and Chaparro 1976). In contrast, drastic changes were introduced in the formation of party coalitions in the elections of the same period.

The results of presidential elections in Chile since 1958, the year when a legal reform abolished local party pacts and induced a more consistent organization of the national party system on the left–right axis, are shown in Table 3.10. As can be seen, the right-wing candidate, Jorge Alessandri (supported by the Conservative and the Liberal parties, lately merged into the National party), won in 1958 with less than a third of popular votes. Alessandri was less than three percentage points ahead of Salvador Allende, the candidate of the united left of Socialists and Communists. As was noted at the time, if the irrelevant, independent leftist candid-ate, Antonio Zamorano, a defrocked priest known as *el cura de Catapilco* (the priest of the little village of that name), had not entered the contest and obtained more than 3 per cent of votes, Allende would probably have won. On the other hand, Alessandri would probably also have won in a second round by majority. Neither of the two top minority runners (Alessandri and Allende), however, was a Condorcet winner or the median voter's candidate since each of them would have been defeated by the intermediate candidate, Eduardo Frei, in pairwise contests.

Fearing victory of the left, the incumbent President's party did not present a candidate of its own in 1964. The National party decided to endorse the centrist candidate, Frei, who, facing an asymmetric number of rivals, obtained an absolute majority of votes from the center and the right. With 56 per cent of popular support, Frei was certainly the median voter's candidate. Exceptional for Chile's modern history, President Frei's party also obtained an absolute majority of seats in Congress in the election held shortly after his inauguration.

Encouraged by his majority support in both the presidential and congressional elections, Frei introduced a constitutional reform reinforcing the president's powers (regarding the president's legislative veto, reserved domains, and the power to call referendums). The unbalanced relation of powers between the

President and Congress created by this reform did not help to build further compromises between the two institutions but rather fostered interinstitutional conflict.

Several attempts at replacing plurality rule with majority rule for the election of President failed: both when the proposal was introduced by Alessandri in the final period of his mandate, by Frei shortly after his election, and by several members of Congress during the discussion of the just-mentioned successful constitutional reform. In each case, the reform of the electoral rule was blocked by minority yet sufficiently large parties with expectations of winning by plurality. The left and the Christians rejected Alessandri's proposal for majority rule in 1964, and the National party prevented the reform during further discussions in 1964 and 1969.

For the election of November 1970, the right again presented its own candidate, Alessandri. National party leaders were troubled by the unusually high concentration of power in the hands of the incumbent President, as well as by the recent leftist ideological turn of the Christian-Democrats, especially after the choice of their new candidate, Radomiro Tomic. The right-wing leaders expected that Alessandri would obtain greater popular support than the centrist candidate (as he certainly did). The other intermediate party, the Radicals, split and the fraction keeping the party name decided, in contrast to previous elections, not to present a candidate of its own but rather to join the Socialists and the Communists (as well as other minor groups) in support of the leftist candidacy of Allende. Facing now two separate candidacies of the center and the right and without rivals on the left side of the spectrum, this time Allende won. Remarkably, in 1970, Allende obtained a smaller proportion of votes, less than 37 per cent, than he had in 1964 (and smaller than the sum of votes the parties supporting him now had obtained in separate candidacies in 1958).

In contrast to previous presidents and the other candidates, Allende was the last preference of a majority of voters. Most voters who supported the Christian-Democratic party's and the National party's candidates would have preferred each other's candidate instead of the leftist one. Even among voters of the 'lower socioeconomic group', according to the polls, Allende was as much rejected as Alessandri (Prothro and Chaparro 1976: 88; Valenzuela 1978: 42). In a majority voting against either candidate, Allende would certainly have been the loser, that is, he was the Condorcet loser.

However, he was elected by Congress with the votes of the Christian-Democrats, together with those of his own supporting parties. In a secret meeting before the election, Allende and Tomic had agreed that the plurality winner would be recognized by the other candidate if he obtained an advantage of at least 30,000 votes over the second most-voted candidate (Fontaine 1972: 66). The agreed sufficient difference was roughly equivalent to 1 per cent of votes and, in face, Allende surpassed Alessandri by slightly more than 39,000 votes, that is, by about 1.3 per cent. With the decision to confirm Allende as the plurality-winning

president, the Christian-Democrats expected to become the leading opposition
party against the leftist government, a strategy that was considered preferable in
the medium term than joining the rightist party's potentially winning candidate as
a minor, subordinate partner. As an exchange for the Christian-Democratic votes,
Allende agreed to support a constitutional amendment or 'Statute of Guarantees'
requiring him to respect civil liberties, elections, and freedom of the press.
Despite of the orders from US President, Richard Nixon, to the CIA, US agents
were unable to bribe Christian-Democratic congressmen or military leaders to
prevent Allende's election by Congress.

The Allende government rapidly undertook a number of radical reforms,
including the nationalization of farms and factories and a wide redistribution
policy. A negative majority was soon formed. Whereas the reinforced President's
legal powers had eroded the traditional spaces of interinstitutional accommodation, a new cooperation between the opposition parties in Congress developed
and combined with street demonstrations and strikes against the government. In
September 1973, in the midst of full political deadlock, a military coup initially
supported by the right and most Christian-Democrats established a dictatorship
which lasted for more than fifteen years. About 3,000 persons were persecuted and
killed in the first few months after the *coup*. The next democratic presidential election took place in 1989, using majority-runoff rule. The Christian-Democratic
candidate, with the support of the Socialists, won the Presidency in the first round.

3.2. MULTIPLE-WINNER RULES

Multiple-winner outcomes can be attained in two stages: (1) elections
with proportional representation; and (2) the formation of assembly multiparty coalitions. As will be discussed in the following pages, the outcomes
of this two-stage process (the Assembly or Cabinet positions and the
corresponding public policies) tend to be more inclusive, moderate, and
stable than the typical outcomes obtained with single-winner rules.

Multiple-winner rules reinforce themselves. By fostering the emergence, strength, and survival of multiple political actors, they obtain broad
support from the corresponding actors and tend to become equilibrium
solutions. Multiple-winner rules will be evaluated here for the social efficiency of their outcomes.

Proportional Representation

The principle of proportional representation in political bodies has been
enunciated on several occasions since the late 18th century, but it was not
linked to practical formulas for its implementation for quite a long time.
One of the first statements in favor of proportional political representation

can be attributed to Honoré Gabriel Riqueti, Count De Mirabeau, in his address to the provincial Estate (Assembly) of Provence on 30 January 1789, that is, in the process of electing the Estates-General which would trigger the Revolution in France.

According to Mirabeau, 'the Estates-General are to the nation what a chart is to its physical configuration; in all its parts, and as a whole, the copy should at all times have the same proportions as the original' (author's translation from Mirabeau 1789, vol. 1: 7). In Mirabeau's view, representation of all parts should prevent the two dominant Estates, the aristocracy and the clergy, from prevailing over the whole nation. His requirements for an acceptable government included universal suffrage, proportional representation, and the power of the representatives to make effective decision—in other words, the basic components of a democratic social choice that were identified in the introduction to this book.

In a lesser known passage of the same speech, Mirabeau stated precisely that 'the nation is not there [in the Estates] if those who call themselves its representatives have not been chosen in free and individual elections, if the representatives of groups of equal importance are not equal numerically and in voting power'. For Mirabeau, was not only a question of faithful representation of society based upon equal voting rights of individual members of the three estates and fair apportionment, but also a question of obtaining socially efficient outcomes. 'In order to know the will of a nation, the votes must be collected in such a way so as to prevent the mistake of taking the will of an estate for one other, or the particular will of certain individuals for the general will' (idem: 7–8).

Within the British utilitarian tradition, proportional representation was promoted with the aim of producing a broader distribution of political satisfaction among different groups in the society than majority rule could produce. John Stuart Mill, most prominently, attacked majoritarian rules because they produce 'class legislation' and 'class rule'. According to Mill, the winner in plurality-rule parliamentary regimes with two stages in the process of decision making (popular elections and Cabinet formation in Parliament), is actually 'a majority of the majority, who may be, and often are, but a minority of the whole'.

In contrast, proportional representation would give power to the majority and the minorities, to all 'interests' or 'classes', in the aim of giving every group 'protection against the class legislation of others without claiming the power to exercise it in their own'. For Mill, a good government should prevent the exclusive rule of a single winning group and favor multiple winners' power-sharing. For this aim, proportional representation was the right institutional choice because it 'makes it impossible for partial interests to have the command of the tribunal, but it ensures them advocates' (Mill 1861, ch. 7).

More formally enunciated, the principles of proportional representation can be found in the work of several 19th-century mathematicians. Specifically, in Charles L. Dodgson's (Lewis Carroll) presentation, desirable principles include that 'the number of unrepresented electors should be as small as possible', and that 'the proportions of political parties in the House should be, as nearly as possible, the same as in the whole body of electors' (1884, in McLean and Urken 1995: 41–54, 300).

As suggested, some early promoters of proportional representation used images like 'chart', 'map', 'picture', 'portrait', 'mirror' 'looking-glass'. (For a collection of quotations using these types of metaphors, see Pitkin 1967: 60ff). The most prominent authors, however, did not intend a mere reproduction of the complexity of society within political institutions. As explicitly stated by the authors quoted above and clearly suggested by the context in which these principles were formulated, they aimed at preventing the maintenance or emergence of a single, absolute winner—the dominant estates, a class rule—and the exclusion of significant groups from the institutional process, in favor of better social choices. Some authors tried to make room for the middle and lower classes previously excluded by aristocratic domination; others wished to prevent the establishment of exclusive working-class rule. Inclusiveness in decision making and power-sharing was expected to produce more satisfactory results. In other words, proportional representation was not only promoted for obtaining fair electoral results as an end in itself, but with the aim of producing political outcomes with greater social utility than more exclusive rules. Lewis Carroll's clever quotation that begins the chapter, describing a race in which 'everybody wins and all must have prizes', makes this point in a flash.

Parallel to the enunciation of these general principles, several mathematical formulas of proportional representation were invented in the United States at the end of the 18th century, although they were not used then for allocating seats to different parties or groups. As stated in the United States Constitution (Article 1, Section 2): 'Representation and direct taxes shall be apportioned among the several States which may be included in this Union according to their respective numbers' of citizens. Several formulas of 'fair apportionment' were thus conceived with the aim of allocating House representatives to the states, although they were going to be elected by plurality rule.

The basic mathematical formulas which were to be used in political elections elsewhere beginning in the late 19th century were invented by the Founding Fathers of the American Constitution. Some formulas divide the number of citizens (or votes) by a series of divisors and allocate seats to the largest quotients obtained. These include Thomas Jefferson's proposal in 1791, which was reinvented by Belgian lawyer Victor d'Hondt for proportional elections in 1878 and (with different counting procedures producing the same result) is also known as Hagenbach-Bischoff, as well as US Senator Daniel Webster's proposal in 1832, which was reinvented by the French mathematician André Sainte-Laguë in 1910. Other formulas allocate seats on the basis of a quota (of citizens or votes) and the greatest remainders, including in particular Alexander Hamilton's proposal in 1792, which was reinvented, quite independently, by English schoolmaster Thomas Wright Hill in 1821, Danish mathematician and politician Carl C. G. Andrae in 1855, and English lawyer Thomas Hare in 1857 (and usually known as The Hare quota). (Other formulas were proposed by former President John Quincy Adams, mathematician James Dean, and statistician Joseph A. Hill; discussants include George Washington and James Madison; see Balinski and Young 1982.)

Pluralistic Voting Procedures

Proportional representation requires multimember districts. But it can be implemented with different ballots in order to select either individual candidates or party lists. The following paragraphs review several pluralistic voting procedures: multimember elections with majoritarian formulas, single transferable vote, and party lists.

Multimember, Majority Elections

When a connection had not yet been established between the principles of proportional representation and the corresponding mathematical formulas, other devices aimed at preserving some minority representation in elections using majoritarian rules were introduced in a number of countries. Limitedly pluralistic, nonproportional procedures include cumulative vote and limited vote.

Cumulative vote allows each voter to concentrate several votes on a single candidate or distribute them among several candidates. In accord with the utilitarian aim of maximizing the sum of individual utilities, this procedure enables voters to express the intensity of their preferences. Yet it is highly vulnerable to strategic vote. By concentrating insincere votes on the most preferred candidate, voters tend to choose in cumulative voting as they would with categoric ballot. Cumulative vote was used in certain elections in Chile and in the South African province of Cape of Good Hope in the 19th century and for the State Assembly of Illinois until 1980.

Limited vote allows each voter to vote for fewer candidates than the number of representatives which are to be elected in the district. Limited vote was used for electing a few members of the British House of Commons in 1886–90, the local Councils of Boston and Philadelphia, as well as the national parliaments of Spain, Portugal, and some Latin-

American countries in the late 19th century. A variant called single nontransferable vote (SNTV), which gives each voter only one vote, was used in Japan after World War II until 1994. (For the effects of multi-member districts with limited vote, see Carroll as discussed by Black 1996; for the Japanese SNTV, see Lijphart, López-Pintor, and Sone 1986; Cox 1997: 100–8, 240–50.)

Single Transferable Vote

This voting procedure requires each voter to rank individual candidates in the ballot. It is an eliminatory method similar to the Australian alternative vote previously discussed, but it is applied to multimember districts. Seats are allocated to candidates who have obtained a quota of votes (usually the Droop quota) while the remaining votes are transferred to the following candidates in voters' ordinal preferences.

Single transferable vote (STV) allows a moderate pluralistic representation (Katz 1984). Yet, like all quota systems, STV may produce nonmonotonic results (Doron and Kronik 1977). It does not prevent strategic voting since it would be possible for some voters to induce an early elimination of less desired candidates in the first counts in order to favor the survival of less popular candidates in further rounds of counting (Brams and Fishburn, 1983). However, the computational effort that would be required to take advantage of this possibility is so enormous, even if there is complete information on voters' preferences, that it would be extremely difficult to pull off a strategic vote. Thus, STV can be considered to be strongly resistant to manipulation (Bartholdi and Orlin 1991).

STV was first invented by Thomas W. Hill in 1821 and first used in local elections in the small colonial town of Adelaide (South Australia) in 1839. On a second, unrelated occasion, STV was devised by Swiss mathematician and Minister of Finances (and later Prime Minister) Carl Andrae and used for the first time in national parliamentary elections in Denmark between 1856 and 1863. Thomas Hare (who was perhaps influenced by Jeremy Bentham, according to a suggestion in Hart 1992: 29) was able to present the procedure in a much more precise manner in 1857 and 1859. He gained fame as its inventor, despite its earlier authors, thanks in great part to public praise of the system by John Stuart Mill and a subsequent opinion campaign and parliamentary proposals.

STV has been used in local elections in former British colonies, including Canada, Tasmania, and South Africa. In the United States, it extended from the town of Ashtabula, Ohio, in 1915 to twenty-two city councils including Boulder, Sacramento, Cleveland, and Cincinatti in the 1920s, and to New York City between 1937 and 1947, where it created the occasion for the election of a few black and Communist aldermen for first time in the city's history. It is nowadays used for the election of the city council and school committee of Cambridge, Massachusetts, and New York City school boards. Single transferable vote is used for national parliamentary elections in the British-inspired political systems of Ireland and Malta since 1920, and for the Australian Senate since 1949; as well as in Estonia in 1992 (at the induction of political scientist Rein Taagepera) (Hoag and Hallet 1926; Weaver 1984, 1986; Mair 1986; Tideman 1995; and author's information).

Party Lists

The principle of proportional representation encourages many parties or candidates to run separately according to their own profile, that is, not to withdraw or merge. The strategy of entering the race independently can be based on the expectation that every candidacy can obtain a sufficient number of votes to be represented in the Assembly and have some further influence in legislation and Cabinet formation. Pure proportional representation is not manipulable because is not a 'single-valued' decision procedure, according to social choice theory. In contrast to single-winner rules, such as plurality or majority rules, proportional representation is not vulnerable to strategies, such as manipulation of the agenda by introducing new alternatives (traditionally known as 'divide and win' tactics), or giving salience to different issue-dimensions (see Nurmi 1987).

In principle, proportional representation also encourages sincere voting by the citizens, since voters can expect that their political preferences will be satisfied to the extent that they coincide with those of other citizens. With a high number of parties or candidates running and sincere votes on the part of citizens according to their preferences, proportional representation usually creates Assemblies in which no party has an absolute majority of seats.

There are, however, some specific effects produced by the different proportional representation formulas. Quota formulas can produce some nonmonotonic results from somewhat unusual combinations of numbers such that an increase in the number of votes (or citizens) may produce a decrease in the number of seats. (This is the 'Alabama paradox' that was discovered on the occasion of allocating US House seats to the states.)

Both the quota formulas and the Webster-Sainte Laguë formula encourage party fragmentation and even the independent running of individual candidates from the same party because it may give a coalition fewer seats than its partners can obtain separately. Under this institutional framework, if different parties are created by political entrepreneurs, they can survive separately; if the initial situation is dominated by a few parties, some of their candidates can find incentives to split from the party and run on their own. In contrast, the Jefferson-d'Hondt formula favors larger parties and thus encourages the formation of electoral coalitions. (Some discussion of the incentives for fragmentation and coalition can be found in Balinski and Young 1982: 87–93. An extreme example of party fragmentation induced by a quota formula of proportional representation is in Colombia; Cox and Shugart 1995; the consequent electoral reform introducing the d'Hondt formula was discussed and supported by international experts see Valenzuela 1999.)

For all the formulas, the higher the number of seats in the district, or district 'magnitude', the more proportional representation is obtained. Specifically, there is an inverse relation between the 'effective threshold' of votes needed by a party to obtain seats and the district magnitude. (Lijphart 1994a; Taagepera 1998). The degree of proportionality of electoral results can be measured with several indices comparing proportions of votes and proportions of seats for each party (see the discussion in Gallagher 1991).

Thus, manipulation may appear in elections by proportional representation to the extent that a small district magnitude tends to exclude some parties and produce significant deviations from proportionality, but not when the allocation of seats approaches full proportionality to each party-vote share. (For other formal analyses of the effects of electoral formulas of proportional representation, see Taagepera and Shugart 1989; and for an empirical survey, see Lijphart, 1994a. A few examples of strategic behavior in systems with quota formulas or small district magnitude are identified in Cox 1997: 108–22.)

Proportional representation on the basis of votes given to different party lists was proposed by Socialist Victor Considerant as early as 1834. His influence on the Swiss writer Morin in the 1860s eventually led to the adoption of proportional representation in the Swiss canton of Ticino in 1891 and in other cantons in the following years. An unrelated publication on the topic was Thomas Gilpin's pamphlet printed in Philadelphia in 1844 (and reprinted in the *Annals of the American Academy of Political and Social Sciences* in 1896).

The Argentinean provinces of Buenos Aires in 1873 and Mendoza in 1895 early on adopted systems of proportional representation based on party lists. Proportional representation was also adopted for party-list national parliamentary elections in Serbia in 1899 (after being used for local elections in 1888), Belgium in 1899, Finland in 1906, Cuba in 1908, Sweden in 1909, the Portuguese districts of Lisbon and Oporto in 1911, Bulgaria in 1911, and Russia in 1916. In the years 1918–20, immediately after World War I and the dissolution of the German, Austrian, and Russian Empires, all the constituent Assemblies which met in the newly created states decided on a list system of proportional representation for national elections, including Austria, Germany, Italy, the Netherlands, Norway, Poland, Romania, Switzerland; the micro-states of Luxembourg,

San Marino, Liechestein, and Danzig; Estonia, Latvia, and Lithuania, as well as Far Eastern Republic (Siberia), Armenia, and Georgia before being annexed to the Soviet Union. Hungary adopted the same principles in 1925 (Hoag and Hallet 1926; Carstairs, 1980).

Most newer democracies established in Western Europe at the end of World War II, and in Southern Europe, Latin America, and Eastern Europe during the last quarter of the 20th century also adopted party-list systems of proportional representation for national political elections (as will be discussed in Chapter 5).

Nearing the year 2000, the Hare quota formula is being used in Bolivia, Colombia, Costa Rica, Germany, and the proportional portion of Lithuania. The d'Hondt (or Hagenbach-Bishoff) formula is used in the Czech Republic, Finland, Iceland, Israel, the Netherlands, Portugal, Slovakia, Spain, Switzerland, and the proportional portions of Hungary and Italy, as well as in Argentina, Brazil, Chile, Ecuador, Peru, Uruguay, and Venezuela. Modified Sainte-Laguë formulas are used in Denmark, Norway, and Sweden. Austria and Belgium combine Hare and d'Hondt formulas.

Multiparty Coalitions

As a result of both partys' and voters' strategies, proportional representation tends to produce multiple winners. Proportional representation does not, however, produce outcomes as directly as do plurality or majority rules. When the latter formulas are used in mass political elections, a single winner (either a parliamentary party led by a candidate for premier or a president) is usually known a few hours after voting. In contrast, parliamentary elections with proportional representation transfer the decision to an additional institutional stage. There, actors can negotiate to form or support a Cabinet.

A series of analytical and empirical studies of Cabinet formation in parliamentary regimes shows that the assumption that parties keep their ideological connectedness when they form coalitions performs better than alternative assumptions, such as those based merely on the size of the coalitions. In parliamentary negotiations, political parties tend to maintain relative policy-ideological positions that are consistent with their relative positions during the previous electoral campaign. They prefer coalition partners located at neighboring positions in the policy-ideology space to those at more distant locations. Within this policy-ideology condition, parties tend to form coalitions without superfluous partners. (For the concept of minimum connected winning coalitions, see Axelrod 1970. For comparative analyses, see Laver and Schofield 1990; Laver and Budge 1992; Laver and Shepsle 1996.)

Minority Cabinets in parliamentary regimes can also be largely explained by the assumption that political parties that might form an alternative majority in parliament on the basis of their numbers of seats abstain from doing so if they occupy too distant policy-ideological positions or are not connected on the left–right axis. Then, a centrist party (or coalition) containing the median seat, even if it is not supported by a majority of seats, can survive noncredible threats to overthrow it from ideologically separate parties on its left and right. (Strom 1990.)

A similar assumption regarding the ideological connectedness of multi-party coalitions (but not regarding the size of the coalitions) can be made for Assemblies in presidential regimes and other nonparliamentary institutional settings in which multiparty majorities are formed. (For the concept of connected winning coalitions, see Colomer 1996*d*; Colomer and Hosli 1997.)

If party policy-ideology positions matter, centrist parties—and especially the party containing the median seat—can be relatively advantaged in parliamentary negotiations to form a majority. Let us remember once again that the median is defined as the position having no more than half of the seats on both its right and left. If parties keep their ideological connectedness on the left–right scale when they form a majority coalition to appoint or support a Cabinet, which is to say if every party is only ready to form a coalition with adjacent parties, then the party containing the median seat is always a necessary partner in gathering a majority or allowing a minority Cabinet to survive. If parliamentary representation is proportional to different voters' preference groups, the median seat corresponds to the median voters' preference. We thus find the paradoxical result that interactions of parties that give prominence to their policy and ideological positions in choosing partners tend to produce ideologically moderate outcomes. This differs from results in elections with alternative formulas, such as plurality rule, in which it is possible to form a majority in parliament without including the position of the median voter.

In order to illustrate this result, Fig. 3.3 compares hypothetical majority coalitions formed from proportional representation, which always include the median voter, and more biased plurality winners. A plurality winner is operationalized as the largest plurality short of a majority. In the following examples, the plurality winners are supported by 40–44 per cent of popular votes (proportions that are quite close to the typical single-party plurality Cabinet in the United Kingdom).

For a distribution of five preferences with roughly the same proportion of voters in a single dimension, only half of the coalitions encompassing the largest plurality (2/5, 40 per cent) include the median voter. For seven preferences, the proportion of coalitions encompassing the largest plurality (3/7, 43 per cent) that include the median voter rises to 60 per cent, and

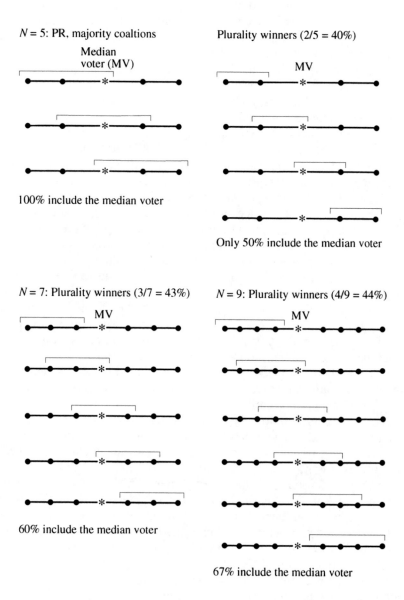

FIG. 3.3. Median-winners by proportional representation (PR) and plurality rule

for nine preferences (and 4/9 plurality, 44 per cent), it rises to 67 per cent. This suggests that the larger the number of voters' groups with different preferences, the more likely it is that the plurality winner will include the median voter. In other words, while coalitions formed on the basis of proportional representation should always include the median voter, the bias against centrist outcomes introduced by single-winner decision rules can be counteracted to some extent by the complexity of the electorate.

The expected advantage of the median party in multiparty parliamentary negotiations can be anticipated by voters in elections with proportional representation and induce strategic votes in favor of those parties with better chances of capturing the median seat, that is, in favor of moderate, rather centrist parties. The basic effect of this strategy is the reinforcement of the moderation of parliamentary and governmental decisions in parliamentary regimes with proportional representation.

Despite the advantageous bargaining position of the median party, the distribution of Cabinet offices among parties can be expected to be relatively proportional to their proportions of seats in parliament. Post-electoral or 'parliamentary deviation' measures the disproportion between the share of seats of each party and its expected share of offices in the Cabinet. The corresponding 'power index' is calculated on the basis of the party contribution in seats to form all the viable winning coalitions to which it can belong. It has been found that parliamentary deviation between proportions of parliamentary seats and proportions of expected Cabinet offices tends to be relatively lower in parliaments with low electoral deviation between proportions of votes and seats (Colomer 1996*b*).

This can be illustrated, by contrast, with the high electoral and parliamentary deviations that are found in the process of forming a single-party majority Cabinet in electoral systems based on plurality rule (such as that of the United Kingdom). Typically, the electoral system transforms a minority of votes for one party into more than 50 per cent of seats, and then the majority party in parliament, which always includes the median seat but usually not the median voter, obtains 100 per cent of portfolios in the Cabinet, depriving all the other parties (which may have received a majority of votes) of parliamentary power. Electoral deviation is thus amplified with parliamentary deviation in the following institutional stage. In contrast, proportional representation from votes to seats tends to distribute expectations of obtaining Cabinet portfolios among several parties in a more proportional way.

Consistent with the above discussion, a comparative analysis of twelve countries has found that multiparty Cabinets based on proportional representation are, on average, substantially closer to the median voters' position than are single-party parliamentary Cabinets based on plurality or majority rules. In this study, the Cabinet's policy positions are calculated as the average position of all the parties in the Cabinet, weighted by their proportion of seats. Results also hold with respect to the position of the median party in the Cabinet coalition. Similar results are found regarding the mean voter. (The sample reported here includes Australia, New Zealand, the United Kingdom, France, Belgium, Denmark, Germany, Ireland, Italy, the Netherlands, Spain, and Sweden in the period 1968–87; Huber and Powell 1994.)

Cases: Efficient Multiparty Cabinets

Socially efficient outcomes produced by proportional representation and multiparty coalitions will be illustrated with several cases of Cabinet formation in parliamentary regimes in Western Europe. The following survey includes two cases that have obtained rather bad scores in certain received opinion, especially for their high levels of ministerial instability: the French Fourth Republic (1945–58) and the Italian First Republic (1945–93). Two cases with a higher reputation in achieving governance are also discussed: the Dutch parliamentary Monarchy (here surveyed for the period since 1945) and the German Federal Republic established in 1949. The following analysis of these countries' institutional formulas will focus upon the inclusiveness of the political representation they promote and the stability and social efficiency of the resulting Cabinet positions and policy outcomes. From this point of view, the performance of proportional representation and the corresponding multiparty coalitions obtains a clearly positive evaluation for the four countries mentioned.

The French Fourth Republic

After the liberation of France from Nazi occupation in 1945, national elections were called with party lists and proportional representation. The electoral rules established in the constituent period 1945–6 included the d'Hondt formula of highest averages (which gives some advantage to larger parties). The ballot was an open list with candidates to be chosen from all parties or *panachage*. The rules admitted '*apparentments*', that is, electoral coalitions between parties running separately in order to allocate all seats in a district to the coalesced parties if their votes added up to an absolute majority (the seats would then be distributed among the winning parties proportionally to their votes).

These rules created incentives for forming broad electoral coalitions prefiguring further parliamentary and Cabinet multiparty coalitions. They were organized around the center, basically including the Socialists, the Radicals, the Christians, and the Conservatives, at the exclusion of the two extremes, the Communists and the Gaullists. The electoral rules permitted voters to select their most preferred individual candidates from the several parties in the coalition. An electoral reform in 1951 introduced additional mechanisms to reinforce the centrist moderation of the expected results. It established a quota formula of highest remainders for the districts in the Paris area in the aim of producing more proportional results and not giving advantage to the larger parties in that region, that is, the Communists and the Gaullists.

Of the six basic parties or blocs that were formed, usually the seats of four were necessary to form a majority in Parliament. The center-left Radicals were always the fifth in votes and in seats (if we take both the Radicals and the independent Conservative candidates as single groups). However, the Radicals always contained the median voter and the median seat and from this advantageous position they became the first party in number of Premiers and in number of Cabinet ministers.

In addition to the median, center-left Radicals, the left Socialists and the center-right Christians were also slightly advantaged in parliamentary bargaining and Cabinet formation because of their proximity to the median position on the policy-ideological space. In contrast, the extreme Communists and Gaullists, which, on average, were only slightly disadvantaged in terms of seats in comparison with their votes, were badly hurt in their expectations of being included in the Cabinet. Table 3.11 shows results in votes and seats, as well as in the further distribution of Cabinet ministers, for the five elections in the period 1945–56 (1945, June and November 1946, 1951, and 1956).

More specifically, the Cabinet coalitions during the constituent period 1945–7 were formed by the Communists, the Socialists, and the Christians with some minor participation on the part of Radicals (first, under the premiership of General de Gaulle and later mostly with Socialist premiers). However, from 1947 to 1958 the Communists were replaced with the Conservatives (also called 'Moderates'). Almost all premiers in this period were members of the more centrist parties within the typical four-party parliamentary coalition, the Radicals and the Christians. One exception in favor of a Conservative seems to have been based on voting miscalculation: the Radicals and the Christians voted for him in the expectation that he would not obtain sufficient votes, but unexpectedly some dissident Gaullists backed the candidate and made him a winner (Leites: 1959, p. 62).

The most common reproach to the French Fourth Republic was the instability of its Cabinets, which lasted only six months on average. Yet this can hardly be attributed to the electoral system of proportional representation and the corresponding multipartism, since a similar degree of Cabinet instability had existed in the previous French Third Republic with majoritarian electoral systems (based on plurality or majority rules). Almost all coalition Cabinets in the period 1875–1939 had been formed around the Republican Conservatives, mostly with the center-left Radicals as partners or, for some periods, the Christians. The Socialists were included in a governmental combination only in the period 1924–32 and in the short-lived experience of the Popular Front formed in 1936–38 by the Radicals, the Socialists, and the Communists. The average dura-

Table 3.11. *Votes, seats, and ministries in the French Fourth Republic (1945–58)*

		Votes	Seats	Ministries
LEFT	Communists	27	25	4
	Socialists	18	20	23
MEDIAN	Radicals	12	12	29
	Christians	20	22	25
	Conservatives	14	13	14
RIGHT	Gaullists	6	5	3
	Others	3	3	2
		100	100	100

Note: Numbers are percentages of votes, seats, and ministries for the five elections and twenty-five cabinets in the period 1945–58. Dotted lines separate Cabinet parties from more extreme or other parties.

Communists: PCF; Socialists: SFIO; Radicals: RGR, UDSR; Christians: MRP; Conservatives (or 'Moderates'): Independent Republicans, PRL, Paysans (PUS, IP); Gaullists: UG, RPF, ARS; Others: mainly 1956 'Poujadistes' (UFF).

Source: Author's own calculations with data in Williams (1958) and La Gorce (1979*a,b*).

tion of Cabinets in the period 1875–1939 was eight months; for the years 1918–39 it was six months, almost exactly the same length of time as for the period following 1945. (Soulier 1939). Despite Cabinet instability, the Third Republic represented by far the longest period of time in France since the fall of the absolutist Monarchy without a significant constitutional change and, as can be argued also for the Fourth Republic, a period of very stable policy.

The instability of Cabinets from 1946 ran in parallel to the long duration of the legislatures (five years in both 1946 and in 1951). This can be explained by a combination of institutional and strategic factors. The dissolution of the assembly was relatively difficult. The Cabinet could call anticipated elections only if two crises provoked by votes of censure or confidence had occurred within the preceding eighteen months. Since the threat of provoking dissolution and an anticipated election was hardly credible, individual ministers from parties in disagreement over some Cabinet policies dared to step down in the expectation of producing a new ministerial combination in which they might have more influence (Petry 1994).

Typically, the Premier and his Cabinet obtained support on the basis of proposals regarding some prominent issue, such as economic policy, European trade agreements, or colonial conflicts, and they were voted down as a consequence of a new divisive issue, such as the European Defence Community or the Church–school issue. The parties taking the initiative of overthrowing Cabinets were not the centrist Radicals or Christians, but those in less moderate positions in the ideological spectrum: the Socialists and the Conservatives, who were pulled towards the extremes by the challenging electoral strength of the Communists, the Gaullists, or the Poujadists. 'The parties that characteristically brought down the Cabinet did so for substantive [policy] reasons more than for calculations of places in future Cabinets, and suspicion that *ministrables* undermined the Cabinet [for office-seeking reasons] find little support in their votes' (MacRae 1967: 9, also 324).

These features reflected the general desire to keep the executive under control and to prevent power from residing in the hands of any one group in order to allow successive Cabinets to promote a variety of issues that would satisfy different group preferences. The effects of frequent reshuffles in favor of power redistribution could be compared to those sought by other institutional devices (such as the rotation in office by lots, as experimented with, for example, in some late medieval city-states), with the differential advantage of being produced under the stable framework of a five-year legislature and with co-responsibility within the four-party coalition.

All the Cabinets of the French Fourth Republic in the period 1945–58 were supported by the parliamentary representatives of the median voter. Continuity in policy was favored by continuity in personnel: 15 individuals held 25 premierships, and 114 individuals held 411 ministerial portfolios (including the previously mentioned premierships), an average of 3.6 offices per person. For instance, the Christian-Democrat Robert Schuman was twice appointed Premier, ten times Minister of Foreign affairs, three times Minister of Finance, and twice Minister of Justice. Some parties or individuals kept certain ministries for long periods despite Cabinet changes, such as the Christians (Schuman and Bidault) in the Ministry of Foreign affairs, the independent Petsche in the Ministry of Finance, and the Socialists and the Radicals in the Ministry of the Interior (author's own calculation, which is very similar to the calculation of ministers and secretaries of state by Dogan 1989, who found an average of 3.4 offices per person).

The achievements of the French Fourth Republic include: the re-establishment of a democratic regime after the authoritarian rule of Marshal Pétain, and the War; dealing with the legacy of the German occupation while remaining one of the powers in the new diplomatic scenario; contributing to the European agreements on coal and steel, atomic energy, and the creation of the European Economic Community; negotiating independence for Tunisia and Morocco; ending the colonial war in Indo-China; and putting into play many long-term projects and legislation. During the Fourth Republic, France's economic recovery and development compared favorably with the rest of Europe. Paris was for a while a highly attractive international capital of the arts and humanities. Pluralistic intellectual life flourished, in contrast to further ideological polarization in the 1960s.

The French Fourth Republic ended as a result of a military coup. By early 1958, the French Army in Algeria began to act without the approval of the French

Cabinet by fighting against the movement for independence. In May, the Army chiefs removed civil officers in the colony and threatened to march on Paris in defence of a 'French Algeria'. General de Gaulle then quickly returned from political retirement and blackmailed the incumbent government with a military takeover if he were not given the premiership. The Gaullist party had obtained 22 per cent of votes in 1951 but its support had fallen to 4 per cent in the following election in 1956. The popular approval of the Premiers and Cabinets of the existing legislature elected in 1956 was as great as for the previous two legislatures (according to the collection of IFOP survey polls compiled by MacRae 1967: 309–13). Yet, under the threat of coup and in a highly unusual move, on June 1958 a majority of the National Assembly voted De Gaulle Premier and gave him special powers.

General de Gaulle eventually curbed the military rebellion and gave Algeria independence. At the same time, he introduced significant institutional changes which created a new Fifth Republic. On the one hand, Cabinet instability was reduced by increasing the requirements for a vote of censure and by giving the President of the Republic (de Gaulle himself) the power of dissolution of the Assembly. On the other hand, proportional representation in the National Assembly was replaced with majority rule. However, as discussed previously, political pluralism in France resisted the restrictive effects of the electoral reform and re-emerged strengthened. At the end of the 20th century, a five-party coalition Cabinet was 'cohabitating' with a President elected with the support of two other parties (one of them, in fact, a multiparty coalition itself).

The Italian First Republic
At the liberation of Italy from Fascism in 1945, national elections were called with party lists and proportional representation. The electoral rules established during the constituent period 1945–7 used the Imperiali quota at the district level and highest remainders at the national level, favoring the allocation of seats to parties according to their votes and the possibility for small parties to obtain parliamentary representation. The ballot admitted preferential vote for three or four individual candidates within a party list.

In the second election, in 1948, the Christian-Democratic party obtained an absolute majority of seats in the Chamber of Deputies with 48.5 per cent of votes. Then the Christians tried to introduce a new, majoritarian electoral rule that would have given two-thirds of seats to the party or electoral coalition of parties running separately that obtained an absolute majority of votes. Obviously, the Christians intended to consolidate their single-party domination with self-reinforcing rules. The electoral campaign of 1953 focused chiefly on this issue, with the opposition parties loudly denouncing 'the tricky law'. But the Christians did not obtain a majority of votes and proportional representation remained stable for the following forty years.

The Christian-Democratic party was dominant from 1946 to 1979. In eight

successive elections it was the median voter party and, thanks to the proportionality of the electoral rules, it also captured the median seat in Parliament. The
Communists were the second party in votes, but their extreme position on the left
side of the ideological spectrum dramatically diminished their chance of entering
into a majority parliamentary coalition. After the initial period of 'national
concentration' governments (1945–7), the Communists were also vetoed as regular partners in national politics, especially for their position on Cold War foreign
policy. The Christians, thus, could form frequent minority single-party Cabinets
in the expectation that they would not be overthrown by a joint action of the
parties on their left (basically Communists and Socialists) and on their right
(Monarchists and Fascists). Alternatively, the Christians formed coalitions with
minor partners of center-right, the Liberals, or center-left, the Republicans and
the Social-Democrats. In 1963, the Socialists were also incorporated into multiparty coalition Cabinets with the Christians. After the election of 1976, even the
Communists supported in Parliament the Cabinet of the Christian Premier Giulio
Andreotti.

During this period, ministerial portfolios within multiparty Cabinets were
distributed in rough proportion to each party's contribution in parliamentary seats
to form a majority. But, as a consequence of frequent minority Cabinets of the
Christians, these obtained in total about four times the number of ministries of the
'lay' parties combined despite having only about twice the number of seats of the
latter (Socialists, Social-Democrats, Republicans, and Liberals). All premiers
were members of the largest, median party.

A different period was initiated with the election of 1979. A higher proportion
of votes for the Communists and a lower proportion for the Christians produced
the effect of moving the median vote and the median seat to the 'lay' space,
despite the fact that the parties in it had not broadened their electoral support.

From the new, advantageous median position, the 'lay' parties increased their
bargaining power with the implicit threat of forming an alternative majority with
the Communists (which in fact happened in a number of regional and local
governments). Several four- and five-party coalition Cabinets were formed in this
period. The Christians continued to have about twice the number of votes and
parliamentary seats than all the 'lay' parties combined, but ministerial portfolios
were now distributed exactly half-and-half from 1980 to 1992. Also, for about
half this period the Premiers were members of minority parties, Giovanni
Spadolini (1981–2), a Republican, and Bettino Craxi (1983–7), a Socialist. Table
3.12 shows results in notes and seats as well as in the further distribution of
Cabinet ministers for the two periods mentioned.

The Christian-Democratic leadership developed formal rules for allocating
ministries to both the parties and its own internal fractions according to some estimated value of the portfolios (the so-called 'Cencelli's manual'). Five categories
of ministries were distinguished. The most important, A, included Foreign
Affairs, Interior, and Finance, all of which were almost always controlled by the

TABLE 3.12. *Votes, seats, and ministries in the Italian First Republic (1945–92)*

		1945–79 (8 elections, 37 cabinets)			1979–92 (3 elections, 12 cabinets)		
		Votes	Seats	Ministries	Votes	Seats	Ministries
LEFT	Communists	25	26	<1	32	32	0
MEDIAN	'Lay' parties	21	18	15 *MEDIAN*	23	21	40
	Christians	40	44	76	35	38	53
	Liberals	4	4	3	2	2	4
RIGHT	Fascists	6	6	0	6	6	0
	Others	3	2	[5]	2	1	[3]
		100	100	100	100	100	100

Note: Numbers are percentages of votes, seats, and ministries. Dotted lines separate Cabinet parties from more extreme or other parties.

Communists: PCI and minor groups (PSIUP, LC, DP); 'Lay': Socialists (PSI), Social–Democrats (PSDI), Republicans (PRI), and Radicals (PR); Christians: DCI; Liberals: PLI; Fascists: Monarchists and MSI. 'Others' for ministries refer to independents.

Source: Author's own calculations with data in Furlong (1994).

Christians. The least important, D, included Tourism and Scientific Research the manual was published by Venditti 1981). In order to round off figures in the distributive calculus, the number of ministries in this period was increased from seventeen to thirty, with up to fifty-eight subsecretaries. Public banks, public companies, social security boards, social assistance agencies, and television channels were also apportioned. During this period the Parliament became gradually weaker, as can be illustrated by the increasing proportion of bills approved at the Cabinet's initiative. The governmental proposals were given a 'privileged path' and Parliament members' secret ballot was abolished in order to give the leaders control of party discipline. The Premier became a most powerful figure (Criscitiello 1994).

Italian politics during the First Republic (1945–92) has been characterized as having 'unstable Cabinets, relatively stable Ministers and Prime Ministers, lasting coalitions, and stagnating policies' (Pasquino 1996: 147). For extensive analyses supporting similar visions, see La Palombara 1987; Hine 1993.) There were eleven elections, thirty changes of premier, and forty-nine cabinets in forty-seven years. This means that the legislature lasted more than four years on average, while the average Cabinet duration was less than a year. Yet only nineteen individuals held the forty-nine Premierships, and seven of these did it for more than half the total time. In particular, Alcide De Gasperi was appointed Premier eight times (in the initial period 1945–53), Giulio Andreotti seven times, Amintore Fanfani six times, and Aldo Moro and Mariano Rumor five times each. All of them were Christian-Democrats. As mentioned, this party almost always controlled some crucial ministries, including those of the Interior, Foreign Affairs, Finance, Education, and Agriculture. Most reshuffles were negotiated by party leaders outside Parliament in order to avoid anticipated dissolution and elections. All of this produced a highly stable, moderate set of public policies from a socially efficient position of the Cabinets.

The First Italian Republic has on its record the re-establishment of a democratic regime after the Fascist period of Mussolini and World War II, its contribution to the creation of the European Economic Community, and a remarkable economic recovery and growth that made many observers speak of the 'Italian miracle'. A very long period of the same major party in power, however, fed clientelar relations between public administration and the ruling political parties, on one hand, and private companies on the other. Illegal private contributions to party finances obtained side-payments in policy decisions and other governmental favors. As mentioned, the executive powers expanded at the expense of parliamentary control, and interparty bargaining eventually distributed power away from the proportions of each party's electoral strength. In the 1992 election, people's support for the party system and certain aspects of the institutional framework had visibly eroded. Yet, it should be noted, contrary to some received opinion, that the decreasing performance of the Italian pluralistic democracy was not due to excessive governmental instability but rather to its opposite—the long-lasting, unchallenged power of the same rulers, a near immobilism.

As a result of baroque multiparty negotiations, the Chamber of Deputies was elected since 1994 with a new mixed system composed of single-member districts with plurality rule and multimember districts with proportional representation. It was expected that this system would promote a higher bipolarization leading to the displacement of the Christian-Democrats from government. Shaken by scandals concerning corruption and becoming the target of new decision rules and judicial prosecution, the Christian party indeed split into several factions, joining opposite electoral coalitions. Two large, heterogeneous multiparty blocs were formed, including as decisive partners the most extreme parties: reformed and unreformed Communists, on one side, and Populists and post-Fascists on the other. The moderate members of each bloc were much closer to each other than to their extreme partners. The two blocs quickly alternated in government in the second half of the 1990s.

Yet, against most expectations, the newly fractionalized political center, approximately corresponding to the legacy of the Christian and the 'lay' parties, was able to develop significant bargaining power. Under the new rules, the small, centrist parties obtained some seats on the basis of proportional representation. At the same time, they could threaten the larger parties of the left and the right with the prospect of running separately in the single-member districts with the aim of making the plurality winner dependent on irrelevant alternatives. As a result of this threat and the corresponding bargaining power, the divided centrist parties were given significant proportions of likely winning candidacies within each of the two large multiparty electoral coalitions. Political pluralism in Italy thus strongly resisted the restrictive effects of the electoral reform of the 1990s. At the end of the 20th century, there were more parties in Parliament than ever before and the incumbent Cabinet was a seven-party coalition.

The Netherlands: From Accommodation to Compromise

In 1918, at the end of World War II, universal suffrage and proportional representation were introduced in the Netherlands. A relatively high number of political parties already existed at that time. The electoral system in use since then is based on a single countrywide district and allocation of seats to parties on the basis of a combination of their quotas of votes and the d'Hondt formula of largest averages. This system produces extremely proportional results and has allowed about four or five major parties to be represented in the Lower House (with up to 14 parties in total in the early 1970s).

The present survey starts after the parenthesis produced by World War II, although major elements of continuity with the previous period can be identified. The major political parties of the Netherlands were initially organized along two different issue-dimensions. First, one Catholic and two major Calvinist parties gave high salience to religious and moral issues. Until the 1963 election, the religious parties together collected a majority of votes and seats in the Lower House. Second, the left, led by the Socialists, and the right, formed by the Liberals, were defined and split on economic issues. Each of the two sets of parties, the religious bloc and the Socialist-Liberal set, gave prominence to different issues and obtained the support of different groups of voters. There was no real competition between the two sets of parties on the same issues nor significant amounts of shifting voters.

During the first twenty years after World War II, the fragmentation of the policy-issue space, as well as the existence of several religious parties, led to the formation of broad multiparty coalitions. All Cabinets included parties with clearly defined positions on each of the two issue-dimensions, which made room for numerically superfluous partners to enter the corresponding coalitions. They were always formed by the Christians together with either the Socialists or the Liberals, or both. This period was the basis for Arend Lijphart's elaboration of his model of 'the politics of accommodation'. Surplus coalitions and consensus politics were presented as essential features of this Dutch-inspired model (Lijphart 1968).

The religious dimension lost prominence in the political agenda and the religious parties ceased to gather together a majority of votes and seats after the election of 1967. The three Christian parties previously alluded to eventually merged into a single candidacy in 1977 and a single party in 1980 (the Christian

Democratic Appeal, or CDA). At the same time, new minor 'lay' parties emerged. The left–right axis became the main organizing dimension of the party system on which all parties tended to compete. Electoral competition and the volatility of voters' choices increased (Irwin and van Holsteyn 1989a, b).

This new situation created some opportunities for higher bipolarization. As a result, the Socialists and the Radicals (Democrats '66) promoted some institutional reforms, including a majoritarian electoral system, in order to facilitate more drastic alternations of parties in government. When these reforms were rejected by the Christians and the Liberals, the Socialists developed a confrontational strategy by forming a common front with two minor radical parties as a commitment to support a more left-oriented Cabinet after the election if they obtained a sufficient number of seats. However, this strategy by the Socialists backfired. In fact, it induced the Christians and the Liberals to respond by choosing each other as preferred Cabinet partners to the exclusion of the Socialists, a coalition which was predominant in the second half of the 1970s and 1980s.

The majority support of the Christian parties, initially, and their central position on the left–right dimensions later, gave them some global advantage in forming governments for fifty years, as reflected in the higher proportion of ministries than shares of votes and seats they controlled. New Cabinet formulas emerged in more recent times, including the one formed by the Socialists and the Liberals. Most Cabinets since 1967 have been based on minimum-winning coalitions without numerically superfluous partners, but there has been a considerable rotation of parties in all ministries and a general sense of compromise when it comes to establishing major public policies (Daalder 1986, 1989). Table 3.13 shows results in volts and seats, as well as in the futher distribution of Cabinet ministers in the period 1946–98.

Cabinet formation is usually a lengthy and laborious process in the Netherlands. Multiparty negotiations may take several months from the election day to completion (with the record at 207 days in 1977). These negotiation costs, a couple of shifting coalitions during the legislature of 1963–7, and some unpredictability of the exact party composition of Cabinets on the basis of the electoral results, moved some politicians and opinion leaders to underline the negative aspects of the consensus politics model and to favor clearer choices. In the 1970s, even Arend Lijphart temporarily suspected that accommodation would be replaced with more adversarial politics (as discussed in Lijphart 1989).

However, the full panorama of Dutch politics since 1945 shows a very high degree of Cabinet and policy stability, moderation, and social efficiency. Post-electoral negotiations are open rather than 'smoke-filled'. Sixty per cent of Cabinets completed their legal terms, the average duration being more than thirty months. Only twelve Premiers led twenty-one Cabinets in fifty-five years, some with long stays in power, such as the Socialist W. Drees for ten years (1948–58) and the Christian R.F.M. Lubbers for twelve years (1982–94). From the point of view of its accomplishments in a growing economy and social well-being, the

TABLE 3.13. *Votes, seats, and ministries in the Dutch parliamentary Monarchy (1946–98)*

	Votes	Seats	Ministries
Socialists	29	30	21
Christians	36	44	55
Liberals	13	14	12
Others	22	12	12
	100	100	100

Note: Numbers are percentages of votes. seats, and ministries for the 16 elections and 21 Cabinets from 1946 to 1998.

Socialists: PvdA; Christians: KP, ARP, CHU (merged into CDA in 1977), and minor KNP, GPV, SGP; Liberals: VVD. 'Others' in ministries include DS '70, D '66, PPR, and independents.

Source: Author's own calculations with data in Daalder (1987), and newspapers.

Netherlands is widely considered to be one of the most successfully governed countries in the world.

Post-war Germany

After the defeat of the Nazis and the end of World War II, military governors in the American, British, and French occupation zones of Germany were gradually replaced with democratic institutions. First, local and Land (*Länder*) parliamentary governments were elected with party-list proportional representation rules (mixed rules in the British zone) in 1946–7. Second, in 1948 the Land governments appointed a Parliamentary Council in charge of building new constitutional rules and choosing the electoral system for national parliamentary elections, which would also be approved by the military governors.

The Christian-Democrats and their permanent allies, the Social-Christians in Bavaria (CDU/CSU), favored plurality rule in single-member districts in the expectation of becoming absolute winners and being able to form single-party Cabinets. Yet the Social-Democrats, which had been the second party in votes at the previous local and Land elections, estimated that, with plurality rule, the likelihood of their becoming absolute winners would be relatively lower and the opportunity of leading majority multiparty coalitions would be unlikely since small parties (like the centrist Liberals-Democrats) might have been eliminated from Parliament. A majority organized by the Socialists and the Liberals thus favored proportional representation, returning in this way to the basic institutional principle of the Weimar Republic (Merkl 1963; for a formal model, see Bawn 1993).

The electoral rules implemented for the 1949 election were based on individual single ballots and two-level districts. First, party lists were allocated seats on the basis of votes at the Land level using the d'Hondt formula of highest averages.

Parties were required to pass a threshold of 5 per cent of votes. Second, single-member districts were used to select individual candidates to fill about half the party seats, but they did not affect, in general, the number of seats allocated to each party. The electoral system was consolidated for the elections from 1953 with the introduction of two separate votes per voter.

This system creates incentives for the voter to split the ticket in favor of small party lists that have weaker or less visible individual candidates in the single-member districts than the two larger parties have. The proportion of voters splitting their tickets, typically in favor of the Liberals or other small parties, was about 7 per cent initially, and has increased since then up to more than 15 per cent. (Barnes *et al.* 1962; Fisher 1973; Jesse 1988; Bawn 1993.)

The Christians made a new attempt to attract the Socialists to a reform establishing plurality rule in the second half of the 1960s, but they again failed due to risk-adverse calculations on the part of the Socialist leadership, as previously discussed in Chapter 2. In 1985, the electoral formula was replaced with the Hare quota and highest remainders, which produce even more proportional representation than did the previous formula.

It must be emphasized that the German system is not a mix of proportional representation and plurality rule, but a personalized proportional representation system giving the voters the opportunity to choose not only a party list but also some of the individual candidates for the corresponding party seats. Only if a party wins more individual candidates than seats obtained by proportional representation does it retain the excess seats and the Parliament is enlarged accordingly. But, to call this an 'additional-member' system may be misleading, since, in fourteen elections from 1949 to 1998, the additional seats have been less than 0.5 per cent of total seats in Parliament. The elections in Germany since 1949 have produced extremely proportional allocations of seats to the parties according to their votes.

In the first few elections after the War, most political parties of the Weimar Republic obtained parliamentary representation (up to eleven parties in 1949, including the Communists and the German Imperialists, but excluding the Nazis). The neo-Nazis in 1953 and the Communists in 1956 were outlawed by the Constitutional Court. The party system was gradually simplified around the larger Christian and Socialist parties with the smaller Liberal party in between. However, this did not prevent the entry of new parties into the institutional scene, especially the Greens in the 1980s and the post-Communists in the 1990s.

All German Cabinets formed from 1949 to 1998 have been multiparty coalitions. The Christians (CDU/CSU) were the median voter party and, thanks to the proportionality of the electoral rules, they also captured the median seat in Parliament in the first three elections in 1949, 1953, and 1957. The Christians formed Cabinets with the support of the Liberal party (FDP) and the German party (DP) on two occasions, and with only the German party on one.

The Liberal party (FDP) became the median voter and the median seat party in all elections from 1961 to 1994. They formed majority coalitions either with the Christians (until 1966 and in the period 1982–98) or with the Socialists (1969–82), with the short interlude of the Christian-Socialist 'Grand Coalition' (1966–9) which encircled the median voter in between the two coalesced parties. The Liberals left the Socialists as Cabinet partners and rejoined the Christians through a censure motion in Parliament in 1982 paralleling a switch in citizens' support. In the following elections, the major parties announced their preferred parliamentary coalitions during the electoral campaigns.

The Liberals have been in government much longer than any of the other parties because of their pivotal position and despite having received, on average, about one-fifth of the votes obtained by the Christians and about one-fourth of those of the Socialists. The Liberals have held a proportion of ministerial portfolios that is almost double that of their average proportion of votes and seats, as can be seen in Table 3.14. The advantage of the Liberals in forming multiparty coalitions in Parliament increased the incentives for some voters to split their two votes between individual candidates of one of the larger parties (generally the Christians) and the small, but usually the pivotal Liberal party list. At least for some of the voters doing this, their sincere preference is for the Christians and they vote strategically for the Liberal party list in order to secure a centrist partner with which the former can form a majority coalition cabinet (see the discussion by Cox 1997: 81–3, 197–8).

The intermediate role of the Liberals moderated the policy effects of successive alternations in power between the two larger parties. They introduced significant elements of stability on relevant issues by always holding the portfolios of Economy, Foreign Affairs, and Justice. Michael Laver and Kenneth Shepsle modelled the allocation of Cabinet portfolios within the long-lasting coalition

TABLE 3.14. *Votes, seats, and ministries in the German Federal Republic (1949–98)*

		Votes	Seats	Ministries
LEFT	Socialists	38	38	27
	Liberals	9	9	16
RIGHT	Christians	44	46	54
	Others	9	7	3
		100	100	100

Note: Numbers are percentages of votes, seats, and ministries for the 14 elections and 16 Cabinets in the period 1949–98.

Socialists: SPD; Liberals: FDP; Christians: CDU/CSU; 'Others' in ministries include the German party (DP) and the Greens.

Source: Author's own calculations with data in Woldendorp *et al.* (1993), Schmidt (1996), and newspapers.

formula of the Christians and the Liberals in the 1980s and early 1990s. They show that, on the basis of each party's preferences for controling different policy issues, the allocation giving the Christians the Ministries of Finance and the Interior, and the Liberals the Ministry of Foreign Affairs (among others) was an equilibrium result maximizing both parties' satisfaction (Laver and Shepsle 1996: 125–39).

In the 1998 election, the Social-Democrats became, for first time, the median voter and the median seat party. This possibly expressed some voters' tiring of the very long period of Christian-Democrat power, as well as a somewhat delayed effect of the incorporation of more leftist East German voters into the electorate in 1990. The Socialists chose the Greens as Cabinet partners in accordance to their own and the Liberals' electoral promises during the previous campaign.

Germany underwent fourteen elections, seven changes of Chancellor (or Premier), and sixteen cabinets in forty-nine years. This means that legislatures tended to complete the legal period of four years and Cabinets were somewhat stable, although reshuffles were relatively frequent (up to twenty-six, or one every two years, on average). In reaction to the experience of the Weimar Republic, the stability of the Cabinets was reinforced by the 'constructive' motion of no confidence, which requires a majority in favor of an alternative candidate to overthrow the incumbent Chancellor. Some of the Chancellors held office for record periods of time, such as Konrad Adenauer for fourteen years (1949–63) and Helmut Kohl for sixteen years (1982–98).

As for the other cases of proportional representation and multiparty coalitions previously discussed, not all government performance in Germany after the War can be attributed to direct effects of such institutional formulas. But, to their credit, these multiple-winner rules produced Cabinet and policy outcomes that presided over the most spectacular case of recovery and prosperity in the second half of the 20th century, the so-called 'German miracle'. Starting from the destruction and humiliation in the aftermath of the War, the government established solid foundatons for the development of a market economy, displayed forceful initiatives in public works and social policy, and per capita income increased threefold. The country regained international respect, achieved reunification with its Eastern part within the previous democratic institutional framework, and played a crucial role in building and enlarging the European Union.

4

What Is Voted For

Social utility requires that there should be but one government; but the diversity of the social elements equally requires that this government should not be
one sole power.

François M. Guizot, *La démocratie en France* (1849)

In simple institutional frameworks, a single election determines a large
number of policies on a varied set of issues. Typically, a national election
in a unitary, unicameral parliamentary regime with plurality rule (the
'Westminster' model) is decisive for all the policy issues which will enter
the government's agenda. However, the outcome of an election dealing
with a large number of issues is immediately unpredictable and dependent
on the specific set of issues that become prominent during the electoral
campaign.

A simple regime based on two major political parties forces voters to
choose a 'package' of policy proposals, many of which they may disagree
with. Logically, the voters tend to choose the party 'package' that is clos-
est to their preferences on the issues they care about most intensely. Yet
voters' information on party policy proposals is usually limited. Voters
have to choose on the basis of the few issue-positions that are aired by
parties and political leaders during the electoral campaign. The winning
party's positions in a simple regime may thus satisfy only some of the
most intense preferences of its supporters, producing relatively low social
utility.

In contrast, complex regimes allow voters to choose according to their
preferences on a greater number of issues. In particular, in multiparty elections based on proportional representation, each party can focus on a
different set of issues, globally enlarging the electoral agenda. The higher
the number of parties, the higher the likelihood that different groups of
voters can find a party whose policy proposals fit their preferences on a
number of relevant issues. Once elected, each party can transfer the corresponding support found among the voters most interested on its proposals
to the further parliamentary stage of coalition formation.

The process of Cabinet formation in parliamentary regimes with
proportional representation usually includes two types of agreements. One
is the distribution of Cabinet portfolios to parties with strong preferences

on different domains (such as social policy or labor for the Socialists, education for the Christians, finances for the Liberals, agriculture for the Agrarians, etc.). The other type of agreement derives from the negotiation of intermediate compromises among the parties involved on some major issue domains (particularly on macroeconomic policy, interior and foreign affairs) (see Budge and Keman 1990; Laver and Shepsle 1994, 1996). This combination of varied multiparty agreements on different issues can produce widely diffused political satisfaction among citizens and high social utility.

Likewise, separate elections for different institutions with significant powers on different policy domains can deal with different sets of issues. This is the case with separate elections for the Assembly and the Presidency in presidential and semi-presidential regimes, as well as for regional assemblies, regional chief executives, mayors, etc., in decentralized states. The higher the number of separate offices, the fewer the number of issues corresponding to each of them. The fewer the number of relevant issues in each electoral campaign, the more predictable and stable the electoral outcome will be. At the same time, the higher the number of separate powers, the broader the global agenda that can be developed by all the elected institutions altogether.

Separate elections for different offices facilitate voters choosing political parties according to their preferences on different issues. Different parties may obtain electoral support in different elections from the same citizens depending on specific proposals on the issues corresponding to the powers of the offices submitted to election. To the extent that separation of powers exists, institutions controlled by different parties can satisfy citizens' preferences on different issues. To the extent that the sharing of powers exists, that is, when separately elected institutions with different political majorities have to collaborate on policy decisions, interinstitutional negotiations may lead to intermediate, moderate compromises able to produce high social utility. Even if some of the separate elections may produce socially biased, minority, inefficient results (for instance, as a consequence of using plurality rule or some other exclusive device), interinstitutional cooperation may counterbalance these drawbacks by approaching more stable and efficient solutions.

Globally, multiple partial winners in multiparty coalition Cabinets and in frameworks of division of powers will be able to satisfy citizens' preferences on many more issues than a single, absolute winner. The number of citizens able to find satisfaction of their preferences on some issues and the corresponding social utility will be higher in complex regimes than in simple regimes.

Unified and Divided Government

In order to analyze different political institutions from the perspective sketched, a primary numerical distinction can be helpful. In classical political theory (as elaborated most prominently by Aristotle) the distinction between the rule of one, the few, or the many was sufficient to define basic types of political regimes, such as 'tyranny', 'oligarchy', and 'democracy' (Aristotle 325–4 BC).

Each of these three institutions alone can define the following extremely simple regimes. (1) The unchallenged rule of one or the Empire (as in modern France with the two Bonapartes). (2) The rule of few, like the typically authoritarian Junta which tends, however, to evolve into a unipersonal dictatorship. (3) The many-member Assembly or Convention republic with only temporary executive councils or committees subject to continuous appointments and dismissals, which tends, however, to be either short-lived or dominated by the rule of a single person invested with the right to interpret the general will.

The threefold numerical distinction can also be useful for identifying different interinstitutional relations in more complex democratic regimes. The rules of one, the few, and the many would correspond to the institutions of unipersonal Premier or President, the few-member Cabinet and the many-member Assembly, respectively. As suggested in regard to single-institutional formulas such as the Junta and the Convention republic, and as will be further discussed, in situations of unified government the most concentrated unit, that is, the institution with the least number of rulers, tends to prevail over the others, in this way further reducing the scope of potential beneficiaries of its decisions. Divided governments, in contrast, allow many-member institutions to develop their influence in the decision making process more effectively.

Historical processes have shaped a variety of formal relationships between the three institutions mentioned above. First, we have the typically English evolution during the 17th to 19th centuries, which was somewhat paralleled in several countries in continental Europe. In this case, rising elected Parliament increasingly challenged the Monarch's absolute powers. This included, first, limiting the Monarch's legislative powers, especially on taxation; second, becoming independent of the Monarch's call or dissolution and taking full legislative powers; and, third, electing a Prime Minister and making the Cabinet accountable to the Assembly.

In the countries that followed this pattern, some intermediate regimes between absolute monarchy and democracy existed for significant periods of time. A nonelected executive and an elected legislative shared powers in the context of a semimonarchical, semi-democratic framework, not only in the United Kingdom but also in France, Russia, and Spain. This kind of intermediate relationship was used during the 20th century by certain monarchies in the Arab world.

However, in most European countries, the process eventually led to a 'parliamentary' democratic regime by extending voting rights and making the Premier and the Cabinet fully dependent on parliamentary election results. Before World War I, most European democracies were parliamentary monarchies, the only exceptions being France and Switzerland. At the beginning of the 21st century, eight of the sixteen parliamentary democracies in Western Europe are still monarchies (while a nonexecutive head of state is elected by the Assembly in four republics and is popularly elected in the other four republics).

The second pattern of institutional evolution from an absolute monarchy included the replacement of the Monarch with an elected President who kept the power to appoint and dismiss the Cabinet, while the Assembly was elected separately, as was initiated in the United States.

The parliamentary example of the Spanish Constitution of 1812 was broadly influential in Latin America at the time of the independence of Spanish colonies, especially in Central America in the 1820s. Brazil (from 1824 to 1889) and Chile (from 1891 to 1925) maintained parliamentary formulas until quite late. Direct presidential elections following the United States model were introduced for the first time in Honduras (1839), Bolivia (1839), El Salvador (1841), Haiti (1843), and Costa Rica (1844). But they were generalized in Latin America only after 1848, under the additional influence of the presidential Second Republic and the Second Empire in France. However, even with presidential formulas, parliamentary control of executive ministers and other parliamentary-like devices were relatively common in later periods. Direct presidential elections were also introduced in a number of other former colonies, especially in Africa at the beginning of the 1960s, in search of a unipersonal executive able to affirm the unity of the new nation.

Further constitutional engineering gave birth to an intermediate formula in which the Premier and the Cabinet depend on the Assembly (as in parliamentary regimes), but the President is directly elected and has significant executive powers (as in presidential regimes). This 'semi-presidential' formula was tried out in Germany at the fall of the empire, lately reinvented in Francein 1958–62, and replicated in some recent democracies, especially in Eastern Europe in the 1990s (Fitzgibbon 1945; Stokes 1945; Bartolini 1984; Blais, Massicotte, and Dobrzynska 1997).

We can thus distinguish three basic models of formal relationship between the three institutions which define different democratic regimes. In one model, the elected Assembly appoints the Premier who in turn appoints the Cabinet. This relationship, known as the parliamentary regime, may produce either a single-party majority in the Assembly and a single-party Cabinet (as in the typical situation in the United Kingdom), or a multiparty Assembly in which no party has an absolute majority of seats leading to a coalition or a minority Cabinet (as in most countries in Western Europe).

In the second constitutional model, the Assembly and the President are elected separately, and the latter appoints the Cabinet. This relationship, known as the presidential regime, may also produce either a single-party majority in both the Assembly and the Presidency, or different party support for the winners in each of the two institutions (as is frequently the case in the United States and Latin America).

In the third intermediate model, the Assembly and the Presidency are also elected separately, but it is the former that appoints the Cabinet. This relationship, known as the 'semi-presidential' regime (or 'premier-presidential', 'dual executive', and, for our purposes, the similar categories of 'semi-parliamentary' or 'premier-assembly' regimes), may also produce either a President's party majority in the Assembly or not (as in France and other countries).

In addition to these 'horizontal' relationships between institutions, 'vertical' relationships can be distinguished as corresponding either to unitary states or to decentralized, federal-type states. In the unitary model, a single, central government holds all relevant powers. In decentralized states, the party in the central government may control different proportions of power in the regional or local governments. Yet, again, the degree of coincidence between the parties in central government and those in decentralized governments, as well as their relationship, can produce different levels of unified or divided government.

In the following pages, two political situations will be distinguished for all the mentioned different constitutional regimes and their variants. Unified government will be considered to exist in all those cases in which a single political party controls all political institutions. This category includes the typical single-party Cabinet in unicameral parliamentarism with plurality rule, as well as situations of unified government in presidential and semi-presidential regimes, unitary states and centralized federalism, despite of their different constitutional formulas, because all of them are single-party rules.

Divided government can be considered to exist in situations of multiparty or minority Cabinets in parliamentarism with proportional representation, as well as in the typical situation of divided government in presidentialism, in 'cohabitation' in semi-presidentialism, and in decentralized federalism, because all of them imply the coexistence or the agreement of multiple partial winners. (For related approaches, see Laver and Shepsle 1991; Tsebelis 1995.) The relative social utility produced by unified or divided governments will be discussed for each type of regime.

This chapter is organized in two sections. The first deals with unified government. The second approaches both 'horizontally' divided government, comparing in particular parliamentarism, presidentialism, and semi-presidentialism, and 'vertically' divided government, or federalism.

4.1. UNIFIED GOVERNMENT

Unified government is one in which a single political party holds absolute legislative and executive powers. As suggested earlier, this situation can be produced in different constitutional frameworks, including the following:

(i) a single party both commands a majority in the Assembly and forms the Cabinet in a parliamentary regime, as frequently happens in parliamentary elections with plurality rule;

(ii) the President's party has a majority in the Assembly, in both presidential and semi-presidential regimes, as tends to happen in concurrent elections;

(iii) the central government's party controls all the regional or local governments, basically by controlling the regional or local chief executives.

When different institutions are in the hands of a single, disciplined political party, the most concentrated institution tends to prevail. It may seem rather obvious that the unipersonal office of Premier or President prevails over the collective Cabinet whose members the former has appointed (even if some executive decisions must be shared with the Cabinet members, as is usually required by constitutional rules). But the Premier or President also tends to prevail over a numerous Assembly in which the Premier's or President's party has a majority, rather than the the other way round, despite the latter having appointed the Premier or having been elected separately from the President. Thus, the relative power of the institutions does not depend mechanically on their principal-agent relations, but is strongly dependent on each institutional unit's capacity for decision making. The tendency toward concentration of power is self-reinforcing. When different institutions fall under control of the same political party, not only do they behave as a single actor, but the most concentrated or 'smallest' unit prevails.

This unbalanced situation is reflected in the usual claims regarding the paradoxical 'decline of parliaments' in parliamentary regimes and the 'executive dominance' in regimes with separate elections for the Assembly and the Presidency. These claims began to be aired as a result of the first elections with actual universal men's suffrage at the beginning of the

20th century in Western Europe and North America. (Bryce 1921). New, broad, complex electorates launched many more demands for provision of public goods and redistributive decisions than had their predecessors in pre-democratic or semi-democratic times and contributed to substantial enlargements of governments' agendas. It is in this context that the relative organizational advantage of unipersonal institutions over the many-member Assembly became prominent. The higher the number of issues to deal with, the more prominent the relative advantage of the unipersonal Premier or President to make effective decisions at the expense of an Assembly facing new costs of decision making. Unchecked leadership and executive domination emerged as temporarily appealing alternatives in comparison to disappointingly ineffective parliaments.

The dominance of the unit with a smaller number of members can be explained by institutional factors, such as organizational efficacy and electoral rules. Organizational efficacy reflects the problems of collective action. A single person or a small organization such as a Presidency or a Cabinet, can decide more quickly than a large organization, such as an Assembly, for reasons of unity of purpose and the time required to collect information, share others' information, bargain and vote, even if all or a majority of the organization's members share similar political preferences. A Cabinet prevails over an Assembly with the same political majority for similar reasons of collective action as the board of managers prevails over stockholders in modern corporations.

This is not a very new idea. For example, during the late Middle Ages in the Italian city of Siena, the people's assembly sometimes appointed a small commission with full power (called a *balia*) to replace the more numerous legislative council for a limited period. It was believed at the time that 'in cases in which quick action must be taken, this can be done better and more efficiently by a *few* than by *many*' (Waley 1988). During the discussion of the United States Constitution in late 18th century, Alexander Hamilton noted: 'Decision, activity, secrecy, and dispatch will generally characterize the proceedings of *one* man in a much more eminent degree than in the proceedings of any greater *number*; and *in proportion as the number* is increased, these qualities will be diminished' (Hamilton, Madison, and Jay:1788: No. 70, emphasis added. For similar, apparently unnoticed suggestions, see Olson 1971, ch. 2).

On the basis of greater effectiveness, a President enjoying a unified government can strengthen the discipline of his or her majority party in the Assembly and impose presidential initiatives even in areas that are constitutionally out of the presidential domain. In the case of the United States, for example, it has been noted that, in times of unified government, the President's party is more cohesive in its party votes in the House than the minority opposition party (King and Ragsdale 1988).

For similar reasons of collective action, an Assembly tends to develop smaller internal organizations, such as committees and subcommittees, in order to accomplish their tasks more effectively. Parliamentary reforms aimed at increasing the power of the Assembly over the Premier and Cabinet always include parliamentary committee specialization, as in the United Kingdom and Germany after the World War II. In contrast, if constitution-makers want to curb the power of the Assembly in favor of the Presidency, they can do so by reducing the number of committees in the Assembly, as happened in the transition from the Fourth to the Fifth Republics in France beginning in 1958. (The French National Assembly, which previously worked with more than twenty committees roughly corresponding to ministerial departments, was reduced to only five committees under the new semi-presidential regime.)

For the same reason of effectiveness, a smaller chamber with sufficient legislative powers like a federal Senate should have less difficulty in passing legislation than the larger, lower chamber, as is the case in symmetrical bicameral regimes like the United States. (For the period 1947–83, on average, the US House was able to pass only 11.7 per cent of its bills, while the Senate was able to pass 37.3 per cent; see the discussion in Brams 1989, 1990 ch. 8; Brams, Affuso, and Kilgour 1989; Petracca 1989.)

A second factor in the dominance of the smaller institutional unit lies in the different strategies induced by the procedures for appointing offices. A multiparty Assembly or a coalition Cabinet are composed of multiple, partial winners: all the parties in the Assembly have some seats, all the parties in the Cabinet have some portfolios. In these situations, parties need to bargain and reach agreements among (at least some of) them in order to make decisions. In contrast, a single-party majority Cabinet or a President is a single, absolute winner which does not share power with other actors. While underdog candidates for Assembly seats or Cabinet portfolios in multiparty settings can be given some portions of the offices at stake, the defeated candidates in a single-party Premiership or the Presidency are completely excluded from power. In interinstitutional relations, the President or the single-party Cabinet tends to reproduce the absolute-winner/absolute-loser logic instead of the negotiating, partial-winner logic of the multiparty Assembly or coalition Cabinet.

The logic of this conflict was already perceived during the discussion of the United States Constitution in 1787, when warnings of reproducing an 'elective monarchy' were heard repeatedly. Similar comments were restated at the first historical introduction of the direct election of President with universal suffrage in France in 1851. Alexis de Tocqueville, who was at the time member of the Drafting Committee of the Constitution, cautioned that a President elected directly by the people, especially in a country emerging from an absolute monarchy and with a strong centralization of the state, that is, with a very high horizontal and vertical concentration of powers, would become an authoritarian monarch. For de Tocqueville, a democratic regime would only be possible, 'either if the sphere of (the President's) powers is strictly curtailed', including a ban on re-election or, 'if the President was to be left with his powers, he should not be elected by the people but by the Assembly and submitted to its control', which corresponds to the institutional relationship in a parliamentary regime (de Tocqueville 1851).

An implication of this analysis is that a President with a single-party majority in the Assembly can be considered to be relatively more powerful than a Premier without such a majority, despite the weaker constitutional powers of the former, since the President will, in practice, hold most decision-making powers while not being submitted to regular parliamentary control. Another important implication is that the many-member Assembly can only balance its relationship with the one-member or a few-member executive when the latter has no majority in the former; otherwise it tends to be dominated by the more concentrated institution of the executive and its Chief.

In modern times, a single-party majority in the Assembly was enjoyed by, among others, powerful British Premiers, such as Winston Churchill (1941–5, 1951–5) and Margaret Thatcher (1979–91); 'monarchical' presidents of France, such as Charles de Gaulle (1962–9) and François Mitterrand (1981–6); and American 'war' or 'imperial' Presidents such as Abraham Lincoln (1861–4), Theodore Roosevelt (1901–8), Woodrow Wilson (1913–18), Franklin D. Roosevelt (1933–45), Harry S. Truman (1945–6, and 1949–52), John F. Kennedy (1961–3), and Lyndon B. Johnson (1963–8).

In the parliamentary United Kingdom, Conservative politician Lord Hailsham (formerly Quintin Hogg) coined the expression 'elective dictatorship' to account for a model of centralized democracy that he contrasted with the model of limited government (Hailsham 1978). The epithet was later, appropriately used to characterize the period of Thatcher's premiership in the 1980s (especially by political scientist Vernon Bogdanor 1988).

In de Gaulle's semi-presidential France, Radical leader Mendès-France characterized unified government as 'the monopolization of power in the hands of a single man', while Socialist candidate in opposition, Mitterrand, denounced de Gaulle's concentrated power as 'the permanent coup d'état' (Mitterrand 1964). Yet, when he became President with an absolute majority in the Assembly, Mitterrand found that the same institutions 'suited him well' (Suleiman 1994).

In the presidential United States, there was an increasing 'appropriation by the Presidency of powers reserved by the Constitution and by long historical practice to Congress', in particular the capture by the Presidency of the decision to go to war (Schlesinger 1973). Initially, the Presidency was given a great amount of foreign-policy powers for its greater ability in responding to a surprise attack or conducting military operations, but 'imperial' presidents expanded these powers to domestic affairs.

Note again that we are dealing with the concentration of power and not with principal-agent relationships. The Premier or the President (the principal) always prevails over his or her Cabinet (the agent), but in parliamentary regimes with a single-party majority, the Cabinet (the agent) prevails over the Assembly (the principal). It does not seem to be a question of agenda power either. The Premier and his or her Cabinet are agenda-setters and tend to prevail over the Assembly in parliamentary regimes, but in presidential regimes the President can prevail over an Assembly with a majority of the President's party despite the fact that the Assembly is usually considered the major agenda-setter in times of divided government.

The most concentrated unit also tends to prevail in schemes of 'vertical' division of powers between the central government and a number of regional, local governments. Even if legal powers in different domains are allocated to various governmental levels, when a single party is in power at the center and in most regional or local units, it tends to promote unification and centralization.

The central government can try to limit the exercise of legislative and executive shared powers by the noncentral units by establishing strongly constraining basic legislation, by expanding new areas of governmental activity under its control, or by redistributing financial resources in favor of the center. It may try to transform the separate powers of the noncentral units into shared powers with the center. Ultimately, the center may try to curb the capability of noncentral units for making the final decision in any domain. The prevalence of political centralization over legal decentralization is reflected in the label 'centralized federalism' which has been used in some countries during periods of vertically unified government, as discussed further below.

Limiting Unified Government

One of the institutional rules aimed at maintaining some balance of power between the Presidency and the Assembly when they are elected separately, or at least limiting the degree of concentration of powers in the hands of the President, especially in periods of unified government, is the ban on re-election or the establishment of term limits for the President. Using a more general argument in favor of reducing rulers' power and the opportunities for their self-interested behavior, term limits for legislative

Assemblies have also been promoted. Sometimes, different proposals for term limits are linked to different term lengths. Since this is a question of interinstitutional relations and relative power, we need to analyze term limits and lengths for all the institutions involved, particularly the Presidency and the Assembly, rather than to evaluate the likely effects of any of these formulas for an isolated institution.

From the analytical approach previously presented, we obtain the following insight. In the case that both the President and Assembly members are banned re-election or have firm term limits imposed, as well as in the case that neither the President nor the Assembly members are limited in their number of terms in office, the President prevails. This is due, as previously remarked, to the greater effectiveness of the unipersonal Presidency in decision making, as well as to its constitutive characteristic of total winner, which induces the President to resist sharing power with the Assembly when no asymmetrical checks are imposed on the former.

Some balance of power can be attained when the President can be re-elected but is submitted to term limits, whereas Assembly members can be re-elected an unlimited number of times. The relationship is, however, more balanced if the President is banned from re-election completely and Assembly members are not. Logically, in the opposite case, if only Assembly members are restricted to term limits, the President will certainly dominate. Revealingly, the latter model has only existed in processes which led to the establishment of a presidential, personal dictatorship.

Table 4.1 presents cases corresponding to three of the four logical possible combinations of rules regarding re-election of the President and the Assembly, as viewed here, in twelve North and South American presidential regimes. As mentioned, the fourth combination of re-election of the President and nonre-election of the Assembly does not exist in reality in democratic regimes. The extremely powerful President that this would create would very closely approach dictatorship, as will be discussed below.

As stated earlier, the combination of rules in the first category—firm limits on re-election of any of the offices—provides an advantage to the Presidency. Mexico is a prominent case in which re-election is banned for all the offices. It also includes a considerable concentration of power in the hands of the President and the longest presidential tenure length on the list: six years. Venezuela moved to a comparable position in 1999 when the previous potentially balanced relationship based upon not immediate re-election of the President and unlimited re-election of Congress was abandoned. It was replaced with two-term limits for both the President, with six-year terms, and the National Assembly, with five-year terms. In

TABLE 4.1. *Re-election of Presidents and Assemblies in North and South America*

PRESIDENT'S ADVANTAGE			<————————>			BALANCED RELATIONSHIP		
President: Term-limits			Two-term re-election			Not immediate re-election		
Assembly: Term-limits			Unlimited re-election			Unlimited re-election		
Mexico (1917)	6	3/6	Argentina (1994)	4	4/6	Bolivia (1994)	5	5/5
Costa Rica (1949)	4	4	Brazil (1997)	4	4/8	Chile (1994)	6	4/8
Venezuela (1999)	6	5	Peru (1993)	5	5	Colombia(1991)	4	4/4
			USA (1951)	4	2/6	Ecuador (1998)	4	2–4
						Uruguay (1966)	5	5/5

Note: Numbers are term lengths (years) for the President and the single or the two chambers of the Assembly, respectively (Ecuador uses a mixed system for the unicameral Assembly). Years refer to the most recent constitutional rules on the matter.

Sources: González (1998): Jones (1995*b*, 1997*a*), Nohlen (1998); Serrafero (1997); http://www.venezuela.gov.ve/constitucion.

the case of Costa Rica, the potential relative advantage of the Presidency is counterbalanced by its extraordinarily limited powers. The President of Costa Rica does not have decree, veto, or exclusive legislative initiative powers. In addition, Costa Rican Assembly members may run again for office after one interim period, while the President must wait no less than thirty years before running again. (For presidential power, see Shugart and Carey 1992, tables 8.1, 8.2.)

At the other extreme (on the right of the Table 4.1), some balance of power can be found when the President is banned from running for a second consecutive term while the Assembly members can be re-elected indefinitely. Bolivia, Chile, Colombia, Ecuador, and Uruguay, belong to this category. In all cases except that of Colombia, constitutional rules allow the President to run again for election after one interim term, but this is a rare occurrence.

Cases: Trading Off Term Limits and Lengths

Two basic patterns in the adoption of rules on term limits and lengths for separately elected institutions can be identified. One of these patterns tends to maintain a balance between the Presidency and the Assembly, as can be seen in the practice and institutional regulations in the United States. The other pattern leads to the reinforcement of the Presidency and increasing authoritarianism, as will be illustrated here with the case of institutional evolution in Mexico. In most Latin American presidential regimes, this issue has been the occasion of frequent constitutional reforms. Four cases in the 1990s will be briefly reviewed below: two moves to relatively balanced institutional relations after processes of redemocratization in Argentina and Brazil, and two moves toward higher concentration of presidential power approaching more authoritarian formulas in Peru and Venezuela. The general relationship between concentration of institutional power and authoritarianism will also be discussed.

Term Limits in the United States

The 1789 United States Constitution did not include explicit regulations on term limits for the Presidency or for Congress. The first President, George Washington, created a precedent by limiting himself to two terms each of four years (1789–97). Presidents Thomas Jefferson (1801–9), James Madison (1809–17), and James Monroe (1817–25) followed his example. The rule of two terms for President, paralleled with the absence of limits for re-election of members of Congress, was considered for some to be an element of the United States' 'unwritten constitution'. Yet for others, the lack of legal restrictions on the length of the Presidency was seen as an 'open door to dictatorship'. Echoing the latter's worries, the US Senate approved a constitutional amendment placing a two-term limit on presidential tenure in 1824, but the House of Representatives did not confirm it. Proposals to limit the Presidency to a single term of either four or six years were made repeatedly by President Andrew Jackson (1829–37) at about the time the President's popular election was introduced. Similar proposals were discussed, but not approved, by the Senate in 1866 and in 1912.

Some Presidents considered running for a third term. They include, in particular, Theodore Roosevelt, who after one acting term and one elected term (1901–9), ran again after one interim break in 1912, but came second in the race. Only after four successive elections of Democratic President Franklin D. Roosevelt in 1932, 1936, 1940, and 1944, who broke the precedent rule twice, while not admitting being terminally ill, and in times of war, was a presidential term limit formally introduced to the Constitution. As soon as the Republicans obtained a majority in Congress, during Democratic Harry Truman's presidency in 1947, they approved the two-term limit. Echoing constitutional discussions of the end of the 18th century, new warnings against the rise of 'autocracy', 'executive dictatorship', 'totalitarianism', and the creation of 'a dynasty' dominated the debates. The Twenty-Second Amendment of the Constitution banning a President to run for a third term of office was ratified by state legislatures in 1951 (Rossiter 1987: 215–22; Sundquist 1992: 46–54).

In contrast to the formal restrictions imposed on presidential terms, the members of the US Congress have not been submitted to term limits in office. One of the clearest disadvantages of Congress as opposed to the Presidency is the relatively short lengths of terms of office: two years for the House and six years for the Senate compared to four years for the President. Amendments proposing longer congressional terms were introduced in every session from 1869 to 1906.

Between 1929 and 1963 there were sixty-four such proposals, in contrast to only nine attempts to limit congressional terms during the same period (Kamber 1995.)

More prominently, a proposal for lengthening terms to four years for the House and eight years for the Senate was discussed in Congress in 1965–6. President Johnson backed the proposal. However, it was not finally approved probably because congressmen realized that it might have had counter-productive effects. With the proposed new lengths of terms of office, Congressional elections would have always been concurrent with Presidential elections. As will be discussed in the next section, concurrent elections for President and for Congress usually play out in favor of the President's party, in contrast to nonconcurrent elections. The likely effect of the reform would thus have been more frequent periods of unified government, that is, of the President's party having a majority in Congress. According to our previous discussion, unified government would have given the unipersonal Presidency a strong advantage over the multimember Congress (Sundquist 1992: 71–4; similar proposals were made by the Committee on Constitutional Reform in 1987, Robinson 1985, 1989).

Term limits for re-election of legislature members were promoted in more recent times. Since 1990, initiatives to limit state Assembly terms of office were passed in twenty-three states. The Republicans came to the 1994 US Congressional elections with the proposal of introducing term limits for members of the two chambers of Congress. Yet these decisions and proposals were overturned by the Supreme Court in 1995 and again in 1997, as well as by some state courts.

A balance of power between a unipersonal President limited to two terms in office and a multimember Congress with unlimited terms, has thus been preserved in the legal framework. In fact, the average length in office of American Presidents from 1945 to 2000 was 5.6 years, the average lengths for congressmen were much longer: 10.4 years for representatives and 10.3 years for senators in the period 1953–2000 (author's calculations with data in Ornstein, Mann, and Malbin 1998).

Revolutionary Nonre-election in Mexico

In contrast to the United States, the Mexicans had several revolutions with the purpose of banning the re-election of the President, but actual results rather favored the concentration of power and authoritarianism. The first experience of authoritarian presidentialism was generated by General Antonio López de Santa Anna. He was elected President of Mexico eleven times beginning in 1833 and became a dictator adorned with monarchical pomp, but he also attained huge failures in both domestic and foreign policy, including a defeat in war and the corresponding loss of territory to the United States. Santa Anna was overthrown and expelled from the country in 1855.

Once the Republic was re-established, Benito Juárez was elected President twice, in 1867 and 1871. After Juárez died in office, acting-President Sebastián

Lerdo de Tejada was elected in 1872 and attempted re-election four years later. Against both Juárez and Lerdo de Tejada, opposition to re-election and proposals to introduce the principle of a single presidential term into the Constitution were promoted, most prominently by General Porfirio Díaz. The issue became central in Mexican politics, to the point that Díaz, referring to his own protest movement in 1871, suggested: 'If no citizen asserts himself and perpetuates himself in power, this will be the last revolution'.

On the basis of this position, Porfirio Díaz was first elected President of Mexico in 1877. Yet he immediately introduced a constitutional reform to allow himself to run again for office after one interim term. Accordingly, he was again elected President in 1884, and again reformed the Constitution in order to allow his own immediate re-election. A further reform in 1890 suppressed any limit and lengthened the presidential term from four to six years. Díaz was elected four more times under the new rules. By the time of his seventh election in 1910, there were increasing accusations of electoral fraud.

The Liberal opposition to Díaz' dictatorship was led by Francisco I. Madero, who organized the Anti-Re-election Party with a program based on the nonre-election of the President and reduction of the presidential term to four years. Social demands for distribution of land to peasants and improvement of workers' conditions were added to the revolutionary political platform. Remarkably, Madero contrasted democracy with 'absolute power' (Madero 1908). In 1911, Porfirio Díaz was overthrown by a revolutionary movement under the motto, 'Effective Suffrage, No Re-election'. The new 1917 Constitution, mostly written by Venustiano Carranza, the first Mexican President who was elected only once, banned re-election of all executive offices: President, Vice-President, state Governors, and municipal Presidents (Brandenburg 1964; Scott 1964).

The Mexican example of limiting the executive was celebrated and imitated in other countries in the area. Ill-fated experiences of *caudillos* and presidential dictators led all Central American governments to commit themselves to maintaining the constitutional principle of nonre-election for the offices of President and Vice-President of the Republic at the General Treaty of Peace and Amity signed in Washington in 1927. The nonre-election principle was also widely adopted in the republics of South America.

However, single-party rule in post-revolutionary Mexico eventually led to a new form of concentration of power to the advantage of the Presidency. First, ex-President Alvaro Obregón broke the existing rules by seeking the approval of re-election in 1927 and the extension of the presidential term from four to six years one year later. He obtained re-election in 1928, but was assassinated almost immediately.

A more successful formula for establishing a new relationship of powers to the advantage of the Presidency was introduced in 1933: nonre-election of the six-year term President, and also nonre-election of three-year deputies and six-year senators. This formula caused the members of Congress, especially the

House, to be permanently unexperienced, as well as dependent on the President for further appointments after their mandates. From that point, the Mexican Congress consisted of rather passive, incompetent, and obedient men. President Lázaro Cárdenas (1934–40) was the first to enjoy the advantages of this new regulation. He also accumulated for the first time the offices of President of the Republic and head of the single ruling party, the Revolutionary National Party (PNR, later PRM and with the name of Institutional Revolutionary Party, PRI, since 1946).

Despite being based on a legal, constitutional scheme of division of powers between the President and Congress, and of being a federal state, Mexico became an authoritarian presidential regime with increasing concentration of powers in the Presidency since the 1930s. The six-year term President is nonre-electable, but, as a consequence of applying the same principle of nonre-election to the other institutions and shorter terms to the House members, he faces a much weaker Congress, as well as diminished state Governors. Until the end of the 20th century, the Mexican President initiated almost all legislation; his veto power over congressional bills was never overruled; he appointed all members of his Cabinet and up to 18,000 paid officers, including military chiefs and judges, without congressional checks. As actual party head, the Mexican President could also appoint and dismiss candidates for about 25,000 other offices (including candidates for state Governors and many at the local level). Until the 1990s, the incumbent President appointed his own successor (a practice known as '*el dedazo*', or pointing out with 'the big finger'). Voting bribes, manipulation, and electoral fraud were widespread. As President Miguel Alemán's aide said in the early 1950s, 'the power of a President of Mexico has no other limits but time, his six years in office'.

A succession of unipersonal, temporary dictators paraded through the presidential residence of 'Los Pinos' in Mexico City for several decades. The concentration of power was even further accentuated after the repressive turn adopted in 1968, at the slaughter of protest students in the Three Cultures square in Tlatelolco, Mexico City, during the presidency of Gustavo Díaz Ordaz (1964–70), as well as during that of Luis Echevarría, who had been Secretary of Governance in 1968 (1970–6). It reached a peak with José López Portillo (1976–82), who was elected without even a symbolic opponent and witnessed the breakdown of the traditional model of state-controlled economic growth. Re-election of Congress members and other nonpresidential offices was a permanent demand of opposition parties in further attempts at democratization (Craig and Cornelius 1995; Weldon 1997; Colomer 1998*b*).

Bargaining Re-election for Accountability

In order to reach some balance of power between separate institutions, a trade-off can be developed between the number of terms in office, the term length, and the legal division of powers between the institutions. If, for example, the President's re-election is accepted, the presidential term length may be shortened and the new combination of rules may produce a similar expected period of presidential tenure. Longer potential tenures can be counterbalanced either with more frequent elections, which make the rulers more accountable to voters, with more relevant interinstitutional checks, or with some reduction in the corresponding legal powers of the institution. (Some ideas along these lines are suggested in Cain 1996; Grofman and Sutherland 1996; Carey 1996.)

Four cases of recent institutional reforms regarding term and length limits are briefly described below. While the cases of Argentina and Brazil seem to have settled on relatively balanced relationships by exchanging presidential re-election for shorter terms, Peru and Venezuela have evolved in favor of a greater concentration of power in the President, and authoritarianism.

Institutional Balance. Recent institutional reforms in Argentina were broadly consensual and led to a remarkably balanced framework. Almost no President of Argentina had been re-elected for about a century since the 1853 Constitution. The only exception was Colonel Juan-Domingo Perón, who promoted a constitutional reform in 1949 in order to be re-elected three years later. However, the possibility of presidential re-election was eliminated after Perón was overthrown in 1955 and, following several periods of authoritarian rule, against at the redemocratization of the country in 1983.

President Raúl Alfonsín, from the Radical party, backed a further reform, elaborated by the Council for the Consolidation of Democracy in 1987, which included a reduction of presidential powers, the creation of the figure of Premier, and interinstitutional relations close to the semi-presidential model (see Nino *et al.* 1992). The Radicals were, however, defeated at the following presidential election in 1989, and the new President, Carlos Menem, from the Justicialist party, prepared an alternative reform, which included the re-election of the President, and which he initially tried to approve by referendum. Yet, at Alfonsín's initiative, the two major parties opened formal negotiations on the issue. These led to the 'Pacto de Olivos' (for the name of the presidential resid-ence) between the two leaders in 1993, which was followed by the election of a Constituent Assembly with no single-party majority and the approval of a new Constitution in 1994.

The intermediate agreement between a move toward parliamentary-like formulas, as initially promoted by the Radicals, and a move toward greater presidential powers, as preferred by the Justicialist leader, was arranged in the following way. The President was permitted to be re-elected for a second term, but the term length was shortened. Instead of a six-year period, a President could be in office for two periods of four years. Under the assumption that the results of the second election were completely uncertain, the new formula would produce, in the long term and on average, an expected period in office similar to the former: $4 + (4 \times 0.5) = 6$. But, it introduces an intermediate occasion of accountability for the incumbent President. In addition, the new Constitution created the post of

Head of the Ministers Cabinet, or Coordinating Minister, which can be submitted to censure by the Assembly. President Menem was re-elected once in 1995 without a majority in the Assembly.

In Brazil, the re-election of the President had never been permitted since the foundation of the Republic in 1889. The most recent process of redemocratization led to the 1988 Constitution, in which the principle of nonre-election was confirmed. In addition, many presidential powers were transferred to the Assembly. A referendum was even called for the introduction of a parliamentary regime (as well as on the re-establishment of the Monarchy) in 1993, but most voters preferred to retain the direct election of the President. A further constitutional review by the Assembly reduced the presidential term length from five to four years.

This trend in favor of restricting presidential powers was somewhat curbed with the election of President Fernando Henrique Cardoso in 1994, although further reforms were approved with rather broad political consensus. Not having a majority in the Assembly, Cardoso formed a multiparty coalition Cabinet with more support than his previous presidential candidacy. In 1997, he obtained Assembly approval for a constitutional amendment permitting the re-election of the President. The previous single term of five years was thus finally replaced with two terms of four years, producing in this way an institutional trade-off between term limits and term length. In 1998, Cardoso was the first Brazilian President to be re-elected in more than a hundred years.

In the President's Advantage. When Alberto Fujimori was elected President of Peru in 1990, constitutional presidential powers were relatively limited. The 1980 Constitution had created the figure of a Prime Minister subject to censure by the Assembly. In addition, the President did not have legislative veto or decree powers, and the assembly had exclusive powers to prepare, amend, and approve the budget. Fujimori had run for office without a structured party behind him and did not have very wide support in the Assembly. After some attempts to use emergency legislative powers and govern illegally by decree, in April 1992 President Fujimori suspended the Constitution and disbanded the Assembly. Fujimori's *'autogolpe'* ('self-coup') was organized with the Armed Forces' support and included deployment of troops in the capital and the arrest of the presidents of the two Assembly chambers, opposition party leaders, and trade union organizers. Requesting full power to implement economic reforms and fight political terrorism and drug-trafficking, Fujimori concentrated all legislative powers and proceeded to reorganize the judiciary.

Fujimori's supporters obtained a majority in a Constituent Assembly called in November 1992 which was boycotted by the opposition. The new Constitution approved in September 1993 introduced the re-election of the President for a second term. The Assembly was reduced to one chamber, giving the President's party a higher likelihood of obtaining a unified government. In 1995, Fujimori was re-elected, while his party obtained a majority in the Assembly in the midst of accusations of electoral fraud. The Assembly, dominated by the President, voted for an 'interpretation' of the rules allowing Fujimori to run for a third term.

Interinstitutional relations had been relatively balanced in democratic Venezuela since 1958. According to the 1961 Constitution, the President was elected for a term of five years and could not be re-elected before two interim terms, while the members of the Chamber of Deputies and the Senate could be re-elected for consecutive terms of five years without limits. However, several formulas that were initially intended to consolidate the democratic regime, eventually led to rigidity. Voters were given relatively limited choice in a system based upon two major political parties, concurrent elections for President and Congress, and a single ballot for the two chambers of Congress in which only the party codes appeared. The leaders of the two larger parties, Social-Democrats and Christian-Democrats, shared key executive, legislative, and judicial appointments and controlled virtually all institutions and social organizations. In the long term, bipartisan politics became a barrier to the entry of new parties, whereas economic crisis and social unrest increased.

Following strong claims of corruption and abuse of power by the old political elites, the presidential election of December 1998 resulted into the victory of Lieutenant- Colonel Hugo Chávez, who had led two attempts of military coup in 1992 (the second from prison). Chávez' supporters also obtained a majority in a Constituent Assembly called in July 1999. The new Constitution approved in December 1999 introduced the immediate re-election of the President for a second term and extended the presidential term length from five to six years. The Assembly was reduced to one chamber, and its members were limited to re-election for two terms of five years. Chávez was allowed to run again for President in 2000 as if it were for his first term.

Unified Authoritarianism

An authoritarian regime is always a unified, highly concentrated government. Democratization processes tend to establish pluralistic formulas and the balanced relationship between institutions, as has been previously suggested by cases of recent democracies and will be more generally discussed in the final chapter of this book. Conversely, attempts at expanding executive powers, imposing unipersonal, effective government, lengthening presidential tenure, multiplying consecutive presidential terms, or absorbing decentralized governmental units tend to lead to nondemocratic regimes.

There are a few, highly prominent cases of Premiers who disbanded a directly elected Parliament that had previously appointed them, and became dictators, including Benito Mussolini in Italy in 1922 and Adolf Hitler in Germany in 1934. But, more frequently, the concentration of powers evolves into dictatorship in presidential regimes. Sometimes, the President and his dominating party can maintain Assembly and Presidential elections with low degrees of competition, as was the case with the ruling leaders in Mexico since the 1930s, Juan-Domingo Perón in Argentina in the 1950s, and a number of other initially elected *caudillos* in Latin America and Africa in the 1950s and 1960s. Some directly elected Presidents have gone so far as to eliminate the elected Assembly. Cases include the early, notorious coup by Louis Napoleon in France in 1851, as well as those by Gabriel Terra in Uruguay in 1931; José M. Velasco Ibarra in Ecuador in 1946, and again in 1970; Mariano Ospina (against an attempt of impeachment by the Assembly) in Colombia in 1949; Ferdinand Marcos in the Philippines in 1972; Juan M. Bordaberry in Uruguay in 1973; Alberto Fujimori in Peru in 1992; Jorge Serrano in Guatemala in 1993; and Boris Yeltsin in Russia (against a partly nondemocratic Assembly) in 1993.

It is relevant to note that, if an authoritarian regime is directly established by a faction of the Armed Forces or by an armed revolutionary movement, they either support the incumbent unipersonal President and close down the numerous Assembly, or dismiss both and install a small-member Cabinet, Committee, or Junta that typically evolves into the domination of a one-person *caudillo* or dictator. Or, the Army might establish a single-man dictatorship from the very beginning. In contrast to authoritarian impositions of unipersonal executives over the Assemblies, almost no case can be cited of an Assembly eliminating the Cabinet or the Presidency (the only exception was perhaps the mercurial revolutionary Convention in France in 1792).

Authoritarian rulers not only eliminate separate powers in 'horizontal' relationships and tend to concentrate powers in a unipersonal executive, but they also tend to intervene or suppress regional and local governments that might limit their power. This, in particular, makes it impossible for a single-party regime to be organized as an actual federal state, despite federalizing legal provisions that can be found in some of them. Party centralization always tends to prevail over division of powers, especially in nondemocratic regimes. The fall of single-party regimes with federal legal structures, such as the Communist-dominated Union of Soviet Socialist Republics and Yugoslavia in the 1990s, reveals the fiction while the country explodes into an array of secessionist movements, as will be discussed below.

4.2. DIVIDED GOVERNMENT

Divided government is one in which different political parties have power in relevant institutions. This situation can arise in a variety of constitutional frameworks, including the following:

(i) a multiparty coalition Cabinet, as is typically the case in parliamentary regimes based on proportional representation;

(ii) a President's party with no majority in the Assembly, in both presidential and semi-presidential regimes (as tends to happen in nonconcurrent elections);

(iii) a central government's party not controlling most regional or local governments.

We will refer to multiparty coalition Cabinets and the division between the President and the Assembly as cases of 'horizontally' divided government, whereas political decentralization will be called 'vertically' divided government. Both types of divided government will be addressed separately in later sections, although a final discussion will allow us to note that some positive relationship exists between the stability of the institutional frameworks of horizontal and vertical divisions of powers.

Politically divided government, both horizontal and vertical, can be the mechanical result of unusual combinations of different electoral rules (even if the same electorate vote the same way for different offices) or, more frequently, of divided vote. As previously suggested, simple regimes induce voters to chose a single-party 'package' of policy proposals on all the issues at the same time. In contrast, in complex regimes, voters are given the opportunity to distinguish party proposals on different issues, to vote differently for various offices, and to divide government among more than one party. In particular, as will be seen in the following pages, while concurrent elections tend to produce higher proportions of unified vote, resulting in unified government, voters tend to divide their votes under the incentives provided by nonconcurrent elections for different offices.

On the basis of separate, exclusive powers of different institutions, a situation of divided government can reflect voters' varied preferences on different issues better than can a unified government. If, in contrast, separately elected institutions share powers, a situation of divided government can force different parties with different electoral support to negotiate and compromise on policy decisions from initially different positions. As a consequence of both separate and joint decisions, there can be a relatively higher number of voters whose preferences are taken into account in the institutional process of decision making in divided government than in a single-party, unified government based on a narrower group of people's support.

Divided Vote

Nonconcurrent elections for different offices provide incentives for both sincere and strategic divided votes in favor of divided government. When elections for the Presidency are nonconcurrent with those for the Assembly, or central elections do not concur with regional, local elections, parties in opposition to the central executive have more opportunities to promote different campaign issues than those promoted by the incumbent President or central government at the previous election. Nonconcurrent elections allow political parties to expand the electoral agenda and enable citizens to reveal a relatively high number of their sincere preferences on different issues.

If the different institutions have separate powers on different issues, voters are given the opportunity of distinguishing political parties on several sets of issues allocated to different offices (say, for instance, foreign policy for the President and domestic policy for Congress, or national defense for the central government and public works for local governments, etc.). The voters may then choose different parties for different institutions on the basis of their sincere preferences on these issues, which is more difficult to do when elections are concurrent, party campaigns overlap, and the available information focuses on a smaller set of issues.

If the different institutions share some powers on the same issues, certain centrist voters whose sincere preferences are located somewhere in between the positions of the two major parties can split their votes on the basis of strategic calculations in favor of divided government. Let us assume that two parties Left and Right (or L and R) offer differentiated platforms on the same set of issues both for the election of the Presidency and for the election of the Assembly (alternatively, the reader can assume separate national and regional elections). Intermediate voters whose ideal preferences are relatively closer to party Left would vote twice in favor of the Left on the basis of their relative distance to each of the two party platforms, as illustrated in Fig. 4.1. However, some of these voters can expect that a divided government between Left and Right will induce the two parties to compromise on some intermediate policy positions which can

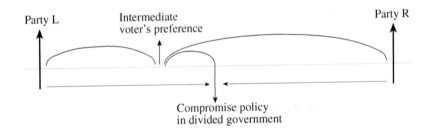

FIG. 4.1. Strategic divided vote

Note: The intermediate voter is closer to party L than party R. But is even closer to the compromise policy between party L and party R produced by divided government

be closer to the voter's sincere preference, as can be seen in Fig. 4.1. Then, centrist voters may favor divided government by splitting their votes between the two parties for different offices (Alesina and Rosenthal 1995).

If there are only separate elections for two offices, a strategic divided vote would be strictly rational only for those voters whose preferences are closer to the expected intermediate, compromising position than to the position of any of the parties. For other intermediate yet more biased voters, it would still be rational to concentrate their votes on a single party. With more than two separate institutions with nonconcurrent elections, as well as with shared powers inducing their holders to negotiate and compromise on intermediate outcomes, the number of intermediate voters with incentives to choose different parties increases. If, for instance, nonconcurrent elections include the Presidency and the Assembly with shared legislative powers, a symmetric second chamber, regional and local governments that share powers with the central government, etc., an intermediate voter relatively close to party Left can vote for party Left on most occasions but also give some votes to party Right for one or a few of the offices. A higher number of voters can expect to be satisfied by interinstitutional compromises in highly complex regimes than they can in less complex regimes. The higher the number of offices with shared powers and nonconcurrent elections, the higher the opportunities for intermediate voters to select some occasions to split their votes.

In contrast to the incentives for vote-splitting just discussed, concurrent elections for different offices tend both to produce a sincere unified vote and to make strategic divided vote more difficult. A disciplined party can develop a single electoral campaign for different offices on the basis of a small selection of issues presented in a compact package. This may move voters to choose candidates or lists of the same party for different offices on the basis of their sincere preference on the few selected campaign issues—the only ones on which the voter has available information. Certainly, some voters can have different policy preferences on different issues. For example, they can have rightist preferences on economic policy (say, in favor of competitive markets) and leftist, liberal preferences on moral issues, or any other combination for any set of issues. However, if some issues are not raised by the candidates during the campaign and parties do not voice their corresponding salient, clearly differentiated positions, voters can be uncertain about their relative closeness to the candidates on those issues. Issues that are not given salience in party campaigns are not likely to be a priority in further legislative or executive agendas either. Since the status quo policy can be expected to prevail in these issues, it is highly risky for voters to choose a party on the basis of nonsalient, rather hypothetical positions on these issues.

Some institutional induction in favor of unified vote can also appear in regional and local elections even when they do not concur with central elections but are held all at the same time. In contrast to the opportunities given by staggered regional elections to parties or candidates for introducing differentiated issues, in simultaneous elections, leaders of disciplined national parties can promote nationwide campaigns in favor of their supported regional, local candidates to the disadvantage of regional, local parties or more independent candidates. This can reduce the scope of the relevant electoral agendas and induce a more unified vote than can staggered elections.

Concurrent elections not only restrict the electoral agenda and induce voters' sincere unified vote, but they also make strategic divided vote more risky, especially if the sophisticated voters able to make strategic calculations are uncertain about the relative electoral chances of the candidates. In order to see this, let us assume that the intermediate voters whose sincere preferences are located between the positions of parties L and R have a strategic interest in promoting divided government between the two parties. Their preferences for candidates for the Presidency and the Assembly can be, for example, as presented in Table 4.2.

This example shows the difficult calculations that sophisticated voters would have to do in order to split their ballots in concurrent elections successfully. Let us assume that the Left candidate for the Presidency is hopeless because the staunch supporters of his rival, Right, are much more numerous, while, in contrast, the race for the Assembly is very uncertain and the strategic vote of the intermediate, centrist voters could decide the winner. The intermediate voters, by voting in accordance to their first preference, L-R, that is, by splitting their vote between Left for the Presidency and Right for the Assembly, can tip the balance in favor of the Right for the Assembly. But, in the hypothetical situation just described, they may waste their votes on a hopeless candidate for the Presidency. The electoral result might then be R-R, that is, a unified government for party Right, the voters' last preference. In contrast, if the sophisticated voters decided to split the ticket the other way round, that is, R-L (their second preference), they would simply increase the majority support for the Right candidate for the Presidency, but could help Left to win in the Assembly race, thus satisfying their second preferred combination, R-L (for which they would have voted).

Whether voting for the first preference, which may help to produce the voter's least preferred outcome, or for the more likely successful second preference, depends on the voter's information regarding the expected chances of every candidate. This information is costly, and may be mistaken, incomplete, or both. Typically, democratic elections involve some degree of uncertainty regarding the winner and do not provide the

TABLE 4.2. *Preferences for a divided government*

	Presidency	Assembly
Most preferred	L	R
	R	L
	L	L
Least preferred	R	R

Note: L, left party; R, right party.

electorate with perfect information in advance. The point is that this problem does exist in concurrent elections. In nonconcurrent elections, in contrast, the voters interested in divided government do not need to know anything about the candidates' expected chances or make sophisticated calculations. They can safely vote for divided government just by choosing against the incumbent President's or central Cabinet's party.

Even in concurrent elections, some voters can split their votes if they are able to identify appropriate candidates in different parties, or simply in order to favor divided government and prevent a single party from imposing its exclusive rule. Nonconcurrent elections, however, can promote both sincere and strategic votes for different parties more readily than concurrent elections.

Concurrent and Nonconcurrent Elections

An empirical survey of the effects of concurrent and nonconcurrent elections is presented here for frameworks of both horizontal division of powers between the President and the Assembly and vertical division of powers between the central government and regional governments.

Horizontally Divided Elections

Separate Presidential and Assembly elections in eight American countries from 1945 to 1995 have produced outcomes according to the institutional inductions previously discussed, as shown in Table 4.3. Concurrent elections have produced divided government in about a half of the cases (53 per cent on average in Costa Rica, Peru, Uruguay, and Venezuela in the aforementioned period, and Brazil in 1945–50). In contrast, divided government has been the typical result in nonconcurrent, or only partly concurrent, elections (in more than 90 per cent of the cases in Ecuador, in Brazil since 1954, and in Chile in 1946–70).

The different effects of concurrent and nonconcurrent elections can also be identified when the two formulas are applied in the same country. In Brazil, for instance, one of the two concurrent elections in the period

TABLE 4.3. *Nonconcurrent elections and horizontally divided government in North and South America (1945–95)*

Concurrent elections		Partly or nonconcurrent elections	
Brazil (1945–50)$_2$	50	Brazil (1954–62, 1989–94)$_8$	100
United States$_{13}$	54	United States$_{14}$	71
Costa Rica$_{11}$	45	Chile (1946–70)$_{13}$	77
Peru (1980–95)$_4$	50	Ecuador$_{16}$	100
Uruguay$_{11}$	55		
Venezuela$_8$	63		
Election average	53		86
Country average	53		87

Note: Numbers are the percentages of elections with different party winners in the presidency and in the Assembly. The subindices are the number of elections accounted for each country between 1945 and 1995. Argentina and Bolivia are not included because a single ballot forces voters to vote en bloc for the same party for the two institutions; in Colombia, the 'National Front' pact created a unified government despite having nonconcurrent elections.

Source: Author's own calculations, with data from Nohlen (1993), *Guide to the U.S. Elections* (1998); *Political Data Base of the Americas* (1999); *Europa World Year Book*. See also Mainwaring and Shugart (1997, table 11.3) for the two chambers in the Assembly.

1945–50 produced unified government, whereas the eight following nonconcurrent elections in two later periods have always produced divided government. Similar institutional effects are also visible in countries with partly concurrent elections, such as the United States. Between1945 and 1998, 54 per cent of the concurrent Presidential and Congressional elections resulted in divided government, in contrast to close to 71 per cent for the mid term nonconcurrent elections. Only concurrent elections have been able to re-establish a single-winner in the Presidency and the House after periods of divided government.

The fact that concurrent elections tend to produce a unified government has induced some politicians in power to manipulate the electoral calendar. When the constitutional rules do not establish fixed terms for the separate offices of the President and the Assembly, as in semi-presidential regimes, an elected President may call an Assembly election immediately after his victory with the aim of becoming a single winner. These quasi-concurrent, 'honeymoon' elections tend to replicate a majority support for the President's party in the Assembly on the basis of the previous presidential campaign (Shugart and Carey 1992). This strategy was successfully used in France by President de Gaulle in 1962 and President Mitterrand in 1981 and 1988. During the French Fifth Republic, all three periods of 'cohabitation' of a President and an Assembly majority from different parties have resulted, in contrast, from nonconcurrent elections (in 1986, 1993, 1997).

Vertically Divided Elections

Vertically divided government can be measured by the proportion of regional chief executives whose party is not in national government. This measure of political decentralization captures the fact that national governments tend to exclude superfluous partners at the national level (as discussed in the analysis of coalition formation in Chapter 3), even if these partners are strong at the regional or local level.

The vertical division of government between different parties is lower in federal countries with concurrent elections for central and regional offices or with separate but simultaneous regional elections than in those with nonconcurrent, staggered elections for regional governments. This is shown in Table 4.4 for 1,765 regional elections in eleven countries during the period 1945–95. Generally speaking, in countries with concurrent elections, less than one-third of the regions are outside the control of the central government's party, whereas in countries with nonconcurrent, staggered regional elections (Australia, Austria, Canada, Germany), about half the regions, on average, are ruled by a party which is not in central government.

TABLE 4.4. *Nonconcurrent elections and vertically divided government (1945–95)*

Concurrent elections		*Nonconcurrent, staggered elections*	
Argentina (1946–73)$_{120}$	12	Argentina (1983–)$_{96}$	60
Brazil (1947–50)$_{52}$	55	Brazil (1954–)$_{182}$	55
India (1952–67)$_{100}$	23	India (1971–)$_{150}$	33
		Australia$_{74}$	50
		Austria$_{120}$	31
		Canada$_{154}$	61
		Germany$_{106}$	50
Partly concurrent		*Nonconcurrent*	
United States$_{761}$	55	Spain$_{69}$	48
• nonconcurrent$_{519}$	62	• staggered (4 regions)$_{17}$	83
• concurrent$_{242}$	41	• simultaneous (13 regions)$_{52}$	37
Malaysia$_{104}$	7	Italy$_{105}$	21
• nonconcurrent (2 regions)$_{16}$	25	• staggered (5 regions)$_{30}$	32
• concurrent (11 regions)$_{88}$	5	• simultaneous (13 regions)$_{75}$	16

Note: Numbers are the percentage of regions with a chief executive whose party is not in central government. The subindices are the number of regional elections in the period 1945–95.

Source: Author's calculations with data from Balestra and Ossona (1983); Cantón (1973); Chaterjee (1997); Feigert (1989); Fisher (1990); Fleischer (1986); Jaensch and Teichmann (1988); Jones (1997*b*); Kallenbach (1977); Ritter and Niehuss (1987); Thayssen (1994); Tribunal Superior Eleitoral (1950–), Zaidi and Zaidi (1976–), *The Book of the States* (Lexington, Ky: Council of State Governments); *Guide to the U.S. Elections*;*Europa World Year Book*; Antonio Agosta, Ministry of the Interior, Italy (personal communication).

In several federal countries (Argentina, Brazil, and India), concurrent regional elections in previous periods were replaced with staggered elections, with the effect of increasing the proportions of regional governments ruled by a party which was not in central government.

Similar effects can be observed within the United States, where, paralleling the increasing frequency of horizontally divided government, vertically divided government has become more prevalent in recent years. The analysis of the figures shows increasing proportions of split-ticket voting, both in concurrent and in nonconcurrent elections. Additionally, institutional changes in a number of states have replaced two-year Governor terms (which produced concurrent elections half of the time) with four-year terms, usually scheduled for nonpresidential election years. In the period 1945–95, less than one-third of state elections were concurrent with Presidential elections (242 out of 761 state elections). The average proportion of winning Governors from the party not holding the Presidency is higher in state elections that are not concurrent with a Presidential election than in those that are concurrent (62 v. 41 per cent, respectively; (author's own calculation).

In a similar vein, empirical analyses of the Land elections in Germany, in periods of both unified and divided central government, (1953–7 and 1972–6, respectively), show that the Chancellor's party, that is, the senior partner of the governing coalition in the national government, tends to lose votes in the land elections following the national election, even if the party is re-elected with a relatively high vote share in the next national election. Since the German federal upper chamber, the *Bundesrat*, is formed by delegates of the Land governments, split-ticket voting is also a means of balance the relationship of forces between majority parties in the two chambers of the national parliament (Lohmann, Brady, and Rivers 1997).

An interesting variant occurs in separate elections for the two chambers of parliament, as can be illustrated with the federal Senate elections in Australia. The elections for the House and for the Senate were concurrent during the period 1946–61, producing only one-third of cases with two different party majorities (in two out of six elections). The elections were nonconcurrent in the ensuing period, 1963–72, always producing different party majorities in the two chambers (in seven elections). Interestingly, although concurrent elections were reintroduced in 1974, many voters have taken benefit from the differences in the electoral systems of the two chambers to maintain their previous tendency to split their votes. Survey results suggest that strategic voters use Senate minor party votes to produce a permanently divided bicameralism (in the nine subsequent elections) (Bowler and Denemark 1993).

Another variant exists in regionalized countries with nonconcurrent elections, such as Spain and Italy, where those regions holding staggered elections have higher proportions of Presidents from parties not in central government than those regions which hold elections simultaneously, as shown in Table 4.4. A more detailed analysis of regional elections in Spain since 1980 shows that this is due to better opportunities, created by staggered elections, for voters to reveal their varied preferences on different issues (especially regional cultural issues), the different participation rates at the different-level elections (which reveal different intensities of preferences on national and regional issues), and a strategic divided vote by a critical sector of centrist voters (Colomer and Martínez 1995; Colomer 1998*a*).

Horizontally Divided Government: Parliamentarism and Presidentialism

The frequency of divided government can be compared for the three types of regime previously distinguished: parliamentarism with majoritarian electoral rules, presidentialism and semi-presidentialism, and parliamentarism with proportional representation. Table 4.5 shows data for 506 elections in forty democratic countries with different institutional combinations during the period 1945–99. In accord with the previous discussion, we see that parliamentary regimes with majoritarian electoral rules tend to produce unified government most of the time. Presidential and semi-presidential regimes produce higher proportions of divided government. Proportional representation tends to produce even more pluralistic effects than division of powers.

In particular, in all the elections with plurality rule in New Zealand (until 1993), and in all minus one in the United Kingdom, a single party has won an absolute majority of seats. In contrast, all the cases but one of parliamentary regimes with proportional representation in the sample have produced divided government most of the time, either multiparty coalitions or minority Cabinets with multiparty support in parliament. In the Czech Republic, Denmark, Finland, the French Fourth Republic, Israel, the Netherlands, and Switzerland, divided government has been the outcome of 100 per cent of the elections.

With regard to pluralistic regimes, the different effects of proportional representation and schemes of division of powers should be identified for the different strategies that they encourage. As previously discussed, proportional representation induces a relatively high number of parties to compete in elections with different agendas and platforms and encourages citizens to vote sincerely for the most part, according to their varied preferences.

Division of powers in presidential and semi-presidential regimes also gives political parties some opportunities to run with different issues and

TABLE 4.5. *Horizontally divided government (1945–2000)*

Parliamentary-majoritarian		Presidential		Parliamentary-proportional representation	
Australia$_{21}$	48	Argentina$_{12}$	33	Austria$_{17}$	71
Canada$_{17}$	41	Bolivia$_5$	100	Belgium$_{17}$	94
India$_{13}$	31	Brazil$_{12}$	90	Czech Rep.$_3$	100
Japan$_{13}$	31	Chile$_{15}$	93	Denmark$_{21}$	100
New Zealand$_{15}$	0	Colombia$_{14}$	29	Finland$_{15}$	100
United Kingdom$_{15}$	7	Costa Rica$_{12}$	42	France, 4th Rep.$_5$	100
		Ecuador$_{16}$	100	Germany$_{14}$	93
		S. Korea$_7$	43	Greece$_{16}$	25
		Peru$_7$	57	Hungary$_3$	67
		Philippines$_5$	60	Ireland$_{16}$	63
		United States$_{27}$	63	Israel$_{13}$	100
		Uruguay$_{11}$	55	Italy$_{11}$	91
		Venezuela$_{10}$	50	Netherlands$_{16}$	100
		Semi-presidential		Norway$_{13}$	61
		Bulgaria$_5$	80	Spain$_8$	73
		France, 5th Rep.$_{17}$	59	Sweden$_{17}$	94
		Poland$_4$	75	Switzerland$_{15}$	100
		Portugal$_{14}$	57		
Election average:	27		63		84
Country average:	26		64		84

Note: Numbers are percentages of parliamentary and presidential elections in which the Premier's or President's party was not a majority in the assembly. Subindices are the number of elections for each country.

Source: Author's own calculations, with data from Bennett (1996); Mainwaring and Scully (1995); Mainwaring and Shugart (1997); Nohlen (1993); Woldendorp *et al.* (1997); *Guide to the U.S. Elections; Political Data Base of the Americas* (1999); *Europa World Year Book*.

the citizens the occasion to choose different parties for different offices. However, the typical single-winner Presidential election introduces a significant degree of unification of citizens' preferences. The popular election of the unipersonal President, which has to be decided by means of some exclusive rule, is always an absolute, single-winner contest. Accordingly, certain parties that would run in parliamentary elections with proportional representation refrain from running in presidential elections. Only candidates with some reasonable expectation of becoming absolute winners tend to compete, especially under plurality rule.

Even if candidates proliferate (as may happen at the first round in a runoff system), the citizens tend to concentrate their support on a few candidates in order not to waste their votes. The reduction of available political alternatives originated by Presidential elections has also some effect on parallel Assembly elections, even if the latter are decided by proportional representation, especially if the campaigns for the Presidency and the Assembly are concurrent. As a result, the degree of political pluralism and the frequency of divided government are relatively lower in presidential and semi-presidential regimes than they are in parliamentary regimes with proportional representation.

Conflict and Cooperation in Parliamentarism and Presidentialism

Both parliamentary, semi-presidential, and presidential regimes provide institutional mechanisms for inducing mutual control and cooperation between the Premier, or the President, and the Cabinet, on one side, and the Assembly, on the other. Some of these mechanisms were primarily designed in medieval England during the process of gradual reduction of the Crown's powers by Parliament. While the King remained formally untouchable, his ministers became increasingly accountable and were made responsible to members of Parliament. In the 138 years between 1321 and 1459, there were no less than thirty-four cases (or one every four years) of King's ministers who were removed from office (they were also frequently fined, imprisoned, or even executed) at the initiative of the Commons and after being submitted to trial by the Lords. After the absolutist interlude of the Tudor dynasty, these practices were renewed and increased in frequency during the 17th century, with at least eighteen cases in the period 1604–28 (or one every year and a half).

Over the years, different procedures were developed, including the so-called 'attainder' and 'address' to the King, as well as the 'impeachment' (from Latin: to hinder, to prevent), also called 'parliamentary judicature' or 'complaint'. Cabinet ministers were dismissed by the English Parliament not only under accusations of criminal behavior, such as corruption, nepotism, malversation, or war profiteering), but also for political conflicts related to religious, financial, or foreign policy issues, as well as for interfering with the Parliament and for introducing 'arbitrary and tyrannical government'.

From 1688, these medieval procedures evolved into more regular instruments of political control of the executive by the legislative body. These practices were diffused across Europe and eventually led to the current procedures of 'vote of confidence' and 'vote of censure' which are established in modern parliamentary regimes.

In parallel, the English colonies in North America had adopted the English impeachment and related procedures in 1635. These procedures became instrumental in the rise of representative Assemblies checking executive and judicial offices, including those of the English patrons. At the moment of independence in 1776, all new state institutions contained some form of removal of governmental officials, including 'impeachment', 'address' to the Governor or the King, and a call for an investiga-

tion. The United States Constitution established the impeachment within
a scheme of separation of powers in order to make all powerholders
responsible not only for private criminal behavior but also for noncrimi-
nal, political wrongdoing. The major concern was to prevent the new
figure of a powerful President from becoming a despot. Impeachments
became rare occurrences at the federal level during the 19th century.
However, traditional mechanisms of control of the executive continued to
be used in the states and were successfully extended to new Latin-American presidential regimes (Black 1974; Ehrlich 1974; Tite 1974; Hoffer
and Hull 1984).

In order to ponder the effectiveness of different institutional incentives
for promoting conflict or cooperation between the Premier or President
and the Assembly, the following classification may be helpful. It will
allow us to proceed to a comparative evaluation of the opportunities for
multiparty and interinstitutional cooperation in the different regime
models: parliamentarism, semi-presidentialism, and presidentialism.
Institutional choices favoring cooperation and consensual decisions can
be considered on the basis of this analytical framework.

Cooperation may be promoted at the initiative of either the Assembly
or the Premier or President. First, the Assembly can foster cooperation by
the appointment or investiture of the Premier and the Cabinet ministers (in
parliamentary and semi-presidential regimes), as well as by giving advice
and consent to presidential appointments of Cabinet members and other
executive and judicial offices (in some presidential regimes).

Second, cooperation can be promoted by the President's veto of legislative decisions, which may be overriden by a qualified majority of the
Assembly (in presidential and semi-presidential regimes).

These two cooperation-inducing mechanisms—parliamentary investiture, presidential veto—can favor broad agreements between different
political actors and political consistency between the executive and the
Assembly. Through interinstitutional agreements, political actors can
introduce innovative decisions regarding the status quo policy and prevent
biased and relatively inefficient decisions.

Instruments of conflict are also available to both the Assembly and the
Premier or President. First, conflict can be promoted by the Assembly by
means of the censure and dismissal of the Premier and the Cabinet
members (in parliamentary and semi-presidential regimes), as well as the
censure and dismissal of Cabinet members and the head of Cabinet, and
the impeachment of the Cabinet members and the President (in presidential regimes).

Second, the Premier or the President can proceed to the dissolution of
the Assembly and call a new election (in parliamentary and semi-presidential regimes). As previously discussed, some Presidents in presidential

regimes have also eliminated the Assembly by unconstitutional means, but this is obviously a more conflictive move than the typical dissolution in the parliamentary framework.

These conflict-producing mechanisms—censure, impeachment, dissolution—can tip the balance in favor of one of the institutions in the short term, thus favoring more biased, possibly minority and less socially efficient outcomes. In some critical situations, however, they can be expedient in establishing a new basis for further political and interinstitutional cooperation.

Institutional incentives for multiparty and interinstitutional cooperation in parliamentarism and semi-presidentialism compare favorably with those in presidentialism. The main element of cooperation for producing consistency between the Premier and the Parliament in parliamentarism and semi-presidentialism, the investiture, is smoother, more predictable, and less distorting than the comparable Assembly's supervision or veto of executive appointments and the President's veto of legislation in presidentialism.

Likewise, the elements of conflict in parliamentarism and semi-presidentialism, mainly the motion of censure of the Premier and the dissolution of the Assembly and call for a new election, are less severe than the impeachment of the President and the suppression of the Assembly, respectively, in presidentialism. Yet, this analysis also suggests a variety of formulas which can create intermediate situations that fall in between the three classical regime models previously described, including, in particular, the positive role of the Assembly in appointing or dismissing Cabinet members and the President's power to dissolve the Assembly in presidential regimes. Constitutional design and reform could also benefit from innovative institutional combinations along these lines.

An empirical survey may clarify the relative effectiveness of the different institutional mechanisms just considered. In parliamentary and semi-presidential regimes in Western Europe, the appointment of the Premier and Cabinet takes different forms. Usually, the most voted party in the election leads the process of forming a multiparty majority coalition in Parliament, especially when the head of state (as in France, Italy, and Spain) or a *'formateur'* appointed by the head of state (as in the Netherlands and Finland) has an active role in the process. Otherwise, and especially if formal investiture in Parliament is not legally required, the bargaining process between political parties is more open and is more likely to lead to the formation of a coalition without the most voted party or to a minority Cabinet (as in Denmark, Norway, and Sweden). However, in all the cases previously discussed, parties tend to maintain policy and ideological connectedness between coalition partners, producing the effect that the party containing the median seat is included in the Cabinet.

There are also different formulas for the motion of censure. In some countries, the Cabinet usually steps down without the need of a formal negative vote, just after being defeated in Parliament on a major bill (as in Belgium, Denmark, Finland, Ireland, Luxembourg, and Sweden). Sometimes, an explicit motion of nonconfidence must be voted on by the Parliament, either by plurality (with abstentions counted as unfavorable to the Cabinet, as in Austria, Italy, the Netherlands, Norway, and the United Kingdom), or by majority (as in France, Greece, Portugal, and Sweden), or by majority in favor of an alternative candidate for Premier in the 'constructive' motion of censure (as in Germany, Spain, and Belgium).

In almost all countries of Western Europe (except Norway), the Premier or President can dissolve Parliament and call a new election, in some cases with temporal restrictions.

These parliamentary mechanisms—investiture, censure, dissolution—produce continuous interactions between the Premier and the Cabinet, on one side, and the parties in Parliament on the other, favoring political consistency between the decisions made by the two institutions.

The institutional variants mentioned have effects on the duration of parliamentary Cabinets (more or less in the order previously presented, from shorter to longer duration). On average, about one-sixth of the Cabinets formed in the sixteen countries of Western Europe mentioned above in the period 1945–90 (60 out of 380 Cabinets) were overthrown either by a successful vote of nonconfidence or by the withdrawal of support by a coalition partner, which can be another way of recreating consistency between the Cabinet and a multiparty majority in Parliament. The country-average duration of parliamentary Cabinets in the countries and the time period mentioned is about twenty-two months (out of forty-eight or sixty months as maximum constitutional terms) (Budge and Keman 1990; Warwick 1994; de Winter 1995; Ieraci, 1996).

Interactions and cooperation between the President and the Assembly are more difficult to develop in presidential regimes because of the asymmetry between the absolute-winner President and the partial-winner Assembly parties, and especially when the President is not the median voter's preference. Interinstitutional cooperation is also difficult because of the lack, or weakness, of mutual control mechanisms.

However, parliamentary-like mechanisms promoting more regular interinstitutional interactions have been introduced in a number of recent constitutional reforms. Regarding the rules enforced in 1999, Cabinet members can be submitted to censure by majority vote of the Assembly in Argentina (only the head of Cabinet), Ecuador, and Peru, and by qualified-majority of the Assembly in Costa Rica, Guatemala, Uruguay, and Venezuela. In Bolivia, the Assembly can censure ministers but this does not imply their dismissal. (In previous periods, Cabinet members were made responsible to the Assembly during two long periods of democratic government in Latin America: Chile from 1891 to 1925 and Uruguay from 1917 to 1933, as well as in Cuba from 1940 to 1952.)

Cases of removal of the President because of impeachment by the Assembly in presidential regimes include the following: Arnulfo Arias (1951) and José R. Guizado (1955) in Panama; Fernando Collor de Mello in Brazil (1992); Carlos Andrés Pérez in Venezuela (1993); Abdala Bucaram in Ecuador (1997); and Raúl Cubas in Paraguay (although he resigned and fled the country a few hours before the final vote in the Assembly, in 1999).

In the United States, between 1797 and 2000, motions of 'censure' not involving the removal of the corresponding officer have been approved by the Congress in the cases of seven senators and four Presidents, the latter being Andrew Jackson in 1834, John Tyler in 1843, James Buchanan in 1859, and Richard Nixon in 1973 and 1974 in the moves toward impeachment. The impeachment procedure was initiated fifty-four times by the House of Representatives in the same period, fifteen of which reached the Senate and, as a result, seven federal judges were convicted and removed from office and two more resigned (while four other judges, one Senator, and one Cabinet member were acquitted).

President Andrew Johnson was impeached by the House but acquitted by the Senate in 1868, Richard Nixon resigned from office after the House Judiciary Committe voted three articles of impeachment against him but before the full House voted in 1974, and William Clinton was impeached by the House but acquitted by the Senate in January 1999 (*New York Times* 13 September 1998; *Washington Post* 8 September 1998 and 19 November 1998).

Conversely, legal dissolution of the Assembly by the President is permitted by 1999 in Chile, Peru, and Uruguay, in the last two cases only as a consequence of successful motions of censure. (Alcántara 1999; Shugart and Carey 1992). Dissolution is also permitted in Russia if the President's candidate for Prime Minister is rejected by the Assembly three times. But this device has not been used so far.

Multiparty Presidents

Interinstitutional cooperation in situations of divided presidential government can be harder to attain in two-party systems than in multiparty systems, due to the greater number of opportunities created by multipartism for the President's party to form legislative and Cabinet coalitions with other parties.

In a two-party system, interinstitutional agreements when the President and the Assembly are supported by different political parties require either difficult unanimous agreements or party indiscipline. Bipartisan, near-unanimous agreements to share power for long periods were attained in Colombia and Venezuela at their redemocratization in 1958, in the so-called 'National Front' and 'Pact of Punto Fijo', respectively. These cooperative agreements were conceived with the aim of supporting a frail, new democratic regime. However, the corresponding apportionment of power between the major parties eventually became exclusive and indirectly fostered the emergence of conflict and anti-system movements (Hartlyn 1994; Coppedge 1994).

In the two-party United States, high levels of party indiscipline allowed several Presidents to gather legislative majorities including congressmen of the opposition party on various issues. Yet, even in the United States, divided government in times of greater party discipline has been difficult to manage, as is discussed below. In general, two-party systems may be compatible with interinstitutional cooperation to the extent that they are internally fractionalized, which is to say, that more than two parties actually exist.

In contrast to the problems of two-party systems in divided government, multiparty systems allow for greater cooperation. If the interinstitutional relationship is sufficiently balanced, that is, if the unipersonal President has somewhat limited power, the Assembly can become the appropriate arena for multiparty negotiations and compromises in a way similar to the typical occurrence in parliamentary regimes.

In fact, most Presidential Cabinets in presidential regimes in Latin America have been multiparty coalitions. An empirical survey by Grace I. Deheza covers 116 Presidential Cabinets in nine South American presidential democracies (Argentina, Bolivia, Brazil, Chile, Colombia, Ecuador, Peru, Uruguay, and Venezuela) from 1958 (the year in which the first coalition Cabinets were formed in Colombia and Venezuela) to 1994. The formation of a new Cabinet is considered when there is a change of President or when the party composition of the Cabinet is modified.

Multiparty coalitions form 59 per cent of the Presidential Cabinets examined, a proportion even higher than multiparty coalition Cabinets in parliamentary regimes in a similar period (which is about 50 per cent, according to the sources mentioned below). Only one-fourth of the multiparty presidential Cabinets correspond to pre-electoral presidential coalitions, while three-fourths result from post-electoral, parliamentary negotiations. The most pluralistic case is Brazil, where all the Presidential Cabinets examined were multiparty coalitions.

Single-party Cabinets in minority in the Assembly are 22 per cent of the cases, but on many of these the President's and Cabinet's party has more than 45 per cent of the Assembly seats and can form *ad-hoc* majority coalitions with minor partners on different issues. Finally, single-party majority Cabinets are only 19 per cent of the cases (including, in particular, all presidential cabinets in two-party Argentina).

Presidential Cabinet portfolios are distributed among the coalition parties roughly in proportion to each party's contribution in seats to form a majority in the Assembly, in a similar way to negotiations in parliamentary regimes. The President's pary usually keeps the most important porfolios, including Economy, Defense, and Interior, but the other parties in the coalition are compensated with proportions of portfolios somewhat greater than their contribution in seats (see Deheza 1997, 1998; for comparable data on parliamentary regimes; Laver and Schofield 1990; Strom 1990).

The opportunities for cooperation and broad agreements created by horizontally divided government have been noted even by Juan J. Linz, the most vocal critic of presidentialism, who holds it was a major factor in democratic breakdown in Latin America in the past. In Linz' words, 'The fact that, of those 10 [presidentialist] countries experiencing breakdowns since 1945 [Argentina, Bolivia, Brazil, Chile, Colombia, Ecuador, S. Korea, Peru, Philippines, Uruguay], at the time of writing [1994] nine are [presidential] democracies shows that democratization is possible in countries with a presidential tradition. Perhaps the societies and their leadership in those presidential democracies have learned from past failures, and we might find in the future presidential systems as stable as parliamentary democracies are in Europe' (Linz 1994: 74; Linz and Valenzuela 1994; see also Colomer 1994; Mainwaring and Shugart 1997).

Cases: Horizontal Interinstitutional Cooperation

Three cases of relatively successful interinstitutional cooperation in schemes of horizontal division of powers will now be examined. First, we will discuss the opportunities and problems of divided government in the two-party, presidential system of the United States. Second, the results of 'cohabitation' between different political majorities supporting the President and the parliamentary Premier in the semi-presidential Fifth Republic of France will be analyzed. Finally, we will review the peculiar institutional conditions for the formation of multiparty coalitions supporting the President in the Assembly in the 'parliamentarized' presidential regime of Bolivia.

Divided Government in Presidentialism: The United States

Divided government tends to be the 'normal' situation in the United States at all levels of its complex division of powers: between the President and the two chambers of Congress, between the federal government and the states, and between state Governors and Assemblies.

Specifically, different party majorities in support of the President and in the Congress have resulted from 42 per cent of the elections during the period 1832–1998. The proportion of federal elections producing divided government is still higher in the more recent period 1945–98: 71 per cent of nonconcurrent elections and 54 per cent of concurrent elections. The average proportion of states with divided representation in the Senate between the two parties was 26 per cent from the first direct election of senators from 1914 to 1954, but increased to 40 per cent in the later period 1956–96. Governors from a party which is not in the White House have won in 55 per cent of the elections during the period 1945–95 (in 421 out of 761 elections). The proportion of states with different parties in the Governorship and in the majority of the Assembly was only 15 per cent in 1945, but had steadily increased to 60 per cent by the mid 1990s (Jacobson 1990 and Cox and Kernell 1991; Brunell and Grofman 1998; author's own calculations; and Fiorina 1992, respectively).

As previously discussed, divided government can be created both by the mechanical effects of certain institutional devices, such as irregular districting in different elections, and by divided vote, helped by the holding of nonconcurrent and staggered elections. Most analysts observe the relatively increasing importance of strategic divided vote or 'ticket-splitting' in producing divided government in the United States. It has been noted, in particular, that in nonconcurrent or 'mid term' congressional elections, in districts in which new candidates from the two parties compete, the voters favor those of the party not holding the Presidency; incumbents from the party not in the Presidency 'surge'; and the margins of victory of non marginal incumbents of the President's party are reduced in comparison with those in concurrent elections (Alesina and Rosenthal 1995).

In the second half of the 20th century, divided government at the federal level was typically created by the election of a Republican President and a Democratic majority in the Congress, as during the presidencies of Dwight Eisenhower (in the period 1955–61), Richard Nixon (1969–74), Gerald Ford (1974–7), Ronald Reagan (1981–9), and George Bush (1989–93). In these situations, the Republican President could gather a congressional majority or adapt to congressional initiatives with relative frequency, thanks to the high level of party indiscipline among Democratic representatives and senators (especially due to differences between Northern liberals and Southern conservatives) which moved the President to bargain with the median congressmen. Many compromises were also reached thanks to the abundance of local issues, 'pork barrel' decisions, as well as logrolling and vote trading between congressmen on different policy issues (King and Ragsdale 1988; Riggs 1988; Cox and McCubbins 1993).

The period of divided government between a Democratic President and a Republican majority in the Congress during the Presidency of William Clinton, in 1995–2001, created a new situation, especially as a result of the higher level of party voting discipline and of policy and ideological commitment of the Republican congressmen elected in 1994. In this framework of two relatively disciplined parties, one could only expect either hard-won agreements by unanimity or inter-party and interinstitutional conflict. However, President Clinton was able to attain significant bipartisan and interinstitutional cooperation by renouncing some of his initial proposed reforms and adopting moderate policy positions, especially regarding free international trade, a series of balanced budgets, 'workfare' policy, as well as the more traditionally bipartisan foreign policy. The most significant sources of potential conflict were reduced to family values and moral issues (which indirectly fostered the salience of sexual scandals, including regarding the President's private behavior). But, during this innovative experience of divided government, the two parties adjusted their major policy positions to each other's more than in any previous period (Quirk and Cunion 1999).

In general, governmental performance in periods of divided government compares not unfavorably with periods of unified government. Regarding legislative production, while Presidents oppose significant legislation more often under divided government, 'there seems to be no relationship between divided government and the amount of significant legislation the administration supports' (Edwards, Barrett, and Peake, 1997). The overall level of executive-legislative conflict in US congressional committees between 1947 and 1990 declined, despite of increasing proportions of divided government (Peterson and Greene, 1993). Out of the 267 significant laws approved between 1946 and 1990, an annual average of 6.4 acts was approved during the eighteen years of unified government, while an annual average of 5.9 acts was approved during the twenty-six years of divided government. Regarding judicial appointments, which must be made with very broad interinstitutional consensus, Presidents were able to name nine justices in situations of unified government (or one every twenty-four months) and fifteen in situations of divided government (or one every twenty-one months) (Mayhew 1991; Fiorina 1992).

Frequent accusations of 'paralysis', 'stalemate', 'deadlock', and 'gridlock' are voiced in periods of divided government (for instance, see Sundquist, 1995). Certainly, unified government allows the President to concentrate extremely strong power and to launch expeditious decisions. But, precisely because they are supported by a single winning actor, many of these decisions are vulnerable to arbitrariness or the influence of special interests and can produce biased and socially inefficient outcomes. In contrast, policy making in situations of divided government can be relatively contentious and take up more legislators' and executive officers' bargaining time. However, there is significant evidence that Presidents without a party majority in Congress tend to promote less partisan confrontation and be more compromising than those in the alternative situation. Policy decisions in periods of divided government tend to be more consensual and socially efficient than those in periods of unified government.

'Cohabitation' in Semi-presidentialism: France
General Charles de Gaulle established new constitutional rules in France during the period 1958–62 as a reaction to the high level of political pluralism of the Fourth Republic (as discussed in Chapter 3). Although the main target of criticism at the time was the instability of Cabinets during the previous regime, de Gaulle's

main aim was to attain a very high level of concentration of power in the hands of a directly elected President. Already during his first occasion as provisional chief executive at the end of the World War II, de Gaulle had revealed his ambition: 'Truly, the unity, the cohesion, and the internal discipline of the French government must be sacred, or else the very leadership of the country will rapidly become powerless and disqualified' (de Gaulle 1946). Once the Fifth Republic was custom-made for himself, he stated: 'The indivisible authority of the state is entirely given to the President by the people who elected him. There exists no other authority, neither ministerial, nor civil, nor military, nor judicial that is not conferred or maintained by him' (in Suleiman 1994).

As was expected, there was unified government in the French Fifth Republic during the presidencies of Charles de Gaulle (1962–9) and Georges Pompidou (1969–74) (when the Gaullist party included independent Republicans in its candidacies), as well as during the presidencies of Socialist François Mitterrand in the years 1981–6, when he aimed at 'exercising, to their fullest extent, the powers conferred upon me by the Constitution', and of Gaullist Jacques Chirac in the years 1995–7, when single candidacies of the Gaullists and other center-right parties were formed.

Yet, some form of divided government has existed for most of the time and been increasingly frequent in the French Fifth Republic. The President's party did not have a majority in the National Assembly not only during de Gaulle's early transitional period between the Fourth and the Fifth Republics in 1958–62, but during most of the Valéry Giscard d'Estaing presidency (1974–81), when the Gaullists and the other center-right parties ran separately in the Assembly elections. During most of Mitterrand's second term (1988–95), the Socialist party also did not have a majority in the Assembly and formed a coalition Cabinet with four center-right ministers.

More prominently, 'cohabitation' between a President and a Premier supported by an alternative political majority in the Assembly has existed during a total of nine years, both between Socialist President Mitterrand and Gaullist Premiers Jacques Chirac (1986–8) and Édouard Balladur (1993–5), and between President Chirac and Socialist Premier Lionel Jospin (1997–2002). In consistency with our previous comparative analysis regarding Presidential and Assembly elections, the President's party has lost its majority in the Assembly, creating divided governments, in all the three nonconcurrent Assembly elections since the first presidential victory of an opponent to de Gaulle in 1981 (in 1986, 1993, 1997).

The label 'semi-presidential' was coined for the French political regime by political scientist Maurice Duverger (1970). Most French constitutional lawyers observed that the regime fitted the high level of concentration of power that is characteristic of presidentialism. Before the actual experiences of cohabitation, Duverger speculated that the existing institutions would produce 'an alternation between presidential and parliamentary phases', in both cases in favor of a single, compact political majority with a single dominant figure, either the President or the

Premier, respectively (Duverger 1978, 1980, the latter being the only of his pieces on the topic available in English). The hypothesis of alternating phases was reproduced in most English-language literature on France (see discussion in Lovecy 1992; Bahro, Bayerlein and Veser 1998). However, the actual experience of cohabitation since the mid 1980s moved Duverger himself to a new analysis of what had been expected to be like a 'parliamentary phase' in favor of recognizing a more significant division of powers in it (Duverger 1986, and especially 1996: 519ff.).

The distinction between unified and divided government can account for political developments during the French Fifth Republic in a more comparative way. First, during the periods in which the President's party has a majority in the Assembly, the regime works much like a presidential regime with unified government, as was desired and anticipated by its designers, but also like a parliamentary regime in similar circumstances of a single-party majority. In all these situations, the unipersonal President (or the single-party parliamentary Premier) becomes the main figure, with considerable powers.

Second, during the both periods of minority Presidents and cohabitation, different political parties or coalitions share power, which forces them to negotiate and form broader multiparty majorities in order to make effective policy decisions. More specifically, the situation of a minority President is, as Duverger noted, 'weaker than that in the British regimes [with parliamentary unified governments] because the major partner of the alliance has only direct command over one of the allied parties' (Duverger 1986: 512). Although the President in a cohabitation situation is certainly weaker than the President in situations of divided government under presidential regimes, he is not completely subordinate to the parliamentary Premier and holds significant powers able, in fact, to limit the Premier's.

Presidential powers in situations of cohabitation include the following: some 'reserved' (actually shared) domains, such as defense (including the ultimate control over the use of nuclear forces), foreign policy (including the paramount consequences of the membership to the European Union on economic and other policies), and justice, including the veto of the appointment of the corresponding three ministers. The President's powers also include: many executive appointments; the chairmanship of the weekly meetings of the Council of ministers and its agenda; actual veto-power of certain rule-decrees and ordonnances approved by the Cabinet after delegation by the Assembly; the possibility of demanding revisions to bills from the Cabinet or Assembly, and appealing to the Constitutional Council regarding legislation; the call of referendums, especially on constitutional matters; and exceptional powers. All these opportunities make the French President much more powerful than any Monarch or elected President in a parliamentary regime. In addition, he has the power to dissolve the Assembly, which is not even in the hands of the typical President in presidential regimes.

All Presidents in situations of cohabitation have exercised their powers in order to block or moderate some Cabinet initiatives, including such issues as privatization of state companies, hospitals, and prisons; public subsidies to private schools; regionalization of colonial dominions; regulation of audiovisual media; rules on worker dismissal by companies; and asylum and citizenship rights. Interinstitutional cooperation has produced consensual compromises for the appointment of members of the Council of Monetary Policy, the Economic and Social Council, and the two French members of the European Commission. An innovative agreement on foreign policy moved to establish the joint participation of the President and the Premier in the summit meetings of the Group of the Seven and of the European Council, in vivid contrast with the divisiveness of French foreign policy in previous periods of unified government.

All country experts agree upon the fact that the first experience of cohabitation in 1986–8, which was received with alarm and the expectation of 'conflict' and 'disharmony' by most observers of the time, was less smooth than the subsequent 'constructive cohabitations' (e.g., Pierce 1991; Gouaud 1996). As noted in Chapter 3, the two following 'cohabitating' Presidents, Mitterrand in 1993–5 and Chirac in 1997–2002, were not the median voter's first preference. But thanks to the interaction of these Presidents with the median voter's Premiers, strongly biased and socially inefficient policy decisions were prevented—in contrast to the high level of bipolarization developed during the period of de Gaulle's presidency. Interinstitutional cohabitation fostered larger compromises and broader majorities in support of consensual policies than those in most parliamentary regimes. Most citizens very quickly recognized the advantages of divided government and largely approved it with their votes and opinions (as reflected, for instance, in the collection of Sofres and BVA polls collected by Duverger 1996: 556ff). (For another positive interpretation in a broader historical and comparative framework, see Furet, Julliard, and Rosanvallon, 1988.)

A 'Parliamentarized Presidentialism': Bolivia

There were 189 military coups in Bolivia between 1826 and 1980, which is to say one every ten months over 154 years, a world record by all accounts. On the basis of the 1967 Constitution (which had been established during the military rule of General René Barrientos), general elections that opened a new historical period of democratization were called in 1979, although their results were only enforced from 1982.

A series of institutional reforms were negotiated among political parties in this way producing successive corrections and adjustments in the institutional mechanisms in favor of democratic stability and consensual politics. From 1991, President Jaime Paz Zamora (from the Revolutionary Leftist Movement, MIR) appointed a Constitutional Reform Commission that was able to obtain successive multiparty accords (some discussion can be found in Toranzo Roca, 1991). Opposition leader Gonzalo Sánchez de Lozada (from the historical nationalist party, Revolutionary National Movement, MNR) relied upon an international group of scholars and experts who took inspiration from the transition to demo-cracy under a parliamentary regime in Spain (see the report in Fundación Milenio, 1997). Constitutional arrangements were attained in favor of both democratization and more effective decision making, including guarantees of civil rights, indigenous people's rights, independence of the judiciary, empowerment of local governments, new forms of popular participation, and electoral reforms.

Under the initial constitutional framework, every Bolivian voted 'en bloc' for many offices, including President, Vice-President, senators, deputies, mayors, and local councilors; in other words, every voter had to chose a single party and all its candidates for all the different offices. The Chamber of deputies (the lower chamber of the bicameral Congress) was elected by proportional representation with the Hare-quota formula and highest remainders. As previously discussed, this formula can promote factionalization because small candidacies can obtain more advantageous representation than large candidacies (in fact, there were up to twenty-six parties with seats in the first Bolivian election of 1979). However, in contrast to the process in Colombia described earlier, the level of party faction-alization in Bolivia was somewhat reduced as a consequence of the vote-en-bloc device for the presidential election. Under this mechanism, some likely small candidacies have incentives not to run separately in order to maintain their support for a potentially winning presidential candidate.

Nevertheless, the Bolivian electoral formula was revised in 1986 by requiring that a party obtains at least one seat based on the quota of votes, in order to be eligible for seats based on vote remainders, in this way reducing the incentives for factionalization. A new electoral system with double-ballot based on the German model (discussed in chapter 3) was introduced in 1994, thus creating some oppor-tunities for divided vote. National and local elections were scheduled for alternate years, also creating incentives for some citizens to divide their votes between different parties for different offices. The Senate was elected in three-member districts in which the most voted party was rewarded with two seats, likely producing different majorities than in the Chamber of deputies.

The President of Bolivia cannot be re-elected in successive terms. If no candid-ate for President achieves an absolute majority of popular votes, the second round is transferred to Congress. According to the 1967 Constitution, Congress could chose among the three top contenders in the first round and only between the two top contenders in further rounds. The 1994 reform reduced the choice for Congress to the two top contenders in three rounds; otherwise, the plurality winner in the popular election is elected President. The latter reform aimed both at reducing institutional distortion of electoral results and at permitting more effective decision making in choosing a winner.

The Bolivian political regime has been labeled 'hybrid presidentialism' and 'parliamentarized presidentialism' (for instance, see Shugart and Carey 1992: 81–5; Gamarra 1997). There are at least two advantages of this type of regime. First, the Bolivian institutional framework prevents unified government from emerging thanks to the significant degree of multipartism permitted by the different electoral systems of the two chambers. Second, in contrast to the usual situ-ation of divided government in presidentialism, it promotes political consistency between the Presidential-Cabinet coalition and the Assembly legislative coalition. This consistency may not be as solid as in parliamentary regimes due to the absence of an effective motion of censure of the executive by the Assembly. However, there are some institutional incentives to maintaining regular interac-tions and cooperation between the two institutions, including the possibility for the Assembly to interpellate Cabinet ministers, to submit them to accounting trials, and to vote motions of censure or disapproval (although not linked to compulsory resignation.)

In three out of five elections in the period 1982–97, the plurality candidate in popular votes was elected President by Congress: the leftist Hernán Siles Suazo in 1980 (having obtained 39 per cent of popular votes); the nationalist Sánchez de Lozada in 1993 (34 per cent of popular votes); and the rightist Hugo Bánzer in 1997 (only 22 per cent of popular votes). On the other two occasions, the front-runner in the popular election was replaced with an alternative candidate supported by a multiparty coalition in Congress. In 1985, the second candidate in votes, Víctor Paz Estenssoro (MNR), was preferred by a majority in Congress to the former dictator Bánzer who had obtained only one and a half percentage points of advantage in popular votes (28 per cent). Perhaps in a reversal of this shift, in 1989 the front-runner candidate, MNR's Sánchez de Lozada, who obtained only 23 per cent of popular votes, was deprived of office. Banzer's party, the second in votes with less than half a percentage point of disadvantage, supported Jaime Paz Zamora, the third candidate in votes (20 per cent). After this experience, as explained above, the election of the third candidate in votes was further prevented by the corresponding electoral reform which reduced the choice to the two most-voted candidates.

In a framework of a considerably balanced relationship of forces among the three larger parties, there have been, thus far, two Presidents from the left, two from the nationalist center, and one from the right. Cabinet and Assembly coali-tions include those between the center and the left, between the center and the right, as well as between the left and the right with additional support from minor populist parties.

Comparative institutional performances should be evaluated in the context of similar economic, cultural, and other relevant conditions. In the particular envir-onment of Bolivia, the incentives provided by 'parliamentarized presi-dentialism' to multiparty, consensual, and effective decision making have allowed significant successes in democratization, alternation in government, and economic policy making, thus producing a wide distribution of relative political satisfaction among different groups of citizens. Considering Bolivia's troubled history, such a long period of democratic stability is in itself no mean achievement.

Vertically Divided Government: Federalism

A vertically divided government is one based on separate powers between central and noncentral institutions. There can be several different origins of schemes of vertical division of powers. One is the development of large-scale common interests among previously separate or newly independent political units. This was the case of thirteen independent colonies forming the United States of America in 1776, twenty-two cantons forming Switzerland in 1848, and eleven Land governments rebuilding the German state in 1949. Similarly, newly independent states with large and disparate territories adopting federal-like structures include Venezuela in 1811, Mexico in 1824, Argentina in 1853, Canada in 1867, Brazil in 1891, Australia in 1901, India in 1947. Another path is the emergence or political promotion of salient local community interests within the borders of a previously existing, yet weak, nation-state domination, including, for instance, Belgium in 1970 and Spain in 1978.

In an efficient distribution of powers, the central government is allocated powers on issues related to large groups' interests, including defense, foreign affairs, foreign trade, money and credit, redistributive policy, and the corresponding taxation powers. Noncentral governments, in contrast, focus on economic issues related to territorial scale or location, such as local commerce, agriculture, and public works, as well as on issues linked to local or regional groups' interests which can be defined on a territorial basis, including education and the management of religious or ethnic differences and languages.

No distribution of powers between institutions is, however, perfectly efficient because, in order to minimize costs, there should be a special unit for each public good that exactly contains its users. Since the users of a highway are different from those of local schools or from those sharing a language, and so forth, the principle of efficiency would result in the creation of an extremely high number of partly overlapping administrative structures, making the whole scheme unaffordably costly (Tullock 1969; Oates 1972).

Accordingly, central, regional, and local governments usually share citizens with common, interlaced interests and share some powers in the form of concurrent jurisdictions and divided functions over certain domains. If every government-level has sufficient separate powers on some issues, partial power-sharing on other issues can promote cooperation and agreements among them in order to complete the process from the approval of initial legislative frameworks to policy decisions and their implementation. Multilateral cooperation in schemes of vertical division of powers tends to produce consensual outcomes. Furthermore, it fosters either reinforced political support for the existing institutions, or new institutional equilibrium solutions.

This approach may enlighten standard definitions of federalism, such as: the relationship between central and regional governments in which they are at the same time 'coordinate and independent [or 'not subordinate'] in their respective spheres' (Wheare 1946), a framework in which each government 'has the authority to make some final decisions independently of the other' (Riker 1964, 1987), a combination of 'self-government' and 'concurrent regimes' (Ostrom 1971) or, even more simply, 'self-rule and shared rule' (Elazar 1987, 1996).

Vertically divided government (or different political majorities in the central and the regional or local governments) can result from a divided vote at different-level elections, as discussed earlier. It can also result from citizens voting for the same party for different offices if the distribution of voters' preferences is sufficiently varied across the territory, that is, if there appear to be a sufficient number of regional or local majorities which are national minorities. In contrast to unitary states, where only those citizens whose preferences coincide with the national majority obtain satisfaction, in vertically divided government the national losers are compensated by becoming partial winners at the regional or local level. In two- or three-level elections, the number of total losers is likely to be smaller than in a single-level election.

The total amount of political satisfaction or social utility produced by vertically divided government depends on the importance given by the voters to the different issues associated with each governmental level. But the number of issues on which the voters can satisfy their preferences is never lower than under a unified government. As a simplification and adaption of the mathematical proof provided by Roland Pennock (1959), Table 4.6 shows an example of the different amounts of social utility that can be obtained by a unitary decision and by decentralized decisions in a situation in which a large-scale (national) minority is a majority at some small scale (regional). In comparison with a single, absolute winner in the unitary framework, different winners in different regions in the decentralized framework can produce higher amounts of social utility.

Many is Better than Few

A high number of differentiated regional units provides a more solid ground for a federal state than a low number. In federations formed by only two or three uneven regional groups, one of them can reasonably expect to dominate the center as well as the other regions and develop the corresponding ambition. This can lead either to the absorbtion of the smaller groups in a unified structure or to conflict and secession.

Schematically, in a simple framework of division of powers between two uneven regions, one 'large' and the other 'small', the large region may prefer dominance to separation. But, since both alternatives would make

TABLE 4.6. *Social utility in unitary and decentralized governments*

		Parties	
		Left	Right
Regions	A	*60*	40
	B	*60*	40
	C	40	*60*
		——	——
Unitary (national winners)		*160*	140
Decentralized (regional winners)		60 + 60 + 60 = *180*	

Note: Numbers are voters in each region (A, B, C) and at the national level. The number of winners with different institutional formulas are in italics.

the large region a single winner, it may relegate parity of powers between the two regions (the typically federal, multiple-winner alternative) to be its least preference. In contrast, the small, predictably dominated region is likely to develop exactly the opposite order of preferences. It will prefer parity of power (which implies over-representation of the small region at the federal level), but separation rather than subordination. The small region might accept subordination, perhaps at the cost of separating or as protection from a foreign power threat. But separation appears to be the intermediate alternative in both preference orders (Table 4.7) on which a bilateral negotiation can converge. (for comparable suggestions, see Elster 1995; Laitin 1995; Riker 1996a.)

Recent failures of newly created two-unit federations in which the smaller, likely dominated group has seceded include the following cases: Great Britain–Northern Ireland after the secession of the Republic of Ireland, with Northern Ireland home-rule eventually suppressed (1920–69); India–Pakistan at their independence (1947), succeeded by

TABLE 4.7. *Preference orders regarding unity, federation, and secession*

Preference	Large group	Small group
First	Unitary (total winner)	Parity (partial winner)
Second	Separation (single winner)	Separation (single winner)
Least	Parity (partial loser)	Unitary (total loser)

West Pakistan–Bangladesh, with secession of the latter (1947–71); South
Africa–South West Africa, with secession of the latter, now called
Namibia (1948–68); Rhodesia–Nyasaland, with secession of Zambia and
Malawi from Rhodesia (1953–63); Egypt–Syria, split up by the latter
(1958–61); Tanzania, where Zanzibar was motivated to approve a separate
constitution from Tanganyka (1964–79); Ethiopia–Eritrea, with secession
of the latter (1952–91); and Czechoslovakia, also with secession of the
latter, smaller unit (1991–2). Nigeria, initially independent in 1960 with
only three regional units, experienced the secession of Biafra in 1967; yet,
interestingly, after a period of military rule, a new Nigerian federation was
created with an initial number of twelve regional units, lately increased up
to thirty.

Unbalanced relationships between a large number of regional units can
be conflictive and unstable if one of the regions is sufficiently large and
sufficiently domineering on some divisive issue as to be able to try to
impose its exclusive rule. In particular, a language, ethnic, or religious
dualism on a territorial basis can be a source of political bipolarization and
an uneven relationship. This seems to be the case in Canada, despite its
having a large number of provinces. As a consequence of the population
evolution toward two linguistically homogenous territories of unequal
size, the minority Quebec fears assimilation by the Anglo component and
secessionist movements have developed. Belgium has also experienced
salient political conflicts in the second half of the 20th century on the
basis of its language dualism between the Walloon and Flemish territories.
A bipolar territorial confrontation developed during the Spanish Second
Republic after a single regional government was established in Catalonia
in 1931, in contrast to the multiregional arrangement adopted during the
following democratic experience in 1978.

More stable federal or federal-type states usually have higher numbers
of regional units, none of which can reasonably feed ambitions of becom-
ing the single dominant one. Cases include: the United States (50),
Mexico (32), Switzerland (26), Brazil (26), India (25), Argentina (24),
Venezuela (20), Italy (20), Spain (17), Germany (16), Malaysia (13),
Canada (11), Austria (9), South Africa (9), Australia (8), as well as the
European Union (15).

Divided Bicameralism

A crucial institutional element of cooperation between the central government and the regional governments in federal states is the upper chamber
of territorial representation.

Upper chambers are fairly common in Assemblies throughout the
world, but their institutional diversity is very great. Upper chambers of
nondemocratic origin in parliamentary regimes were deprived of signifi-

cant powers by giving the lower chamber the decisive role in case of disagreement (as in Britain, France, and even in some regionalized countries like Austria, Belgium, and Spain). In other cases, the upper chamber is elected by procedures which tend to replicate the political composition of the lower chamber, thus making strong political disagreements between the two chambers unlikely (as in Austria, Italy, and Japan). Or the upper chamber is appointed by some unelected office (as in Canada).

In most of these cases of asymmetric bicameralism, the second chamber does not represent voters' preferences which are significantly different from those represented in the lower chamber. The second chamber can only introduce delays and improvements in the approval of bills, especially if it can initiate legislation, if the two chambers can go through a high number of negotiating rounds before the lower one makes a final decision, or the subordinated second chamber has a single-winner party facing a multiparty lower chamber (Tsebelis and Money 1997).

The second chamber is only a genuinely decisive actor if it has both significant legislative powers and a differentiated political majority from the lower chamber. These conditions of symmetry are only fulfilled in upper chambers of territorial representation in federal states. Symmetric bicameralism usually requires either the indirect election of the chamber by the regional governments or parliaments (as in Germany, India, and Russia) or differentiated regional districts and nonconcurrent popular elections able to produce winners different from those in the lower chamber (as in Argentina, Australia, Brazil, Switzerland, the United States, and Venezuela). In contrast to the relatively proportional allocation of seats according to the population that usually occurs in the lower chamber, typically, every region is given equal representation in the federal upper chamber, independently of its population (or the smaller units receive over-representation). Disagreements between the two chambers in a federal state can be solved through negotiations among delegates of the two chambers in a conference committee (as in Germany, Switzerland, and the United States) or by a decision of the two chambers in a joint session (as in Australia, India, Venezuela and, for some issues, Brazil).

Bicameralism reunites some effects of both horizontal and vertical division of powers. First, it offers the parties an incentive to broaden the agenda of issues while it allows the citizens to divide their votes as they may in 'horizontally' separate elections. At the same time, federal upper chambers can promote 'vertical' cooperation between the central and regional governments in public policy decision making.

A symmetric bicameralism with sufficient mechanisms of cooperation can have effects similar to those of inclusive decision rules (such as the two-thirds majority which is required for decisions on many constitutional issues in Belgium, the two-thirds majority in any of the two chambers used in Argentina, or the double-majority requirement regarding the cantons in Switzerland, which will be discussed below). Requiring the concurrence of two-chamber different majorities to make a decision is like requiring a supermajority. Even if each of the chambers makes decisions by simple majority rule, joint decisions by two politically differentiated chambers will be negotiated or be found around moderate, intermediate alternatives. These will likely be supported by an inclusive majority, thus giving satisfaction to larger numbers of citizens than would a single-chamber decision (Riker 1992*a*, *b*.)

Cases: Vertical Interinstitutional Cooperation and Conflict

Three cases of interinstitutional cooperation and supermajority decisions in schemes of vertical division of powers will now be surveyed. First, we will analyze the combination of federal government and cantonal referendums leading to permanent supermajority Cabinets in Switzerland. Second, we will look at the multiparty consensual decisions produced by symmetrical bicameralism in federal Germany. Third, we will approach the ongoing evolution in the European Union towards a federal-like institutional structure, as particularly fostered by the multiparty European Parliament. In all these cases, multilateral cooperation keeps pluralist institutional frameworks in equilibrium.

In contrast, the disgreggation of authoritarian federal Yugoslavia shows that compound states in which one of the units is sufficiently large to become dominant can find themselves in disequilibrium once they move to a democratic context.

The Swiss 'Magic Formula'

The Federal Assembly of Switzerland makes decisions by very large majority and appoints 'Grand Coalition' Federal Councils (or parliamentary Cabinets). In particular, the so-called 'magic formula' of Cabinet coalition between the Radical, Christian, Populist, and Socialist parties, together encompassing up to 85 per cent of popular votes and parliamentary seats, has been maintained without interruption since 1959.

Supermajority decisions and highly consensual politics in Switzerland result from incentives provided by an unusual institutional combination: a national parliamentary regime and cantonal referendums. Switzerland, a land of small homogeneous communities which used direct democracy in the late medieval and the early modern era (as discussed in Chapter 2), was organized as a federal state based on twenty-two cantons at the end of the 1847–8 civil war. The federal Assembly has two chambers. The upper chamber, or Council of the States, is formed by two representatives per canton, independently of its population. The lower chamber, or National Council, was initially elected in cantonal multimember districts with majority-plurality-runoff. For about forty years, the winners of the civil war, the Radicals (or Free Democrats, lately FDP), were the dominant party, but representation then was based largely on cantonal parties with loose national ties.

A series of crucial institutional innovations then followed. In 1874, the citizens were given the possibility of demanding referendums on legislation (by collecting 30,000 signatures; increased to 50,000 in 1977). While any bill submitted to popular referendum must be approved by a majority of Swiss voters, constitutional reforms and international treaties need both a majority of voters and a majority of voters in a majority of cantons. Since 1891, referendums on constitutional amendments, which were previously compulsory for Assembly proposals, have also been permitted for popular initiatives.

The growth of new parties, the Conservatives in the late 19th century (lately named Christian-Social and Christian-Democrats, CVP) and the Socialists (SPS) in the early 20th century, moved to introduce proportional representation in 1918. The new electoral system was based on cantonal districts, a quota formula with highest remainders (later replaced with d'Hondt), and open ballot allowing the voter to choose candidates from different party lists. The three major parties, the Radicals, the Conservative-Christians, and the Socialists, have obtained similar proportions of votes since then, each around 25 per cent, while new minor parties, particularly the Populists (or Agrarians, lately People's party, SVP), have also obtained representation. (Gruner 1978; Linder 1994).

From 1874 to 1959, the number of referendums on federal legislation steadily rose from an average of one every two and a half years to one every four months, especially at the initiative of parties excluded from national government. Regarding constitutional amendments, given that many cantons contain a small number of voters, a national minority formed by a set of small cantonal major-ities can veto a proposal. Precisely, if the 'no' votes in a referendum were distributed among the cantons in an optimal way, the minimum number of votes able to defeat an amendment proposal at the national level would be less than 10 per cent (Germann 1992).

The permanent threat of referendums prevents the Assembly from making certain legislative decisions—more than the actual veto itself. Despite the fact that the Assembly may approve legislation by simple majority, the fear of further defeat in referendum moves legislators to build very large parliamentary major-ities (Neidhart 1970).

The seven members of the Federal Council, which includes an annually rotating chair, are appointed in joint sessions of the two chambers of the Federal Assembly. For a very long time, the Constitution formally required that no two Council members may come from the same canton (until the formal rule was abolished by popular vote in February 1999). Other rigidly obeyed customs are that the Council must include representatives of the two largest German-speaking cantons, Bern and Zurich, and no fewer than two representatives of 'Latin' cantons (usually a member from the largest French-speaking canton, Vaud, and one other either from another French canton or from the Italian-speaking canton of Ticino, or both). This is roughly in proportion to the distribution of family languages among the population: about 70 per cent German, 20 per cent French, 9 per cent Italian (and 1 per cent Romanche). In recent years, the inclusion of at least one woman in the Council has become an informal rule. The posts in the Council are usually filled only one or two at a time, typically at the proposal of the corresponding party whose member is being replaced, and according to the expected language-area origin. The combination of rules regarding canton, language, and gender, as well as political party's preferences, usually make the number of potential candidates very small.

On the basis of the electoral evolution previously sketched and the threat of referendum, these rules led to stable Council coalitions between the Radicals and the Conservatives beginning in 1891, as well as the coalition's enlargement with the Populists since 1929 and the Socialists temporarily during the war and post-war period, 1943–54. The more stable 'magic formula' was not adopted, however, until after the 1959 election, when, exceptionally, four Council members had to be replaced (three of them because of ill health). This opportunity for a major renewal again opened the door to Socialist candidates, this time supported by the Conservative-Christians. Since then, the corresponding distribution of offices in the Council for the Radicals, the Christians, the Socialists, and the Populists is 2: 2: 2: 1, respectively, in close proportion to each party's votes and seats.

In order to have reasonable expectations of winning a referendum in most cantons, a national majority coalition should have a majority or at least include the median voter's parties in most cantons. In addition, a significant number of voters in a referendum may not follow the position adopted by the party they vote for in elections, especially on issues that strongly affect minority interests, or they may abstain on issues on which they have no intense preferences or are indifferent. Even national party leaders cannot always count on the support of all their cantonal, still quite independent sections (Steiner 1983).

In the crucial election of 1959, the Conservative-Christians obtained an absolute majority of votes and were thus the median voter's party only in six cantons, while the Radicals obtained a majority in only one canton. In contrast, the Socialists were the most voted party in eight cantons, including the two largest German-speaking cantons, Bern and Zurich, and were *à la pair* with the Radicals in the largest French-speaking canton, Vaud—all of them regular providers of Council members, as mentioned above.

All these factors led to the rational formation of surplus majorities in the Federal Assembly and the Federal Council by political parties with reasonably self-interested motives. In the two-chamber Assembly elected in 1959, a narrow minimum-winning coalition might be formed by the Radicals and the Conservative-Christians, gathering together 130 seats out of 244. The two parties had collected 50.1 per cent of total popular votes, but they had obtained together a majority support in only twelve of the twenty-two cantons, not including the

French-speaking Vaud and Geneva. An alternative surplus majority formed by the Radicals, the Conservative-Christians, and the Populists would have been based on 59 per cent of popular votes and 64 per cent of seats, but its partners had together obtained a majority support in only sixteen cantons, again not including the two largest French ones. In contrast, only the four partners of the 'magic formula', including the Socialists, which had together collected 85 per cent of popular votes and of parliamentary seats, had obtained a majority of votes in all the twenty-two cantons, allowing the corresponding legislative majority and the Council to be confident about facing the challenge of popular referenda (author's own calculations with data in *Statistisches Jahrbuch der Schweiz*, Basle1964).

In fact, following the adoption of the 'magic formula' in 1959, the proportion of all governmental proposals (including constitutional amendments, laws, decrees, treaties, and urgent decrees deviating from the Constitution) that were defeated in referendum decreased from 40 per cent in the previous period to 25 per cent (Kobach 1993; Trechsel and Sciarini 1998).

A simplified model of the situation discussed here is shown in Table 4.8. Cantons of different size with uneven support for political parties may produce a narrow national majority which is a minority in most cantons, as well as a surplus 60 per cent national majority which is still a minority in some cantons, while, in contrast, a four-party majority based on about 85 per cent of popular votes obtains a majority support in all the cantons.

Consensual politics in federal Switzerland has largely been explained as an outcome of political leaders' cooperative strategies. Arend Lijphart remarked that 'consociational' decision making, as opposed to 'competitive' decision making, developed despite the existence of rather fragmented subcultures and homogenous cantons (Lijphart, 1968, 1979). Other authors, such as Jürg Steiner, placed an 'amicable agreement' pattern of decision making in the more favorable context of cross-cutting language, religious, and economic cleavages (Steiner 1974, supported by Bohn 1980).

The approach developed here points out the fact that a consensual outcome, such as the surplus multiparty coalition usually referred to as the 'magic formula', and the corresponding moderate, stable policy making, may not result from cooperative strategies. The consensual, cooperative outcome can result from competitive party strategies not substantially different from those typically adopted by political leaders in stable democracies, yet developed under the precise incentives provided by an institutional framework with a double-majority requirement. Although repeated experiences of negotiation may develop self-sustaining informal norms of behavior, the stability of a particular coalition formula ultimately depends on the stability of the distribution of votes and seats among political parties. In fact, party coalition formulas in Switzerland have changed at various historical moments. In the election of October 1999, the Populists increased dramatically their number of votes and asked for a second office in the Council, at the expense of the weakened Socialists. The 'magic formula' stayed, but it

What Is Voted For

TABLE 4.8. *National and cantonal majorities*

| | Cantons | | | National |
	A	B	C	total
Radicals	10	10	6	26
Christians	5	15	5	25
Socialists	10	5	10	25
Populists	10	0	0	10
Others	5	5	4	14
Total	40	35	25	100

Note: The hypothetical national majority formed by Radicals and Christians, with (26 + 25) 51% of votes, is a majority in only canton B (25/35). The surplus national majority formed by Radicals, Christians, and Populists, with (26 + 25 + 10) 61% of votes, is a majority in only two cantons, A (25/40) and B (25/35). Only the even larger four-party coalition formed by Radicals, Christians, Populists, and Socialists together gathers 86% of votes and a majority in all the cantons.

could again change if there were significant shifts in the distribution of voters' preferences among political parties.

Swiss citizens have benefited from several fortunate circumstances in modern history which established the foundation for their well-being. Not the least of these has been federal institutions introducing joint requirements of both national and cantonal majorities in policy decision making. The corresponding legislative and executive supermajorities have permitted the peaceful development of a great degree of cultural and political pluralism and a very remarkable policy and democratic stability.

The German Cooperative Federalism

Federalism was established in Germany by the occupying forces at the end of World War II in the aim of weakening the German state and preventing new authoritarian experiments. However, the federal structure of Germany has produced unintended effects in favor of highly effective decision making and consensual politics, both at the regional and the national levels.

After the defeat of the Nazis in 1945, while the Soviets desired a new unified government in Germany, which they eventually established in the Eastern part of the territory, the Americans, British, and French gave priority to the creation of new regional, or Land, democratic governments. In the words of the American Secretary of State in 1947, the United States opposed a strong central government because 'it could be too readily converted to the domination of a regime similar to the Nazis'. The British Foreign Minister wanted 'all powers vested in the Länder except such as are expressly delegated to the central government'. His French colleague went as far as to conceive of the center as a mere 'coordination' of Lands with the national Assembly consisting only of a chamber of Lands (Golay 1958: 5).

At the behest of the Western Allies in 1948, the newly elected eleven Land governments in the Western part of Germany appointed a Constituent Assembly (which was modestly called 'Parliamentary Council') to 'draft a democratic constitution which will establish for the participating states [*Länder*] a governmental structure of federal type', under the supervision of the occupying Allied powers.

Three basic conditions of an efficient and stable federal state, which have been previously identified in the general discussion of this chapter, were fulfilled in the 'Basic Law (Provisional Constitution)' approved in Bonn in 1949. First, the number of regional units was relatively high: eleven (provisionally excluding West Berlin). Although only Bavaria, Bremen, and Hamburg could claim continuity as historic German states from the imperial era, and the territorial limits of the other Lands were new creations, new Land constitutions were adopted and significant local interests developed. After the 1999 reunification with the Eastern part of the country, the number of Lands increased to sixteen.

Second, an effective division of powers between the Land governments and the central government was established. In particular, the Lands were given exclusive powers in education, cultural and religious affairs, and local government; concurrent powers on a number of other domains, including health care and welfare; as well as control of the assessment and collection of major taxes.

Third, an upper chamber of territorial representation, the *Bundesrat*, was established in parallel to the national lower chamber, the *Bundestag* (whose election, party composition, and decision making is discussed in Chapter 3). The *Bundesrat*, or upper chamber, is a key institution in the federal structure of Germany. It is both the guardian of the division of powers in favor of the Lands and the main institutional setting for cooperation among the Land governments in federal policy making.

The German upper chamber is composed of members of the Land governments (in a democratic adaption of the old imperial tradition) with some over-representation of the smaller Lands. Each Land delegation is required to vote en bloc in accordance with the instructions of the Land government. The composition of the upper chamber changes frequently as a result of staggered regional elections. In contrast to the lower chamber, the upper chamber cannot be dissolved by the Chancellor.

As previously discussed, the emergence of different political majorities in the two chambers can be partly explained by the salience given to different issues in national elections and in staggered Land elections, but also by the indirect effect of voters choosing to split their votes between different parties for strategic reasons in the elections for the national lower chamber and for the Land governments.

The Christian-Democrats dominated the Cabinets and enjoyed a majority in the two chambers during 1949–69 and 1982–90. However, different political majorities around the Christians and the Socialists in the two chambers, or divided bicameralism, have been alternately produced during the periods of both Socialist-dominated governments in 1969–82, Christian-dominated governments from the reunification with East Germany in 1991 until 1998, and Socialist-dominated governments since 1999. Divided bicameralism has thus existed during 46 per cent of the period between 1949 and 2002 (and 75 per cent of the period since 1969).

According to the Constitution, the upper chamber has powers equal to those of the lower chamber regarding constitutional amendments, some suspensory veto right over federal legislation in general (which may be overriden by the lower chamber), and absolute veto on legislation affecting Land interests. The latter were initially identified as decisions on the territory of the Lands, some taxes and finances, and the creation of new federal administrative agencies in the legal domains of the Lands. The upper chamber also has extensive control over the federal administration, including the implementation of federal legislation by the ministries.

Yet the 'elastic clause' regulating which issues can be considered to affect Land interests has worked strongly in favor of the Land governments and the upper chamber in controversies over the division of powers. It has eventually produced symmetrical bicameralism, that is, the *Bundesrat*, representing the regional governments, has achieved in practice powers equal to those of the lower chamber. Important factors of this development have been: the increasing salience of Europe-wide legislation, especially with regard to economic policy, which affects the territorial distribution of powers; frequent different political majorities in the two chambers; and the support of the independent constitutional court (Golay 1958).

Horizontally divided government between the two chambers, as produced by a vertical division of powers and separate elections at different institutional levels, forces the corresponding negotiations between the two major parties and their coalition partners for passing legislation on relevant issues with broad political support. In 1949, only 10 per cent of all federal laws required the upper chamber's approval. But by the mid 1990s, the proportion of federal legislation submitted to the absolute veto right of the upper chamber had increased to about 60 per cent. Most legislation has thus actually been approved with the support of the Christians, Liberals, the Socialists, together gathering an average of 90 per cent of popular votes. Despite the fact that the upper chamber does not intervene formally in the appointment or censure of the Chancellor and the Cabinet, it is considered to have had a relevant role in the resignations of Christian-Democrat Chancellor Konrad Adenauer in 1963 and Socialist Chancellor Willy Brandt in 1974 (Dalton 1993).

Legislative performance in periods of bicameral divided government compares favorably with periods of unified bicameral government, that is, with the same political majority in the two chambers. The number of bills passed annually by the lower chamber in the period of divided bicameral government 1969–81 was 103, while the corresponding numbers in the periods of unified bicameral government were 120 for 1949–69 and 92 for 1982–90, with a total average of 111. The proportion of laws requiring the approval of the upper chamber that were promulgated was 53 per cent in the above-mentioned period of divided bicameralism, and 50 and 56 per cent in the two above-mentioned periods of unified bicameralism, with a total average of 52 per cent (author's own calculations with data in Thayssen 1994).

A Federalizing European Union

The institutional relations in the European Economic Community closely corresponded to those of an international organization for about thirty years (1957–86). According to the 'intergovernmental' model of institutional relations, most decisions were made by unanimity of delegates of state governments, as represented in the Council of Ministers and in the regular meetings of government heads in the European Council. Stagnation and immobility gradually emerged, especially after successive enlargements of the European Community from six to twelve member-states, because any member of the Council could veto any innovative decision (as discussed in Chapter 3).

New decision rules fostering federalizing interinstitutional relations were established by a series of constituent-like regulations, including the European Single Act (1986), the Maastricht Treaty of the European Union (1992), and the Amsterdam Treaty (1997). They introduced different decision procedures requiring the major institutions of the European Union (EU), that is, the Council, the European Parliament, and the European Commission, to share powers. Under the impulse of Europe-wide aggregative political parties, they promoted more innovative decisions towards an 'ever-closer' Union, including a common market and a common currency, as well as a further enlargement to fifteen member-states.

The deployment of the 'federal' model of the European Union would require further increases in the powers of the European Parliament and more balanced interinstitutional relations, but it is anticipated by these developments. The federal model is based upon a double criterion of representation. While the Council, formed by representatives of state governments, could be considered an upper chamber of territorial representation, the Parliament would act as the repres-enta-tive body of European citizens at large. According to the typical relations in a parliamentary regime, the Commission, or executive body, would be appointed by the two parliamentary chambers and would be responsible to them.

Under the existing framework, the Council of Ministers and the European Parliament are elected separately and with different rules. This usually produces the possibility that different political party majorities can be formed in each chamber, as in the typical symmetrical bicameralism of federal states previously discussed. As a result, interinstitutional decisions have to be based on very broad agreements. In particular, the members of the European Commission, including its President, which were traditionally appointed by the Council (in practice by the state governments), need the approval of the Parliament since the implementation of the Amsterdam Treaty in 1999. The requirement of two majorities in the Council and in the Parliament tends to produce a consensual supermajority not substantially different in party composition from the support given to the Commissions appointed under previous procedures. But it makes the executive body of the European Union more accountable to representatives of the European citizens.

Federalizing interinstitutional relations according to the model here sketched have been fostered by aggregative European political parties. Successive enlargements of the European Union led to an increasing number of national parties obtaining representation in the institutions, from about 40 at the first direct election of the European Parliament in 1979, to up to 110 in 1999. Yet, remarkably, the absolute number of European Political Groups in the Parliament decreased following the elections of 1994 and 1999, and the degree of party fragmentation in Parliament decreased steadily in each of the five elections in the period 1979–99 (as measured, for instance, by the effective number of parties or other similar indices of fractionalization). Despite representing fifteen member-states with their own party systems, the European Parliament in the late 20th and early 21th centuries is less fragmented than the parliaments of several European countries, such as Belgium, Denmark, Finland, and the Netherlands.

The European Socialist Party was the largest group in the European Parliament after the first four elections, with an average of about one-third of seats, and the only group integrating national parties from all the member-states since the first election. It also includes the Italian post-Communist party of the Democratic Left since 1994. The European People's Party, which initially gathered together Christian-Democratic parties from nine countries, was successively enlarged with the British Conservatives and some minor allies in 1992, Forza Italia in 1995, and the French Gaullists in 1999, all having previously formed their own national-istic groups. It became the largest group in Parliament after the fifth election in 1999.

The two European Political Groups mentioned, the Socialists and the Populars, have always encompassed together more than half the members of the European Parliament and this proportion is increasing at every election. The Socialists and the Populars, together with the intermediate Liberals, which are the third group in number of seats, tend to form 'connected' coalitions around the center, especially on economic and foreign policy issues. Some alternative coalitions emerge, such as the so-called 'majority of progress' organized around the Socialists, with the Greens, the Communists, and the Liberals as potential partners, especially with respect to social policy and human rights issues. Center-right coalitions without the Socialists have also been formed, including for the election of the Parliament chair (Jacobs, Corbett, and Shakleton 1995; Gaffney 1996; Raunio 1997).

The formation of increasingly aggregative European Political Groups and of viable majority coalitions has made the European Parliament much more effective since the late 1980s than in previous periods. To the extent that the Parliament is capable of making decisions, interinstitutional relations corresponding to the federal model of the European Union are fostered. Political parties in the European Parliament benefit from the opportunities given by the existing institutional rules at any given moment. But, at the same time, they create these opportunities by promoting treaties and constitutional-like regulations that reduce the traditional 'democratic deficit' of the European institutions and replace the dominant role of the Council with more complex formulas. As nationalistic groupings cede room to larger Europe-wide groups, further decisions towards a closer union find less nationalistic resistance. The intergovernmental model which had led to 'Eurosclerosis' and 'Europessimism' in the early 1980s, has gradually been replaced with federalizing interinstitutional relations able to promote more optimistic prospects (Colomer and Hosli 1997; Colomer 1999c).

The Disintegration of Yugoslavia
The dispersion of Yugoslavia in the 1990s is a dramatic example of the implausibility of a multinational federation in a democracy when one of the groups is large enough to try to become dominant. An uneven composition to the advantage of previously independent Serbia was the major weakness of the country since its foundation.

At the end of World War I, Slovenia and Croatia, liberated by the fall of the Austro–Hungarian Empire and fearing Italian expansionism, joined the Great Serbia to form the so-called United Kingdom of the Serbs, Croats, and Slovenes (in this order), under Serbian Monarchy. Simply put, the Serbian political institutions, as had been designed in the Serbian Constitution of 1903, were extended to other territories in 1918. The basic formulas of a unitary state and unicameral parliamentary regime, promoting a high concentration of power, were maintained. Only one nationality was established and even a single language, 'Serbo–Croatian–Slovenian', was proclaimed. The three peoples considered themselves to be Slavs and shared the Christian religion, although they had accumulated two previous imperial memberships (Turkish and Austrian), two ecclesiastical obediences (Eastern Orthodox and Roman Catholic), and two alphabets (Cyrillic and Latin).

During the unitary experience, the Serbs being about half of the total population (out of 17 million people), they dominated most political decisions. Almost all Cabinets were led by the Serbian Radical party, sometimes with the help of the small Muslim minority. Serbian domination was challenged by Croatian parties, provoking relatively high Cabinet instability. In the face of stable Serbian-led majorities, secessionist movements soon developed among the Croats. In 1929, the Serbian King, Alexander, reacted to ethnic turmoil by abrogating the Constitution, disbanding the Parliament, and establishing himself as dictator. At that very moment the new unitary name, Yugoslavia (literally, 'Southern Slavs'), was coined and adopted (Dragnich 1983, 1992).

The German occupation and World War II included a series of civil wars in the Balkans, especially between the Croats and the Serbs. With the victory of the Communists in 1945, Yugoslavia was refounded as a federal republic. The Communist leader, Marshall Josip Broz Tito (from a Slovenian–Croatian family and a Croatian himself) tried to curb feared Serbian domination with a new territorial redistribution of power. On one side, the borders of Croatia were enlarged (not accepting, for instance, the autonomy of Dalmatia). On the other side, Serbia was diminished by the creation of the separate republics of Bosnia–Herzegovina (with an ethnically mixed population), Montenegro (which was Serbian in religion and language), and Macedonia, formerly South Serbia (whose language was standardized with new alphabet and orthography only in 1948 and was recognized as a 'nation' only in 1967). Within Serbia, two small, ethnically mixed provinces were created, Vojvodina and Kosovo. The two provinces were given equal representation in the federal bodies: the Federal Council, the bicameral Federal Assembly created in 1953, as well as the collective State Presidency lately created by Tito as a provision for his succession. In 1974, they were also given *de facto* veto power in the Serbian parliament.

The initial union of three peoples with two cultural traditions was thus transformed into a conglomeration of four languages, five nations, six republics, and eight political units with equal powers in federal government. The Serbian Republic was reduced to one of the eight units with a fourth of the total population, although the Serbs, now territorially dispersed, were still the largest group (about 40 per cent of the total population in the 1980s) (Curtis 1990).

The Communist-dominated federation was but a temporary fiction because a single party actually monopolized power. After the death of Tito and, especially, at the fall of Communism in Central and Eastern Europe in 1989, ethnic conflict arose. Resentment for past grievances added to sentiments of unfair distribution of institutional power. A crucial decision for the later political developments was the call of the first multiparty elections in 1990 at the republic level, instead of the one federal election. This promoted the salience of nationalistic issues and the corresponding popular support of nationalist and secessionist movements (sim-ilar to what had happened in the Soviet Union at about the same time and in contrast to Spain in 1977, as was remarked by Juan Linz 1992). However, the electoral schedule reflected general doubts about the future of the authoritarian federal fiction. Tito's constitutional engineering in favor of new republics and provinces eventually provoked unintended effects. Once competitive elections were called, they became platforms for the promotion and manipulation of sentiments of belonging and 'identity' which fostered disarray and disintegration.

Beginning in 1989, the newly elected Serbian president, former Communist (renamed Socialist) Slobodan Milosevic, led the project of 'Serbian reunifica-tion'. First, he secured his political party's control over the government of Montenegro and the administrative control of Vojvodina, while the Assembly and the government of Kosovo were suppressed. In 1991, the declaration of independ-ence of ethnically homogeneous Slovenia, where almost no Serbs lived, was soon followed by the withdrawal of Serbian-led federal troops. In fact, the Slovenian secession could have given the Serbs a clearer majority in the rest of Yugoslavia. The independence of Croatia in 1992, in contrast, provoked a Serb attempt to conquest Eastern Slavonia, as well as the proclamation of the Serbian Republic of Krajina, although Croatia eventually reconquered the territory in 1995. The clash between Serbs and Croats was very bloody in the war of Bosnia–Herze-govina during 1992–5 (causing about 250,000 deaths), which was settled with the actual partition of the country into the Croatian–Muslim federation of Bosnia–Herzegovina and the Serbian Republic of Bosnia. 'Ethnic cleansing' took place (on both sides) in Kosovo, even under NATO's bombing in 1999.

The leader of the Great Serbia project, Milosevic, who ruled over about a fourth of former Yugoslavia's total population, forcefully tried to reshape the map of the Balkans in a way that would have allowed him, as the new president of the rump of Yugoslavia, to rule over more than half of the same population. But all the minority groups resisted the attempt and choose to secede (Bennett 1995; Udovicki and Ridgeway 1997).

Horizontal and Vertical Division of Powers

A horizontally unified government tends to eliminate vertical division of powers. As previously discussed, the Premiership or the Presidency in a situation of unified government tends to dominate, curb, or even suppress the Assembly in order to become a single, absolute winner. For similar motives of expediency and the concentration of powers, a unified central government tends to reduce or eliminate the autonomy of regional and local governments.

If a single party has an absolute majority in the central government and also in the noncentral governments, the party becomes the single dominant actor in both horizontal and vertical interinstitutional rela-tions. The legal division of powers between the central government and the noncentral units may survive, but is actually eliminated by the homogeneous political control of all institutions. Alternatively, if a single party has an absolute majority in the central government, but does not control the noncentral governments, it may try to replace the legal scheme of vertical division of powers with a unitary formula in order to eliminate alternative sources of power and become the only dominant actor.

In contrast, an effective vertical division of powers is more likely to exist and survive in the framework of divided central government, whether in the form of multiparty coalition Cabinets or the coexistence of different party majorities in the Presidency and the Assembly. If no party is an absolute winner and several parties share power in the central institutions, they will tend to negotiate and compromise with other parties in the noncentral governments in order to expand their shares of power to the territorial institutions. The latent internal competition between partners in the central government can lead them to search for other partners with powerful positions in noncentral governments, in this way expanding the scope of multiparty agreements.

Noncentral governments can maintain and defend their separate powers on some issues or their share of powers on others, which is to say, they can sustain vertical division of powers by introducing division into the central government. An upper chamber of territorial representation, in particular, can make regional governments decisive actors at the federal level and prevent a single party with an absolute majority in the lower chamber from becoming a total winner monopolizing all powers. Also, an independent judiciary not controlled by a single party can help to keep the balance of decentralization (Bednar, Eskridge, and Ferejohn 1995).

Several cases can illustrate that vertical division of powers is relatively more stable and effective when it parallels horizontal division of powers than when it coexists with a unified central government. For example, federalism is better grounded in Germany than in Austria. As previously discussed, the Federal Republic of Germany, which is organized into sixteen Lands, is based upon a system of proportional representation in the national lower chamber producing multiparty coalition Cabinets and a symmetric upper chamber with frequently changing majorities. In contrast, in Austria, where there are only nine Lands, there have been significant periods of single-party absolute majority or Grand Coalition in the central government, while the federal council is usually considered, rather than a second chamber, 'a second-rate chamber'. As a result, while Germany is one of the most decentralized countries in Europe, the Austrian Lands have no separate powers and very few significant shared powers, as well as little co-decision in federal affairs. (For a comparative presentation of federalism in Europe, see Hesse and Wright 1996.)

Similarly, federalism in the United States is more robust than in Canada. As previously noted, the United States, which has fifty states, has frequent periods in which the federal government is divided between the Presidency and Congress. There exists a clear correlation between the periods of unified government in Washington and those of increasing centralization, including, in particular, the 'Reconstruction' period in the

1860s, the 'New Deal' period in the 1930s and 1940s, and the 'Great Society' period in the 1960s. Meanwhile, decentralization has been generally recognized to be higher in periods of divided central government, as it was in the 1980s.

In contrast, Canada, which has only eleven provinces, has frequent single-party national Cabinets while the upper house, which is appointed by the British General Governor, is ineffective at representing provincial concerns. An additional restriction over the power of provincial governments occurred with the abolition of the role of the British Privy Council as independent judiciary in 1947–9, followed by its replacement by the Supreme Court of Canada, which is less independent of party politics. This change led to the decline of judicial protection of the provinces. The subsequent demands from Quebec to restore the provinces' veto right have not been satisfied. As several attempts to attain a new compromise on the definition of the federal relationship failed, secessionist tendencies and internally divisive conflicts in the province have arisen (Breton 1964; Watts 1996*a*).

More generally, federalism has had a difficult time surviving in simple, British-style political regimes based upon elections by plurality rule and a unicameral parliamentarism. Former British colonies that were organized as federal states have experienced the erosion of vertical division of powers and the corresponding tensions between the center and some regions. In India, the constitutional rules go as far as to give the central government the right to dismiss state governments and to replace them with direct rule from the center, legally only for reasons of public order, but in fact also for partisan concerns. The centralizing process in India, especially during the long period of absolute majority of the Congress party in the central government in Delhi, encouraged secessionist movements, particularly in Kashmir, Punjab, and Uttar Pradesh (Thakur 1995; Lijphart 1996).

Conversely, decentralization and vertical division of powers can develop in relatively favorable conditions, even if there is no explicit constitutional mandate for federalism, under the pressure of regional parties in a context of divided central governments. Countries like Belgium and Spain, for example, have developed significant levels of political, administrative, and financial decentralization in favor of regional governments in favorable conditions created by national electoral systems of proportional representation, multipartism, and the corresponding absence of a single-party absolute majority in the center. These noninstitutionalized processes, however, are more vulnerable to conflict than those including more robust federal mechanisms of multilateral cooperation.

Case: The Very United Kingdom

In the mid 18th century, the political regime of England was considered to be the best example of 'one nation in the world that has for the direct end of its constitution political liberty' founded on the principle of separation of powers (Montesquieu, 1748, book XI). In contrast, by the mid 20th century, political students widely agreed that the United Kingdom was 'both the original and the best-known example' of the model of democracy based on concentration of powers (see, for example, Lijphart 1984: 5).

In fact, the old 'England' had become a complex territorial compound of England and Wales, Scotland (since 1707), and Ireland (in 1801–1921). For some time after the union with Scotland, the central government in London respected Scottish autonomy, especially in matters of religion, private law, and the judiciary system. Britain was also highly decentralized in favor of local governments at least until the early 19th century (North and Weingast 1989; Weingast 1995).

However, the British regime was particularly vulnerable to unifying tendencies due to the fact that the initial horizontal division of powers was based upon the coexistence of the House of Commons with nondemocratic institutions, namely a monarchical executive and an aristocratic upper chamber. With the steady expansion of voting rights during the 19th and 20th centuries (as discussed in Chapter 2), the popularly elected House of Commons came to prevail over the nonelected King and House of Lords. But the Commons were elected by means of a highly restrictive electoral system based on plurality rule, typically producing a two-party system and single-party Cabinets. Thus, democratization implied increasing concentration of powers in the hands of a single-winning actor, the party in Cabinet, and, more precisely, the Premier. As a result of this evolution, the judiciary also became vulnerable to the corresponding majority in Parliament. Unification in national government also caused increasing centralization. Whereas some traditional Scottish institutions were curbed, in the case of Ireland, it seceded before it could be dominated, in 1920. Later, violent conflict in Northern Ireland led to the suppression of the local Assembly by the central government in 1969. Local governments were weakened by the central government through the 1980s, including the abolition of the Greater London Council.

Major institutional reforms in favor of restablishing pluralism were only initiated at the initiative of those excluded from power during a long period without governmental alternation. Turns between the Labour and the Conservative parties had averaged less than seven years from 1945 to 1979. Yet the Labourites did not manage to replace the Conservatives in the Cabinet again until eighteen years after Margaret Thatcher's first victory, that is, after four successive elections giving the Conservatives an absolute majority of seats in the House of Commons (always based on a minority of popular votes), a period almost three times longer than the previous average.

On the basis of some risk-adverse calculations, the new Labour leadership then went on to prefer the expectation of regular power-sharing (mostly with the Liberals, who had been permanently in opposition) rather than bet on maintaining institutions which produced such uncertain alternation between absolute winners and absolute losers. The Labour Cabinet elected in 1997, led by Anthony Blair, promoted the corresponding institutional reforms.

Interestingly, elements of both horizontal and vertical division of powers were introduced in parallel. First, local governments were strengthened, in particular by introducing the direct election of a London mayor and proportional representation for the separated election of the corresponding local Assembly. Regional Assemblies and governments were created in Scotland and Wales (the latter with no legislative or taxation powers) on the basis of proportional representation. An agreement between the British and the Irish governments, together with all the parties in the region, led to conditional devolution of self-rule to Northern Ireland and the establishment of a framework of confederal-like relationship between the states of the two islands.

At the horizontal level, an initiative for a major electoral reform of the House of Commons was launched. As a first step, the United Kingdom ceased to be an exception in Europe when, in 1999, the representatives to the European Parliament were elected by proportional representation (as in all the other member-states of the European Union). The Government had established an Independent Commission on the Voting System, led by former Labour minister and leader of the Liberals in the House of Lords, Lord Jenkins of Hillhead (formerly Roy Jenkins), with collaboration from a selection of outstanding British political scientists (or 'psephologists', as they were called). In December 1998, the Commission issued a report recommending the replacement of the several centuries-old electoral system based on plurality rule with an 'additional member-system' able to produce higher proportionality in repres-entation (Jenkins 1998; simulations of electoral results with alternative elect-oral systems can be found in Dunleavy, Margetts, and Weir 1998; Dunleavy and Margetts 1999).

The above reforms might indeed produce a dramatic reversal of the British political regime's previous historical trends by moving it from concentration of powers to vertically and horizontally divided government. From the approach presented in the previous pages, however, a few remarks should be added.

First, the absence of provisions for the establishment of regional governments across England might induce either unified government (if the national government party obtains a majority in the regions) or bipolarization between the central and the Scotland governments, rather than inter-regional cooperation.

Second, although the House of Lords was deprived of most of its hereditary members, it was not replaced with a corresponding upper chamber of territorial representation, which also reduces the opportunities for multilateral exchanges.

In short, the fate of the new vertical division of powers in the United Kingdom may depend on the further extension of decentralization to other regional units and the development of institutions of multiregional cooperation, as well as on the emergence of horizontally divided government in the form of multiparty coalition national Cabinets.

5

Choosing Socially Efficient Institutions

In contriving any system of government, and fixing the several checks and controls of the constitution, every man ought to be supposed a *knave*, and to have no other end, in all his actions, but private interest. By this interest we must govern him and, by means of it, make him cooperate to public good, notwithstanding his insatiable avarice and ambition.

David Hume, *Of the Independency of Parliament* (1741)

Social choice theory has guided our search for the institutional variables which appear to explain different degrees of social efficiency of political outcomes. The simplified, abstract questions identified from the initial model: who can vote, how votes are counted, and what is voted for, have led us to more detailed analyses of voting rights, voting rules, and schemes of division of powers, respectively. These institutional variables have not been selected for their influence on the dynamics of the decision-making process, but rather from a policy outcome-oriented perspective.

Social utility can be considered to be relatively high when the outcomes of the institutional process fulfill certain conditions. Specifically, socially efficient outcomes can be obtained from processes leading to the formation of parliamentary Cabinets or executive Presidents when the winner includes the median voter's preference. As discussed earlier, the median is the position that minimizes the sum of the distances from voters' preferences and maximizes citizens' political satifaction or social utility.

Likewise, in schemes of division of powers, social utility is higher when different winners are able to give satisfaction to different groups of voters' preferences. Efficient results can be obtained either by allocationg different issues to different institutions according to citizens' intensity of preferences, or by interinstitutional cooperation able to produce broader, consensual majorities than there would be with a unified government.

From this perspective, the question of the best political regime can be answered in the following way. First, broad suffrage rights are better than restrictive rights because they give more opportunities to more individuals and larger groups to develop their demands and obtain political satisfaction of their preferences. A stable democracy, as a formula based on pluralistic elections of rulers by the greatest number of citizens, is, on average and in the long-term, always better, that is, more socially efficient, according to the categories of social choice theory, than nondemocratic regimes.

Early in this book, we surveyed a number of historical experiences of small, homogeneous communities in which collective decisions obtained broad consensus through using virtual universal suffrage and unanimity or quasi-unanimity rules. In modern times, small political communities have proliferated in all parts of the world. This is due, in part, to the fact that open trade and communications make the economic and cultural advantages of large scale states less relevant, while the costs of their political decision making become more visible.

The advantages of small political communities for collective decision making can be tested with the fact that, of the independent countries with more than five thousand and less than one million inhabitants, 70 per cent (28 out of 40 countries) are democracies, mostly with simple institutional formulas, while the proportion of democracies among countries with more than one million inhabitants is only 42 per cent (64 out of 151 countries). (Author's own calculation with data in Freedom House 1999, and United Nations 1998. In addition to 191 independent countries, Freedom House also reports nine microterritories, four of which are recognized by the United Nations—but none of the two lists includes the Vatican.)

In large political communities encompassing complex societies, the institutional devices that are necessary to produce socially efficient results require more sophistication. In general, pluralist institutional formulas, including proportional representation, as well as 'horizontal' and 'vertical' division of powers, are able to produce higher social utility than simple formulas based on majoritarian voting rules that favor the concentration of power in a single winner.

More specifically, and according to the analyses previously presented, the best opportunities for satisfying citizens' preferences and producing high social utility can be created by parliamentary regimes with proportional representation, as well as by decentralized, bicameral federalism. In these frameworks, the existence of multiple winners and the institutional incentives for multiparty cooperation tend to produce highly satisfactory results.

Also, 'horizontal' division of powers between the President and the Assembly can produce relatively high levels of consensus and social utility if the incentives for interinstitutional and multiparty cooperation are effective is preventing deadlock and conflict. More specifically, semi-presidential formulas with divided government, that is, 'cohabitation' of different political majorities supporting the parliamentary Cabinet and the Presidency, and other intermediate, parliamentarized variants of horizontal division of powers, are better at fostering interinstitutional cooperation than pure presidential regimes with unified government or more rigid, potentially conflictive schemes of separation of powers.

Finally, unicameral parliamentary regimes with majoritarian electoral rules, which usually produce unified government, that is, a single, absolute winner, should be considered less socially efficient than the alternatives previously mentioned. Unitary states also perform worse than decentralized ones.

These findings from the perspective of social utility are consistent with previous contributions in a variety of approaches regarding the economic and social performance of different types of democratic regimes. They include the following. First, the British model of a simple regime based upon parliamentarism and plurality rule was analyzed as a source of 'adversary politics'. The social effects of this institutional model can be summarized in two points. First, it tends to produce socially minority and biased governments which satisfy only the preferences of small groups of citizens and are prone to be captured by minority interests. Second, the complete alternation of parties in government without intermediate bridges causes policy reversal and instability which in turn discourage investment and long-term plans among private actors in the society (Finer 1975, 1982).

Second, certain statistical correlations show that pluralistic regimes compare favorably to regimes favoring the concentration of power with regard to certain economic and social variables. Specifically, it has been found that parliamentary regimes with proportional representation are associated with higher levels of political participation and lower levels of political violence than alternative democratic formulas (Powell 1982). 'Collegially ruled' political regimes with executive power-sharing, especially coalition Cabinets, have been associated with higher levels of per capita income and lower levels of protest demonstrations, political strikes, riots, armed attacks, political assassinations, and political deaths, than 'monocratically ruled' political regimes (Baylis 1989).

Data for eighteen countries show that pluralistic democracies, especially parliamentary regimes with proportional representation, are associated with lower levels of unemployment and income inequalities, as well as with higher levels of electoral turnout and female representation than 'majoritarian' or 'Westminster' democracies. No significant differences are found regarding inflation, economic growth, and public order (Lijphart 1991, 1994b; Crepaz 1996; Birchfield and Crepaz 1998).

Finally, available survey polls on citizens' subjective opinion support the hypothesis that pluralistic institutions produce widespread political satisfaction. Data from the Euro-Barometer for eleven European democracies in 1990 show that there is always a gap in satisfaction with the way democracy works between winners and losers, that is, between those citizens who voted for the party or parties in government and those who voted for the parties in opposition. Yet, winners tend to be more satisfied with democracy the more a country's political institutions approximate simple, 'majoritarian' regimes with a high concentration of powers (the extreme case in the sample being the United Kingdom). At the same time, losers who live in pluralistic, 'consensual' democracies show a higher level of satisfaction than the losers living in majoritarian democracies. The more pluralistic the system, the more likely the losers will be satisfied with the way democracy works (the extreme case in the sample being the Netherlands). In other words, political satisfaction is more widely and evenly distributed in pluralistic regimes than in majoritarian ones (Anderson and Guillory 1997).

The Choice of Pluralistic Political Institutions

The analytical links between political institutions and social utility established in this book can be extended to the analysis of institutional change. A strategic explanation of institutional change, which can be valid both for the trespassing between nondemocratic and democratic regimes and within democratic regimes, has been sketched in some of the previous chapters. The basic assumptions of the model that will be elaborated here are the following. First, political actors are self-interested in terms of power, including in particular the incumbent rulers. Second, in situations of uncertainty regarding the future, political actors tend to develop risk-adverse institutional preferences favoring power-sharing or likely alternation in power rather than to bet on exclusive institutions which create permanent absolute winners and absolute losers. (Some ideas of this sort are in Przeworski 1991, ch. 2; Elster 1991, 1993; Lijphart 1992*b*; Colomer 1995*c*; 2000*a*, ch. 6; Dunleavy and Margetts 1995; Geddes 1996).

More specifically, the process of institutional change can be stylized in the following way. A situation of uncertainty appears when the incumbent rulers are challenged by new groups' demands. If the existing institutional framework is restrictive, that is, if it permits only the absolute victory of one actor at the expense of all the others, whether the winner is defined as a social class, an ethnic group, or a political party, the incumbent rulers risk becoming absolute losers. The emerging challengers may feed expectations of becoming new absolute winners and replacing the incumbent rulers under the existing institutions. Yet, if some degree of uncertainty regarding future outcomes is also shared by the challengers, they may develop risk-adverse preferences similar to those of the challenged rulers in favor of more inclusive and pluralistic institutions.

As has been suggested in the previous chapters, actors with uncertain expectations of staying in or gaining power can promote or accept institutional changes in favor of more openness and inclusiveness. Changes such as these include broader voting rights, especially if they are introduced in parallel to new voting rules favoring the formation of multiple winners and power-sharing; proportional representation inducing the formation of multiparty coalitions; and separate elections for different offices able to produce multiple winners. With these changes, both challenged incumbent rulers and emerging challengers can expect to prevent their complete defeat and exclusion from power and to guarantee a minimum amount of power for themselves in the long term.

Actors' support for either the existing or the newly established institutions depends on the corresponding distribution of power. If significant actors are and expect to be permanently (that is, for a very long period) excluded from power—as may happen in institutional frameworks producing absolute winners and absolute losers—they may prefer to challenge the existing institutions and try to replace them with alternative formulas. In contrast, if significant actors have reasonable expectations of gaining or sharing power within the existing institutional framework, they are likely to support it. While 'majoritarian' democracy allows the winners to implement their preferred policies unchallenged, pluralistic democracy can be widely preferred because it compensates the losers.

A political regime is in equilibrium, that is, it becomes a stable, self-enforcing game if it promotes actors' strategies complying with the existing institutional rules. The actors' play within the rules of the game (in particular, actors' participation in electoral competition) tends to reinforce the rules themselves. The very actors whose existence is viable under the prevailing institutional framework will support the existing institutions and will resist the introduction of adverse changes. If the existing institutions favor or permit the creation and survival of multiple winners, the former will obtain wide, endogenous support, and will generate broad resistance toward less inclusive rules. In other words, pluralistic democratic institutions that produce widespread political satisfaction and relatively high social utility are more likely to stay in equilibrium than more exclusive formulas.

Some implications of this model can be submitted to empirical observation. Following the above reasoning, pluralist democratic institutions should obtain relatively high endogenous support and, as a consequence, they should have greater longevity than exclusive or simple institutions favoring the concentration of power. If this implication resists the test of facts in the long term, it will be possible to state that institutions chosen by actors with self-interested strategies will approach increasingly high levels of social utility. At least in the field of the choice of political institutions, self-interested behavior could produce socially efficient results.

More specifically, the implications are the following. First, attempts to establish pluralistic democratic regimes should obtain higher rates of success, in other words, higher proportions of self-consolidation and long-term duration, than more simple, majoritarian democracies. Second, as a consequence of this trend, the number and the proportion of surviving pluralist democracies should be higher than those of simple, majoritarian democratic regimes.

Data for 123 attempts of democratization and major democratic institutional changes in 85 countries with more than one million inhabitants during the 127-year period 1874–2000 are summarized in Table 5.1 (more details are in Tables 5.2 and 5.3). The starting point chosen is the introduction of elections for relevant offices with universal men's suffrage when have maintained democratic continuity. (Note, however, that universal men's suffrage was established in France and Spain in earlier periods and that some of the surviving institutional formulas in other democracies, such as the United Kingdom and the United States, were established before the period mentioned.)

Following the categories used in this book, democratic institutional formulas are distinguished as parliamentary-majoritarian, presidential and semi-presidential, and parliamentary-proportional representation, in the presumed order of lower to higher social efficiency. Institutional changes are grouped in the three historical periods, or democratizing 'waves', usually established: 1874–1943, 1944–73, and 1974–2000.

The numbers of institutional changes recorded are 31 in the first wave, 48 in the second wave, and 44 in the third wave. The numbers of successful attempts of democratization, that is, the numbers of presently existing democracies that were established in different periods, are increasing: 9 from the first wave, 18 from the second wave, and 37 from the third wave (plus five major institutional changes in established democracies).

The corresponding rates of success, or proportions of democratizing attempts which have resulted in enduring democracies that continue to exist, are the following: 42 per cent for parliamentary-majoritarian, 56 per cent for presidential and semi-presidential, and 69 per cent for parliamentary-proportional representation regimes. This seems to confirm our previous hypothesis regarding the relatively higher capability of pluralistic democratic regimes to obtain endogenous support and endure.

The rates of success were relatively favorable for the parliamentary-majoritarian formula, the British model, during the first wave of democratization before World War II, with 62 per cent success. But this rate was obtained for a small number of cases: only eight attempts of democratization with this institutional model. Moreover, Switzerland moved from a majoritarian electoral system to proportional representation within the period. During the second wave, in contrast, the rate of success of the

TABLE 5.1. *Political institutions and successful democratization (1874–2000)*

	Parliamentary-majoritarian	Presidential and Semi-presidential	Parliamentary-proportional representation	Total
1st wave (1874–1943)	5 (3)	1 (8)	4 (10)	10 (21)
2nd wave (1944–73)	6 (15)	4 (13)	9 (1)	19 (29)
3rd wave (1974–99)	2 (0)	27 (4)	11 (0)	40 (4)
Total	13 (18)	32 (25)	24 (11)	69 (54)
Success rate	42%	56%	69%	

Note: 'Plain' numbers are the cases of 'successful' or enduring democracies (i.e. those that have lasted until 2000); numbers in parentheses are the cases of 'failed' democracies (i.e. those that have not lasted until 2000). 'Success rates' are the proportion of successful democratization cases out of the total number of democratizing attempts.

Source: Author's own elaboration with data for countries with more than one million inhabitants from Huntington (1991); Alvarez *et al.* (1996); Gasiorowski (1996); Power and Gasiorowski (1997); Prze-worski *et al.* (forthcoming), Freedom House (1972–99), and newspapers. See also Tables 5.2 and 5.3.

British model was only 29 per cent, partly due to the failure of simple, restrictive democratic institutions in a number of former colonies in Africa and Asia with pluralistic ethnic, religious, or language composition. During the third wave, the number of democracies with more than one million inhabitants has more than doubled, from twenty-seven to sixty-four, but, at the end of the 20th century, the number of democratic regimes using parliamentarism and majoritarian electoral rules remains the same as in 1973: ten. The addition of two new cases, Papua-New Guinea and Thailand, was cancelled out by institutional changes to pluralistic formulas in two previously established majoritarian democracies, Japan and New Zealand.

In contrast, parliamentary-proportional representation formulas performed very well in terms of duration after both the second and third waves, with 90 per cent and 100 per cent of success in establishing enduring democratic regimes, respectively. Note that several cases of proportional representation formulas recorded as 'failures' at the first wave could be attributed not to institutional performance but to foreign invasion (Belgium, Czechoslovakia, Denmark, the Netherlands, and Norway), while only one case, France, could be dropped from the list of failures of majoritarian formulas with the same criterion.

Presidential and, especially, semi-presidential formulas have obtained very high levels of success at the third wave, 83 per cent and 100 per cent of cases, respectively, having lasted until now. These formulas have been mainly re-established in Latin America during the process of redemocratization, but they have also been chosen in Eastern Europe, Africa, and Asia by newcomers to democracy. The global performance of the presidential and semi-presidential formulas in all the three waves is about the average of all attempts of democratization: 55 per cent. The evolution of the three democratic institutional variants over time is shown in Fig. 5.1.

A more detailed analysis of institutional changes favors the idea that pluralistic formulas can obtain relatively large support. Regarding parliamentary elections, it is interesting to observe that of the eleven European democracies with proportional representation that broke down during the 1920s and 1930s, all re-established proportional representation at their redemocratization: seven at the end of World War II (Austria, Belgium, Denmark, Germany, Italy, the Netherlands, and Norway) and four at the fall of Communism in the 1990s (Czechoslovakia, Estonia, Latvia, and Lithuania). Among the new countries using proportional representation, two had used majoritarian electoral formulas in previous failed democratic experiences (Greece and Spain) and four were newcomers to democracy (Hungary, Israel, Slovenia, and South Africa).

As already mentioned, three parliamentary-majoritarian democracies changed to more pluralistic alternatives without democratic fracture. Switzerland joined the European general trend of new democracies at the end of World War I. (Rappard 1936). New Zealand replaced single-member districts and plurality rule, having produced the purest two-party system in the world, with proportional representation producing multipartism and coalition Cabinets after a decision in referendum in 1993 (Vowles 1995; Jackson and McRobie 1998). Japan replaced a majoritarian system based upon multimember districts and limited vote with a mixed system of proportional representation in 1994 (Shiratori 1995).

Moves from proportional representation include France in the passage from the Fourth to the Fifth Republics from 1958 on. But, as previously discussed in Chapters 3 and 4, French multipartism resisted the new electoral rule of majority-runoff. At the same time, a new element of institutional pluralism was introduced with the direct election of the President. At the beginning of the 21st century, France is a more pluralistic democracy than the Fourth Republic by all accounts.

In Italy, as also mentioned in Chapter 3, proportional representation was replaced with a mixed electoral system after a referendum in 1993. However, the number of political parties under the new framework became even higher than before (Donovan 1995; D'Alimonte and Bartolini 1997). Attempts to suppress the portion of seats elected with proportional representation by

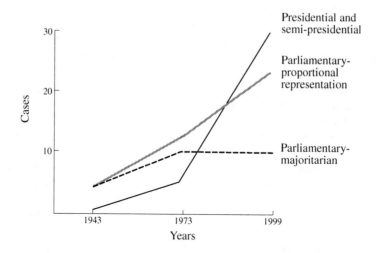

Fig. 5.1. Types of democratic regimes in democratization waves

referendum failed twice, in 1999 and 2000. In parallel, new divisions of powers were introduced: the direct election of a President was supported by the major parties; in 1999, the regions were given new powers, and the regional presidents were to be elected directly.

The capability of presidential democracies to survive has been submitted to intense discussion (Linz 1990, 1994; Mainwaring 1993; Power and Gasiorowski 1997; Blais, Massicotte, and Dobrzynska 1997). Yet, empirical observation in a broad and long-term perspective suggests that once installed, direct presidential elections are not easily abandoned. There have been a few instances of reverse moves, such as Germany after Nazism. But in almost all cases, further redemocratization after an authoritarian period has been followed by a reinstatement of direct presidential elections, especially in Latin America in the 1980s. The proposal of suppressing presidentialism was explicitly defeated in a 1993 referendum in Brazil. The performance of presidential elections has improved with the replacement of plurality rule with the relatively less socially inefficient rule of majority-runoff in twelve Latin-American countries during the period 1978–99 (as has been discussed in Chapter 3). New cases of direct election of the chief executive include France, as already mentioned, and Israel, where the parliamentary regime was modified with the introduction of the direct election of Prime Minister in 1996 (Diskin 1995).

In sum, in addition to 118 attempts of democratization, five major institutional changes without democratic breakdown have been identified. Of the latter, three are moves from parliamentary-majoritarian to parliamentary-proportional representation formulas (Switzerland in 1918, New Zealand in 1993, and Japan in 1994), and two are moves from parliamentary-proportional representation to presidential-like formulas (France in 1958 and Israel in 1996). No established democracy has so far changed in favor of a parliamentary-majoritarian regime. Even the United Kingdom has introduced some proportional electoral rules and decentralization, as discussed at the end of Chapter 4.

Changes in favor of federalism and other formulas of 'vertical' division of powers can be approached in a similar way. Four long-established democracies have maintained federal structures from the beginning: Australia, Canada, Switzerland, and the United States. Four large Latin-American countries have maintained federal formulas even during authoritarian periods or have re-established them at their redemocratization, Argentina, Brazil, Mexico, and Venezuela. Changes from unitary or imperial states to federal or regional structures during processes of democratization or during democratic periods include Austria, Belgium, Germany, India, Italy, South Africa, and Spain (cf. Elazar 1987, table 2.2; Watts 1996*b*, table 2).

Federations tend to fail if they are formed by only two units or if they are designed under authoritarian regimes, as discussed in Chapter 4. But no reversal moves seem to exist for multilateral federations in democratic contexts. When multiple winners have been created in a territory, they effectively resist further attempts to simplify the corresponding political structure.

At the end of the 20th century, out of sixty-four democratic regimes in countries with more than one million inhabitants, only 16 per cent are parliamentary regimes with majoritarian electoral rules, while 50 per cent are presidential or semi-presidential regimes, and 34 per cent are parliamentary regimes with proportional representation, as shown in Table 5.3. At least 23 per cent have a federal-like division of powers. The relative success of pluralist formulas must be submitted to the observation of their survival in the future. However, the empirical analysis presented here allows us to maintain the hypothesis concerning the higher capability of socially efficient, pluralistic political institutions for obtaining stable support.

Table 5.2. *Political institutions and democratization, per country (1874–2000)*

	Parliamentary-majoritarian	Presidential and Semi-presidential	Parliamentary-proportional representation
1st wave (1874–1943)	Australia (1902) Canada (1891) New Zealand (1876) Switzerland (1874–1918) United Kingdom (1885)	United States (1879)	Finland (1907) Ireland (1920) Sweden (1910) Switzerland (1918)
FAILED	France (1870–1940) Portugal (1910–26) Spain (1869–73, 1890–1923, 1931–6)	Argentina (1912–30) Chile (1925–73) Colombia (1903–49) Costa Rica (1920–48) Cuba (1940–52) France (1848–51) Uruguay (1918–73) *Semi-presidential* Germany (1918–33)	Austria (1918–33) Belgium (1899–1940) Czechoslovakia (1918–39) Denmark (1915–40) Estonia (1922–34) Italy (1919–22) Latvia (1922–34) Lithuania (1922–6) Netherlands (1917–40) Norway (1897–1940)
TOTAL: Enduring democracies Failed democracies	5 3	1 8	4 10
2nd wave (1944–73)	Botswana (1966) India (1947, 1977) Jamaica (1962) Japan (1952–1994) Mauritius (1968) Trinidad (19620	Colombia (1958) Costa Rica (1953) Venezuela (1958) *Semi-presidential* France (1958)	Austria (1945) Belgium (1945) Denmark (1945) France (1945–1958) Germany (1948) Israel (1948) Italy (1945) Netherlands (1945) Norway (1945)
FAILED	Burma (1948–62) Ghana (1969–72) Greece (1946–67) Indonesia (1955–66) Kenya (1963–6) S. Korea (1960–1) Laos (1954–8) Malaysia (1957–69) Nigeria (1960–5) Pakistan (1947–54) Sierra Leone (1961–6) Sri Lanka (1948–83) Sudan (1956–57, 1965–68) Thailand (1975–76) Turkey (1961–80)	Argentina (1946–55) Bolivia (1952–64) Brazil (1945–64) Ecuador (1948–61) Guatemala (1944–54) Honduras (1957–62) Madagascar (1960–71) Nigeria (1979–82) Panama (1952–68) Pakistan (1972–6) Peru (1956–67) Philippines (1946–72) *Semi-presidential* Somalia (1960–8)	Lebanon (1943–76)
TOTAL: Enduring democracies Failed democracies	6 15	4 14	9 1

Table 5.2. *Continued*

	Parliamentary-majoritarian	Presidential and Semi-presidential	Parliamentary-proportional representation
3rd wave (1974–99)	Papua-New Guinea (1977) Thailand (1983)	Argentina (1983) Bolivia (1982) Brazil (1982) Chile (1990) Dominican Rep. (1978) Ecuador (1979) El Salvador (1984) Guatemala (1985) Honduras (1982) Israel (1996) S. Korea (1988) Malawi (1994) Mali (1992) Mexico (1997) Namibia (1990) Nicaragua (1990) Panama (1994) Philippines (1986) Taiwan (19960 Uruguay (1984) *Semi-presidential* Benin (1991) Bulgaria (1990) Lithuania (1992) Mongolia (1992) Poland (1989) Portugal (1976) Romania (1996)	Czech Rep. (1990) Estonia (1992) Greece (1975) Hungary (1990) Japan (1994) Latvia (1994) New Zealand (1993) Slovakia (1994) Slovenia (1991) South Africa (1994) Spain (1977)
FAILED		Ghana (1979–82) Nigeria (1991–2) Peru (1980–92) Uganda (1980–4)	
Total: Enduring democracies	2	27	11
Failed democracies	0	4	0

Sources: As for Table 5.1

TABLE 5.3. *Democracies in 2000*

Parliamentary-majoritarian	Presidential and Semi-presidential	Parliamentary-proportional representation
Australia (1902)	Argentina (1983)	Austria (1945)
Botswana (1966)	Bolivia (1982)	Belgium (1945)
Canada (1891)	Brazil (1982)	Czech Rep. (1990)
India (1947)	Chile (1990)	Denmark (1945)
Jamaica (1962)	Colombia (1958)	Estonia (1992)
Mauritius (1968)	Costa Rica (1953)	Finland (1907)
Papua-New Guinea (1977)	Dominican R. (1978)	Germany (1948, 1990)
Thailand (1983)	Ecuador (1979)	Greece (1975)
Trinidad (1962)	El Salvador (1984)	Hungary (1990)
United Kingdom (1885)	Guatemala (1985)	Ireland (1920)
	Honduras (1982)	Italy (1945)
	Israel (1948) (1996)	Japan (1952, 1994)
	S. Korea (1988)	Latvia (1994)
	Malawi (1994)	Netherlands (1945)
	Mali (1992)	New Zealand (1876), 1993)
	Mexico (1997)	Norway (1945)
	Namibia (1990)	Slovakia (1994)
	Nicaragua (1990)	Slovenia (1991)
	Panama (1994)	South Africa (1994)
	Philippines (1986)	Spain (1977)
	Taiwan (1996)	Sweden (1910)
	United States (1879)	Switzerland (1874, 1918)
	Uruguay (1984)	
	Venezuela (1958)	
	Semi-presidential	
	Benin (1991)	
	Bulgaria (1991)	
	France (1945, 1958)	
	Lithuania (1991)	
	Mongolia (1991)	
	Poland (1989)	
	Portugal (1976)	
	Romania (1996)	
TOTAL	10	32 · 22
	16%	50% · 34%

Source: As for Table 5.1.

References

Alcántara, Manuel (1999). *Sistemas políticos de América Latina*. Madrid: Tecnos.

Alesina, Alberto and Rosenthal, Howard (1995). *Partisan Politics, Divided Government, and the Economy*. New York: Cambridge University Press.

Alonso, Paula (1996). 'Voting in Buenos Aires, Argentina, Before 1912', in Eduardo Posada-Carbó (ed.) *Elections Before Democracy: The History of Elections in Europe and Latin America*. New York: St. Martin's Press, 181–200

Alvarez, Mike, Cheibub, José Antonio, Limogi, Fernando, and Przeworski, Adam (1996). 'Classifying Political Regimes', *Studies in Comparative International Development*, 31, 2, 3–36.

Anderson, Christopher J. and Guillory, Christine A. (1997). 'Political Institutions and Satisfaction with Democracy: A Cross-National Analysis of Consensus and Majoritarian Systems', *American Political Science Review*, 91, 1, 66–81.

Anderson, Eugene N. and Anderson, Pauline R. (1967). *Political Institutions and Social Change in Continental Europe in the Nineteenth Century*. Berkeley: University of California Press.

Annino, Antonio (ed.) (1995). *Historia de las elecciones en Iberoamérica, siglo XIX*. Mexico: Fondo de Cultura Económica.

—— (1996). 'The Ballot, Land and Sovereignty: Cádiz and the Origins of Mexican Local Government, 1812–1820', in Eduardo Posada-Carbó (ed.) *Elections Before Democracy: The History of Elections in Europe and Latin America*. New York: St. Martin's Press, 61–86.

Anthony, Susan B. [1875] (1968). 'Social Purity', in Aileen S. Kraditor (ed.) *Up From the Pedestal. Selected Writings in the History of American Feminism*. Chicago: Quadrangle Books.

Aristotle [325–4 BC] (1997). *The Politics* (Peter L. Phillips Simpson ed.). Chapel Hill and London: University of North Carolina Press.

Arrow, Kenneth [1951] (1963). *Social Choice and Individual Values* (2nd edn). New York: Wiley.

Axelrod, Robert. (1970). *Confict of Interest*. Chicago: Markham.

Babeau, Albert (1882). *Le village sous l'Ancien Régime*. Paris: Didier.

—— (1894). *La province sous l'Ancien Régime*. Paris: Firmin-Didot. (Reprint AMS Press, New York, 1972)

Bahro, Horst, Bayerlein, Beernhard H., and Veser, Ernst (1998). 'Duverger's Concept: Semi-presidential Government Revisited', *European Journal of Political Research*, 34, 201–224.

Baker, Keith Michael (ed.). (1987). *The Old Regime and the French Revolution*. Chicago: University of Chicago Press.

Baldwin, Marshall W. (1968). *Alexander III and the Twelfth Century*. New York: Newman Press.

Balestra, R. and Ossona, J. L. (1983). *Qué son los partidos provinciales*. Buenos Aires: Sudamericana.

Balinski, Michel L. and Rachev, Svetlozar T. (1997). 'Rounding Proportions: Methods of Rounding', *Mathematical Scientist*, 22, 1–26.

—— and Young, H. Peyton (1982). *Fair Representation: Meeting the Ideal of One Man, One Vote*. New Haven: Yale University Press.

Barante, M. de (1863). *Vie politique de M. Royer-Collard, ses discours et ses écrits*. Paris: Didier, in Henri Baudrillart (1979). *Publicistes Modernes*. New York: Arno Press.

Barberà, Salvador (1977). 'The Manipulation of Social Choice Mechanisms that Do Not Leave "Too Much" to Chance', *Econometrica*, 45, 7, 1573–88.

Barnes, Samuel H., Grace, Frank, Pollock, James K, and Serlich, Peter W. (1962). 'The German Party System and the 1961 Federal Election', *American Political Science Review*, 56, 899–914.

Bartholdi III, John J. and Orlin, James B. (1991). 'Single Transferable Vote Resists Strategic Voting', *Social Choice and Welfare*, 8, 341–54.

Bartolini, Stefano (1984). 'Sistema partitico ed elezione diretta del capo dello stato in Europa', *Rivista Italiana di Scienza Politica*, 2, 209–22.

Bastid, Paul. (1948). *L'Avènement du suffrage universel*. Paris: Presses Universitaires de France.

Bawn, Kathleen (1993). 'The Logic of Institutional Preferences: German Electoral Law as a Social Choice Outcome', *American Journal of Political Science*, 37, 4, 965–89.

Baylis, Thomas A. (1989). *Governing by Committee: Collegial Leadership on Advanced Societies*. Albany: State University of New York Press.

Becker, Lydia E. [1872] (1987). 'The Political Disabilities of Women', Westminster Review, in Jane Lewis (ed.). *Before the Vote Was Won: Arguments For and Against Women's Suffrage*. London: Routledge & Kegan Paul, 118–58.

Bednar, Jenna, Eskridge, William, and Ferejohn, John. (1995). 'A Political Theory of Federalism', Stanford University working paper. (Forthcoming in John Ferejohn, Jack Rakove, and Jonathan Riley (ed.) *Constitutions and Constitutionalism*. New York: Cambridge University Press)

Bennett, Christopher (1995). *Yugoslavia's Bloody Collapse: Causes, Course and Consequences*. New York: New York University Press.

Bennett, Scott. (1996). *Winning and Losing. Australian National Elections*. Melbourne University Press.

Benson, Robert L. (1968). *The Bishop-elect. A Study in Medieval Ecclesiastical Office*. Princeton: Princeton University Press.

Bentham, Jeremy [1789] (1970). *Introduction to the Principles of Morals and Legislation*, in *Collected Works* (James H. Burns and Herbert L. Hart ed.). London: Athlone.

—— [1830] (1983). *Constitutional Code*, in *Collected Works* (Frederick Rosen and James H. Burns ed.). Oxford: Oxford University Press.

Birchfield, Vicki and Crepaz, Markus M.L. (1998). 'The Impact of Constitutional Structures and Collective and Competitive Veto Points on Income Inequality in Industrialized Democracies', *European Journal of Political Research*, 34, 175–200.

Bishop, Cortlandt F. (1893). *History of Elections in the American Colonies*. New York: Columbia College.

Bismarck, Otto Fürst von [1899] (1966). *The Memoirs*. New York: Howard Fertig.

Bisson, Thomas N. (1964). *Assemblies and Representation in Languedoc in the Thirteenth Century*. Princeton: Princeton University Press.

Black, Charles L. (1974). *Impeachment: A Handbook*. New Haven: Yale University Press.

Black, Duncan. (1948*a*). 'On the Rationale of Group Decision Making', *Journal of Political Economy*, 56, 23–34.

—— (1948*b*). 'The Decisions of a Committee Using a Special Majority', *Econometrica*, 16, 245–261.

—— (1958). *The Theory of Committees and Elections*. Cambridge: Cambridge University Press.

—— (1996). *A Mathematical Approach to Proportional Representation: Duncan Black on Lewis Carroll* (Iain McLean, Alistair McMillan, and Burt L. Monroe ed.). Boston: Kluwer.

Blais, André, Massicotte, Louis, and Dobrzynska, Agnieszka (1997). 'Direct Presidential Elections: A World Summary', *Electoral Studies*, 16, 4, 441–55.

Blanc, Louis [1848] (1971). *1848. Historical Revelations*. New York: Howard Fertig.

Bogdanor, Vernon (ed.) (1988). *Constitutions in Democratic Politics*. Aldershot, UK: Gower.

Bohn, David E. (1980). 'Consociational Democracy and the Case of Switzerland', *Journal of Politics*, 42, 165–79.

Borda, Jean-Charles de [1784] (1995). 'On Elections by Ballot', in Iain McLean and Arnold B. Urken (ed.) *Classics of Social Choice*. Ann Arbor: University of Michigan Press, 83–7.

Botana, Natalio (1995). 'Comentarios finales', in Antonio Annino (ed.) *Historia de las elecciones en Iberoamérica, siglo XIX*. Mexico: Fondo de Cultura Económica, 469–79.

Bowler, Shaun and Denemark, David (1993). 'Split Ticket Voting in Australia: Dealignment and Inconsistent Votes Reconsidered', *Australian Journal of Political Science*, 28, 19–37.

Brams, Steven J. (1975). *Game Theory and Politics*. New York: Macmillan.

—— (1982). 'Polls and the Problem of Strategic Information and Voting Behavior', *Society*, 19, 4–11.

—— (1989). 'Are the Two Houses of Congress Really Coequal?', in Bernard Grofman and Donald Wittman (ed.) *The Federalist Papers and the New Institutionalism*. New York: Agathon, 125–41.

—— (1990). *Negotiation Games: Applying Game Theory to Bargaining and Arbitration*. New York: Routledge.

—— and Affuso, Paul J. (1985). 'New Paradoxes of Voting Power in the EC Council of Ministers', *Electoral Studies*, 4, 187–91.

—— Affuso, Paul J., and Kilgour, D. Marc (1989). 'Presidential Power: A Game-Theoretic Analysis', in Paul Brace, Christine Harrington, and Gary King (ed.) *The Presidency in American Politics*. New York: New York University Press.

—— and Fishburn, Peter C. (1983). *Approval Voting*. Boston: Birkhäuser.

—— Kilgour, D. Marc, and Zwicker, William (1998). 'The Paradox of Multiple Elections', *Social Choice and Welfare*, 15, 2, 211–36.

—— and Nagel, Jack (1991). 'Approval Voting in Practice', *Public Choice*, 71, 1–17.

Brandenburg, Frank (1964). *The Making of Modern Mexico*. Englewood Cliffs, NJ: Prentice Hall.

Breton, Albert (1964). 'The Economics of Nationalism', *Journal of Political Economy*, 72, 4, 376–86.

Bridge, John S. C. (1921). *A History of France from the Death of Louis XI*. Oxford: Clarendon Press.

Brucker, Gene (1962). *Florentine Politics and Society, 1343–1378*. Princeton: Princeton University Press.

—— (1977). *The Civic World of Early Renaissance Florence*. Princeton: Princeton University Press.

—— (1983). *Renaissance Florence*. Berkeley: University of California Press.

Brunell, Thomas L. and Grofman, Bernard (1998). 'Explaining Divided U.S. Delegations, 1788–(1996): A Realignment Approach', *American Political Science Review*, 92, 2, 391–400.

Bryce, James (1921). *Modern Democracies*. New York: Macmillan.

Buchanan, James and Tullock, Gordon (1962). *The Calculus of Consent. Logical Foundations of Constitutional Democracy*. Ann Arbor: University of Michigan Press.

Budge, Ian (1993). 'Issues, Dimensions, and Agenda Change in Postwar Democracies: Longterm Trends in Party Election Programs and Newspaper Reports in Twenty-three Democracies', in William Riker (ed.) *Agenda Formation*. Ann Arbor: University of Michigan Press, 41–79.

—— and Keman Hans, (1990). *Parties and Democracy. Coalition Formation and Government Functioning in Twenty States*. Oxford: Oxford University Press.

—— Robertson, David, and Hearl, David (ed.) (1987). *Democracy, Strategy and Party Change*. Cambridge: Cambridge University Press.

Bushnell, David (1972). 'La evolución del derecho del sufragio en Venezuela', *Boletín Histórico* (Caracas), 29, May, 189–206.

Cadart, Jacques (1952). *Le régime électoral des États Généraux de 1789 et ses origines (1302–1614)*. Paris: Librairie du Recueil Sirey.

Cain, Bruce E (1996). 'The Varying Impact of Legislative Term Limits', in Bernard Grofman (ed.) *Legislative Term Limits: Public Choice Perspectives*. Boston: Kluwer, 21–36.

Campbell, Peter (1965). *French Electoral Systems and Elections Since 1789*. Hamden, CT: Archon Books.

Cánovas, Antonio (1884–90). *Problemas contemporáneos*. Madrid: Clásicos castellanos, 3 vols.

Cantón, Darío (1973). *Elecciones y partidos políticos en la Argentina: historia, interpretación y balance*. Buenos Aires: Siglo XXI.

Capel, Rosa M. (1992). *El sufragio femenino en la II República española*. Madrid: Horas y Horas.

Carey, John (1996). *Term Limits and Legislative Representation*. New York: Cambridge University Press.

Carr, Raymond (1966). *Spain 1808–1939*. Oxford: Clarendon Press.

Carroll, Lewis [1865, 1871] (1970). *The Annotated Alice: Alice's Adventures in Wonderland and Through the Looking Glass*. Harmondsworth, UK: Penguin.

Carstairs, Andrew McLaren (1980). *A Short History of Electoral Systems in Western Europe*. London: Allen & Unwin.

Castles, Francis and Mair, Peter (1984). 'Left–Right Political Scales: Some Experts Judgements', *European Journal of Political Research*, 12, 83–8.

Chang Rodríguez, Eugenio (1985). *Opciones Políticas Peruanas*. Lima: Centro de Documentación Andina.

Chaterjee, Partha (ed.) (1997). *State and Politics in India*. Delhi: Oxford University Press.

Chavarri Sidera, Pilar (1988). *Las elecciones de diputados a las Cortes generales y extraordinarias (1810–1813)*. Madrid: Centro de Estudios Constitucionales.

Chiaramonte, José Carlos (1995). 'Vieja y Nueva Representación: los procesos electorales en Buenos Aires, 1810–1820, in Antonio Annino (ed.) *Historia de las elecciones en Iberoamérica, siglo XIX*. Mexico: Fondo de Cultura Económica, 19–64.

Chirinos Soto, Enrique (1962). *Cuentas y Balances de las Elecciones de 1962*. Lima: Ediciones Perú.

—— (1984). *La nueva Constitución y los partidos*. Lima: Centro de Documentación Andina.

Clark, Martin (1996). *Modern Italy 1871–1995*, London: Longman.

Cole, Alistair and Campbell, Peter (1989). *French Electoral Systems and Elections Since 1789*. Brookfield, VT: Gower.

Colomer, Josep M. (1987). *El utilitarismo. Una teoría de la elección racional*. Barcelona: Montesinos.

—— (ed.) (1991). *Bentham. Antología*. Barcelona: Península.

—— (1994). 'The Blame Game of Presidentialism', in H. E. Chebabi and Alfred Stepan (ed.) *Politics, Society, and Democracy: Comparative Studies, Essays in Honor of Juan J. Linz*. Boulder: Westview, 110–14.

—— (1995a). *Game Theory and the Transition to Democracy: The Spanish Model*. Aldershot, UK/Brookfield, VT: Edward Elgar.

—— (1995b). 'Leadership Games in Collective Action', *Rationality and Society*, 7, 2, 225–46.

—— (1995c). 'Strategies and Outcomes in Eastern Europe', *Journal of Democracy*, 6, 2, 74–85.

—— (ed.) (1996a). *Political Institutions in Europe*. London: Routledge.

—— (1996b). 'Measuring Parliamentary Deviation', *European Journal of Political Research*, 30, 1, 87–101.

—— (1996c). 'The Catholic Church "Conventions". Voting Rules and Heresthetics in the Election of the Pope', mimeo, New York University.

—— (1996d). 'Measuring Power in Committees and Parliaments', mimeo, New York University.

—— (1998a). 'The Spanish 'State of Autonomies': Non-Institutional Federalism', *West European Politics*, 21, 4, 40–52.

—— (1998b). 'México: democracia a medias', *Claves*, 87, 41–9.

—— (1999a). 'On the Geometry of Unanimity Rule', *Journal of Theoretical Politics*, 11, 4, 543–53.

—— (1999b). 'Las ventajas de la segunda vuelta', *Proceso* (Mexico), 1169, 28 March.

—— (1999c). 'Governance of the European Union: How Political Parties Rather than State Governments Are Fostering Federalizing Institutional Relations'. Paper given at the 95th Annual Meeting of the American Political Science Association, Atlanta, Georgia.

—— (2000a). *Strategic Transitions. Game Theory and Democratization in Eastern Europe*. Baltimore: The Johns Hopkins University Press.

—— (2000b). 'El sistema electoral de la guerra civil', *Claves*.

—— and Hosli, Madeleine O. (1997). 'Decision-Making in the European Union: The Power of Political Parties', *AussenWirtschaft*, 52, 255–80.

—— and McLean, Iain (1998). 'Electing Popes: Approval Balloting and Qualified-Majority Rule', *Journal of Interdisciplinary History*, xxix: 1, 1–22.

—— and Martínez, Florencio. (1995). 'The Paradox of Coalition Trading', *Journal of Theoretical Politics*, 7, 1, 41–63.

Committee on the Constitutional System (1987). 'A Bicentennial Analysis of the American Political Structure: Report and Recommendations of the Committee on the Constitutional System', Washington, DC, in Arend Lijphart (ed.) (1992). *Parliamentary versus Presidential Government*. Oxford: Oxford University Press, 78–89.

Conacher, J. B. (ed.) (1971). *The Emergence of British Parliamentary Democracy in the Nineteenth Century. The Passing of the Reform Acts of 1832, 1867, and 1884–1885*. New York: Wiley.

Condorcet, Jean-Antoine-Nicolas de Caritat, Marquis de [1792] (1994). *Foundations of Social Choice and Political Theory* (Iain McLean and Fiona Hewitt ed.). Aldershot, UK: Edward Elgar.

Constant, Benjamin [1815] (1957). *Principes de politique*, in Oeuvres. Paris: Gallimard.

Coppedge, Michael (1994). 'Venezuela: Democratic despite Presidentialism', in Juan J. Linz and Arturo Valenzuela (eds.), *The Failure of Presidential Democracy*. Bultimore: The Johns Hopkins University Press. Vol. 2, 322–47.

Coroleu Inglada, Josep and Pella Forgas, Josep [1876] (1993). *Las Cortes catalanas: estudio jurídico y comparativo*. Valencia: Librería París.

Cox, Gary W. (1987). *The Efficient Secret. The Cabinet and the Development of Political Parties in Victorian England*. Cambridge: Cambridge University Press.

—— (1997). *Making Votes Count*. Cambridge: Cambridge University Press.

—— and Kernell, Samuel (1991). *The Politics of Divided Government*. Boulder: Westview.

—— and McCubbins, Matthew D. (1993). *Legislative Leviathan: Party Government in the House*. Berkeley: University of California Press.

—— and Shugart, Mathhew S. (1995). 'In the Absence of Vote Pooling: Nomination and Vote Allocation Errors in Colombia', *Electoral Studies*, 14, 4, 441–60.

Craig, Ann L. and Cornelius, Wayne A. (1995). 'Housed Divided Parties and Political Reform in Mexico', in Scott Mainwaring and Timothy E. Scully (ed.) *Building Democratic Institutions. Party Systems in Latin America*. Stanford: Stanford University Press.

Crepaz, Markus M. L. (1996). 'Consensus vs. Majoritarian Democracy: Political Institutions and Their Impact on Macroeconomic Performance and Industrial Disputes', *Comparative Political Studies*, 19, 1, 4–26.

Criscitiello, Annarita (1994). 'The Political Role of Cabinet Ministers in Italy', in Michael Laver and Kenneth A. Shepsle (ed.) *Cabinet Ministers and Pariamentary Government*. Cambridge: Cambridge University Press.

Crombez, Christophe (1996). 'Legislative Procedures in the European Community', *British Journal of Political Science*, 26, 199–228.

Curtis, Glenn E. (1990). *Yugoslavia: A Country Study*. Washington, DC: Library of Congress.

D'Alimonte, Roberto and Bartolini, Stefano (ed.) (1997). *Maggioritario per caso*. Bologna: Il Mulino.

Daalder, Hans (1986). 'Changing Procedures and Changing Strategies in Dutch Coalition Building', *Legislative Studies Quarterly*, 9, 4, 507–31.

Daalder, Hans (ed.) (1987). *Party Systems in Denmark, Austria, Switzerland, the Netherlands and Belgium*. London: Pinter.

—— (1989). 'The Mould of Dutch Politics: Themes for Comparative Inquiry', *West European Politics*, 12, 1, 1–20.

—— and Mair, Peter (ed.) (1983). *Western European Party Systems*. London: Sage.

Dalton, Russell J. (1993). *Politics in Germany.* New York: Harper Collins.

Dante (Alighieri) [1265–1321] (1982). *Divina Commedia.* Berkeley: University of California Press.

Davies, Norman (1982). *God's Playground. A History of Poland.* New York: Columbia University Press.

Davis, Otto A., Hinich, Melvin J, and Ordeshook, Peter C. (1970). 'An Expository Development of a Mathematical Model of the Electoral Process', *American Political Science Review,* 64, 426–48.

de Gaulle, Charles [1946] (1992). 'The Bayeux Manifesto', translation by Eva Tamm Lijphart in Arend Lijphart (ed.) *Parliamentary versus Presidential Government.* Oxford: Oxford University Press, 139–41.

de Tocqueville, Alexis [1851] (1970). 'The Drafting Committe for the Constitution', in Tocqueville, *Recollections.* New York: Doubleday.

de Winter, Lieven (1995). 'The Role of Parliament in Government Formation and Resignation', in Herbert Döring (ed.) *Parliaments and Majority Rule in Western Europe.* Frankfurt/main: Campus.

Deheza, Grace Ivana (1997). *Gobiernos de coalición en el sistema presidencial: América del Sur,* doctoral dissertation. Florence: European University Institute.

Deheza, Grace Ivana (1998). 'Gobiernos de coalición en el sistema presidencial: América de Sur', in Dieter Nohlen and Mario Fernández (ed.) *El presidencialismo renovado: Institucionalismo y cambio político en América Latina.* Caracas: Nueva Sociedad, 151–69.

Delors, Jacques (1989). *Address by Mr. Jacques Delors, President of the Commission of the European Communities, Bruges, 17 October (1989).* Brussels: European Communities.

Demélas-Bohy, Marie-Danielle and Guerra, François-Xavier (1996). 'The Hispanic Revolutions: The Adoption of Modern Forms of Representation in Spain and America, 1808–1810', in Eduardo Posada-Carbó (ed.) *Elections Before Democracy: The History of Elections in Europe and Latin America.* New York: St. Martin's Press.

Dinkin, Robert J. (1977). *Voting in Provincial America. A Study of Elections in the Thirteen Colonies, 1689–1776.* Westport: Greenwood.

—— (1982). *Voting in Revolutionary America. A Study of Elections in the Original Thirteen States, 1776–1789.* Westport: Greenwood.

Diski, Hanna and Abraham. (1995). 'The Politics of Electoral Reform in Israel', *International Political Science Review,* 16, 1, 31–46.

Dogan, Mattei (1989). *Pathways to power: Selecting leaders in pluralist democracies.* Boulder: Westview.

Donovan, Mark (1995). 'The Politics of Electoral Reform in Italy', *International Political Science Review,* 16, 1, 47–64.

Doron, Gideon and Kronik, Richard (1977). 'Single Transferable Vote: An Example of a Perverse Social Choice Function', *American Journal of Political Science,* 21, 2.

Dowding, Keith (1997). 'Equity and Voting: Why Democracy Needs Dictators', *L'Année Sociologique,* 47, 2, 39–53.

Downs, Anthony (1957). *An Economic Theory of Democracy.* New York: Harper.

Doyle, William (1980). *Origins of the French Revolution.* Oxford: Oxford University Press.

—— (1989). *The Oxford History of the French Revolution.* Oxford: Clarendon.

Dragnich, Alex N. (1983). *The First Yugoslavia.* Stanford: Hoover Institution Press.

—— (1992). *Serbs and Croats. The Struggle in Yugoslavia.* New York: Harcourt Brace Jovanovich.

Duhamel, Alain (1983). *Les prétendants.* Paris: Gallimard.

Dulles, John W. F. (1970). *Unrest in Brazil. Political-Military Crises 1955–1964.* Austin: University of Texas Press.

Dunleavy, Patrick and Margetts, Helen (1995). 'Understanding the Dynamics of Electoral Reform', *International Political Science Review*, 16, 1, 9–30.

—— and Margetts, Helen (1999). 'Mixed Electoral Systems in Britain and the Jenkins Commission on Electoral Reform', *British Journal of Politics & International Relations*, 1,1, 12–38.

—— Margetts, Helen, and Weir, Stuart (1998). *Making Votes Count and Making Votes Count 2.* London: Democratic Audit.

Duverger, Maurice (1970). *Institutions politiques et droit constitutionnel.* (11th edn). Paris: Presses Universitaires de France.

—— (1978). *Echec au Roi.* Paris: Albin Michel.

—— (1980). 'A New Political System Model: Semi-presidential Government', *European Journal of Political Research*, 8, 2, 168–83.

—— (ed.) (1986). *Les régimes semi-présidentiels.* Paris: Presses Universitaires de France.

—— (1996). *Le système politique français* (21st edn). Paris: Presses Universitaires de France.

Edwards, George C., Barrett, Andrew, and Peake, Jeffrey (1997). 'Legislative Impact of Divided Government', *American Journal of Political Science*, 41, 2, 545–63.

Ehrlich, Walter. (1974). *Presidential Impeachment: An American Dilemma.* St. Charles, MO: Forum.

Elazar, Daniel J. (1987). *Exploring Federalism.* University of Alabama Press.

—— (1996). 'From Statism to Federalism. A Paradigm Shift', *International Political Science Review*, 17, 4, 417–29.

Elster, Jon (1991). 'Constitutionalism in Eastern Europe: An Introduction', *The University of Chicago Law Review*, 58, 2, 447–82.

—— (1993). 'Constitution-Making in Eastern Europe. Rebuilding the Boat in the Open Sea', *Public Administration*, 71, 2, 169–217.

—— (1995). 'Transition, Constitution-Making and Separation of Czechoslovakia', *Archives Européenes de Sociologie*, 36, 1, 105–34.

Engels, Friedrich [1895] (1972). 'The Tactics of Social Democracy', in *The Marx–Engels Reader* (Robert C. Tucker ed.). New York: Norton.

Europa World Year Book (previously *Europa Year Book*) (1945–99). London: Europa Publications.

Farnetti, Paolo (1978). 'Social Conflict, Parliamentary Fragmentatuon, Institutional Shift, and the Rise of Fascism: Italy', in Juan J. Linz and Alfred Stepan (ed.). *The Breakdown of Democratic Regimes.* Baltimore: The Johns Hopkins University Press, vol. 2, 3–33.

Feigert, Frank B. (1989). *Canada Votes, 1935–1986.* Durham, NC: Duke University Press.

Ferejohn, John A., McKelvey, Richard D., and Packel, Edward W. (1984). 'Limiting Distributions for Continuous State Markov Voting Models', *Social Choice and Welfare*, 1, 45–67.

Ferro, Víctor (1987). *El dret public català. Les institucions a Catalunya fins al Decret de Nova Planta.* Vic: Eumo.

Feuchtwanger, E. J. (1993). *From Weimar to Hitler: Germany, 1918–1933.* New York: St. Martin's Press.

Finer, Samuel E. (ed.) 1975. *Adversary Politics and Electoral Reform.* London: Anthony Wigram.

—— (1982). 'Adversary Politics and the Eighties', *Electoral Studies,* 1, 221–30.

Finlay, Robert (1980). *Politics in Renaissance Venice.* New Brunswick, NJ: Rutgers University Press.

Fiorina, Morris (1992). *Divided Government.* New York: Macmillan.

Fishburn, Peter C. (1973). *The Theory of Social Choice.* Princeton: Princeton University Press.

Fisher, Claus A. (ed.) (1990). *Wahlhandbuch für die Bundesrepublik Deutschland: Daten zu Bundestags-, Landstags- und Europawahlen in der Bundesrepublik Deutschland, in den Ländern und in der Kreisen, 1946–1989.* Paderborn: Ferdinand Schöningh.

Fisher, Stephen (1973). 'The Wasted Vote Thesis: West German Evidence', *Comparative Politics,* 5, 293–99.

Fitzgibbon, Russell H. (1945). 'Constitutional Developments in Latin America: A Synthesis', *American Political Science Review,* 39, 3, 511–22.

Fleischer, David (1986). 'Brazil at the Crossroads: The Elections of 1982 and 1985', in Paul W. Drak and Eduardo Silva (ed.) *Elections and Democratization in Latin America, 1980–1985,* San Diego, CA: Center for Iberian and Latin American Studies, University of California.

Fondation Nationale des Sciences Politiques (1967). *L'élection présidentielle des 5 et 19 décembre 1965.* Paris: Armand Colin.

Fontaine, Arturo A. (1972). 'Revolución en papel sellado', in Tomas P. MacHale (ed.) *Visión crítica de Chile.* Santiago de Chile: Portada.

Freedom House (R. D. Gastil and Adrian Karatnycky ed.) (1972–99). *Freedom in the World. The Annual Survey of Political Rights and Civil Liberties.* New Brunswick: Transaction (http://www.freedomhouse.org).

Fundación Milenio [International experts: Bolívar Lamounier, Juan J. Linz, Carlos Nino, Carina Perelli, and Arturo Valenzuela] (1997). *Proyecto de reforma a la Constitución política del Estado 1991–1992.* La Paz: Fundación Milenio.

Furet, François, Julliard, Jacques, and Rosanvallon, Pierre (1988). *La République du centre. La fin de l'exception française.* Paris: Calmann Levy.

Furlong, Paul (1994). *Modern Italy: Representation and Reform.* London: Routledge.

Gaffney, John (ed.) (1989). *The French Presidential Elections of 1988. Ideology and Leadership in Contemporary France.* Aldershot, UK: Darmouth.

—— (1996). *Political Parties and the European Union.* London: Routledge.

—— (1997). 'The Mainstream Right: Chirac and Balladur', in John Gaffney and Lorna Milne (ed.) *French Presidentialism and the Election of 1995.* Aldershot, UK: Ashgate.

Gallagher, Michael (1991). 'Proportionality, Disproportionality and Electoral Systems', *Electoral Studies,* 10, 1, 33–51.

Gamarra, Eduardo A. (1997). 'Hybrid Presidentialism and Democratization: The Case of Bolivia', in Scott Mainwaring and Matthew S. Shugart (ed.) *Presidentialism and Democracy in Latin America.* New York: Cambridge University Press, 363–93.

Gasiorowski, Mark J. (1996). 'An Overview of the Political Regime Change Dataset', *Comparative Political Studies,* 29, 4, 469–83.

Geddes, Barbara (1996). 'Initiation of New Democratic Institutions in Eastern Europe and

Latin America', in Arend Lijphart and Carlos H. Waisman (ed.) *Institutional Design in New Democracies*. Berkeley: University of California Press.

Germann, Raimund E. (1992). 'Switzerland's Future in Europe: Isolation or Constitutional Change', *Governance*, 5, 2, 224–34.

Gibbard, Allan (1973). 'Manipulation of Voting Schemes: A General Result', *Econometrica*, 41, 587–601.

Gil, Javier (1991). 'Las Cortes de Aragón en la edad moderna: comparación y reevaluación', in *Les Corts a Catalunya*. Barcelona: Generalitat de Catalunya, 304–17.

Gillespie, J. David. (1992). *Politics at the Periphery. Third Parties in Two-Party America*. Columbia, SC: University of South Carolina Press.

Giolitti, Giovanni [1922] (1967). *Memorie della mia vita*. Milan: Garzanti.

Golay, John F. (1958). *The Founding of the Federal Republic of Germany*. Chicago: University of Chicago Press.

González, María Lourdes (1998). 'Organos electivos: composición y períodos electorales', in Dieter Nohlen, Sonia Picado, and Daniel Zovatto (ed.) *Tratado de derecho electoral comparado de América Latina*. México: Fondo de Cultura Económica, 59–64.

González Antón, Luis (1978). *Las Cortes de Aragón*. Zaragoza: Librería General.

Goodin, Robert E. (1995). *Utilitarianism as a Public Philosophy*. New York: Cambridge University Press.

Gouaud, Christiane (1996). *La cohabitation*. Paris: Ellipses.

Gragg, Florence A. and Leona C. Gabel (ed.) (1959). *Memoirs of a Renaissance Pope. The Commentaries of Pius II*. New York: Putnam's Sons.

Graham, Richard (1995). 'Formando un gobierno central: Las elecciones y el orden monárquico en el Brasil del siglo XIX', in Antonio Annino (ed.) *Historia de las elecciones en Iberoamérica, siglo XIX*. Mexico: Fondo de Cultura Económica, 347–380.

Grofman, Bernard and Sutherland, Neil (1996). 'The Effect of Term Limits when Competition is Endogenized: A Preliminary Model', in Bernard Grofman (ed.) *Legislative Term Limits: Public Choice Perspectives*. Boston: Kluwer, 175–80.

Gruner, Erich (1978). *Les élections au Conseil national suisse 1848–1919*, 4 vols. Bern: Francke.

Gueniffey, Patrice (1993). *Le nombre et la raison. La Révolution française et les élections*. Paris: École des Hautes Études en Sciences Sociales.

Guide to the U.S. Elections (1999). Washington, DC: *Congressional Quarterly*.

Guidi, Guidubaldo. (1992). *Lotte, pensiero e istituzione politiche nella Repubblica Fiorentina dal 1494 al 1512*. Florence: Leo S. Olschki.

Guizot, François M. [1849] (1974). *Democracy in France*. New York: H. Fertig.

Hailsham of Saint Marylebone, Baron (Quintin Hogg) (1978). *The Dilemma of Democracy: Diagnosis and Prescriptions*. London: Collins.

Hamilton, Alexander, Madison, James, and Jay, John [1788] (1974). *The Federalist*. Cambridge, MA: Harvard University Press.

Hart, Jenifer (1992). *Proportional Representation: Critics of the British Electoral System 1820–1945*. Oxford: Clarendon Press.

Hartlyn, Jonathan (1994). 'Presidentialism and Colombian Politics', in Juan J. Linz and Arturo Valenzuela (eds.), *The Failure of Presidential Democracy*. Baltimore: The Johns Hopkins University Press vol. 2, 220–53.

Harvey, Anna L. (1998). *Votes Without Leverage. Women in American Electoral Politics, 1920–1970*. Cambridge: Cambridge University Press.

Hause, Steven C. (1987). *Hubertine Auclert: the French Suffragette*. New Haven: Yale Univeristy Press.

—— with Kennedy, Anne R. (1984). *Women's Suffrage and Social Politics in the French Third Republic*. Princeton: Princeton University Press.

Haworth, Paul L. (1906). *The Hayes–Tilden Disputed Presidential Election of 1876*. Cleveland: Burrows Brothers.

Hayes-Renshaw, Fiona and Wallace, Helen (1997). *The Council of Ministers*. New York: St. Martin's Press.

Head, Randolph C. (1995). *Early Modern Democray in the Grisons. Social Order and Political Language in a Swiss Mountain Canton, 1470–1620*. Cambridge: Cambridge University Press.

Hermens, Ferdinand A. [1941] (1972). *Democracy or Anarchy? A Study of Proportional Representation*. New York: Johnson Reprint.

Hesse, Joachim and Wright, Vincent (ed.) (1996). *Federalizing Europe? The Costs, Benefits, and Preconditions of Federal Political Systems*. Oxford: Oxford University Press.

Hine, David (1993). *Governing Italy: The Politics of Bargained Pluralism*. Oxford: Clarendon Press.

Hinich, Melvin J. and Munger, Michael C. (1997). *Analytical Politics*. New York: Cambridge University Press.

Hirschman, Albert O. (1991). *The Rhetoric of Reaction. Perversity, Futility, Jeopardy*. Cambridge, MA: Harvard University Press.

Hoag, Clarence Gilbert, and Hallet, George Harvey (1926). *Proportional Representation*. New York: Macmillan.

Hoffer, Peter C. and Hull, N.E.H. (1984). *Impeachment in America, 1635–1805*. New Haven: Yale University Press.

Howard, Robert (1930). 'Parliaments in the Middle Ages and the Early Modern Period', *Catholic Historical Review*, XVI, July.

Huard, Raymond. (1991). *Le suffrage universel en France (1848–1946)*. Paris: Aubier.

Huber, John D. and Inglehart, Ronald (1995). 'Expert Interpretations of Party Space and Party Locations in 42 Societies', *Party Politics*, 1, 1, 73–111.

—— and Powell Jr, G. Bingham. (1994). 'Congruence Between Citizens and Policymakers in Two Visions of Liberal Democracy', *World Politics*, 46, 3, 291–326.

Hughes, Colin (1990). 'The Rules of the Game', in C. Bean, I. McAllister, and J. Warhurst (ed.) *The Greening of Australian Politics: The 1990 Federal Election*. Melbourne: Longman Cheshire.

—— and B. D. Graham. (1968). *A Handbook of Australian Government and Politics*. Canberra: Australian National University Press.

Hume, David [1741–2] (1994). *Political Essays* (Knud Haakonssen ed.). Cambridge: Cambridge University Press. [Spanish version: *Ensayos politicos* (Josep M. Colomer ed.). Madrid: Tecnos, 1987]

Huntington, Samuel (1991). *The Third Wave. Democratization in the Late Twentieth Century*. Norman: University of Oklahoma Press.

Hyde, J. K. (1973). *Society and Politics in Medieval Italy. The Evolution of the Civil Life, 1000–1350*. New York: St. Martin's Press.

Ieraci, Giuseppe (1996). ' "Events" and "Causes" in Cabinet Termination and Survival: Is Explanation Still Possible?', *West European Politics*, 19, 1, 51–68.

Irwin, Galen A. and van Holsteyn, J. J. M. (1989a). 'Decline of the Structured Model of Electoral Competition', *West European Politics*, 12, 1, 21–42.

—— (1989b). 'Towards a More Open Model of Competition', *West European Politics*, 12, 1, 112–38.

Irwin, William J. (1991). *The 1993 Cortes Elections. Origin of the Bienio Negro*. New York: Garland.

Jackson, Gabriel (1965). *The Spanish Republic and the Civil War*. Princeton: Princeton University Press.

Jackson, Keith and McRobie, Alan (1998). *New Zealand Adopts Proportional Representation. Accident? Design? Evolution?* Aldershot, UK: Ashgate.

Jacobi, Mary Putnam [1894] (1968). ' "Common Sense" Applied to Woman Suffrage', in Richard Hofstadter (ed.) *Ten Major Issues in American Politics*. New York: Oxford University Press, 85–92.

Jacobs, Francis, Corbett, Richard, and Shackleton, Michael (1995). *The European Parliament*. London: Stockton.

Jacobson, Gary C. (1990). *The Electoral Origins of Divided Government. Competition in U.S. House Elections, 1946–1988*. Boulder: Westview.

Jaensch, Dean and Teichmann, Max (1988). *The Macmillan Dictionary of Australian Politics*. Melbourne: Macmillan.

Jenkins of Hillhead, Lord (Roy Jenkins) (ed.) (1998). *The Report of the Independent Commission on the Voting System*, 2 vols. London: The Stationnery Office.

Jesse, Eckhard (1988). 'Split-Voting in the Federal Republic of Germany: An Analysis of the Federal Elections from 1953 to 1987', *Electoral Studies*, 7, 109–24.

—— (1990). 'Electoral Reform in West Germany: Historical, Political and Judicial Arguments', in Serge Noiret (ed.) *Political Strategies and Electoral Reforms. Origins of Voting Systems in Europe in the 19th and 20th Centuries*. Baden-Baden: Nomos, 365–93.

Jones, Colin (1988). *The Longman Companion to the French Revolution*. New York: Longman.

Jones, Mark P. (1995a). *Electoral Laws and the Survival of Presidential Democracies*. Notre Dame, IN: University of Notre Dame Press.

—— (1995b). 'A Guide to the Electoral Systems of the Americas', *Electoral Studies*, 14, 15–21.

—— (1997a). 'A Guide to the Electoral Systems of the Americas: An Update', *Electoral Studies*, 16, 13–5.

—— (1997b). 'Evaluating Argentina's Presidential Democracy: 1983–1995', in Scott Mainwaring and Matthew S. Shugart (ed.) *Presidentialism and Democracy in Latin America*. Cambridge: Cambridge University Press.

Kallenbach, Joseph E. and Jessamine, S. (1977). *American State Governors, 1776–1976*. Dobbs Ferry, NY: Oceana.

Kallina, Edmund F. (1988). *Courthouse Over White House. Chicago and the Presidential Election of 1960*. Orlando: University of Central Florida Press.

Kamber, Victor (1995). *Giving Up on Democracy: Why Term Limits Are Bad for America*. Washington, DC: Regnery.

Katz, Richard S. (1984). 'The Single Transferable Vote and Proportional Representation', in Arend Lijphart and Bernard Grofman (ed.) *Choosing an Electoral System*. New York: Praeger, 135–45.

Keohane, Robert O. and Hoffmann, Stanley. (1990). 'Institutional Change in Europe in the

1980s', in William Wallace (ed.) *The Dynamics of European Integration*. London: Pinter.

King, Gary, and Ragsdale, Lyn (1988). *The Elusive Executive: Discovering Statistical Patterns in the Presidency*. Washington, DC: Congressional Quarterly.

Klingemann, Hans-Dieter, Hofferbert, Richard I., and Budge, Ian (ed.). (1994). *Parties, Policies, and Democracy*. Boulder: Westview.

Kobach, Kris W. (1993). *The Referendum: Direct Democracy in Switzerland*. Aldershot, UK: Dartmouth.

Kolb, Eberhard (1988). *The Weimar Republic*. London: Unwin Hyman.

Konopczynski, Ladislas (1930). *Le liberum veto. Étude sur le dévelopement du principe majoritaire*. Paris: Librairie Ancienne Honoré Champion/Warsaw: Librairie Gebethner et Wolff.

Knutsen, Oddbjørn. (1998). 'Expert Judgements of the Left–Right Location of Political Parties: A Comparative Longitudinal Study', *West European Politics*, 21, 2, 63–94.

Kraditor, Aileen S. (1965). *The Ideas of the Woman Suffrage Movement, 1890–1920*. New York: Columbia University Press.

—— (ed.) (1968). *Up From the Pedestal. Selected Writings in the History of American Feminism*. Chicago: Quadrangle Books.

Kramer, Gerald H. (1977). 'A Dynamical Model of Political Equilibrium', *Journal of Economic Theory*, 16, 310–34.

La Gorce, Paul-Marie de (1979a). *L'Après-guerre 1944–1952*. Paris: Bernard Grasset.

—— (1979b). *Apogée et mort de la IVe République 1952–1958*. Paris: Bernard Grasset.

La Palombara, Joseph G. (1987). *Democracy, Italian Style*. New Haven: Yale University Press.

Laitin, David (1995). 'National Revivals and Violence', *Archives Européennes de Sociologie*, 36, 1, 3–43.

Lamartine, Alphonse de (1850). *The Past, Present and Future of the Republic*. New York: Harper.

Lamounier, Bolivar (1994). 'Brazil: Toward Parliamentarism?', in Juan J. Linz and Arturo Valenzuela (ed.) *The Failure of Presidential Democracy*. Baltimore: The Johns Hopkins University Press, vol. 2, 179–219.

Lane, Jan-Erik, McKay, David, and Newton, Kenneth (1991). *Political Data Handbook: OECD Countries*. Oxford: Oxford University Press.

Laver, Michael and Budge, Ian (ed.) (1992). *Party Policy and Government Coalitions*. London: Macmillan.

—— and Schofield, Norman (1990). *Multiparty Government: The Politics of Coalition in Europe*. Oxford: Oxford University Press.

—— and Shepsle, Kenneth A. (1991). 'Divided Government: America is Not Exceptional', *Governance*, 4, 3, 250–69.

—— and Shepsle, Kenneth A. (ed.) (1994). *Cabinet Ministers and Parliamentary Government*. Cambridge: Cambridge University Press.

—— and Shepsle, Kenneth A.(1996). *Making and Breaking Governments. Cabinets and Legislatures in Parliamentary Democracies*. Cambridge: Cambridge University Press.

Lector, Lucio (1894). *Le conclave*. Paris: Lethielleux.

Leites, Nathan (1959). *On the Game of Politics in France*. Stanford: Stanford University Press.

Lepsius, M. Rainer (1978). 'From Fragmented Party Democracy to Government by Emergency Decree and National Socialist Takeover: Germany', in Juan J. Linz and Alfred Stepan (ed.) *The Breakdown of Democratic Regimes*. The Baltimore: Johns Hopkins University Press, vol. 2, 34–79.

Lesnodorski, Boguslaw (1959). 'La Diète de la Pologne d'autrefois', in *La Diète polonaise*. Warsaw: Arkady.

Levillain, Philippe (1994). *Dictionnaire historique de la papauté*. Paris: Fayard.

Lewin, Leif (1988). *Ideology and Strategy. A Century of Swedish Politics*. Cambridge: Cambridge University Press.

Lewis, Jane (ed.) (1987). *Before the Vote Was Won: Arguments for and Against Women's Suffrage*. London: Routledge & Kegan Paul.

Lijphart, Arend (1968). *The Politics of Accommodation. Pluralism and Democracy in the Netherlands*. Berkeley: University of California Press.

—— (1979). 'Religion vs. Class Voting: The "Crucial Experiment" of Comparing Belgium, Canada, South Africa and Switzerland', *American Political Science Review*, 73, 442–68.

—— (1984). *Democracies: Patterns of Majoritarian and Consensus Government in Twenty-One Countries*. New Haven: Yale University Press.

—— (1989). 'From the Politics of Accommodation to Adversarial Politics in the Netherlands: A Reassessment', *West European Politics*, 12, 1, 139–52.

—— (1991). 'Constitutional Choices for New Democracies', *Journal of Democracy*, 2, 72–84.

—— (ed.) (1992*a*). *Parliamentary versus Presidential Government*. Oxford: Oxford University Press.

—— (1992*b*). 'Democratization and Constitutional Choices in Czechoslovakia, Hungary and Poland 1989–91', *Journal of Theoretical Politics*, 4, 2, 207–23.

—— (1994*a*). *Electoral Systems and Party Systems*. Oxford: Oxford University Press.

—— (1994*b*). 'Democracies: Forms, Performance, and Constitutional Engineering', *European Journal of Political Research*, 25, 1–17.

—— (1996). 'The Puzzle of Indian Democracy: A Consociational Interpretation', *American Political Science Review*, 90, 2, 258–68.

—— López Pintor, Rafael and Sone, Yasunori. (1986). 'The Limited Vote and the Single Nontransferable Vote: Lessons from the Japanese and Spanish Examples', in Bernard Grofman and Arend Lijphart (ed.) *Electoral Laws and Their Political Consequences*. New York: Agathon, 154–69.

Linder, Wolf (1994). *Swiss Democracy*. New York: St. Martin's Press.

Lines, Marji (1986). 'Approval Voting and Strategy Analysis: A Venetian Example', *Theory and Decision*, 20, 155–72.

Linz, Juan J. (1978). 'From Great Hopes to Civil War: The Breakdown of Democracy in Spain', in Juan J. Linz and Alfred Stepan (ed.) *The Breakdown of Democratic Regimes*. Baltimore: The Johns Hopkins University Press, vol. 2, 142–215.

—— (1990). 'The Perils of Presidentialism', *Journal of Democracy*, 1,1, 51–69.

—— (1992). 'Political Identities and Electoral Sequences: Spain, the Soviet Union, and Yugoslavia', *Daedalus*, 121, 2, 123–40.

—— (1994). 'Presidential or Parliamentary Democracy: Does It Make a Difference?', in Juan J. Linz and Arturo Valenzuela (ed.) *The Failure of Presidential Democracy*. Baltimore: The Johns Hopkins University Press, vol. 1, 3–87.

Linz, Juan J. and de Miguel, Jesús (1977). 'Hacia un análisis regional de las elecciones de 1936 en España', *Revista Española de la Opinión Pública*, 48, 27–67.

—— and Stepan, Alfred (ed.). (1978). *The Breakdown of Democratic Regimes*, 4 vols. Baltimore: The Johns Hopkins University Press.

—— and Stepan, Alfred (1996). *Problems of Democratic Transition and Consolidation*. Baltimore: The Johns Hopkins University Press.

—— and Valenzuela, Arturo (ed.). (1994). *The Failure of Presidential Democracy*. Baltimore: The Johns Hopkins University Press.

Lively, Jack and Rees, John (ed.) (1978). *Utilitarian Logic and Politics. James Mill's 'Essay on Government', Macaulay's Critique and the Ensuing Debate*. Oxford: Clarendon Press.

Lloyd, Henry D. (1907). *A Sovereign People. A Study of Swiss Democracy*. New York: Doubleday.

Llull, Ramon [1283]. (1982). *Blanquerna*. Barcelona: Edicions 62. (A fragment trans. in Iain McLean and Arnold B. Urken (ed.) *Classics of Social Choice*. Ann Arbor: University of Michigan Press (1995), 71–3).

—— [1299] (1937). 'De Arte Electionis', in H. Finke (ed.) *Gesammelte Aufsätze zur Kulturgeschichte Spaniens*, P. I, §6, 252–309. Münster: Aschendorffschen. (Trans. in Iain McLean and Arnold B. Urken (ed.) *Classics of Social Choice*. Ann Arbor: University of Michigan Press, 1995, 73–5).

Lohmann, Susanne, Brady, David W., and Rivers, Douglas (1997). 'Party Identification, Retrospective Voting, and Moderating Elections in a Federal System. West Germany, 1961–1989', *Comparative Political Studies*, 30, 4, 420–4.

Lovecy, Jill (1992). 'Comparative Politics and the Fifth French Republic. "La fin de l'exception française" '. *European Journal of Political Research*, 21, 385–408.

Ludwig, Emil (1927). *Bismarck. The Story of a Fighter*. New York: Little, Brown.

Mabillon, Johanne and Germain, Michaele (1689). *Musei Italici. Tomus II. Complectens Antiquos Libros Rituales Sanctae Romanae Ecclesiae*. Paris: Vidua Edmund Martin, Johannen Boudot e Stephanum Martin.

Mackie, Thomas T. and Rose, Richard (1991). *The International Almanac of Electoral History*. Washington, DC: .

MacRae, Jr., Duncan (1967). *Parliament, Parties, and Society in France 1946–1958*. New York: St. Martin's Press.

Macridis, Roy and Brown, Bernard E. (1960). *The De Gaulle Republic. Quest for Unity*. Hommenvod, IL: Dorsey.

Madero, Francisco I. [1908] (1986). *La sucesión presidencial en 1910*. Mexico: Instituto Nacional de Estudios Históricos de la Revolución Mexicana.

Mainwaring, Scott (1993). 'Presidentialism, Multipartism, and Democracy: The Difficult Combination', *Comparative Political Studies*, 26, 198–228.

—— (1997). 'Multipartism, Robust Federalism, and Presidentialism in Brazil', in Scott Mainwaring and Matthew S. Shugart (ed.) *Presidentialism and Democracy in Latin America*. New York: Cambridge University Press, 55–109.

—— and Scully, Timothy E. (ed.) (1995). *Building Democratic Institutions. Party Systems in Latin America*. Stanford: Stanford University Press.

—— and Shugart, Matthew S. (ed.) (1997). *Presidentialism and Democracy in Latin America*. New York: Cambridge University Press.

Mair, Peter. (1986). 'Districting Choices under the Single-Transferable Vote' in Bernard

Grofman and Arend Lijphart (ed.) *Electoral Laws and Their Political Consequences.* New York: Agathon, 289–307.

Major, J. Russell (1951). *The Estates General of 1560.* Princeton: Princeton University Press.

—— (1980). *Representative Government in Early Modern France.* New Haven: Yale University Press.

Manin, Bernard (1995). *Principes du gouvernement représentatif.* Paris: Calmann Lévy.

Marín-Bosch, Miguel (1987). 'How Nations Vote in the General Assembly of the United Nations', *International Organization*, 41, 4, 705–24.

Marongiu, Antonio (1968). *Medieval Parliaments. A Comparative Study.* London: Eyre & Spottiswoode.

Martines, Lauro (1979). *Power and Imagination. City-States in Renaissance Italy.* New York: Knopf.

Marx, Karl [1852] (1987). 'British Political Parties', in David McLellan (ed.) *Selected Writings.* Oxford: Oxford University Press.

May, Kenneth O. (1952). 'A Set of Independent, Necessary and Sufficient Conditions for Simple Majority Decision', *Econometrica*, 20, 680–4.

Mayhew, David R. (1991). *Divided We Govern: Party Control, Lawmaking, and Investigations, 1946–1990.* New Haven: Yale University Press.

McClintock, Cynthia (1994). 'Presidents, Messiahs, and Constitutional Breakdowns in Peru', in Juan J. Linz and Arturo Valenzuela (ed.) *The Failure of Presidential Democracy.* Baltimore: The Johns Hopkins University Press, vol. 2, 286–320.

McKelvey, Richard D. (1976). 'Intransitivities in Multidimensional Voting Models and Some Implications for Agenda Control', *Journal of Economic Theory*, 12, 472–82.

—— (1979). 'General Conditions for Global Intransitivities in Formal Voting Models', *Econometrica*, 47, 1085–1112.

—— (1986). 'Covering, Dominance and Institution Free Properties of Social Choice', *American Journal of Political Science,* 30, 283–314.

McLean, Iain and Urken, Arnold B. (ed.) (1995). *Classics of Social Choice.* Ann Arbor: University of Michigan Press.

Mendès-France, B. and Laumonier, L. (1967). 'Une application des méthodes de l'analyse statistique à l'estimation des déplacements de voix entre les deux tours des élections présidentielles de 1965', *Revue Française de Science Politique*, XVII, 1, 110–14.

Merkl, Peter H. (1963). *The Origins of the West German Republic.* New York: Oxford University Press.

Merrill III, Samuel. (1988). *Making Multicandidate Elections More Democratic.* Princeton: Princeton University Press.

—— and Nagel, Jack (1987). 'The Effect of Approval Balloting on Strategic Voting Under Alternative Decision Rules', *American Political Science Review*, 81, 509–24.

Michener, James A. (1989). *Presidential Lottery. The Reckless Gamble in Our Electoral System.* New York: Random House.

Mill, John Stuart [1861] (1963). *Considerations on Representative Government*, in *Collected Works.* Toronto: University of Toronto Press, vol. 18.

—— [1869] (1963). *The Subjection of Women*, in *Collected Works.* Toronto: University of Toronto Press, vol. 14.

Miller, Nicholas R. (1983). 'Pluralism and Social Choice', *American Political Science Review*, 21, 769–803.

Miller, Nicholas R., Grofman, Bernard, and Feld, Scott L. (1989). 'The Geometry of Majority Rule', *Journal of Theoretical Politics*, 1, 379–406.

Mirabeau [Honoré-Gabriel Riqueti, Count De Mirabeau] [1789] (1834). 'Discours prononcé à la Tribune Nationale. États de Provence. Aix, 30 janvier 1789', in *Oeuvres*. Paris: Lecointe et Pougin, vol. 1, 3–27.

Mitchell, B. R. (1992–5). *International Historical Statistics*. New York: Stockton.

Mitterrand, François. (1964). *Le coup d'état permanent*. Paris: Plon.

Montesquieu [Charles Louis de Secondat, Baron de la Brède et de Montesquieu] [1748] (1964). *L'Esprit des lois*. In *Oeuvres complètes*. Paris: Seuil.

Mori, Arturo (1933). *Crónica de las Cortes Constituyentes de la Segunda República Española*. Madrid: Aguilar.

Myers, Alec R. (1975). *Parliaments and Estates in Europe to 1789*. London: Thames & Hudson.

Najemy, John M. (1982). *Corporatism and Consensus in Florentine Electoral Politics, 1280–1400*. Chapel Hill: University of North Carolina Press.

Neidhart, Leonhard (1970). *Plebiszit und Pluralitüre Demokratie. Eine Analyse der Funktionen des Schweizerischen Gesetzesreferendums*. Bern: Francke.

Nicholls, Anthony J. (1991).*Weimar and the Rise of Hitler* (3rd edn). New York: St. Martin's Press.

Niemi, Richard, and Riker, William H. (1976). 'The Choice of Voting Systems', *Scientific American*, 234, 6, 21–7.

Nino, Carlos S. (ed.) (1992). *El Presidencialism puesto a prueba: con especial referencia al sistema presidencialista latinoamericano*. Madrid: Centro de Estudios Constitucionales.

Nixon, Richard M. (1990). *Six Crises*. New York: Simon & Schuster.

Nohlen, Dieter (ed.) (1993). *Enciclopedia electoral latinoamericana y del Caribe*. San José, Costa Rica: Instituto Interamericano de Derechos Humanos.

—— (1998). 'La reelección', in Dieter Nohlen, Sonia Picado, and Daniel Zovatto (eds.) *Tratado de derecho electoral comparado de América Latina*. México: Fondo de Cultura Económica, 140–4.

Noiret, Serge (ed.) (1990). *Political Strategies and Electoral Reforms. Origins of Voting Systems in Europe in the 19th and 20th Centuries*. Baden-Baden: Nomos.

—— (1994). *La nascita dei partiti nell'Italia contemporanea. La proporzionale del 1919*. Manduria: Lacaita.

North, Douglass C. (1990a). 'A Transaction Cost Theory of Politics', *Journal of Theoretical Politics*, 2, 4, 355–67.

—— (1990b). *Institutions, Institutional Change and Economic Performance*. New York: Cambridge University Press.

—— and Thomas, Robert P. (1973). *The Rise of the Western World: A New Economic History*. Cambridge: Cambridge University Press.

—— and Weingast, Barry W. (1989). 'The Evolution of Institutions Governing Public Choice in 17th Century England', *Journal of Economic History*, 49, 803–32.

Nugent, Neill. (1994). *The Government and Politics of the European Union*. Durham, NC: Duke University Press.

Nurmi, Hannu (1987). *Comparing Voting Systems*. Dordrecht: Kluwer.

O'Gorman, Frank (1982). *The Emergence of the British Two-Party System 1760–1832*. New York: Holmes & Meyer.

—— (1989). *Voters, Patrons, and Parties. The Unreformed Electoral System of Hanoverian England, 1734–1832*. Oxford: Clarendon Press.

Oates, Wallace E. (1972). *Fiscal Federalism*. New York: Harcourt Brace Jovanovich.

Olson, Mancur (1971). *The Logic of Collective Action*. Cambridge, MA: Harvard University Press.

Ornstein, Norman J., Mann, Thomas E., and Malbin, Michael J. (1998). *Vital Statistics on Congress 1997–98*. Washington, DC: *Congressional Quarterly*.

Ostrom, Vincent [1971] (1987). *The Poltical Theory of a Compound Republic*. Lincoln: University of Nebraska Press.

Owen, Robert (1993). *Selected Works* (Gregory Claeys ed.). London: W. Pickering.

Pasquino, Gianfranco (1996). 'Italy: A Democratic Regime Under Reform', in Josep M. Colomer (ed.) *Political Institutions in Europe*. London/New York: Routledge, 138–69.

Patil, Anajali V. (1995). *The UN Veto in World Affairs. 1946–90*. Sarasota, FL: Unifo.

Pavone, Claudio (1991). *Una guerra civile. Saggio storico sulla moralità della Resistenza*. Turin: Bollati Boringhieri.

Peirce, Neal R. (1968). *The People's President. The Electoral College in American History and the Direct-Vote Alternative*. New York: Simon & Schuster.

Pennock, J. Roland. (1959). 'Federal and Unitary Government. Disharmony and Frustration', *Behavioral Science*, 147–57.

Peterson, Paul E. and Greene, Jay P. (1993). 'Why Executive-Legislative Conflict in the U.S. Is Dwindling', *British Journal of Political Science*, 24, 33–55.

Petit-Dutaillis, Charles (1947). *Les communes françaises, caractères et évolution*. Paris: Albin Michel.

Petracca, Mark (1989). 'The Distribution of Power in the Federal Government: Perspectives from The Federalist Papers—A Critique', in Bernard Grofman and Donald Wittman (ed.) *The Federalist Papers and the New Institutionalism*. New York: Agathon, 158–72.

Petry, François. (1994). 'The Role of Cabinet Ministers in the French Fourth Republic', in Michael Laver and Kenneth A. Shepsle (ed.) *Cabinet Ministers and Parliamentary Government*. Cambridge: Cambridge University Press.

Phillips, John A. (1982). *Electoral Behavior in Unreformed England, 1761–1802*. Princeton: Princeton University Press.

—— (1992). *The Great Reform Bill in the Boroughs: English Electoral Behaviour, 1818–1841*. Oxford: Oxford University Press.

Pierce, Roy (1991). 'The Executive Divided Against Itself: Cohabitation in France (1986–88)', *Governance*, 4, 3, 270–94.

—— (1995). *Choosing the Chief. Presidential Elections in France and the United States*. Ann Arbor: University of Michigan Press.

Pinder, John (1995). *European Community. The Building of a Union* (2nd edn). Oxford: Oxford University Press.

Pisano, Giorgio (1965–6). *Storia della guerra civile in Italia (1943–45)*, 3 vols. Milan: FPE.

Pitkin, Hanna Fenichel (1967). *The Concept of Representation*. Berkeley: University of California Press.

Piven, Frances Fox and Cloward, Richard A. (1988). *Why Americans Don't Vote*. New York: Pantheon.

Plott, Charles (1967). 'A Notion of Equilibrium and its Possibility Under Majority Rule', *American Economic Review*, 57, 787–806.

Plumb, J. H. (1967). *The Origins of Political Stability in England, 1675–1725*. Boston: Houghton Mifflin.

—— (1969). 'The Growth of the Electorate in England, 1600–1715', *Past and Present*, 45, 90–116.

Political Data Base of the Americas (1999). Georgetown University and Organization of American States (http://www.georgetown.edu/pdba).

Porter, Kirk H. (1969). *A History of Suffrage in the United States*. New York: Greenwood.

Posada-Carbó, Eduardo (ed.) (1996). *Elections Before Democracy: The History of Elections in Europe and Latin America*. New York: St. Martin's Press.

Powell, G. Bingham (1982). *Contemporary Democracies: Participation, Stability and Violence*. Cambridge, MA: Harvard University Press.

Power, Timothy J. and Gasiorowski, Mark J. (1997). 'Institutional Design and Democratic Consolidation in the Third World', *Comparative Political Studies*, 30, 2, 123–55.

Prothro, James W. and Chaparro, Patricio E. (1976). 'Public Opinion and the Movement of Chilean Government to the Left, 1952–72', in Arturo Valenzuela and J. Samuel Valenzuela (ed.) *Chile: Politics and Society*. New Brunswick, NJ: Transaction Books, 67–114.

Proudhon, Pierre-Joseph (1923). *Oeuvres complètes*. Paris: M. Rivière.

Przeworski, Adam (1991). *Democracy and the Market*. Cambridge: Cambridge University Press.

—— Alvarez, Mike, Cheibub, José Antonio, and Limogi, Fernando (forthcoming). *Democracy and Development. Political Institutions and Material Well-Being in the World, 1950–1990*. Cambridge: Cambridge University Press.

Quirk, Paul J., and Cunion, William (1999). 'Clinton's Domestic Policy: The Lessons of a "New Democrat" ', in Colin Campbell and Bert A. Rockman (ed.) *The Clinton Legacy*. New York: Chatham House, 200–25.

Rae, Douglas W. (1975). 'The Limits of Consensual Decision', *American Political Science Review*, 69, 1270–94.

Ramírez y Berrios, M. Guillermo. (1963). *Examen espectral de las elecciones del 9 de junio de 1963*. Lima.

Ranzato, Gabriele (1991). 'La forja de la soberanía nacional: las elecciones en los sistemas liberales italiano y español', in Javier Tusell (ed.) *El sufragio universal*. Madrid: Ayer, 115–38.

Rappard, William E. (1936). *The Government of Switzerland*. New York: Van Nostrand.

Raunio, Tapio (1997). *The European Perspective: Transnational Party Groups in the 1989–1994 European Parliament*. Brookfield, VT: Ashgate.

Reeves, Thomas C. (1991). *A Question of Character. A Life of John F. Kennedy*. New York: Free Press.

Riggs, Fred W. (1988). 'The Survival of Presidentialism in America: Para-constitutional Practices', *International Political Science Review*, 9, 4, 247–78.

Riker, William H. (1964). *Federalism: Origin, Operation, Significance*. Boston: Little, Brown.

—— (1965). *Democracy in the United States*. New York: Macmillan.

—— (1980). 'Implications from the Disequilibrium of Majority Rule for the Study of Institutions', *American Political Science Review*, 74, 432–46.

—— (1982). *Liberalism Against Populism: A Confrontation Between the Theory of Democracy and the Theory of Social Choice*. San Francisco: Freeman.

—— (1983). 'Political Theory and the Art of Heresthetics', in Ada Finifter (ed.) *Political Science: The State of the Discipline*. Washington, DC: American Political Science Association, 47–67.

—— (1986). *The Art of Political Manipulation*. New Haven: Yale University Press.

—— (1987). *The Development of American Federalism*. Boston: Kluwer.

—— (1992a). 'The Merits of Bicameralism', *International Review of Law and Economics*, 12, 166–8.

—— (1992b). 'The Justification of Bicameralism', *International Political Science Review*, 13, 1, 101–16.

—— (ed.) (1993). *Agenda Formation*. Ann Arbor: University of Michigan Press.

—— (1996a). 'European Federalism: The Lessons of Past Experience', in Joachim J. Hesse and Vincent Wright (ed.) *Federalizing Europe? The Costs, Benefits, and Preconditions of Federal Political Systems*. Oxford: Oxford University Press.

—— (1996b). *The Strategy of Rhetoric: Campaigning for the American Constitution* (Randall L. Calvert, John Mueller, and Rick K. Wilson ed.). New Haven: Yale University Press.

Ritter, Gerhard A. (1990a). 'The Social Bases of German Political Parties, 1867–1920', in Karl Rohe (ed.) *Elections, Parties and Political Traditions. Social Foundations of German Parties and Party Systems, 1867–1987*. New York: Berg.

—— (1990b). 'The Electoral Systems of Imperial Germany and Their Consequences for Politics', in Serge Noiret (ed.) *Political Strategies and Electoral Reforms. Origins of Voting Systems in Europe in the 19th and 20th Centuries*. Baden-Baden: Nomos, 53–75.

—— and Merith Niehuss (1987). *Wahlen in der Bundesrepublik Deutschland: Bundestags- und Landtagwahlen 1946–1987*. Munich: C.H. Beck.

Robinson, Donald L. (1985). *Reforming American Government: The Bicentennial Papers of the Committe on the Constitutional System*. Boulder: Westview.

—— (1989). *Government for the Third American Century*. Boulder: Westview.

Romero Maura, Joaquín (1973). 'El caciquismo: tentativa de conceptualización, *Revista de Occidente*, 127, 15–44.

Rosanvallon, Pierre (1992). *Le sacré du citoyen. Histoire du suffrage universel en France*. Paris: Gallimard.

Rosen, Frederick (1983). *Jeremy Bentham and Representative Democracy*. Oxford: Oxford University Press.

Rosenstone, Steven J., Behr, Roy L., and Lazarus, Edward H. (1996). *Third Parties in America. Citizen Response to Major Party Failure*. Princeton: Princeton University Press.

Rossi-Landi, Guy (1967). 'Majorité et opposition avant les élections législatives. Note sur quelques sondages' *Revue Française de Science Politique*, XVII, 1, 70–7.

Rossiter, Clinton (1987). *The American Presidency*. Baltimore: The Johns Hopkins University Press.

Rousseau, Jean-Jacques [1762] (1997). *The Social Contract*. Cambridge: Cambridge University Press.

Rubinstein, Nicolai (1966). *The Government of Florence under the Medici (1434 to 1494)*. Oxford: Clarendon Press.

Sani, Giacomo and Sartori, Giovanni (1983). 'Polarization, Fragmentation and Competition in Western Democracies', in Hans Daalder and Peter Mair (ed.) *Western European Party Systems*. London: Sage.

Satterwhaite, Mark A. (1975). 'Strategy-Proofness and Arrow's Conditions: Existence and Correspondence Theorems for Voting Procedures and Social Welfare Functions', *Journal of Economic Theory*, 10, 187–217.

Schlesinger, Arthur M. (1973). *The Imperial Presidency*. Boston: Houghton Mifflin.

Schmidt, Manfred G. (1996).' Germany: the Grand Coalition State', in Josep M. Colomer (ed.) *Political Institutions in Europe*. London: Routledge, 62–98.

Schofield, Norman (1978). 'Instability of Simple Dynamic Games', *Review of Economic Studies*, 43, 575–94.

Scott, Robert E. (1964). *Mexican Government in Transition*. Urbana: University of Illinois Press.

Sen, Amartya K. (1966). 'A Possibility Theorem on Majority Decisions', *Econometrica*, 34, 491–9.

—— (1970). *Collective Choice and Social Welfare*. San Francisco: Holden-Day.

—— and Pattanaik, Prasanta K. (1969). 'Necessary and Sufficient Conditions for Rational Choice under Majority Decision', *Journal of Economic Theory*, 1, 178–202.

Serrafero, Mario D. (1997). *Reelección y sucesión presidencial. Poder y continuidad. Argentina, América latina y EE. UU.* Buenos Aires: Belgrano.

Serrano García. R. (ed.) (1993). *La revolución liberal en Valladoid (1808–1874)*. Valladolid: Grupo Pinciano.

Seton-Watson, Christopher (1967). *Italy from Liberalism to Fascism 1870–1925*. London: Methuen.

Seymour, Charles [1915] (1970). *Electoral Reform in England and Wales. The Development and Operation of the Parliamentary Franchise 1832–1885*. London: Archon Books.

—— and Donald Paige Frary (1918). *How the World Votes. The Story of Democratic Development in Elections*, 2 vols. Springfield, MA: C. A. Nichols.

Shepsle, Kenneth A. (1979). 'Institutional Arrangements and Equilibrium in Multidimensional Voting Models', *American Journal of Political Science*, 23, 27–59.

—— (1986). 'Institutional Equilibrium and Equilibrium Institutions', in Herbert Weisberg (ed.) *Political Science: The Science of Politics*. New York: Agathon, 51–81.

—— (1989). 'Studying Institutions: Some Lessons from the Rational Choice Apprach', *Journal of Theoretical Politics*, 1, 131–49.

—— and Weingast, Barry R. (1981). 'Structure-Induced Equilibrium and Legislative Choice', *Public Choice*, 37, 503–19.

Shiratori, Rei (1995). 'The Politics of Electoral Reform in Japan', *International Political Science Review*, 16, 1, 79–94.

Shugart, Mathew S. and Carey, John M. (1992). *Presidents and Assemblies. Constitutional Design and Electoral Dynamics*. Cambridge: Cambridge University Press.

Skidmore, Thomas E. (1967). *Politics in Brazil, 1930–1964: An Experiment in Democracy*. New York: Oxford University Press.

Soulier, A. (1939). *L'instabilité ministerielle sous la Troisième République*. Paris: Recueil Sirey.

Steiner, Jürg (1974). *Amicable Agreement versus Majority Rule. Conflict Resolution in Switzerland*. Chapel Hill: University of North Carolina Press.

—— (1983). 'Reflections on the Consociational Theme', in Howard R. Penniman (ed.) *Switzerland at the Polls*. Washington, DC: American Enterprise Institute for Public Policy Research, 161–76.

Stepan, Alfred (1971). *The Military in Politics: Changing Patterns in Brazil.* Princeton: Princeton University Press.

—— (1978). 'Political Leadership and Regime Breakdown: Brazil', in Juan J. Linz and Alfred Stepan (ed.) *The Breakdown of Democratic Regimes.* Baltimore: The Johns Hopkins University Press, vol. 2, 110–37.

Stokes, William S. (1945). 'Parliamentary Government in Latin America', *American Political Science Review*, 39, 3, 522–37.

Strom, Kaare (1990). *Minority Government and Majority Rule.* New York: Cambridge University Press.

Suleiman, Ezra N. (1994). 'Presidentialism and Political Stability in France', in Juan J. Linz and Arturo Valenzuela (ed.) *The Failure of Presidential Democracy.* Baltimore: The Johns Hopkins University Press, vol. 1, 157–61.

Sundquist, James L. (1992). *Constitutional Reform and Effective Government.* Washington, DC: The Brookings Institution.

—— (1995). *Back to Gridlock? Governance in the Clinton Years.* Washington, DC: The Brookings Institution.

Taagepera, Rein (1998). 'Effective Magnitude and Effective Threshold', *Electoral Studies*, 17, 4, 393–404.

—— and Shugart, Mathew S. (1989). *Seats and Votes.* New Haven: Yale University Press.

Taylor, Miles (1997). 'Interests, Parties and the State: the Urban Electorate in England, c.1820–72', in John Lawrence and Miles Taylor (ed.) *Party, State and Society. Electoral Behavior in Britain Since 1820.* Aldershot, UK: Scholar Press.

Temple, Nora (1973). 'Municipal Elections and Municipal Oligarchies in Eighteenth-century France', in J. F. Bosher (ed.) *French Government and Society 1500–1850.* London: Athlone.

Thakur, Ramesh Chadra (1995). *The Government and Politics of India.* New York: St Martin's Press.

Thayssen, Uwe (1994). *The Bundesrat, the Länder and German Federalism.* Baltimore: The Johns Hopkins University Press.

Tideman, Nicolaus (1995). 'The Single Transferable Vote', *Journal of Economic Perspectives*, 9, 1 27–38.

Tite, Colin G.C. (1974). *Impeachment and Parliamentary Judicature in Early Stuart England.* London: Athlone.

Toranzo Roca, Carlos F. (ed.) (1991). *Aspectos básicos de la reforma del Estado.* La Paz: ILDIS.

Trechsel, Alexander and Sciarini, Pascal (1998). 'Direct Democracy in Switzerland: Do Elites Matter?', *European Journal of Political Research*, 33, 1, 99–124.

Tribunal Superior Eleitoral (1950–). *Dados estatísticos.* Río de Janeiro: Departamento de Imprensa Nacional.

Tsebelis, George (1995). 'Decision Making in Political Systems: Veto Players in Presidentialism, Parliamentarism, Multicameralism, and Multipartyism', *British Journal of Political Science*, 25, 289–326.

—— and Money, Jeanette (1997). *Bicameralism.* New York: Cambridge University Press.

Tudesq, André-Jean (1965). *L'élection présidentielle de Louis-Napoléon Bonaparte, 10 decembre 1848.* Paris: A. Colin.

Tullock, Gordon (1969). 'Federalism: Problems of Scale', *Public Choice*, 6, 19–29.

Tusell, Javier (1971). *Las elecciones del Frente Popular*. Madrid: Cuadernos para el diálogo.

—— (1976). 'The Popular Front Elections in Spain, 1936', in Stanley G. Payne (ed.) *Politics and Society in Twentieth-Century Spain*. New York: New Viewpoints.

—— (1982). *Las constituyentes de 1931: Unas elecciones de transición*. Madrid: Centro de Investigaciones Sociológicas.

—— (ed.) (1991). *El sufragio universal*. Madrid: Ayer.

—— (1997). 'Los intentos reformistas de la vida política durante el reinado de Alfonso XIII', in Salvador Forner (ed.) *Democracia, elecciones y modernización en Europa. Siglos XIX y XX*. Madrid: Cátedra, 295–312.

Udovicki, Jasminka and Ridgeway, James (ed.) (1997). *Burn This House: The Making and Unmaking of Yugoslavia*. Durham, NC: Duke University Press.

Ull Pont, Eugenio J. (1976). 'El sufragio universal en España (1890–1936)', *Revista de Estudios Políticos,* July–October, 105–130.

United Nations Population Division (1998). *World Population Prospects* (http://www.popin.org/pop1998).

Valenzuela, Arturo (1976). 'Political constraints to the Establishment of Socialism in Chile', in Arturo Valenzuela and J. Samuel Valenzuela (ed.) *Chile: Politics and Society*. New Brunswick, NJ: Transaction Books, 1–25.

—— (1978). *The Breakdown of Democratic Regimes, Chile*. Baltimore: The Johns Hopkins University Press.

—— (1994). 'Party Politics and the Crisis of Presidentialism in Chile: A Proposal for a Parliamentary Form of Government', in Juan J. Linz and Arturo Valenzuela (ed.) *The Failure of Presidential Democracy*. Baltimore: The Johns Hopkins University Press, vol. 2, 91–150.

Valenzuela, Arturo (ed.), Josep M. Colomer, Arend Lijphart, and Matthew Shugart (1999). *Sobre la Reforma Política en Colombia*. Washington, DC: Georgetown Analytics.

Varela Ortega, José (1977). *Los amigos políticos. Partidos, elecciones y caciquismo en la Restauración (1875–1900)*. Madrid: Alianza.

Venditti, Renato (1981). *Il manuale Cencelli. Il prontuario della lottizzazione democristiana. Un documento sulla gestione del potere*. Rome: Riuniti.

Vowles, Jack (1995). 'The Politics of Electoral Reform in New Zealand', *International Political Science Review*, 16, 1, 95–115.

Waley, Daniel (1988). *The Italian City-Republics*. New York: Longman.

Warwick, Paul V. (1994). *Government Survival in Parliamentary Democracies*. New York: Cambridge University Press.

Watts, Ronald L. (1996a). 'Canada: Three Decades of Periodical Federal Crises', *International Political Science Review*, 17, 4, 353–71.

—— (1996b). *Comparing Federal Systems in the 1990s*. Kingston: Queen's University, Institute of Intergovernmental Relations.

Weaver, Leon (1984). 'Semi-proportional and Proportional Representation Systems in the United States', in Arend Lijphart and Bernard Grofman (ed.) *Choosing an Electoral System*. New York: Praeger, 191–206.

—— (1986). 'The Rise, Decline and Resurrection of Proportional Representation in Local Governments in the United States' in Bernard Grofman and Arend Lijphart (ed.) *Electoral Laws and Their Political Consequences*. New York: Agathon, 139–53.

Weber, Robert (1995). 'Approval Voting', *Journal of Economic Perspectives*, 9, 1, 39–50.

Weingast, Barry R. (1979). 'A Rational Choice Perspective on Congressional Norms', *American Journal of Political Science*, 23, 245–62.

—— (1995). 'The Economic Role of Political Institutions: Market-Preserving Federalism and Economic Development', *The Journal of Law, Economics and Organization*, 7, 1, 1–31.

Weldon, Jeffrey (1997). 'Political Sources of Presidencialismo in Mexico', in Scott Mainwaring and Matthew S. Shugart (ed.) *Presidentialism and Democracy in Latin America*. New York: Cambridge University Press.

Wheare, Kenneth C. (1946). *Federal Government*. London: Oxford University Press.

Wiel, Alethea (1895). *Venice*. New York: Putnam.

Williams, Philip (1958). *Politics in Post-War France. Parties and the Constitution in the Fourth Republic*. London/New York: Longman.

—— with Goldey, David and Harrison, Martin (1970). *French Politicians and Elections 1951–1969*. Cambridge: Cambridge University Press.

Williamson, Chilton (1960). *American Suffrage: From Property to Democracy, 1760–1860*. Princeton: Princeton University Press.

Wilkinson, Bertie (1972). *The Creation of Medieval Parliaments*. New York: Wiley.

Woldendorp, Jaap, Keman, Hans, and Budge, Ian (1993). *Handbook of Democratic Government. Party Government in 20 Democracies (1945–1990)*. Dordrecht: Kluwer.

Wollstonecraft, Mary [1792] (1996). *A Vindication of the Rights of Woman*. Mineola, NY: Dover.

Wright, Jack F. H. (1984). 'An Electoral Basis for Responsible Government: The Australian Experience', in Arend Lijphart and Bernard Grofman (ed.) *Choosing an Electoral System. Issues and Alternatives*. New York: Praeger, 127–34.

—— (1986). 'Australian Experience with Majority-Preferential and Quota-Preferential Systems', in Bernard Grofman and Arend Lijphart (ed.) *Electoral Laws and Their Political Consequences*. New York: Agathon.

Zaidi, A. M. and Zaidi, S. G. (ed.). (1976–). *Encyclopaedia of the Indian National Congress*. Delhi: Indian Institute of Applied Political Research, 28 vols.

Zenatti, Oddone (ed.). (1984). *Dante e Firenze*. Florence: Sasoni.

Index

aboriginals 44, 53
Adams, J. Q. 119
Adelaide 120
Adenauer, K. 140, 196
Affuso, P. J. 148
Africa 43, 53
African-Americans 26–7, 44, 50–2
Agrarians
    Finland 65
    Norway 65
    Spain (PA) 88–91
    Sweden 64
Alabama paradox 104–5, 121
Alcántara, M. 175
Alemán, M. 156
Alesina, A. 163, 178
Alessandri, J. 114–15
Alexander I Karageorgevic 200
Alexander III (Rolando Bandinelli) 75
Alfonsín, R. 157
Algeria 95, 131
Allende, S. 113–16
Alonso, P. 28
Alvarez, M. 213
American Congressional Union for Women's
    Suffrage 40
American Revolutionary Popular Action
    (APRA) 109–10
Amsterdam Treaty (1997) 83
Anarchists, Spanish 90
Anderson, C. J. 210
Anderson, E. N. 35
Anderson, P. R. 35
Andrae, C. C. G. 119
Andreotti, G. 132, 134
Anglo model 42–4, 46–53, 102
Annino, A. 28
Anthony, S. B. 40–1
Aragonese Corts 73, 77–9
Argentina 28, 69, 106–8, 122–3
Arias, A. 175
Aristotle 1, 143
Armenia 123
Arrow, K. 3
Ashtabula 120
Asia 13, 53

Asians in North America 51, 53
Auclert, H. 41
Australia
    suffrage rights 43–4, 53
    voting rules 69, 86–7, 91–3, 102, 120,
    127
Austria/Austrian Empire 18, 60, 69, 80,
    122–3
Axelrod, R. 123
Azaña, M. 87–8

Babeau, A. 22
Baden 60
Bahro, H. 181
Baker, K. M. 23
Baldwin, M. W. 75
Balestra, R. 167
Balinski, M. L. 89, 119, 122
Balladur, E. 96–8, 180
Bánzer, H. 184
Barante, M. 38
Barberà, S. 3
Barcelona 59, 77–8
Barnes, S. H. 138
Barre, R. 96–7
Barrett, A. 179
Barrientos, R. 182
de Barros, A. 111–12
Bartholdi, J. J. 120
Bartolini, S. 144, 214
Basle 193
Basque regionalists 88
Bastid, P. 35
Bavaria 62, 137
Bawn, K. 137–8
Bayerlain, B. H. 181
Baylis, T. A. 209
Becker, L. E. 33
Bednar, J. 202
Behr, R. L. 52
Belaúnde Terry, F. 109–10
Belgium 69, 81, 122–3, 127
Bennett, C. 201
Bennett, S. 170
Benson, R. L. 74
Bentham, J. 6, 120

Bergamo 21
Bernstein, E. 40
biased presidents 95–8
bicameralism, divided 188–90
Bidault, G. 130
Bilbao 59
Birchfield, V. 209
Bishop, C. F. 24, 26
von Bismarck, O. F. 34–5, 60–1
Bisson, T. N. 22
Black, C. L. 172
Black, D. 3, 120
blacks 26–7, 44, 50–2
Blair, A. 205
Blais, A. 144, 215
Blanc, L. 35
Blanqui, L.-A. 35
Bogdanor, V. 149
Bohn, D. E. 193
Bolivia 69, 106–7, 123
    parliamentarized presidentialism 182–4
Bologna 19, 21
de Borda, J.-C. 100–1
Bordaberry, J. M. 160
Boston 119
Botana, N. 28
Boulder 120
Bourbons 79
Bowler, S. 168
Brady, D. W. 168
Brams, S. J. 5, 80, 100–1, 120, 148
Brandenburg, F. 155
Brandt, W. 196
Brazil 28, 69, 102, 106–8, 111–13, 123
Breton, A. 203
Bridge, J. S. C. 23
Britain *see* United Kingdom
Brown, B. E. 94
Brucker, G. 20–1
Brunell, T. L. 178
Bryce, J. 147
Bucaram, A. 175
Buchanan, J. 5, 104, 175
Budge, I. 69, 123, 142, 174
Buenos Aires 28, 122
Bulgaria 69, 122
Bundesrat 60
Bundestag 60
Bush, G. 178
Byrd, H. F. 104–5

Cadart, J. 22
Cain, B. E. 157
Calvinists 135

Cambridge, Massachusetts 121
Campbell, P. 56, 94
Canada 43–4, 53, 69, 102–3, 120
Cánovas, A. 38–9
Cantón, D. 167
Cape of Good Hope 119
Capel, R. M. 36
Cárdenas, L. 156
Cardoso, F. H. 158
Carey, J. M. 106, 152, 157, 166, 175, 183
Carr, R. 58
Carranza, V. 155
Carroll, L. 66, 118, 120
Carstairs, A. M. 65, 123
Castille 77–8
Castles, F. 69
Catalan Regionalists 59, 88
Catalonia 73, 77–9
Catholics/Catholicism 73–5, 77–8, 83
    Netherlands 135
    Spain 58, 88–91
    suffrage rights 26, 31, 33–5, 57, 61
CEDA 89–90
Cencelli's manual 132–3
Center Party
    Spain 90
    Sweden 64
Chamber of Deputies
    Brazil 112
    Italy 131, 134
Chang Rodriguez, E. 109
Chaparro, P. E. 114–15
Chaterjee, P. 167
Chavarri Sidera, P. 28
Chávez, H. 159
Chiaramonte, J. C. 28
Chicago 106
Chile 69, 102, 106–8, 113–16, 119, 123
China 80
Chirac, J. 95–8, 180, 182
Chirinos Soto, E. 110
Christian Democrats
    Brazil 111
    Chile 113, 115–16
    France 95, 97, 130
    Germany 62, 137
    Italy 131–2, 134
    Peru 109–10
Christian parties 27
    France (MRP) 127–30
    Germany (CDU/CSU) 61, 137–40
    Italy (DCI) 133
    Netherlands 135–7
Church *see* Catholics/Catholicism

Churchill, W. 149
CIA (Central Intelligence Agency) 116
Cincinatti 120
Civil War, American (1861–65) 50–2,
    104
Clark, M. 57
Clemenceau, G. 36
Cleveland 120
Cleveland, G. 104
Clinton, W. 104, 175, 178–9
Cloward, R. A. 51
Cole, A. 56, 94
Collor de Mello, F. 175
Colombia 69, 106–8, 122–3
colonies
    former British 17–18, 25–7, 32, 43, 52
    voting rules 99, 102, 120
    Spanish 17
Colorado 51
Committee of Permanent Representatives
    82
Common Foreign and Security Policy 83
Communists
    Australia 93
    Brazil 111–12
    Chile 114–15
    Communist International 57
    France (PCF) 93–4, 96, 127–30
    Germany 35, 61–2; post-Communists
        63, 138
    Italy 132–4
    Peru 109
    Spain (PCE) 39, 89–91
Conacher, J. B. 47
Concordat of Worms (1122) 74
de Condorcet, J.-A.-N. 84
Condorcet winners 84, 87, 95, 108, 110
Congress Party (India) 100, 103
Conservatives 29–30
    Australia 92
    Canada 103
    Chile 114
    France (Moderates) 93, 127–30
    Germany 60–1
    Norway 65
    Spain 38–9, 58
    Sweden 63–4
    UK 48–9, 102–3
Considerant, V. 122
Constant, B. 38
Constituent Assembly (France) 54–5
Constitution
    Brazil (1946) 111
    Cádiz (1812) 27–8, 58

Chile (1925) 113
Finland (1919) 65
France (1851) 54–5
United States (1789) 27, 118
Constitutional Court (Germany) 138
Cook County, Chicago 106
Coppedge, M. 176
Corbett, R. 199
Cornejo, H. 109
Cornelius, W. A. 156
Coroleu Inglada, J. 79
Correa, J. 110
Costa Rica 69, 106–8, 123
Council of Ministers 73, 81–3
Cox, G. W. 5, 47, 120, 122, 139, 178
Craig, A. L. 156
Craxi, B. 132
Crepaz, M. M. L. 209
Criscitiello, A. 133
Crombez, C. 83
Cuba 106, 122
Cunion, W. 179
Curtis, G. E. 200
Czech Republic 69, 123

Daalder, H. 69, 136–7
Daley, R. 106
D'Alimonte, R. 214
Dalton, R. J. 196
Dante, A. 21
Danzig 123
Davies, N. 80
Davis, O. A. 6, 85
de Gaulle, C. 82, 93–6, 128, 131, 149
    and divided government 166, 179–80,
        182
de Winter, L. 174
Dean, J. 119
Deheza, G. I. 176–7
Delors, J. 83
Demélas-Bohy, M.-D. 28
Democratic Center (France) 95–6
Democrats
    Italy 56
    USA 52, 103–5
Democrats '66 (Dutch Radicals) 136–7
Denemark, D. 168
Denmark 69, 83, 120, 123, 127
d'Hondt, V. 118–19
d'Hondt formula 65, 123, 127, 135, 138
Díaz, P. 155
Díaz Ordaz, G. 156
Dinkin, R. J. 25–7
District of Columbia 104

divided government 141–6, 160–206
  concurrent and nonconcurrent elections
    165–9
  divided vote 161–9
  horizontally 201–3; concurrent and
    nonconcurrent elections 165–6;
    interinstitutional cooperation 177–84;
    parliamentarism and presidentialism
    169–77; conflict and cooperation
    171–5; multiparty presidents 175–7
  vertically 201–3; concurrent and
    nonconcurrent elections 167–9;
    federalism 185–90; divided
    bicameralism 88–90; interinstitu-
    tional cooperation and conflict
    190–201
Dobrzynska, A. 144, 215
Dodgson, C. L. 118
Dogan, M. 130
Dominican Republic 106
Donovan, M. 214
Doron, G. 120
Dowding, K. 3
Downs, A. 85
Doyle, W. 23
Dragnich, A. N. 200
Drees, W. 136
Duhamel, A. 97
Dulles, J. W. F. 113
Dunleavy, P. 205, 210
Dutra, E. 111
Duverger, M. 180–2

Echevarría, L. 156
Ecuador 69, 106–8, 123
Edwards, G. C. 179
Ehrlich, W. 172
Eisenhower, D. 178
El Salvador 106
Elazar, D. J. 186, 212
Electoral College, US Presidential 104–6
Elster, J. 210
Engels, F. 39–40
England 17, 37, 39
  parliament 23–5, 99
Eskridge, W. 202
Estates-General (France) 17, 22–3, 117
Estonia 121, 123
Europe 77, 123
  Central 13, 17
  Northern 43, 60, 63–5, 77
  unanimity 81–3
  Western 13, 123, 127
European Assembly 81

European Commission 81, 83
European Community 80, 83
European Council 83
European Defence Community 129
European Economic Community 81–2, 130,
  134
European Parliament 81, 83
European Union 140, 197–9

Fanfani, A. 134
Far Eastern Republic (Siberia) 123
Farnetti, P. 57
Fascists
  of Falange 90
  Italy 58, 131–4; post 134
  Spanish (FE) 89–91
federalism 185–90
Feigert, F. B. 167
Feld, S. L. 85
Ferejohn, J. A. 85, 202
Ferro, V. 79
Feuchtwanger, E. J. 62
Filho, C. 112
Finer, S. E. 209
Finland 43–4, 46, 63, 65, 69, 122–3
Finlay, R. 20
Fiorina, M. 178–9
Fishburn, P. C. 5, 100, 120
Fisher, C. A. 167
Fisher, S. 138
Fitzgibbon, R. H. 144
Fleischer, D. 167
Florence 20–1
Florida 104
Fondation Nationale des Sciences Politiques
  96
Fontaine, A. A. 115
Ford, G. 178
Founding Fathers of the American
  Constitution 118
France
  cohabitation in semi-presidentialism
    179–82
  Estates-General 17, 22–3, 117
  National Assembly 54, 87, 93–5, 131
  suffrage rights 33–5, 37–9, 41, 43–6,
    54–6, 62
  voting rules 69, 77, 80–4, 86–7, 127–31,
    137
Franco, F. 59
Frary, D. P. 24, 26, 47, 53, 60
Frederick I (Barbarossa) 75
Free Trade Party (Australia) 92
Frei, E. 114–15

Freiburg 19
French Union for Women's Suffrage 33–4
Fujimori, A. 158–60
Furet, F. 182
Furlong, P. 133

Gabel, L. C. 75
Gaffney, J. 97–8, 199
Gallagher, M. 122
Gamarra, E. A. 183
García, A. 110
Garfield, J. 104
Gasiorowski, M. J. 213, 215
De Gasperi, A. 134
Gaullist Rally for the Republic (RPR) 94–8,
    127–31
Gaytani, J. 101
Geddes, B. 210
General Assembly 80–2
Genoa 19, 21
Georgia 26, 123
Germain, M. 101
German Imperialists 138
German Party (DP) 138–9
German-Austrian Confederation 60
Germann, R. E. 191
Germany
    cantons and communes 17–19
    cooperative federalism 194–7
    East 63, 140
    Empire 35, 77, 79, 122
    suffrage rights 39–40, 43–4, 46, 59–63
    voting rules 69, 81–3, 122–3, 127, 130,
        137–40
Gibbard, A. 3
Gil, J. 79
Gillespie, J. D. 52
Gilpin, T. 122
Giolitti, G. 56–7
Giscard d'Estaing, V. 95, 97, 180
Gladstone, W. E. 36
God's will 66, 83–4
Golay, J. F. 195–6
González, M. L. 152
González Antón, L. 78
Goodin, R. E. 6
Gouaud, C. 182
Goulart, J. 111–13
Gragg, F. A. 75
Graham, B. D. 53
Graham, R. 28
Great Council, Italian 19–20
Greece 69
Green Party (Germany) 138–40

Greene, J. P. 179
Grofman, B. 85, 157, 178
Gruner, E. 191
Guatemala 106
Gueniffey, P. 54
Guerra, F.-X. 28
Guidi, G. 20
Guillory, C. A. 210
Guizado, J. R. 175
Guizot, F. M. 141

Habsburg monarchs 18, 78
Hagenbach-Bishoff formula *see* d'Hondt
    formula
Hailsham, Lord 149
Hallet, G. H. 121, 123
Hamilton, A. 119, 147
Hare, T. 119–20
Hare quota 123, 138
Harrison, B. 104
Hart, J. 99, 120
Hartlyn, J. 176
Harvey, A. L. 34
Hause, S. C. 36, 41
Haworth, P. L. 104
Haya de la Torre, V.-R. 109–10
Hayes, R. 104
Hayes-Renshaw, F. 83
hazard 34–6
Head, R. C. 19
Hearl, D. 69
Helvetic Confederation 19
Hermens, F. A. 61–2
Herrero, S. 36
Hesse, J. 202
Hill, J. A. 119
Hill, T. W. 120
Hine, D. 133
Hinich, M. J. 6, 85
Hirschman, A. O. 31
Hitler, A. 159
Hoag, C. G. 121, 123
Hoffer, P. C. 172
Hofferbert, R. I. 69
Hoffmann, S. 83
Hogg, Q. 149
van Holsteyn, J. J. M. 136
Honduras 106
Hosli, M. O. 124, 199
House of Burgesses (Virginia) 25
House of Commons 24, 32, 49, 102, 119
House of Representatives
    Australia 87, 91
    USA 52, 103, 121

Howard, R. 23
Huard, R. 54
Huber, J. D. 6, 69, 107
Hughes, C. 53, 92
Hull, N. E. H. 172
Hume, D. 207
Hungary 69, 123
Huntington, S. 213
Hyde, J. K. 19

Iberian-American colonies 27–9
Iceland 123
Ieraci, G. 174
IFOP polls 98, 131
Illinois 106, 119
India 69, 100, 102–3
Indo-China 130
Inglehart, R. 69, 107
innocuousness 31–4
Innuit 44
interinstitutional cooperation 177–84,
    190–201
Ireland 69, 121, 127
Irwin, G. A. 136
Irwin, W. J. 89
Israel 69, 123
Italy
    communes 17, 19–21
    First Republic 131–5
    suffrage rights 35–6, 43–6, 54, 56–8
    voting rules 69, 74, 81, 122–3, 127

Jackson, A. 153, 175
Jackson, G. 90
Jackson, K. 214
Jacobi, M. P. 33
Jacobs, F. 199
Jacobson, G. C. 178
Jaensch, D. 167
Japan 69, 120
Jay, J. 147
Jefferson, T. 118–19, 121–2, 153
Jenkins, R. 205
Jesse, E. 63, 138
John of England, King 76–7
Johnson, A. 175
Johnson, L. B. 149, 154
Jones, C. 23
Jones, M. P. 69, 107, 152, 167
Jospin, L. 96, 98, 180
Juárez, B. 155
Julliard, J. 182

Kallenbach, J. E. 167

Kallina, E. F. 106
Kamber, V. 154
Katz, R. S. 120
Kautsky, K. 39
Keman, H. 142, 174
Kennedy, J. F. 104–6, 149
Kent, V. 36
Keohane, R. O. 83
Kernell, S. 178
Kilgour, D. M. 5, 148
King, G. 147, 178
Klingemann, H.-D. 69
Knutsen, O. 69
Kobach, K. W. 193
Kohl, H. 140
Kolb, E. 62
Konopczynski, L. 77, 80
Kraditor, A. S. 34, 40, 51
Kramer, G. H. 85
Kronik, R. 120
Kubitschek, J. 111–12

La Gorce, P.-M. 129
La Palombara, J. G. 133
Labour Party
    Australia 92–3
    New Zealand 103
    Norway 64–5
    UK 49–50, 62, 102–3
Laitin, D. 187
Lamartine, A. de 55
Lamounier, B. 110
Länder 137
Languedoc 22
Lassalle, F. 60
Latin America 43
    military coups 108–16
    from plurality to majority presidents
        106–8
    voting rules 86, 99, 102, 119–20, 123
Latin model 43–6, 52–9
Latvia 123
Laumonier, L. 96
Laver, M. 5, 69, 123, 139–42, 145, 177
Lazarus, E. H. 52
Le Pen 96
Lecaneut, J. 95–7
Lector, L. 76
Left-Republicans (Spain) 88–9
Left-Socialists (Spain) 89
Leites, N. 128
Lenin, V. I. 39
Leon 77
Lepsius, M. R. 62

Lerdo de Tejada, S. 155
Lesnodorski, B. 79
Levillain, P. 74
Lewin, L. 36
Lewis, J. 36
L'Express 98
Liberal Parties 29
  Australia 92
  Canada 103
  Chile 114
  Finland 65
  France 38
  Germany (FDP) 35, 60–1, 63,
    138–40
  Italy (PLI) 56–7, 132–3
  Netherlands (VVD) 135–7
  Norway 65
  Spain 36, 58–9, 88–9
  Sweden 63–4
  UK 37, 49–50, 62, 102
Liberal-Democrats (Germany) 137
Liechtenstein 123
Lijphart, A. 120, 122, 135–6, 193, 203–4,
  209–10
Lincoln, A. 104, 149
Linder, W. 191
Lindman, A. 63–4
Lines, M. 20
Linz, J. J. 89–90, 177, 200, 215
Lisbon 122
Lithuania 79, 123
Lively, J. 33, 37
Lloyd, H. D. 19
Lloyd George, D. 49
Llull, R. 84
Lohmann, S. 168
López Portillo, J. 156
López-Pintor, R. 120
Louisiana 104
Lovecy, J. 181
Lower House
  Australia 86, 93
  Netherlands 135
Lubbers, R. F. M. 136
Lucca 21
Ludwig, E. 35
Luxembourg 81, 122–3
Luxembourg compromise (1966) 82
Luz, C. 112

Maastricht Treaty (1992) 83
Mabillon, J. 101
Macauley, T. B. 37
McClintock, C. 109

McCubbins, M. D. 178
Machado, I. R. 111
McKelvey, R. D. 5, 85
Mackie, T. T. 44
McLean, I. 76, 101, 118
MacRae, D. 130–1
Macridis, R. 94
McRobie, A. 214
Madero, F. I. 155
Madison, J. 119, 147, 153
Madrid 59
Magna Carta (1215) 76–7
Mainwaring, S. 69, 107, 110, 215
  and divided government 166, 170,
    177
Mair, P. 69, 121
Major, J. R. 22–3
Malbin, M. J. 154
Malta 121
Manin, B. 17
Mann, T. E. 154
Maoris 53
Marcos, F. 160
Margetts, H. 205, 210
Marín-Bosch, M. 81–2
Marongiu, A. 77
Martines, L. 21
Martínez, F. 169
Marx, K. 39
Maryland 25
Massachusetts 26, 50, 121
Massicote, L. 144, 215
Maura, A. 59
May, K. O. 5
Mayhew, D. R. 179
Medici 20
Mendès-France, B. 96, 149
Mendoza 122
Menem, C. 157–8
Merkl, P. H. 137
Merrill, S. 5, 101
Mexico/Mexicans 28, 51, 106
  revolutionary non re-election
    154–6
Michener, J. A. 104
Middle East 81
de Miguel, J. 89
Mill, J. 32–3, 37
Mill, J. S. 40, 117, 120
Miller, N. R. 5, 85
Milosevic, S. 201
Ministry of Agriculture (Italy) 134
Ministry of Economy (Germany) 139
Ministry of Education (Italy) 134

Ministry of Finance
France 130
Germany 140
Italy 132–4
Ministry of Foreign Affairs
France 130
Germany 139–40
Italy 132–4
Ministry of the Interior
France 94, 130
Germany 140
Italy 132–4
Ministry of Justice (Germany) 139
Ministry of Scientific Research (Italy) 133
Ministry of Tourism (Italy) 133
Missouri 106
Mitchell, B. R. 44
Mitterand, F. 95–8, 149, 166, 180, 182
Moderates
France 93, 127–30
Norway 65
von Mohl, R. 35
Monarchists
Italy 132–3
Spain 58, 88–90
Money, J. 5, 189
Monroe, J. 153
Montesquieu, C. L. 14, 204
Montpelier 22
Mori, A. 88
Moro, A. 134
Morocco 130
Munger, M. C. 6
Muslims 77
Mussolini, B. 134, 159
Myers, A. R. 77

Nagel, J. 101
Najemy, J. M. 20
Napoleon III (Louis Napoleon) 39, 55, 58,
93, 160
National Assembly (France) 54, 87, 93–5,
131
National Democratic Union (UDN) 111
National Front
Colombia 108
Spain 89–90
National Party
Australia (Country) 92
Chile 114–15
Germany 62
New Zealand 103
National Union for the Republic (UNR) 94
Native American Indians 26–8, 44

Navarre 77
Nazis (National-Socialists) 61–2, 127,
137–8
Neidhart, L. 191
Nelken, M. 36
neo-Nazis 138
Netherlands 69, 81, 122–3
from accommodation to compromise
135–7
Parliamentary Monarchy 127
New Brunswick 53
New England 26, 50
New Hampshire 26
New Jersey 50
New York 26, 50, 120–1
New Zealand 43–4, 53, 69, 102–3, 127
Nicaragua 106
Nicholls, A. J. 62
Niehuss, M. 167
Niemi, R. 5
Nimes 22
Nino, C. S. 157
Nixon, R. M. 104–6, 116, 175, 178
Nohlen, D. 107, 152, 166, 170
Noiret, S. 57
Nordic model 43–6, 59–65
North, D. C. 4, 204
North America 13, 17, 25, 32, 103
see also Canada; United States
North Carolina 26, 50
North German Confederation 34–5, 60
Norway 43–4, 46, 63–4, 69, 122–3
Nova Scotia 53
Nugent, N. 83
Nurmi, H. 5, 121

Oates, W. E. 185
Obregón, A. 155
Odría, M. 109
O'Gorman, F. 25
Ohio 120
Olson, M. 147
Oporto 122
Ordeshook, P. C. 6, 85
Oregon 104
Orlin, J. B. 120
Ornstein, N. J. 154
Ospina, M. 160
Ossona, J. L. 167
Ostrom, V. 186
Owen, R. 35

Pacific Islanders 53
Packel, E. W. 85

Panama 106
Paraguay 106–7
Paris 54, 128, 130–1
parliamentarism and presidentialism
    169–77
Pasquino, G. 133
Patil, A. V. 81–2
Pattanaik, P. K. 3
Pavia 19, 21
Pavone, C. 58
Paysans 129
Paz Estenssoro, V. 184
Paz Zamora, J. 182, 184
Peake, J. 179
Peirce, N. R. 105–6
Pella Forgas, J. 79
Pennock, J. R. 5, 186
Pennsylvania 26
Pérez, C. A. 175
Perón, J.-D. 157, 160
Peru 69, 102, 106–10, 123
Pétain, H. P. 130
Peter the Great 78
Peterson, P. E. 179
Petit-Dutaillis, C. 22
Petracca, M. 148
Petry, F. 129
Philadelphia 119, 122
Philippines 27, 69
Phillips, J. A. 25
Pierce, R. 182
Pinder, J. 83
Pisa 19
Pisano, G. 58
Pitkin, H. F. 118
Pius II, Pope 75
Piven, F. F. 51
Plott, C. 5, 85
Plumb, J. H. 25
plurality/pluralistic 10, 69, 98–101
    parliamentary and presidential elections
        102–16
    political institutions 210–16
    voting procedures 119–23
Plymouth (USA) 25–6
Poland 69, 122–3
    Polish Diet 73, 77, 79–80
political institutions
    choice of pluralistic 210–16
    choosing socially efficient 207–19
    study of 4–5
Polk, J. 104
Pompidou, G. 95, 180
Popular Action Party (PAP) 109

Popular Front
    France 128
    Spain 89–91
Popular Party
    Italy 57, 134
Porter, K. H. 25, 51
Portugal 28–9, 69, 77, 119–20, 122–3
Posada-Carbó, E. 28
Poujadists (UFF) 129–30
Powell, G. B. 6, 209
Power, T. J. 213, 215
presidentialism 96–8, 169–77
Progressives
    Brazil (PSP) 111
    USA 52
Protectionist party (Australia) 92
Prothro, J. W. 114–15
Proudhon, P.-J. 35
Provence 117
Prussia 60, 80
Przeworski, A. 210, 213
PTB (Brazilian Labour Party) 111–13

Quadros, J. 111–12
Quakers 26
Quebec 53
Quirk, P. J. 179

Rachev, S. T. 89
Radicals
    Chile 115
    France 95, 97, 127–30
    Germany 35
    Italy (PR) 56–7, 133
    Netherlands (Democrats '66)
        136–7
    Spain (PRR) 88–90
    UK 49
Radical-Socialists, Spanish (RS)
    88–9
Rae, D. W. 5
Ragsdale, L. 147, 178
Ramirez y Berrios, M. G. 110
Ranzato, G. 56
Rappard, W. E. 214
Raunio, T. 199
Reagan, R. 178
Rees, J. 33, 37
Reeves, T. C. 106
Reform Acts (UK, 1832, 1867 & 1885)
    47–8
Reform Party
    Italy 56
    New Zealand 103

Republicans
  France (PRL) 97, 128–9
  Italy (PRI) 132–3
  Spain 58–9, 88–91
  USA 52, 103–5
Rhode Island 26
Ridgeway, J. 201
Riggs, F. W. 178
Riker, W. H. 4–5, 51, 69, 186–7, 190
Rio de la Plata 28
Riqueti, H. G. 117
Ritter, G. A. 61, 167
Rivers, D. 168
Robertson, D. 69
Robinson, D. L. 154
Roca, T. 182
Romania 122–3
Rome, Treaty of (1957) 81
Romero Maura, J. 58
Roosevelt, F. D. 149, 153
Roosevelt, T. 149, 153
Rosanvallon, P. 34, 54, 182
Rose, R. 44
Rosen, F. 6
Rosenston, S. J. 52
Rosenthal, H. 163, 178
Rossi-Landi, G. 97
Rossiter, C. 153
Rousseau, J.-J. 84
Royer-Collard, P.-P. 37–8
Rubinstein, N. 20
Rumor, M. 134
Russia 57, 80, 122
  Russian Empire 65, 122

Sacremento 120
Sagasta, P.-M . 59
Sainte Laguë formula 65, 119, 121, 123
Salaverry Avenue pact 110
Salgado, P. 111–12
San Francisco 80
San Marino 123
Sánchez de Lozada, G. 182–3
Sani, G. 69
Santa Anna, A. L. de 154
Sardinia 77
Sartori, G. 69
Satterwhaite, M. 3
Schlesinger, A. M. 150
Schmidt, M. G. 139
Schofield, N. 5, 69, 123, 177
Schuman, R. 130
Schwyz 18
Sciarini, P. 193

Scott, R. E. 155
Scully, T. E. 69, 107, 170
Security Council 73, 80–2
Sen, A. K. 3
Senate
  Australia 91, 121
  Italy 19
Serbia 122
Serrafero, M. D. 152
Serrano, G. R. 36
Serrano, J. 160
Seton-Watson, C. 57
Seymour, C. 24, 26, 47, 53, 60
Shakleton, M. 199
Shepsle, K. A. 5, 123, 139–40, 142, 145
Shiratori, R. 214
Shugart, M. S. 106, 122, 152
  and divided government 166, 170, 175, 177, 183
Siberia 123
Sicily 77
Siena 19, 21
Siles Suazo, H. 184
Single European Act (1986) 83
Single Transferable Vote 120–1
Skidmore, T. E. 113
Slovakia 123
São Paulo 111–12
social choice 1–13
  a model 7–11
  social utility 5–7
  theory of 2–11
Social Democrats
  Brazil (PSD) 111–13
  Finland 65
  France 97
  Germany 40, 62, 137, 140
  Italy (PSDI) 132–3
Socialists 29
  Chile 114–16
  France 39, 94–8, 127–30
  Germany (SPD) 35, 60–2, 137, 139–40
  Italy (PSI) 57, 132–3
  Netherlands (PvDA) 135–7
  Peru 109
  Spain 59, 88–91
  Sweden 63–4
Social-Progressives (Peru) 109
Sone, Y. 120
Soulier, A. 129
South Africa 119–20
South America 13, 17
South Carolina 26, 50, 104
South Korea 69

Soviet Union 80–1, 123
  see also Russia
Spadolini, G. 132
Spain 69, 119–20, 123, 127
  Aragonese and Catalan 'Dissentimiento'
    77–9
  pre-civil war 87–91
  suffrage rights 27–9, 36–9, 43–6, 54,
    58–9, 62
State-Rights Democrats (USA) 52
Steiner, J. 192–3
Stepan, A. 113
Stokes, W. S. 144
Strom, K. 124, 177
suffrage rights 14–65
  complex electorates 29–65; Anglo model
    42–4, 46–53, 102; arguments on
    suffrage 30–41; Latin model 43–6,
    52–9; Nordic model 43–6, 59–65;
    voting rights strategies 41–5
  simple electorates 15–29; communes,
    parliaments and colonies 17–29
Sulieman, E. N. 149, 180
Sundquist, J. L. 153–4, 179
Superior Electoral Tribunal (Brazil) 112
Sutherland, N. 157
Sweden 69, 122–3, 127
  suffrage rights 43–7, 59–60, 63, 65
Swedish People's party (Finland) 65
Switzerland 17, 69, 122–3
  communes and cantons 18–19
  magic formula 190–4

Taagepera, R. 121–2
Tasmania 53, 120
Tavora, J. 111–12
Taylor, M. 25, 48
Taylor, Z. 104
Teichmann, M. 167
Temple, N. 22, 34
Terra, G. 160
Thakur, R. C. 203
Thatcher, M. 83, 149, 204
Thayssen, U. 167, 197
Third Lateral Council (1179) 75
Thomas, R. P. 4
threat 36–41
Ticino 122
Tideman, N . 121
Tilden, S 104
Tite, C. G. C. 172
Tito, J. B. 200
de Tocqueville, A. 55, 148–9
Tomic, R. 114–15

transformismo 56–7
Trechsel, A. 193
Truman, H. S. 104, 149, 153
Tsebelis, G. 5, 145, 189
Tudesq, A.-J. 55
Tullock, G. 5, 185
Tunisia 130
Tusell, J. 58–9, 89, 91
Tyler, J. 175

UDF (Union of French Democracy) 94–5,
  97–8
Udovicki, J. 201
Ull Pont, E. J. 59
unified government 141–60
  limiting 150–2
  trading off term limits and lengths
    152–60; re–election and
    accountability 156–9; unified author-
    itarianism 159–60
United Australia party 92
United Kingdom
  divided government 204–6
  suffrage rights 35–7, 40, 43–50, 53, 56,
    62
  voting rules 69, 80–3, 100–2, 117,
    124–7, 137
  see also England
United Nations 73, 80–2
United States
  Anglo-American colonies 25–7
  divided government in presidentialism
    177–9
  minority White House 104–6
  suffrage rights 17, 33, 37, 41–7, 50–3,
    56
  term limits 153–4
  voting rules 69, 80–1, 99–103, 116–21,
    137
  see also African-Americans; Native
    American Indians
Unterwalden 18
Uri 18
Urken, A. B. 118
Uruguay 69, 106–8, 123

Valencia 59, 77–8
Valenzuela, A. 113, 115, 122, 177
Varela Ortega, J. 58
Vargas, G. 111–12
Velasco Ibarra, J. M. 160
Venezuela 69, 106–7, 123
Venice 19–20, 75

Veser, E. 181
Virginia 25–6
voting rules 66–140
  efficient median voter 68–70
  multiple-winner rules 116–40; efficient
    multiparty cabinets 127–40; multi-
    party coalitions 123–7; proportional
    representation 116–23, pluralistic
    voting procedures 119–23
  single-winner rules 70–116; majority
    83–7, parliamentary/presidential
    elections 87–98; medieval organiza-
    tions 73–83, consensual medieval
    parliaments 76–80, God's single will
    74–6, intergovernmental organizations
    80–3; plurality 98–101, parliamen-
    tary/presidential elections 102–16,
    unanimity 71–3, bias and inefficiency
    71–3
Vowles, J. 214
Voynet, D. 96

Waley, D. 19, 147
Wallace, H. 83
Warwick, P. V. 174
Washington, G. 119, 153
Watts, R. L. 203, 212
Weaver, L. 121
Weber, R. 101
Webster, D. 119

Weimar Republic 61, 137–8, 140
Weingast, B. R. 5
Weingast, B. W. 204
Weir, S. 205
Weldon, J. 156
Wheare, K. C. 186
Whigs (US) 103–4
Wiel, A. 19
Wilkinson, B. 77
Williams, P. 94, 129
Williamson, C. 26
Wilson, W. 104, 149
Woldendorp, J. 139, 170
Wollstonecraft, M. 40
women's suffrage 33–7, 40–8, 50–3,
    61–5
Wright, J. F. H. 91–2
Wright, V. 202
Wright Hill, T. 119
Würtemberg 60

Yeltsin, B. 160
Young, H. P. 119, 122
Yugoslavia, disintegrating 199–201

Zaidi, A. M. 167
Zaidi, S. G. 167
Zamorano, A. 114
Zenatti, O. 21
Zwicker, W. 5

CPSIA information can be obtained
at www.ICGtesting.com
Printed in the USA
FFOW02n1018220116
20650FF